IN
FREUD'S
SHADOW_____

Adler in Context

IN
FREUD'S
SHADOW⎯⎯⎯⎯⎯⎯⎯⎯

Adler in Context

Paul E. Stepansky

 THE ANALYTIC PRESS
1983

Distributed by
LAWRENCE ERLBAUM ASSOCIATES, PUBLISHERS
Hillsdale, New Jersey   London

Distributed solely by
Lawrence Erlbaum Associates, Publishers, Inc.

The Analytic Press
365 Broadway
Hillsdale, N.J. 07642

Library of Congress Cataloging in Publication Data

Main entry under title:
Stephansky, Paul E.
    In Freud's shadow.

    Bibliography: p.
    1. Psychoanalysis—History.   2. Adler, Alfred,
1870–1937.   I. Title.   [DNLM: 1. Psychoanalytic theory—
Biography.   WZ 100 A2373s]
BF175.S664   1983   150.19'53   83-8979
ISBN 0-88163-007-1

Printed in the United States of America
10 9 8 7 6 5 4 3 2 1

for Deane

Contents

Preface   *ix*

Note on Translations   *xiii*

Introduction   1

1. From Socialism to Pedagogy: Prelude to Adlerian Theory   8

2. From Medicine to Psychiatry: The Foundations of Adlerian Theory, Part I   32

3. From Medicine to Psychiatry: The Foundations of Adlerian Theory, Part II   55

4. Adler in Freud's Circle: I. The Vicissitudes of Discipleship   81

5. Adler in Freud's Circle: II. The Anatomy of Dissension   112

6. Adler in Freud's Circle: III. *The Nervous Character* and its Critic   150

7. Adler in Freud's Circle: IV. The Psychology of
        Repudiation   175

8. The Psychologist as Pedagogue: Adler and the
        Education of the Child   206

9. The Psychologist as Prophet: Adler and
        Gemeinschaftsgefuehl   242

Appendix: The Hidden Adler in Freud   280

References   293

Index   313

Preface

I have been drawn to the study of Adler for several reasons. Initially, I was intrigued by his problematic status within Freud's earliest group of disciples. The incompatible explanations of Adler's split from Freud provided by Freudians and Adlerians have long been unsatisfying to me, and the wealth of documentary material contained in Otto Rank's *Minutes of the Vienna Psycho-Analytic Society* and recently published collections of Freud's correspondence makes a critical and synthetic reconstruction possible.

I have also been drawn to Adler out of my interest in the relationship between psychotherapy and medical practice. Adler is noteworthy in this respect. He began his career as a general practitioner serving Vienna's urban poor, and he retained important aspects of his medical identity throughout his career. In fact, the development of his psychological nomenclature, as I demonstrate, grows largely out of his earliest clinical concerns. By demonstrating the consistency of Adler's clinical outlook, I hope my study contributes to an understanding of his psychological categories for what they are: not superficial analogues to Freudian concepts, but ideas rooted in the methods and subject matter of clinical medicine. It is unfortunate that Adler's work has received no attention within the tradition of psychosomatic medicine. His theory of organ inferiority and his early notion of *Ueberempfindlichkeit* are important landmarks pointing toward a modern psychosomatic orientation, and his system of Individual Psychology does much to illuminate the ramifying interconnections between medical illness and certain types of psychopathology.

I have been drawn to the study of Adler for a third and more basic reason. Of all Freud's "deviant" disciples, it is Adler whose theories have received the most cursory dismissals by outsiders and the most self-limiting endorsements by "Adlerian" insiders. In both cases, Adler's thought has been deprived of a critical estimation that ranges outside the framework provided by a particular psychological tradition. He is therefore a ripe subject for historical treatment. The present study, in undertaking such treatment, is testimony to my belief that the history of psychoanalysis represents unexploited terrain for the historian of ideas. By this, I mean both that the subject matter of psychoanalysis is sufficiently important to warrant critical historical treatment and that our comprehension of this subject matter can be enriched if it is elaborated in a historical way. I do not presume to have provided an analysis of Adler's ideas that is in any sense definitive or complete. I do hope, however, that I have raised certain questions that clarify the historical import of Adler's ideas and thereby make these ideas interesting to those who have no vested interest in the fate of Adler's psychological movement.

This study has grown out of a doctoral dissertation under the direction of Professor Franklin Baumer, Department of History, Yale University. I must thank Professor Baumer not only for helpful critical advice, but also for patient insistence that I could present my material in a manner accessible and appealing to a wide academic and clinical readership. At the dissertation stage, the study also profited greatly from the critical reading of my friend and colleague, Professor Jeffrey Merrick, now of the Department of History, Barnard College. His perceptive and penetrating comments repeatedly challenged me to reconsider the structure and adequacy of my arguments, and his suggestions have saved me from many a pitfall in matters of both style and substance. Dr. Ernst Prelinger, Department of University Health, Yale University, gave the "Freud" chapters and the appendix an incisive psychoanalytic reading and made several valuable suggestions for sharpening the presentation in this part of the study. During the course of my research, I received supportive correspondence from Professors Erna Lesky and Manfred Skopec of the *Institut fuer Geschichte der Medizin* of the University of Vienna. I am particularly indebted to Professor Lesky for sending me copies of Adler's early socialist editorials from the Viennese *Aerztliche Standeszeitung*. Unpublished letters from Adler to Hans Vaihinger of 5 June 1912 and 22 January 1913 and from Freud to Vaihinger of 27 January 1925 are quoted with the permission of the library of the University of Bremen. Unpublished letters from Adler to Eugen Relgis of 2 November 1929 and from Adler to Yohanan Twersky of 1 April 1929 are quoted with the permission of the Department of Manuscripts & Archives, The Jewish National & University Library, Jerusalem.

My research was supported during 1976–1977 by a Kanzer Fund Fellowship for Psychoanalytic Studies in the Humanities, and I am grateful to Dr. Mark Kanzer and the Yale Kanzer Committee for facilitating my work in this way.

In taking the study beyond the scope and import of the dissertation, I have been no less fortunate in the assistance I have received. Special thanks go to two able colleagues in the study of psychoanalytic history. Peter Swales graciously brought to my attention unpublished Adler correspondence uncovered in the course of his archival investigations; he is likewise responsible for a valuable addition to Adler's bibliography that has been incorporated into this study, Adler's book review of Wilhelm Fliess's *Das Jahr im Lebendigen* published in the Berlin *Vossische Zeitung* in 1918. David Joseph was of major assistance in tracking down several of Adler's early German articles that initially eluded my grasp. More importantly, his unwavering support and friendship were instrumental in my decision to pursue this project through difficult times. I am additionally grateful to my friend and editorial colleague Nick Cariello for discussing various portions of the manuscript with me, to Jim Blight for his substantive and helpful critique of the manuscript, to John Workman for his heroic labors in translating a number of Adler's script letters, and to Judith Augusta and Maeve Byrnes for their conscientious attention to detail in typing successive drafts of the manuscript.

Finally, a special word of thanks to my publisher Lawrence Erlbaum for his enthusiastic commitment to this project and for his understanding and guidance along the path to its publication.

One inevitably reaches the juncture in any preface where one must deal with those special people for whom prefaces really exist, but to whom no prefatory acknowledgment is ever fully adequate. My parents, Selma and William Stepansky, have by now seen me through the best and worst of scholarly times. Their unfailing support and abiding belief in my work have been, and are, a continual source of emotional strength and intellectual renewal. It is with special pride and gratitude that I acknowledge their central role in my scholarship and, more especially, in the value I assign to the very pursuit of scholarship. It is with joy that I acknowledge the contribution of my son, Michael David Stepansky, whose presence brightened my days and reminded me that there is more to life than the pursuit of scholarship.

My wife, Deane Rand Stepansky, at this point knows more about Adler, Freud, and the history of psychoanalysis than any spouse should have to know. She has fulfilled the many offices that devolve upon spouses—those of counselor, critic, sounding board, editor, and proofreader—and she has fulfilled them lovingly, tirelessly, and expertly from the start. Over the years of thinking and rethinking, of writing and rewriting, she has alternately soothed me, revived me, and revitalized me; she has constantly sustained me. In this project and in all projects, she has been the greatest and most inspiring of partners.

Paul E. Stepansky
January, 1983
Bloomfield, New Jersey

Note on Translations

Although I have used German editions of Adler's works whenever possible, my references include citations to extant English translations of these works whenever available. Two general collections of Adler's writings, *The Individual Psychology of Alfred Adler: A Systematic Presentation from his Writings,* edited and annotated by H. L. Ansbacher & R. R. Ansbacher (New York: Harper & Row, 1956) and *The Practice and Theory of Individual Psychology,* translated by P. Radin (Paterson, N.J.: Littlefield, Adams, 1963), are simply cited as "Ansbacher" and "Radin," respectively, throughout the volume. I should note that I have frequently altered the translations on behalf of increased precision and literalness. Adler's different translators have not fully standardized his clinical vocabulary, and this has mitigated against an adequate comprehension of his thought. A key term like *Persoenlichkeitsgefuehl,* for example, has been variously translated as "individuality-feeling," "self-esteem," and "feeling of personality." I have consistently translated the term "ego feeling" as an updated expression of what Adler intended. This translation does justice to Adler's concept as an article of his "ego psychology," and it further illuminates the comparison with Freud. I have translated *Gemeinschaftsgefuehl* as "community feeling," not as "social feeling" or "social interest." The term *Gemeinschaft* literally means community; had Adler intended to write about "social feeling," he had the perfectly conventional expression *sozial Gefuehl* at his disposal. It is in the concrete sense of "community," moreover, that Adler's idea is most amenable to the comparative sociohistorical treatment accorded it in the latter chapters of this study.

IN
FREUD'S
SHADOW⸺⸺⸺⸺
Adler in Context

Introduction

It is a revealing oversight in the history of modern psychiatry that Alfred Adler has yet to be accorded his just due. Despite Adler's important role in the history of psychoanalysis and his obvious stature as the founder of Individual Psychology, the study of his thought and the explication of his system have remained the preserve of committed partisans.[1] In the course of the continuing polemical exchanges between "Freudians" and "Adlerians," Adler's thought has been deprived of the critical and contextual examination it warrants. Caught between the violently disjunctive perspectives of disciples and detractors, therapists, social scientists, and historians have all been the losers. They have been compelled to choose one "Adler" or the other without the benefit of a viable middle ground informed by critical scholarship. Although there are numerous accounts of Adlerian psychology (e.g., Wexberg, 1929; Dreikurs, 1933; Way, 1950), they are the exclusive product of confirmed Adlerians and generally ignore the historical questions that must be raised in order to assess the critical status of Adler's psychological doctrines. Apart from Henri Ellenberger's important reassessment of Adler's life and work in *The Discovery of the Unconscious* (1970), there has really been no critical historical study of Adler at all. What we have is simply a series of impressionistic and often contradictory reminiscences of Adler by colleagues (Sperber, 1926, 1970; Furtmueller, 1946) and protégés (Bottome, 1939;

---

[1]Henri Ellenberger's treatment of Adler in *The Discovery of the Unconscious* (1970) is a partial exception to this claim. Ellenberger does not write as a "committed partisan," but his summary of Adler's work is more didactic than interpretive. When it comes to assessing Adler's influence, moreover, Ellenberger is beneficent to the point of being uncritical.

1

Orgler, 1939; Rom, 1966). These accounts generally end up devoting much more space to elementary explications of Adler's theories than to the historical development of these theories, and they do not discuss the impact and social repercussions of Adler's thought beyond the closed organizational development of the Individual Psychology movement proper.

For the Adlerians, this is all that is necessary. Their Adler is a psychological theorist of indisputable preeminence, and the validity of his theory of psychological development and effectiveness of his therapeutic strategies can be the only true measure of his historical stature. Seen from the vantage point of his later career as therapist, educator, and social reformer, Adler's early status as a Freudian warrants no more than passing mention. Indeed, Adler's eight-year membership in Freud's circle is accorded only negative significance. Psychoanalysis was, from the beginning, a circuitous bypath that obliquely touched the fundamental truths of Individual Psychology. Adler used the psychoanalytic forum as the medium for promulgating his own views at a time when he was unaware of the extent to which Freud's early formulations were tantamount to an inscrutable and exclusionist dogma. Freud, according to the Adlerians, inevitably became the obstacle that Adler had to overcome in the course of his own theoretical liberation. The responsibility for the rift was Freud's because the ''neurotic'' need for uncritical and unoriginal disciples and the authoritarian expectation of obedience from these disciples were also Freud's.

Freudians take a different view of the situation. Their Adler is a renegade protégé who resisted and subsequently disavowed psychoanalytic insight for a variety of personal and professional reasons. The later development of Adlerian theory, moreover, represented the flawed exaggeration of certain insights that had been present in Freudian theory all along. Adler's theoretical innovations, according to these critics, did no more than restate certain aspects of psychoanalysis in the guise of a new and less satisfactory terminology. Because Freudians discredit the motivation underlying the inception of Adler's theories, they see little point in examining critically the subsequent development of Individual Psychology as an autonomous school of psychotherapy.

In the decades following Freud's death, only two theorists of any psychoanalytic stature have expressed indebtedness to the work of Adler—and their work, it should be noted, falls considerably outside the psychoanalytic mainstream. In the early 1940s, Ives Hendrick (1942, 1943a) postulated an ''instinct to master'' which, he claimed, accounted for more behavior in children during the first two years of life than the need for sensual pleasure. This ''instinct to master'' aimed at ''the pleasure in executing a function successfully, regardless of its sensual value'' (1942, p. 41), and Hendrick admitted it was ''essentially the same as Alfred Adler's 'will to power' '' (1943b, p. 563). Twenty years later, Robert White (1960, 1963) sought to amend psychoanalytic instinct theory by expounding a novel theory of "independent ego energies" which aimed at feelings of efficacy and social competence; he explained that this concept of competence was tantamount to Adler's striving for superiority or perfection, having earlier observed (1957) that Adler had taken the "first pioneering steps toward an ego psychology within psychoanalysis." These theories have, at best, constituted minor appendages in the evolution of psychoanalytic theory. For the overwhelming majority of analysts, Adler's system retains significance only as the antithesis of psychoanalytic insight. Individual Psychology, for them, is simply an historical deviation from psychoanalysis, a noteworthy attempt to frame psychological explanations around a descriptive and superficial psychology of the ego that evades the unsettling foundations of psychoanalysis: the theories of the unconscious, repression, and infantile sexuality. For the first generation of psychoanalytic ego psychologists, it was sufficient to stress the radical discontinuity between *Adler's* ego psychology, with its perspectivistic and ultimately misguided emphasis on the adaptive and social functions of the ego, and a *psychoanalytic* ego psychology "built only upon consolidated knowledge of the 'unconscious'" (Rapaport, 1957, p. 683; cf. Kris, 1938, pp. 350–351; Hartmann, 1939, p. 5; Rapaport, 1951, p. 359; 1954, pp. 587–588).

In accord with this disparaging estimation of Adler's psychology, psychoanalysts have dismissed all too summarily those topical Adlerian formulations that impinge on psychoanalysis. Few and far between are analysts like J. C. Flugel (1945, pp. 45–47), for example, who willingly concedes that Adler's notion of the "guiding fiction" represents a "very real" contribution to the understanding of the "ego ideal" component of superego development. More characteristic is the grudging acknowledgment that Adler's work on "lowered self-esteem" and its compensatory outcome points to an issue of ego development that has been insufficiently studied, even if Adler's own "highly oversimplifed views" on the subject must be rejected (Sandler, 1960, p. 157). Few analysts indeed would question David Rapaport's categorical verdict that "the role of [Adler's] work in the science of psychology amounts to no more than 'grease for the wheels of history'" (1957, pp. 683–684). At his best, then, the Adler of the psychoanalysts is the author of "valuable clinical insights without a theoretical framework which could give them lasting impact" (Rapaport, 1957, p. 684). Less charitably, he is the "intellectual ancestor" of all revisionist analysts whose apparent "progressivism" masks a retreat to pre-Freudian ideas.[2] To the extent that Adler warrants any special mention, it is only because

---

[2]This is also the verdict of R. Jacoby (1975, pp. 20–34), who approaches Adler from the standpoint of the Frankfurt School of social criticism.

his retreat from psychoanalysis, unlike those of his successors, was unequivocal and explicit: he, at least, "was clear about what he did" (Waelder, 1956, pp. 7–8).

It is the radical disjunction between the "two Adlers" that clarifies the problem confronting the intellectual historian. Adlerians esteem Adler's Individual Psychology so highly that they are unwilling to reconstruct the circumstances surrounding Adler's allegiance to psychoanalysis. Content to work backwards and evaluate Adler's psychoanalytic years from the vantage point of his own school of psychology, they are disinclined to examine critically Adler's eight-year status as a Freudian. The Freudians, for their part, spend so much time discrediting the quality of Adler's discipleship and the grounds for his split from Freud that they are uninterested in examining the significance of Adler's psychoanalytic collaboration for his subsequent development as an Individual Psychologist. The job of the historian is to do justice to the orientations of both Adlerians and Freudians, but to fuse the selective emphases of these rival camps into a framework that is comprehensive and consistently critical. This task involves abandoning the propagandistic assumptions that have proved so self-limiting in the past. If, following the Freudians, Adler broke with Freud for personal reasons that are suspect and even disreputable, it hardly follows that the subsequent development of Individual Psychology is nothing but an outgrowth of these factors that does not warrant critical examination. If, following the Adlerians, Adler broke with Freud for legitimate doctrinal reasons, it hardly follows that his emergent Individual Psychology must be a substantive and self-evidently meaningful theory that transcends the need for critical examination on its own terms.

In place of the old assumptions, the study of Adler requires a new paradigm. Surely, Adler's status as a Freudian deserves a critical treatment that has not been forthcoming from Adlerians, but it must be a treatment that operates outside preformed psychoanalytic preconceptions. In short, such treatment requires a new sense of the trajectory of Adler's own development, both antedating and extending beyond the critical years of his psychoanalytic collaboration. Before reassessing the responsibility for the "split," in other words, it is essential to understand the theoretical and clinical assumptions that Adler brought to the encounter with Freud. Only in this way can the relationship with Freud become part of Adler's intellectual history and not part of Freud's. Surely, Adler's later system of Individual Psychology must be examined against the backdrop of his Freudian years, but critical assessment of this system should not be a simple function of one's perspective on the Freud-Adler "split." Evaluation of Adler's status as an educator and psychiatrist, that is, should not be restricted to the evaluative referents of either psychoanalysis *or* Individual Psychology. It should, instead, strive to explain the historical timeliness of Adler's psychotherapeutic strategies by focusing on contextual questions that range beyond the perspectivistic contours of either school and that place Adler's doctrines in a wider cultural and intellectual matrix.

The present study of the development of Adler's thought addresses itself to these wider concerns. It is *not* a comprehensive biography of Adler and pays little attention to the formal institutional development of Individual Psychology. Instead, it strives to clarify and reevaluate three central issues that serve as landmarks in Adler's career: (1) the development of his ideas up to the time of his participation in Freud's circle, (2) the character of his collaboration with Freud's circle and the grounds for his eventual split from Freud, and (3) the critical status of the educational and psychotherapeutic ideas that preoccupied him after World War I. To the extent that I succeed in shedding new light on these issues, I believe I have not only contributed to our understanding of Adler, but provided scholars with a useful building block for the comprehensive history of the psychoanalytic movement that remains to be written (cf. Cranefield, 1970).

In endeavoring to answer the questions I pose for myself, I have introduced comparative historical material that is not aimed at establishing direct ''influences'' on Adler's ideas, but rather at situating his theories within a broader intellectual framework than is normally found in studies by psychologists and psychoanalysts. I wish I could have uncovered extensive new material pointing to the direct influence of earlier thinkers on Adler. Unfortunately, with the exceptions of Vaihinger and Smuts—and of course Freud—there simply do not seem to be any thinkers who exerted a major influence on Adler in his psychological and social theorizing. Given the lack of concrete historical referents for Adler's ideas, I have decided that the best (and really the only) way to enrich a study of his thought historically is to draw on the climate of opinion that existed throughout his career—to refer to certain important intellectual trends in the social and philosophical thought of the period that provide a contextual backdrop against which to refract the distinctive qualities of his rather narrowly conceived theories. In this way, I hope to provide an historical framework that facilitates a critical appreciation of Adler's ideas on their own terms. Elaboration of the ''climate of opinion'' is hardly a radical procedure in the history of ideas (see C. Becker, 1932; Baumer, 1949); it is one methodological approach that helps us arrive at historical understanding of a thinker who otherwise lacks direct historical connectedness with his milieu. In the manner of Dilthey, I have tried to enter into Adler via sympathetic insight (*verstehen*), and to introduce historical referents that seem to make sense of his intellectual concerns as they have become part of my own intellectual history (cf., on Dilthey's approach to the history of ideas, Hodges, 1944, 1952; Kluback, 1956).

There are of course major questions that the present work does not address. The final two chapters of this study are synthetic and analytical distillations of ''late'' Adlerian thought. In adopting this topical format, I have not attempted to chart chronologically the evolution of Adler's ideas after World War I. In the process, I have ignored one facet of Adler's intellectual biography that is of special interest to social historians: the nature and scope of Adler's impact in America during his later years. We know that Adler began commuting to the United States for six months a year in 1926 to lecture at the New School for Social Research, subsequently held a visiting teaching appointment at Columbia University between 1929 and 1931, accepted a full-time appointment in medical psychology at the Long Island Medical College in 1932, and permanently emigrated from Austria in 1934. Yet, Adler's case has never been examined within the framework of the contemporaneous exodus of European intellectuals to America, and the reception accorded Individual Psychology has been generally ignored in accounts of the migration of psychoanalysis and the development of ego psychology during this period (e.g., Fleming & Bailyn, 1969; Fermi, 1971; Hughes, 1975). We consequently know virtually nothing of Adler's perceptions of his emigration to America, of the way American psychotherapists reacted to his theories, and most importantly, of the extent to which the American cultural milieu fitted or induced modifications in the content of Adlerian theory. To attempt an answer to the first of these questions, it would be necessary to consider directly the fate of Adler's work in America. Although we have numerous accounts of Adler's public educational activities in Austria, we have no idea of how his espousal of community therapeutics worked itself out during his years in America, to what degree he advocated therapeutic models that were applicable to the community mental health and mental hygiene movements of the 1920s and 1930s, and to what extent he was personally involved in American social reform movements that ostensibly incorporated ''Adlerian'' premises about the importance of community mental health.

Beyond the question of Adler's interaction with American reform movements, the entire matter of his influence on modern psychiatric and psychological thought remains hazy. It has been pointed out, repeatedly, that there is a strong affinity between Adler's theories and the development of current neo-Freudian theories of ego psychology (e.g., H. Ansbacher & R. Ansbacher, 1956; White, 1957). But no attempt has been made to distinguish the actual *influence* of his work from the incontestable *compatibility* of his ideas with many psychologies now in vogue. Henri Ellenberger's (1970) otherwise useful portrait of Adler does not clarify matters in this respect. He terms the shift of psychoanalysis toward ego psychology largely "an adaptation of former Adlerian concepts" (p. 638), and he refers, furthermore, to the "subtler and more diffuse influence" of Adler's ideas "on the main body of the psychoanalysts" (p. 641). Ellenberger's ascription of "influence," however, demonstrates nothing but the simple congruence of Adler's ideas with certain developments in psychoanalytic theory. He spends eight pages, in this connection, cataloguing the work of recent "neo-Adlerians" who do not even mention Adler in their published writings, much less acknowledge any "Adlerian" influence on their ideas (pp. 636–645).

Future students of Adler would be well advised to pay attention to the problematic status of the concept of "influence" as it exists in the history of ideas.[3] It may be that the allegedly "Adlerian" quality of American psychoanalytic thought is testimony less to Adler's "influence" than to certain incidental convergences between Adlerian ideas and American social conditions during the 1930s and 1940s. Methodologically, the question of Adler's "influence" will probably be best charted if it is explored in delimited terms. Instead of pointing to similarities between Adler's work and the theories of Karen Horney, Harry Stack Sullivan, Erich Fromm and others, it would be a useful first step to ascertain Adler's fate in America: whether he had any ties with American institutional psychiatry and whether he interacted with any currents in American social reform (e.g., the mental hygiene movement or the child guidance clinic movement) after he began lecturing regularly in the United States in 1926.

Although the present study does not address the question of Adler's influence directly, it does seek to provide an interpretive framework that will facilitate research in this direction. By clarifying the status of Adler's postwar educational and therapeutic ideas, that is, I hope to convey a richer sense of what there was in Adler that might have been "influential," above and beyond the overworked inferiority-superiority paradigm that has been taken to be the cornerstone of his historical identity.

---

[3]Dunn (1968) and Skinner (1969) have taken impressive first steps toward the needed clarification of this concept.

1

From Socialism to Pedagogy: Prelude to Adlerian Theory

Studies of Alfred Adler have long had their conventions. Sympathetic disciples and explicators generally try to locate the origins of Individual Psychology in the early physical and psychological vulnerabilities of the movement's founder. In the rickets, spasms of breathlessness, and rachitis that plagued Adler during childhood, they see the origins of his later sensitivity to the theme of "inferiority" in his medical and psychological work. In his childhood decision to pursue a career in medicine following a bout with pneumonia during which he overheard his doctor pronounce him "lost," they see the kind of "compensatory" strategy at work that would figure so prominently in Adler's theory of psychological development. In Adler's youthful resolve to become an able mathematics student after great difficulty with the subject, and in his early recollection of overcoming an inhibitory fear of walking through a local cemetery, they see the germ of the kind of successful "overcompensations" that Adler's system of therapy later sought to cultivate.[1]

In accepting the connections between these childhood experiences and the development of Adlerian psychology, such explicators have done no more than acknowledge the verdict Adler himself popularized during the 1920s and 30s. During his later career in America, the founder of Individual Psychology constantly referred to autobiographical experiences in order to document the therapeutic optimism that was at the core of his psychological *Weltanschauung*.

---

[1]On Adler's early physical and psychological vulnerabilities, see, e.g., Rom (1966, pp. 25–33) and Sperber (1970, pp. 14–17).

He began one lecture series by attempting to explain how he himself had "experienced" Individual Psychology:

> To begin with, I would say I was born a very weak child suffering from certain weaknesses, especially from rickets which prevented me from moving very well. Despite this obstacle, now, nearly at the end of my life, I am standing before you in America. You can see how I have overcome this difficulty. Also, I could not speak very well early in my life; I spoke very slowly. Now, though you are probably not aware of it in my English, I am supposed to be a very good orator in German. I have also overcome this difficulty.[2]

It is at once suggestive and predictable that Adler should anchor his psychological insights in the disabilities of his own childhood. Unfortunately, documentary studies of Adler's career can presently do little more than reiterate Adler's impressionistic claims. Until the archival research of the late Hans Beckh-Widmanstetter is organized and published, there will be no basis for confirming or amending the reputed connection between Adler's psychology and Adlerian psychology.[3]

In fact, we know very little about Adler's formative years. Basic genealogical work by Beckh-Widmanstetter has traced Adler's parents back to the Burgenland province that served as a buffer state between Austria and Hungary and established their residence in several Viennese suburbs during the 1860s and 70s. We know that Adler was born in the Viennese suburb of Rudolfsheim on 7 February 1870, that he was the second child in a family of six children, and that he spent most of his youth in the Jewish suburb of Leopoldstadt and the outlying rural area of Waehring. Adler's father, Leopold Adler, was an unsuccessful grain merchant whose family was apparently subjected to financial difficulties during this time.

Despite the fact that he grew up in Jewish neighborhoods, Adler remained strikingly indifferent to the question of his religious identity. He neither made

---

[2]The quotation is from the first page of a lecture deposited with the Adler collection at the Library of Congress, Washington, D.C. The lecture quoted is a typescript that is simply identified "Lecture of March 12th, Dr. Adler, Tuesday." It is certainly a lecture Adler delivered in America during the early 1930s. The lecture is in Adler's awkward and imperfect English, and I have therefore slightly rephrased it. See also Adler (1930a).

[3]Before his death in 1970, Beckh-Widmanstetter made some of his data on Adler's ancestry and an unpublished typescript entitled "Alfred Adler's Childhood and Youth Until His Contact with Sigmund Freud in 1902" available to Henri Ellenberger. Ellenberger subsequently incorporated this material into his account of Adler in *The Discovery of the Unconscious* (1970, pp. 571ff.). Although I was ultimately unable to obtain a copy of this manuscript, I am grateful to Professors Erna Lesky and Manfred Skopec of the Institute for the History of Medicine at the University of Vienna for their efforts on my behalf and for sending me other unpublished Beckh-Widmanstetter material pursuant to my research.

positive identification with his Jewishness nor experienced any anti-Semitism in the rural outskirts of Vienna. Although nominally observant of the Jewish holidays, Adler's parents practiced a "pallid, watered-down version of Judaism" that left little imprint on their children (Ellenberger, 1970, p. 573; Sperber, 1970, p. 28). Alfred attended the Synagogue during Jewish holidays, and perhaps on the Sabbath, but he developed no elective affinity for Judaism. His parents' home in Rudolfsheim, moreover, was practically adjacent to a playground used only by gentile working-class children. It was at this Rudolfsheim playground that Adler picked up the Viennese dialect of "Gstetten" and came to identify himself entirely with the social community of his Christian playmates (Beckh-Widmanstetter, 1966, pp. 39–40; Ellenberger, 1970, p. 579; Sperber, 1970, p. 29). As a young man, Adler underwent baptism and became a Protestant. He never commented on his conversion and his biographers have been unable to provide a satisfactory explanation, given Adler's insulation from social anti-Semitism and subsequent indifference to questions of religious belief. The best they can do is to link Adler's conversion to his secular identity as a "Viennese" and to his intellectual distaste for the very prospect of anti-Semitism.[4]

Of Adler's formal education, we know very little. In 1879, at the age of nine, he attended the same Sperlgymnasium that Sigmund Freud had entered 14 years earlier. In 1881, when his family moved to Hernals, Adler was enrolled in the Hernalser Gymnasium. He attended this school until his eighteenth year, but the destruction of the school archives during World War II precludes any detailed investigation of his student career. Upon completion of the Gymnasium course, Adler registered at the Faculty of Medicine at the University of Vienna for the winter semester of 1888–1889.

Adler's medical education was conventional and restricted in scope. He trained at a time when the Vienna Medical Faculty was steeped in a tradition of scientific positivism that contributed to its fascination with diagnosis and relative neglect of therapy. One historian of the period has recently invoked the concept of "therapeutic nihilism" to describe the modest therapeutic expectations that accompanied the Viennese Faculty's scientific pretensions during this time (Johnston, 1972, p. 223).[5] Given the prevailing preoccupation with pure medical research, it is not surprising that Adler's obligatory course of training did not range outside the subject matter of medicine, surgery, and pathology. He re-

---

[4]See Furtmueller (1946, p. 331) and Sperber (1970, pp. 30–32). Ellenberger (1970, p. 573) notes that two of Adler's younger brothers converted to Catholicism while his older brother left the Jewish community without declaring any religious adherence. Hopefully, Beckh-Widmanstetter's research will help clarify Adler's relation to Judaism.

[5]On Adler's medical education, see Ellenberger (1970, pp. 581–582). On the positivism of the Vienna medical faculty, particularly with respect to diseases of the nervous system, see Lesky (1965, pp. 373ff.).

ceived no psychiatric training. After a notably undistinguished academic performance as a medical student, Adler completed his medical studies in 1895, interned briefly at the Viennese Poliklinik, and satisfied his obligatory military service in the Hungarian unit of a military hospital at Pressburg from 1 April to 30 September 1896. Between 1897 and 1899 Adler claimed to have undertaken further postgraduate training at both the Poliklinik and Vienna's General Hospital, spending time on the psychiatric, medical, and opthalmologic services.[6] In 1899, he established a general practice in the Czerningasse at No. 7, a popular street not far from the Prater.

This skeletal outline must, at present, suffice for our knowledge of the young Adler. Students of Adler's thought, however, are fortunate to have a more convenient starting point. The earliest signpost of Adler's intellectual development, and the earliest printed source available to his biographers, is the small collection of socialist material that Adler published in the first years of his medical career. Focusing on the subject matter of "social medicine," this material includes Adler's first publication, the *Health Book for the Tailoring Trade* of 1898, and the small collection of editorials he contributed to a Viennese medical journal, the *Aerztliche Standeszeitung,* between 1902 and 1904. However suggestive it is that Adler should resort to autobiographical incidents in validating the claims of his later psychology, this strategy may tell us more about the explanatory pretensions of Individual Psychology in the 1930s than about the origins of Adler's thought at the turn of the century. It is the publications on social medicine that provide us with the documentary foothold from which to examine the historical origins of Adler's psychological theories. To be sure, these intriguing contributions reveal a facet of Adler's career that has been generally overlooked by his psychologist disciples and is worthy of documentation in its own right. But for the intellectual biographer the socialist publications have additional importance: they encapsulate the therapeutic concerns that would guide Adler first to the province of psychosomatic medicine and eventually to clinical psychiatry.

I.

It is difficult to ascertain the precise nature and extent of Adler's early socialist affiliation. In 1946, his friend and colleague Carl Furtmueller recounted Adler's aloofness during his medical student days (1888–1895) when "only personal

---

[6]The claim was made in 1915 in Adler's application to the Medical Faculty of the University of Vienna for appointment as a Privatdozent in neurology. See Beckh-Widmanstetter (1965, p. 182). Ellenberger (1970, p. 582), it should be noted, relying on Beckh-Widmanstetter's own archival investigations, could find no documentary evidence of Adler's postgraduate studies, beyond the brief interlude of 1896 that preceded the completion of his military service.

friendship connected him with members of the socialist group." As a young doctor, however, Adler "joined the group, appeared in their debating meetings and was also seen now and then in big popular meetings." He participated, Furtmueller recollected, not as a "speaker and debater," but as a "listener" on whom the sociological conception of Marxism "had a decisive influence" (p. 333). In 1970, Manes Sperber, a Marxist Individual Psychologist who broke with Adler in the 1920s, stated that Adler had joined a "League of Socialist Students" before 1898 and become one of the group's prominent members. Sperber went on to claim that Adler read Marx's *Communist Manifesto, Critique of Political Economy,* and early philosophical works during this time (1970, pp. 17–18). Although it is at present impossible to confirm these accounts or to elaborate further the extent of Adler's involvement in socialist circles, there is no reason to doubt the fact of Adler's early socialist sympathies. Between 1898 and 1904 he published a 30-page pamphlet and a number of editorials that are broadly "socialist" in their import. During 1908, we know that Adler was the friend and therapist of A. A. Joffe, a close associate of Trotsky and the chief contributor to the newspaper that Trotsky was publishing in Vienna during this time. A comment in Trotsky's memoirs (1970, pp. 220, 227) indicates that he and his family were personal friends of Adler as well. We have a record of the well-received lecture on the "Psychology of Marxism" that Adler presented to the Vienna Psychoanalytic Society on 10 March 1909. In his later career, moreover, when the content of his writings never ranged outside his own psychological preconceptions, Adler still contributed three editorials to Vienna's socialist daily, the *Arbeiter-Zeitung* (1923, 1924, 1925). On the other hand, it was during the mid-1920s that Adler dissociated himself from the work of Marxist disciples like Manès Sperber and Alice and Otto Ruehle (Sperber, 1970, pp. 129–131, 223).

What can we say interpretively about Adler as socialist? Although Adler himself never expressly commented on the path that led him from his medical studies to socialism, several issues of historical context are relevant to understanding the significance of this little-known phase of his career.

In the last decades of the nineteenth century, Vienna witnessed a striking interchange between complementary currents of political and medical activism. Max Gruber, the distinguished Viennese physician who later influenced Victor Adler to pursue a career in science, redirected the pan-German and socialist activism of his student days toward the application of medical science to social problems. Following his participation in the radical *Leseverein der deutschen Studenten* (Reading Society of Viennese and German Students) during his university days, Gruber studied medicine in Vienna and proceeded to a series of professorships of hygiene in Germany and Austria where he conducted bacteriological experiments that were instrumental in confirming Robert Koch's theory of the origin of infectious illnesses.[7] Theodor Meynert, Vienna's most distinguished professor of psychiatry during this time, was not only an honorary member of the student *Leseverein*, but hired the group's leader, Engelbert Pernerstorfer, as tutor for his children. He was on close personal terms with his student Victor Adler as well (see Stockert-Meynert, 1930, pp. 78–80 and McGrath, 1974, p. 42).

More specifically, it is interesting to observe that Alfred Adler was not the only Viennese physician to arrive at socialism through his everyday observations as an *Armenarzt*—a physician serving the urban poor. It is noteworthy that the career of Victor Adler (not related to Alfred), the founder of a unified Social Democratic party in Austria in the mid-1880s, paralleled Alfred Adler's career in this important respect. Like Alfred Adler, Victor Adler began his medical career with a small general practice in a working-class section of the city. In 1883, his interest in the health of the Austrian laboring classes led him to accept a temporary position as a government factory inspector, a post established under new labor legislation sponsored by the Austrian Prime Minister Taaffe. In this official capacity, he toured industrial sites in Germany, Switzerland, and England and, on his return, issued a report criticizing the factories in these countries and recommending passage of a worker's health law in Austria.

Victor Adler's recommendations were not acted upon, and he did not receive a permanent government appointment after his tour was completed. His experience as a medical factory inspector, however, did have a crucial effect on his subsequent career: it led him, in 1886, to the Austrian workers' movement. The physical plight of the working poor was henceforth to be addressed not through isolated medical interventions, but through the politics of socialist reform (Ermers, 1932, pp. 104, 109–112; Braunthal, 1965, pp. 37–39). Victor Adler never forsook the medical rationale that informed his political activism, however, and Max Ermers has contended that his socialism was from the outset a kind of "philanthropic medical socialism," a socialism that represented a consistent application of principles derived from medicine and the requirements of social hygiene (1932, pp. 248–249).

More than a decade after Victor Adler's conversion from medicine to politics, Alfred Adler too espoused a species of "philanthropic medical socialism" that addressed itself to the social dimension of medical practice. Although the younger Adler's observations were not abetted by official appointment to the

---

[7]On Gruber, see Frank (1928) and Gruber's own reminiscences (1923). On the student *Leseverein*, see McGrath (1974, chapter 1).

post of factory inspector, his medical-socialist ideology was the product of a comparable kind of first-hand inspection. Instead of extensive observations of a cross section of the European laboring population, Adler opted for an intensive examination of a single group within that population. He chose to write a detailed case study of the medical plight of one of Austria's dying home industries as the basis for his medical-socialist recommendations. The result was the *Health Book for the Tailoring Trade* of 1898.

One crucial difference remains, however, between the unifier of Austrian socialism and the founder of Individual Psychology. When Victor Adler returned from his tour of European industrial sites and presented his findings to the Austrian authorities, he was on the verge of relinquishing his medical identity on behalf of his new allegiance to the Austrian workers' movement. With Alfred Adler, there was never an outright transfer of allegiance. In the handful of "socialist" publications written between 1898 and 1904, Adler did not use his medical background as the basis for a new political identity. Instead, he arrived at his distinctively medical identity through the animus of his early socialist indignation. Adler's goal was to moralize medical practice, and he sought to accomplish this moralization by indicting the academic medical establishment ("*Schulmedizin*") for failing to understand physical illness as the product of remediable social circumstances. Once the theory of disease causation was broadened to include social-environment factors, Adler insisted that the "medical" requirements for health would dovetail with the political demands of the laboring classes, and that medicine and political reform would jointly provide the basis for a new concept of "social medicine."

II.

The *Health Book for the Tailoring Trade* (1898) was Adler's most impressive attempt to document the claim that medical practice was obliged to acknowledge the claims of "social medicine." His formal intent was to document the many ways in which specific occupational practices accounted for specific occupational diseases, and thereby to demonstrate the need for a broadened conception of disease etiology. To this end he fixed on the Austrian tailor trade, a dying *Hausindustrie* whose ongoing victimization by the industrial revolution translated into the increasing misery of its remaining practitioners. Plagued by erratic seasonal work, subject to the erratic wage practices of *Kleinmeister* themselves in the employ of large entrepreneurs, forced to labor in filthy homes 16 to 18 hours a day when work was available, the typical tailor suited Adler's purpose admirably.

It is altogether understandable that Adler should have used his medical experience as the basis for a piece of socialist criticism during this early part of his career. After the period of repressive legislation that accompanied Taaffe's "draconic regime" of the mid-1880s, the Social Democrats made steady progress in Austria following Victor Adler's success in unifying the party's moderate and radical wings. During the 1890s, emergency legislation against the Social Democrats was discontinued, Austrian trade unions were incorporated into the Social Democratic organization, and significant socialist gains were registered in the parliamentary elections of 1897. From 1898 onward, the Social Democrats made steady political progress during the very period when Austrian parliamentary life disintegrated under the impetus of the "nationalities" question (see Bruegel, 1925, pp. 228–234, 298–301, 305–312, 324–325). The quiet growth of the Austrian trade union movement accompanied the success of the Social Democrats. After the Second Trade Union Congress of 1897, Austrian trade unions underwent expansion and centralization. The growth of the movement was abetted by the passage of a federal law in 1898 which extended the competence of trade union courts (*Gewerbegerichte*) to all industries. Unfortunately, the Austrian clothing industry did not share in this growth; they failed to unionize, owing to the inequality between provincial shoemakers and urban tailors (Deutsch, 1929, pp. 355–360).

Although Vienna itself remained under the control of Karl Lueger and the Christian Socialist party from 1897, Lueger undertook a far-reaching program of municipal socialism that revolutionized Viennese life at the turn of the century. In 1898, the year Adler's *Health Book* appeared, Lueger instituted a municipal electric system, to be supplemented the following year by a municipal gas works. Lueger's civic mindedness far transcended the realm of public utilities, however, and included a number of measures to improve the level of urban hygiene. In addition to increasing the amount of municipal land set aside for parks, gardens, and forest preserves, he began construction of both a municipal waterworks and a new hospital. He also established a system of sanitary ambulances and a network of public baths for the city poor (See Kuppe, 1947, pp. 105ff.; Jenks, 1960, pp. 56ff).

In the atmosphere of hygienic improvement that accompanied such municipal reforms, it is not surprising that a Viennese general practitioner in a working-class district of the city should turn his attention to the occupational diseases besetting one of the city's oldest trades. There is nothing particularly subtle about Adler's elaborate documentation of the many diseases related to the conditions under which Austrian tailors worked and lived. What is noteworthy, however, is the skillful way in which Adler fused medical analysis with prescriptive political advice. His persuasive argument was that the many diseases that victimized the hapless tailors would not be medically remediable until a critique of the so-cioeconomic structure of the tailoring trade itself was accepted as a valid medical prerogative.

Adler was not content to catalogue the diseases of the tailor trade in order to indict the medical profession for simple insensitivity to occupational disease. His intent was rather to indict physicians for harboring the simple presumption that they could even understand (much less treat) disease in vacuo. The plight of the tailor trade served this aim because the broad range of diseases endured by tailors was not merely overdetermined in a way that eluded simple medical treatment, but was so tightly wedded to the economic conditions of the trade that tailors were desensitized to the very significance of "health" altogether. This, indeed, was the most dire implication of Adler's study. He showed that occupational diseases necessarily confounded the traditional medical perspective on illness because the economic conditions underlying these diseases had serious psycho-logical consequences; they made the members of the trade unreceptive to the medical *ideal* of health. This is what Adler meant when he denied that the excessive illness in the tailor trade could be derived from any special inaus-piciousness (*Ungunst*) related to the occupation itself. Rather, he claimed that the overall economic plight of the trade produced actual "hostility" toward health. It was this psychological attitude, in conjunction with the noxiousness of the trade, that heightened the tailors' vulnerability to disease (Adler, 1898, p. 11).

How could the medical profession presume to diagnose and treat the dispro-portionate amount of lung illness in the tailor trade? Adler explained that this illness was inherent in the very occupational methods (*Beschaeftigungsweise*) of the trade. The physical posture of the tailor hindered the development of the lungs, while the fabric-laden dust in the air he breathed facilitated the develop-ment of lung disease. Beyond this, the undernourishment of the tailor and the cramped unventilated residential quarters he occupied—these things made him a constitutionally weakened organism without the ability to resist lung disease.

How was the physician to cope with the many stomach disorders of the tailor? Adler claimed, again, that the curved physical posture of the tailor impeded blood flow from the heart. This caused excess blood to accumulate in the stom-ach and resulted in stomach disorders, bowel irregularities, and rectal fistulas. In addition to these deleterious consequences of the tailor's working posture, Adler once more pointed to the unbalanced diet of the tailor as a significant cause of stomach illness. He added that the long durations for which the tailor maintained his debilitating posture also led to crookedness of the spine and scoliosis. The tailor's overuse of his hands and contact with poisonous dyes led to various skin diseases, callouses, and panaritium. By biting off dyed thread in his mouth, the tailor developed serious dental problems. The prolonged close work increased near-sightedness and the chances of eye injuries. Constant use of the hands and arms, teamed with poor nourishment and unsanitary living conditions, also promoted muscle cramps, rhematism, and arthritis (pp. 15–19).

The catalogue of occupationally induced debilities is almost pathetic in its comprehensiveness. Adler ended his dreary recital by citing official statistics that consigned 12 to 27 percent of the tailor trade to a condition of total illness (*Gesammtkrankenstand*). "Misery is profoundly tied to the tailor trade," he wrote, "striking repeatedly with illnesses and breeding ever new forms of misery" (p. 19).

What lessons could be drawn from the demoralizing plight of the tailor trade? Adler clearly hoped his findings would prompt the passage of effective trade laws. He criticized the growing number of middlemen who depressed the earnings of the tailor, and he recorded the current progress of social labor legislation that had already won the tailor obligatory health insurance. Despite such progress, Adler was more concerned with enumerating the different areas in which existing social labor legislation had bypassed the plight of the small trades. He complained, for example, that accident insurance and factory inspection had, to date, been restricted to the large industries. Adler was "Marxist" enough, moreover, to append to his "revisionist" demands a bleak indictment of unregulated capitalism. What was the use of demonstrating the plight of the trade and trying to regulate its abuses by statute, he complained,

> if it is the unbridled competition of the world market that compels the small master to rely on the cheapest help he can get, to the most far-reaching exploitation of his assistants, and to recourse to seasonal work [p. 27].

More significantly, Adler made his political criticism dovetail with a more pointed indictment of the political indifference of the medical establisment. The lesson he drew from his investigation was that the Institute of Physicians was ineffectual against the great mass illnesses (*Volkskrankheiten*) of the day, and would remain so until it recognized the "social" dimension of medical treatment. "A successful conquest of tuberculosis," he wrote, "is unthinkable if the physician's range of activity extends only to the sick individual, if the patient merely learns the name of his illness, receives medication or some medical advice, and returns to the place where death awaits him" (p. 28). For Adler, the solution to occupational diseases depended on the medical profession's acceptance of a new level of social responsibility, and he directly implicated the physician in his proposals for remedying the plight of the tailor. Beyond improved labor legislation, Adler's chief demand for the tailors was the establishment of industry workshops. Medical factory inspectors would be necessary to examine these proposed workshops and see that the basic requirements of hygiene were met. The medical inspectors would underwrite specific hygienic rules to ensure tailors adequate air, space, and light, to determine the length of the work day, and to see that tailors were educated about the dangers of their trade. Since the diseases of the trade were abetted by unsanitary living conditions, moreover, Adler saw the officially appointed doctors, relying on strengthened building codes, as the key agents ensuring the implementation of new hygienic standards in the home (pp. 29, 30).

III.

The *Health Book for the Tailoring Trade* represented the empirical basis of Adler's call for a newly politicized medical profession. In a series of feuilletons written for Heinrich Gruen's *Aerztliche Standeszeitung* between 1902 and 1904, Adler generalized the verdict he had reached in 1898 and polemicized about the need for a new sense of social responsibility to his colleagues. In these editorials, Adler seized on the idea of ''prophylaxis'' as the medical concept that embodied the new political dimension of disease causation. Prophylaxis, which Adler designated ''the most valuable fruit that scientific medicine has offered the people,'' became the beacon light redirecting medicine toward a revitalized sense of social responsibility (1902a, p. 1; 1902b, p. 3). This was because the commitment to preventive medicine necessarily directed medical hygiene to the common principle that underlay all human illness: social misery (*soziale Elend*). In order to practice prophylactic medicine, the physician had to direct his attention to ameliorating the worker's lot by securing him hygienic living and working conditions.

This concept of prophylaxis derived, of course, from the study of the tailor trade, but Adler's conclusions were now absorbed in a broader critique of modern medical practice. For Adler the political requirements of preventive medicine had converted modern health care to a ''public problem'' that ''occupies lawyers and technicians perhaps as much as it occupies physicians.'' He informed his colleagues, without regret, that important questions pertaining to occupational hygiene and mass illnesses like tuberculosis and venereal disease were beginning to be evaluated over the heads of physicians:

The actual causes of this development have been largely established—that the physician had to be taken in tow by the condition of the profession and by the government, instead of marching at the forefront of this tendency. Perhaps there was a time when a brighter ray of light directed this profession, but in the little worries of daily life, in the always illusory expectations attached to elegant research projects, the medical profession again lost the long-range vision [1902, p. 3].

In ensuing editorials, Adler offered his own prescriptive recommendations for restoring the lost prophylactic vision to contemporary medicine. In an editorial entitled "An Academic Chair for Social Medicine," he proposed the establishment of a university professorship that would serve as the central office for promulgating hygiene to the people. Equipped with the authority of the government and medical science, the new chair and its affiliated seminars

would finally provide the undergirding for a system to replace the presently involved tangle of our hygiene. And the illumination that would be ignited there would also bring light not only to the heads and hearts of all listeners, but to the people themselves. Ten years of hygienic popular education, the freeing of hygience from the fetters of politics and bungling exploitation (*Beutemacherei*)—and then we will be able to discuss the mass epidemics! [1902a, p. 2].

In a three-part editorial of 1903 entitled "City and Country" (1903a), Adler stressed the need for uniform sanitary protection laws that would apply to both the cities and rural areas of Austria. Hygienic regulations confined to cities ignored the increasing interaction between urban and rural areas. Adler observed that only national laws regulating the water and food supplies could protect the cities from epidemics originating in rural villages.

In an editorial entitled "State Help or Self Help?" (1903b), Adler returned to the diminished stature of the medical profession at the level of national hygienic policies. He appealed to doctors themselves to counter the growing extent to which national medical policies rested in the hands of technicians and bureaucrats insensitive to the insights of physicians. He discounted, moreover, the possibility that the government itself would take an active role in revitalizing the medical profession. There was a Marxist tinge to Adler's criticism of the state that was missing in his earlier editorials, as well as an explicit reference to the class interests that directed state policy. On the one hand, he questioned the likelihood that the government would ever implement adequate hygienic regulations: ". . . no government can affect anything in its work, beyond conducting the business of politically influential strata whose interests it perceives." On the other hand, he doubted whether the state would be receptive to impartial medical advice on matters of health policy. The state, "the manager of the politically influential classes, cared for medical help only as long as it had to . . . what remains now of the medical profession no longer has unconditional importance" (1903a, No. 18, pp. 1, 3).

To become socially necessary once more, the medical profession had to make its quest for hygienic betterment subserve the political goals of the working class. For Adler, this verdict was testimony to the interdependence of medical science and political reform. The complete vindication of medical hygienic demands, he submitted, was "increasingly a question of the social and political elevation of the working class" (1903a, No. 18, p. 3; 1903b, No. 21, p. 1). By placing its skills at the disposal of the working people and documenting the indispensability of the physician for the hygienic elevation of the people, the medical profession would regain its political significance in society. Only by reaffirming its solidarity with the demands of the working class, moreover, would the medical profession acquire the political leverage to free itself from the straitjacket of state regulation. Adler complained that official authorities tended to put a brake on developments in medical science, inasmuch as research was constrained by "the hesitating social precautions of our time." He criticized the extent to which medical faculty appointments in Vienna were controlled by the state, and went so far as to adjudge the decline of the Vienna medical school "a gain for our ruling classes of the first order" (1903b, No. 21, p. 2; No. 22, pp. 1–2). His plan for the political reawakening of the medical profession thus represented a simultaneous plea for its liberation from outside political control.

IV.

As a socialist, Adler sounded the call for a program of hygienic betterment that would tie the medical profession to the goals of the Austrian working-class movement. Institutionally, he did no more than sound the call. Unlike Victor Adler and Max Gruber, Adler was content simply to articulate the socialist rationale behind the new "social medicine." He did not let the critical bent of his medical insights redefine his professional identity as a medical doctor, and he assumed no leadership role in the subsequent history of Austrian socialism. In the editorials written for the *Aerztliche Standeszeitung* during 1902 and 1903, Adler broached "prophylaxis" as a political goal for the entire medical profession. In a lengthy editorial of 1904, however, he examined the idea of prophylaxis at the level of concrete medical practice, and thereby relinquished the political tone of his earlier editorials for the neutral tone of the educational psychologist. Adler still extolled the concept of prophylaxis, but after 1903 he was content to explore the concept at the level of individual physicians treating individual patients. At this level, Adler's message became prescriptive rather than critical: he wanted physicians to practice preventive medicine in their daily work by becoming psychologists whose knowledge of child development would help them steer young patients away from the path of future illness. This was the level at which "hygiene" and "prophylaxis" was henceforth to be construed.

"The Physician as Educator," printed in three successive issues of the *Aerztliche Standeszeitung* in 1904 and reprinted in article form in 1914, is a remarkable preliminary statement of Adlerian psychology. It is immensely revealing that the article was editorialized in the *Aerztliche Standeszeitung* along with Adler's more polemical "socialist" contributions, for it reveals the therapeutic orientation that accompanied Adler's espousal of "prophylactic" medicine. Even more impressive is the content of the article; written in 1904, it contains basic insights that would guide Adler in all his post-Freudian educational and therapeutic activities. Adler's basic argument was that the treating physician was really an educator, and that it was through educational guidance that he could best practice "prophylactic" medicine. "The educational power of physicians and of medical science is enormous," he contended, and it was this power that left "imperishable traces" in all areas of prophylaxis and "spurs the best of the *Volk* to active collaboration" (1904, p. 2).

The physician was to implement prophylactic care by directing the "mental education" of the child and by interpreting such education in the broadest possible sense. He was to counsel only "healthy" couples without inherited illnesses to undertake propagation. He was to monitor the parental education of the child, seeing that the child was loved but not pampered, punished but not abused. He was to see that the child grew up "with a clear consciousness of finding in his parents always impartial and fair judges, but at the same time loving protectors" (p. 6). In particular, he was to take "preventive" action against two general vices of childhood—obstinacy and lying—and he was to orient such preventive measures around the development of a "courageous" (*mutig*) character in the child.

Adler warned that the physician must be especially prepared to treat the fearful, anxious, oversensitive (*ueberempfindlich*) child prone to become the useless "coward" of the next generation. Such children, unable to adapt to the social requirements of school and family life, withdrew into a solitude that was antithetical to the requirements of social life. Adler claimed that the physican had to direct these withdrawn children toward occupations that would absorb their hostilities in socially useful ways. With medical guidance, the antisocial child of today could be transformed into the butcher, hunter, or surgeon of tomorrow. The necessity for active medical intervention flowed from Adler's certainty that the withdrawn, hostile child was at heart a "coward" who was destined to remain "culturally inferior" in life (pp. 7, 8).

Adler's therapeutic perspective in these matters was clearly judgmental, but it was already judgmental in a way that had nothing to do with a socialist *Weltanschauung*. In this ostensibly "socialist" editorial of 1904, Adler did not explore the social or economic circumstances that contributed to the antisocial psychopathology of childhood. He never ventured any Marxist explanation as to why parents could not acculturate their children without engendering psychological conflicts. Finally, he never questioned, as Wilhelm Reich later would, the moral assumption that the physician could only "heal" by "educating" the deviant child to conform to society as it presently existed.

It is equally noteworthy that Adler's prescriptive editorial skirts the entire issue of "social Medicine" as it had figured in his editorial appeals of 1902 and 1903. Nineteen hundred and four, ironically, is a watershed in the popular education movement that had developed as a wing of the Austrian social reform movement during the last two decades of the nineteenth century; it is the year the Vienna Society for Popular Education (*Wiener Volksbildungsverein*) finally obtained its own building in the Ottakring (Fuchs, 1949, pp. 145–147). Yet, it is "The Physician as Educator" presentation of 1904 that signifies Adler's abandonment of his earlier commitment to the physician's role as a "popular educator" destined to sensitize the public to the importance of "hygiene" and "prophylaxis" as collective social goals.

V.

Adler's article on "The Physician as Educator" is an important transition piece. Written as a series of editorials in the socialist *Aerztliche Standeszeitung,* it betrays Adler's refusal to link the developmental problems of childhood to the social-class referents he had invoked in his study of the tailor trade and in his earlier espousal of "hygiene" as a working-class goal. In fact, from 1904 on, the political dimension is essentially missing from Adler's writings altogether. There are occasional scattered references to the concepts of hygiene and preventive medicine, but the concepts are only invoked from the perspective of Adler's new psychomedical categories. Indeed, after 1904, Adler's politics became psychologized altogether in the sense that political analogies were merely illustrative of the therapeutic values that emerged from medical psychology. By 1907, for example, the appeal to hygienic ideals became an idiom for the new theory of organ inferiority; hygiene henceforth aimed at securing the "compensation" of inferior organs (1907a, p. 13). An essay on the "Heredity of Illness" written a year later again demonstrated the strictly illustrative role of political relationships in elaborating the theory of organ inferiority. Adler believed that all injuries and illnesses suffered by an organism induced embryological changes in offspring that predisposed them to the "inferiority" in question. His intention in the following passage was to propound this Lamarckian inheritance of acquired organ damage as part of the organ inferiority theory and to show, in true Lamarckian fashion, that organ injuries could only be passed on to future generations if they impressed themselves on the reproductive cells:

> If we see the development, the exertion, and the damage of our organs as interrelated to economic conditions, if we see the strengths and illnesses of the human organism as mutually dependent on the developed level of commodity production, then we must acknowledge the same connections as applying to the reproductive organs which furnish the embryological material with the same strengths and weaknesses possessed by the struggling organism [1908a, p. 44].[8]

Culture, we shall see, was destined to play a crucial role in the theory of organ inferiority. After 1907, Adler insistently claimed that the fate of an organic overcompensation depended on the limitations of culture (1907a, p. 19). In addition, he was always quick to include environmentally induced injuries among the material of organic inheritance. He never chose, however, to use the cultural dimension of organ inferiority as the basis for a political critique of society. In his paper on inherited illnesses, for example, he mentioned alcoholism, syphilis, and tuberculosis as the three great injuries to the embryological material, but added that one could include with equal justification "all instances of assault (*Angriffsmomente*) of a social nature." But he never chose to expound the nature of such social injuries, and he never attempted to relate social injuries to particular forms of sociopolitical organization.

Conversely, whenever Adler did make pointed reference to the existing political order, his goal was not to inspire social or political reform, but to provide a political referent from which to present the new ideology of Individual Psychology. Adler's early socialist affiliation did not provide the ideology of his later psychology. Rather, his psychology supplanted politics as the ideological framework through which the original goals of preventive medicine were to be reached. After 1903, the goal of hygiene was no longer to be achieved in alliance with the political goals of the working class. It was to be reached, instead, through alliance with the pedagogical goals of the Individual Psychology movement. Although Adler's formal involvement with public education would await

---

[8]Sulloway (1979, p. 94n) has pointed out that Freud too subscribed to a version of this aspect of Lamarckian theory.

the end of World War I, his psychology was squarely pedagogical from the outset. His earliest psychological paper, "The Physician as Educator," depoliticized the quest for prophylaxis by reducing it to the level of pedagogical guidance to be dispensed by the physician. In the period following 1903, Adler proceeded to depoliticize the very notion of "hygiene" by divorcing it from the political conditions of the marketplace and anchoring it instead in the requirements of his own prescriptive pedagogy. The key to prophylaxis and to the revitalization of the medical profession was no longer the progress of the working class, but the growth of the physician's own psychopedagogical sensibilities.[9] In the attempt to allay social unhappiness, the quest for a "social medicine" was supplanted by the quest for a pedagogical psychology. By 1910, Adler was certain that important connections existed between educational influence and all manner of nervous disturbance. He was equally certain that Individual Psychology was qualified to determine the principles of sound pedagogy (1910a, p. 84).

Admittedly, certain political assumptions were embedded in the therapeutic strictures of Individual Psychology from the outset, and these assumptions became increasingly transparent in Adler's later career. In the broadest sense, Adler's prescriptive pedagogy retained "political" meaning by incorporating implicit normative assumptions about the kind of "community" to which children were to be socialized by their physicians. At the same time as Adler depoliticized the quest for community hygiene, in other words, he added a latent political dimension to the very meaning of medical treatment. In fact, by construing psychological values as the basis for educational socialization, Adler arrived at a position that constructively addressed the concerns of his earlier social criticism.

In the absence of an explicit statement by Adler as to why exactly he abandoned his call to political action after 1903, these last observations seem to provide a reasonable explanation for his definitive "shift" to psychology in 1904. It must be borne in mind that Adler's call to action was never much of a call to action in the first place. His socialist publications bespeak neither a ranging commitment to political reform nor an aggressive identification with the

---

[9]It is worth noting that Adler's abandonment of his "political" viewpoint in 1904 followed shortly after the beginning of his participation in Freud's Wednesday Evening Discussion Group. Beyond observing that the psychoanalytic meetings provided Adler with a weekly forum for expounding his new psychopedagogical viewpoint, it seems plausible to suggest that the exchanges within Freud's circle absorbed Adler's earlier political animus and thereby contributed to the abandonment of his socialist interests. Unfortunately, Adler's polemical reflections on Freud and psychoanalysis provide no evidence to support such conjecture.

political goals of the working class. Instead, they revolve around his focused preoccupation with the potentially ameliorative social impact of a politicized medical profession. By 1904, Adler probably recognized the futility of trying to reanimate the medical establishment with a socially informed concept of "prophylaxis." Apparently frustrated at the inability of both government and the medical profession to promote hygiene at the community level, Adler proceeded to formulate therapeutic guidelines that would enable the physician to cultivate hygiene at the individual level. In this sense, his advocacy of a prescriptive psychopedagogy did not signal the outright abandonment of his circumscribed political concerns, but a decision to atomize political reform by reducing it to the therapeutic relation between physician and patient.[10] In the course of this atomization, therapy was implicitly politicized, but any previous link to an established political ideology was severed.

This is not to suggest that Adler never mentioned general political considerations once he became a psychologist. In communicating the importance of his pedagogical psychology to a wider audience, he occasionally referred to cultural and political hindrances to proper child rearing. The point, however, is that after 1903, his criticisms operated entirely within the preconceptions of his psychology. He referred to such obstacles not to promote political reform, but to sensitize his audience to the importance of his psychopedagogical recommendations. In the opening paragraph of a 1907 paper on the "Developmental Defects of the Child," Adler prefaced his advice to parents with a lyrical panegyric on the importance of children for the future of the people. On behalf of the child, Adler made the same appeal for "air, light, and nourishment" that he had made in 1898 on behalf of the tailoring trade. In 1907, however, his comments lacked any political referent. The struggle that he invoked on behalf of the child was one for mental freedom (*Geistesfreiheit*). It was a struggle to be waged within the individual home by aroused parents whose mission was pedagogical rather than political. He wrote:

> In our children rests the future of the people (*Volk*)! All the creations of peoples, all urging forward, the destruction of old barriers and prejudices, usually happen for the sake of the progeny and are meant first of all to help them. While today the struggle for mental freedom rages, while we are shaking the pillars of superstition and serfdom, tomorrow our children will sun themselves in the mild light of freedom and drink from the fountains of pure knowledge, unconcerned about the threats of a decaying manner of thought. Whereas today the old and rotten collapses, having lost its right of existence, some day the church of true humanity will

---

[10]I owe this suggestion to Professor Jeffrey Merrick, Department of History, Barnard College.

arise more proud and daring than our thoughts can comprehend, before which any falsehood and deceit will be reduced to dust. For our children! They shall enjoy that to which we yearningly aspire: air, light, nourishment, which today are still kept from the people—our children shall fully partake of them! We are fighting for sanitary housing, adequate wages, for the dignity of labor, for solid knowledge, that these may some day be assured for our children. Our sweat is their peace; their health is our struggle [1907b, p. 33].

This fervent appeal might serve as the prologue to any reformist political ideology. Adler, however, appended to it a long catalogue of the physical and emotional ''inferiorities'' that complicated child development. Though he mentioned undernourishment of the parents, overwork of the pregnant mother, inadequate dwellings, and pressure on the child to perform prematurely, among the ''unfavorable social conditions'' that led to childhood inferiorities (1907b, pp. 34–35), he did not evaluate these conditions from the standpoint of the existing political order, and he never intimated that such conditions were remediable through broad-based social reform. He was content simply to call these factors to public attention, convinced that heightened psychological awareness was the key to genuine prophylaxis.

Adler adopted a comparable strategy in his important paper of 1910 on ''Defiance and Obedience.'' He pronounced the preeminence of masculinity the arch evil (*Krebsschaden*) of present culture that interfered with the healthy psychological development of females. He never commented on this evil from the standpoint of social or political structures, however, and his proposed palliatives eschewed political reform for a reformed individual pedagogy. At the end of the paper, Adler confessed that the cure of neurotic ''defiance'' entailed a loss of some part of the child's belief in authority. He did not regret this eventuality, however, noting that

We [thereby] contribute to a time when every person is self-reliant and free, and will realize his justly deserved station no longer in the service of a person but in the service of the common idea of physical and mental progress [1910a, p. 93].

But what did the ''common idea of physical and mental progress'' entail from the standpoint of the organization of society? Here Adler was once more silent. He never considered ''defiance'' as a neurotic strategy conditioned by particular kinds of socioeconomic structures, and he showed no desire to link the future time of self-reliance to concrete forms of socioeconomic reorganization. Even in 1910, his psychological ideals were formulated in vacuo and presented as neutral pedagogic strictures that subserved medical hygiene.

VI.

Once Adler had translated his earliest social criticism into the language of his medical psychology, his political thought was basically at an end. Henceforth his political opinions would be no more than thinly veiled exercises in applied Individual Psychology. This verdict applies especially to the several "political" publications that grew out of his experiences in World War I. In 1916, as the military situation in Austria deteriorated, Adler was drafted as an army physician and sent to the neuropsychiatric section of the military hospital of Semmerling. He was subsequently transferred to the neuropsychiatric section of the Garrison Hospital No. 15 in Cracow, and later, in November, 1917, to the military hospital of Grinzing where he was responsible for the care of typhus patients (Ellenberger, 1970, pp. 586–587). During this interval of military service, Adler was newly sensitized to the political victimization of the common soldier on the front. This sensitivity translated into an open conflict concerning his medical responsibilities. Adler was inclined to use his medical authority to relieve wounded soldiers of further active duty, but this normal medical prerogative was actively countered by the pressure exerted by military authorities anxious to have the wounded return to the front lines (1919, p. 5). As a civilian physician transplanted into a structured military hierarchy, Adler was disconcerted by the opposing pressures exerted on him, and his professional unhappiness canalized into active loathing toward the war. *The Other Side* (1919), a pamphlet published in Vienna shortly after the conclusion of the war, was the key expression of the disillusionment engendered by his military service.

Adler's point in this polemical pamphlet was to exonerate the German peoples from any responsibility for the war. His apologetic was in this respect entirely unexceptional; he claimed the *Volk* had been unwittingly indoctrinated to the virtues of docile obedience through the efforts of the ruling classes and the media. He debunked the authenticity of the people's reputed "will to war," claiming they had been "enslaved" and manipulated by deceptive leaders.[11] As

---

[11]Adler returned to this issue a decade later in a letter to Eugen Relgis of 2 November 1929 (Jewish National & University Library, Ar. Ms. Var. 563/1). In this intriguing document, he is content to explain the willingness of peace-loving individuals and groups to endorse the war as a "mass phenomenon that can only be explained mass psychologically as a search for a collectively sanctioned way of regaining the satisfaction associated with the exercise of individual responsibility." Adler thereby posed a strategy of exoneration that was a variant of his psychological understanding of "inferiority" and "superiority." He believed that the social conditions of war robbed individuals of their sense of self-worth by robbing them of a sense of individual responsibility for the events shaping their lives. Support for the war effect thereby became a reactive, virtually overcom-

an army physician caught in the "middle," Adler recollected the lengths to which soldiers had gone in order to elicit a medical excuse for not returning to the front (p. 6). As a psychiatrist, he questioned the integrity of those soldiers who enlisted voluntarily, suggesting that such volunteers had simply made a virtue out of necessity. These soldiers actually sought war no more than their recruited counterparts. They had merely

> found the desired escape. Now they were no longer whipped dogs who were surrendered against their will to the shower of bullets—no, they were heroes, defenders of the fatherland and their honor. They themselves had uttered the call and they thereby came forward as defenders of right in the holy struggle [p. 14].

Adler claimed that the German peoples were entirely unprepared for the reality of the war. He stated that the *Volk* was "underage" (*unmuendig*),

> and would have retained its minority with every means of cunning and force. It possessed no means of resistance, it possessed no leader whose voice it could listen for. Its defeat was effectively accomplished by the beginning of the war, and it payed to its rulers a war contribution for which the rulers have never granted a hearing: the most costly blood flows, hunger and sickness cry out of faces, the minds of children are terribly poisoned, agriculture and industry lie fallow [pp. 11–12].

Yet, what kind of analytic insights did Adler offer to explain this sad predicament? Here the social critic retreated to the sterile nomenclature of psychology. Because he refused to range beyond his intractable psychological preconceptions, Adler could not offer a psychological explanation of the German peoples' vulnerability in the prewar period that had any analytic content. Instead, he was content to invoke a nonreductive psychological category to identify the missing ingredient that would have potentiated the people's resistance to the war. What the soldiers lacked, Adler observed, was "the unifying bond of a mutually trusting, a strong, trained community feeling (*Gemeinschaftsgefuehl*)." It was this absence of community feeling that made the people vulnerable to leaders

---

pensatory attempt to regain the self-worth associated with the exercise of individual responsibility. It was the lack of individual accountability for the war, Adler wrote, that makes the vast majority of normally peace-loving people feel "deprived of their rights and robbed of their ability to make decisions. In the feeling of abandonment, in the feeling of the deepest human degradation, in the agonizing feeling of inferiority, in the knowledge of their complete worthlessness, they search for a support (*Halt*). One finds such a support in their recognition of the rightness of their country and their acceptance of superstitions about the vile acts of their enemy, in their readiness to acquiesce to all lies and in their belief in the success of their own 'good' cause."

who cultivated "war lust" (*Krieglust*) and prevented the nations of the Austro-Hungarian empire from staging a unified public revolt against the war. In the aftermath of the war, Adler added, "only a powerful current of growing community feeling" could bring salvation to the defeated peoples (pp. 9, 10, 12).

But why did the German peoples lack community feeling and how might one go about cultivating it? On these points, Adler was predictably silent. In all his clinical and educational writings following World War I, he expounded the notion of *Gemeinschaftsgefuehl* as the only genuine psychological virtue, and he used the term both as an index of man's inborn sociability and as the paramount objective of education and psychotherapy.[12] Yet, Adler's notion was never intended to be anything but a psychosocial truism; he never imparted any analytical substance to the idea that gave it meaning outside of his own subjective psychological preconceptions. In the polemical protest against World War I, Adler's psychological subjectivism was plainly in evidence. He bypassed any attempt to ground the concept of community feeling in particular socioeconomic or historical conditions, and he never considered why such conditions were missing in Germany and Austria during the prewar years. Adler's political point was nothing but a suppositional psychological point; it presupposed, and was simply illustrative of, Adler's own psychological values.

The same attempt to translate psychological values into political prescription characterized Adler's essay on "Bolshevism and Psychology" that he published in the Swiss *Internationale Rundschau* in 1918. *Gemeinschaftsgefuehl* was once again the only evaluative referent in Adler's political vocabulary. He reiterated that the people had been seduced to a "war lust" that ran counter to its true nature and had reached enlightenment only after enduring the horrors of the Great War. The great lesson learned was that the striving for domination poisoned the collective life of man: "Whoever wants the community, must renounce the striving for power" (1918a, p. 597). Out of the agony of the war, a revitalized German nation had given to the world this fundamental cultural insight—that community sense (*Gemeinsinn*) and not the striving for power had to become the "guiding idea" underlying cultural development.

For Adler, the new appreciation of the community was tied to the emergence of socialism in Germany. Capitalism, with its "uncontrollable greed for subjugation," had suppressed community sense and glorified power strivings. Socialism, conversely, had posited community sense as the ultimate goal of man's collective life. In this connection, Adler lauded Marx because his discovery of the common struggle of the proletariat against the ruling classes pointed the way

---

[12]See chapters 8 & 9, below.

to the final implementation of community feeling (1918, p. 598). He denounced the Bolshevik takeover of Russia, however, because the Bolsheviks had turned their backs on the requirements of community feeling. Although seeking to implement many of the goals of socialism, the Bolshevik solution was imposed through the traditional deployment of power. In the process, the Bolsheviks had willfully disavowed the psychological value that was the principal legacy of political socialism. However beneficent their goals, their tactics, for Adler, were necessarily ill-fated: "Wherever questions of power (*Machtfragen*) come into question, the individual's will to power is stimulated and opposition results, regardless of the excellence of the aims and goals involved" (p. 599). Counter force was the necessary "psychological side" of any power struggle, and Adler was therefore fatalistic in his prognosis: "The domination of Bolshevism is, as with all previous governments, grounded on the possession of power. With this, its fate is proclaimed." Once power was invoked, the goal of community feeling was the necessary victim. If those Bolsheviks presently entranced by *Macht* were to be called back, on the other hand, it could only be through potentiating the memory of the "wonder of *Gemeinschaftsgefuehl* . . . that can never succeed through the application of force" (p. 600).

In both of these postwar publications, Adler's theoretical vantage point could hardly have been plainer. His political commentary was never more than a metaphor for his psychopedagogical recommendations, and his vague advocacy of "socialism" was nothing but a pretext for the imposition of the single psychological concept that was invoked in these recommendations. In short, Adler has no significance as a socialist after he became a psychiatrist, and it is misleading to submit, as Ellenberger (1970) does, that during the postwar period, "Adler's socialist opinions again came to the fore although in an original and renewed fashion" (p. 587). Adler's disenchantment with his untenable medical role in the war was obviously heartfelt, but he made no serious attempt to explore the basis of this disenchantment as a socialist. Rather, he used his disenchantment as the occasion for restating the psychological assumptions he brought to his wartime duties.

These assumptions revolved around the idea of community feeling. For Adler, the absence of community feeling was at the root of the German peoples' unwitting participation in the war, and the new cultural preeminence of community feeling was the positive legacy of the suffering of the war. Yet, Adler never considered the sociohistorical meaning of the concept in the context of prewar German society, just as he would never explore the epistemological status of the concept in his postwar psychological lectures. When he indicted capitalism, it was because capitalist organization cultivated an "uncontrollable greed for subjugation'' that aggravated power strivings and subverted the healthy growth of community feeling. When he appealed to Karl Marx, it was only to record Marx's status as a proto-Adlerian whose vision of the proletariat's struggle ''showed the way toward the final realization of community feeling'' (1918a, p. 598). Never did Adler's insight range beyond his theoretical commitments as psychiatrist and physician.

What, however, was the actual range of theoretical commitments that informed Adler's appeal to community feeling after World War I? Between Adler's early advocacy of ''hygiene'' and ''prophylaxis'' as medico-socialist ideals and his eventual promulgation of community feeling as the preeminent psychological value, there is the entire matter of his theoretical development. When Adler abandoned his short-lived attempt at social criticism in 1903, he did not thereby become a full-time psychiatrist devoted to the psychopedagogical implementation of his socialized ''hygienic'' ideals. In this respect, Adler's 1904 paper on ''The Physician as Educator'' is exceptional. It embodies many of the key insights of his later Individual Psychology and wrongly implies that Adler's transition from socialism to psychotherapy was direct and unmediated.

This was hardly the case. When Adler ''psychologized'' the quest for community hygiene in papers written between 1908 and 1910, he was not merely picking up where he had left off in 1903. In reality, Adler's identity until about 1909 was at least as ''medical'' as it was ''psychiatric,'' and his psychopedagogical recommendations were grounded in certain medical observations that followed his investigation of the tailor trade in 1898. Medicine was the bridge that took Adler from community hygiene to individual hygiene, and within the context of his medical work, it was the theory of organ inferiority that mediated the transition.

2

From Medicine to Psychiatry: The Foundations of Adlerian Theory, Part I

The traditional perspective on Adler's 1907 *Study of Organ Inferiority and its Psychical Compensation,* the clinical chef d'oeuvre that initiated his transition from medicine to psychiatry, has been one of charitable aloofness. We learn from Ernest Jones (1955, p. 131) that Adler's book was well received by the Vienna analysts at the time of publication; Freud himself later acknowledged it to be a valuable addition to the knowledge of neurosis (1914, p. 99). Although Jones appended the qualifier that the work was largely independent of psycho-analysis, he still conceded its importance as a valid pioneering attempt to circumscribe the question of neurotic "predisposition" that Freud and his colleagues recognized as important.[1]

This circumspect evaluation has proved doubly convenient for psychoanalysts interested in placing Adler's putative therapeutic achievement inside the parameters of Freud's intellectual development. On the one hand, this judgment credits Adler with a certain degree of investigative originality that produced a credible clinical achievement. On the other hand, by appraising Adler's study as an acceptable contribution to the question of neurotic "predisposition" *as Freud recognized it,* psychoanalytic critics like Jones provide themselves with a useful theoretical baseline from which to evaluate Adler's subsequent "split" from the

---

[1]This published estimation of Adler's theory of organ inferiority was not entirely retrospective. Gaston Rosenstein, an occasional participant in the discussions of the Vienna Psychoanalytic Society, praised Adler for attempting to give Freud's *Neurosenlehre* a biological foundation in a *Jahrbuch fuer Psychoanalytische Forschungen* article of 1910.

Freudians. If the study of organ inferiority was a valid psychoanalytic contribution, it means that Adler was at one time theorizing within the framework of Freud's psychoanalysis, and that his "deviation" represents a subsequent development to be explained through an examination of Adler's perverse therapeutic ambitions. Instead of exploring at face value the textual implications of Adler's early work, in other words, critics have pigeonholed the significance of his organ theory of inferiority in order to clarify and justify the historical question they are most intent on raising: why did Adler, one of the original participants in Freud's Wednesday evening discussion group and the first president of the Vienna Psychoanalytic Society, "abandon" his commitment to psychoanalytic principles through "deviant" formulations and "split" from Freud and his followers?

The psychoanalytic standpoint on Adler's medical theories has proved misleading in a second sense. By emphasizing the compatibility of the theory of organ inferiority with psychoanalysis, critics like Jones have presumed a basic discontinuity between Adler's early medical work and his later anti-Freudian psychology. In reality no such discontinuity exists. Adler's system of Individual Psychology is no more than a logical elaboration of psychological assumptions that underlay his medical theorizing from the outset. It will be the task of the next two chapters to elaborate these assumptions, and to chart chronologically the gradual liberation of Adler's psychological categories from their medical trappings during the period between 1907 and 1910. Such detailed consideration of Adler's early ideas serves an essential purpose: it demonstrates the degree to which Adler's system of psychotherapy was erected on foundations provided by his work in clinical medicine. By clarifying the underlying continuity between Adler's psychomedical categories, moreover, such consideration provides an important context for reevaluating the relationship between Adler's system and Freud's psychoanalysis.

I.

The verdict of academic medicine on Adler's theory of organ inferiority has not been charitable. Julius Wagner-Jauregg, the ranking Viennese psychiatrist who rejected Adler's application for appointment as a Privatdozent in neurology in 1915, found his work "clever" (*geistreich*) but scientifically vacuous. Anyone could demonstrate the existence of inherited organ inferiorities, he pointed out, if the very concepts of "organ" and "inferiority" were used as elastically as Adler employed them. For Adler, the eye, the visual "organ," did not simply denote the eyeball; it included all the muscles attached to it as well as that part of the nervous system implicated in the act of seeing. Comparably, the notion of an inherited "inferiority" embraced dispositions to entirely unrelated illnesses. For Adler, the same congenital inferiority of the skin that caused hives in a mother accounted for an outbreak of boils in her son. Adler's "astonishing association of ideas" (*verblueffende Ideenverbindungen*), Wagner-Jauregg suggested, was a product of subjective intuition; it had nothing to do with natural scientific inquiry (Beckh-Widmanstetter, 1965, pp. 183–184, 187).

There is clearly merit to this judgment, but in its estimation of Adler's theory from the standpoint of academic medicine, it is no less misleading than the psychoanalytic judgment that Adler's theory was intended to illuminate the "medical" factors that predisposed certain individuals to become neurotic. Both perspectives belie Adler's eminently practical, therapeutic intent. He subtitled his book "a contribution to clinical medicine," and he invoked the concept of the "inferior organ" for a discrete diagnostic reason: it helped account for the fact that certain diseases were both inherited and confined to particular organ systems, however broadly construed these systems might be. By morphologic inferiority, Adler referred to the deficient development of an organ as characterized by hereditary character, inferior size, form, position, as well as by the various stigmata of degeneration. By functional inferiority, he referred to the functional result of the morphologic anomaly: the inability of the organ to perform a quantity or quality of work sufficient to satisfy a standard of required effectiveness. In both cases, it is immediately clear that Adler's basic intent was not to supplement Freud's psychoanalytic explanation of neurosis by postulating an organic "predisposition" that underlay neurosis. Instead, he sought to provide a heuristic clinical device that would help the physician evaluate certain confusing disease states (1907c, pp. 5–17; 1907d, pp. 1–11).[2]

By linking organic pathology to organ systems that manifested "inferiorities" both morphologically and functionally, Adler offered a clinical theory that represented an original amalgamation of certain aspects of the rival "functional" and

---

[2]It is suggestive of the *clinical* vantage point from which Adler propounded the theory of organ inferiority that the most elaborate and well-documented demonstration of the theory did not appear in the *Study* itself, but in the substantive urological contribution "On the Etiology, Diagnosis and Therapy of Nephrolithiasis [Kidney Stones]" (1907e) that appeared in the *Wiener Klinische Wochenschrift* several months after the appearance of the monograph. Adler argued that kidney stones really constituted a sign of a more encompassing, hereditary inferiority of the urinary tract that could be traced back to fetal development. In arguing his point, he amassed an impressive amount of clinical evidence pointing to the fact that kidney stones were usually accompanied by a variety of systemic urinary tract disturbances. His conclusion was that "In most cases of nephrolithiasis, it is not a question of a grossly obvious retarded development of the kidneys per se . . . Such obvious retardation of kidney development is valuable for our argument because it constitutes a clear sign of the inferiority of the urinary apparatus as a discrete organ system" (p. 1536).

"anatomic" theories of disease that dominated European psychiatric thought during the latter half of the nineteenth century. To the extent that he traced pathology back to morphologically inferior organs, Adler offered a generalized variant of the "pathoanatomical" orientation that sought to explicate mental disorders in terms of the pathological anatomy of the brain. This approach to mental disorder, which received its foremost exemplification in the work of Wilhelm Griesinger and Theodor Meynert, sought to detect actual anatomical lesions in the brain that corresponded to different psychiatric and neuropathic syndromes.[3] By claiming that brain lesions caused all mental abnormalities, the German pathoanatomical psychiatrists propounded a restrictive neurological equivalent of Adler's general theory—they believed that different psychiatric syndromes necessarily corresponded to different kinds of anatomically demonstrable "inferiorities" of the brain. Although Adler formulated his theory of organ inferiority from the standpoint of clinical medicine rather than academic psychiatry, he seemed aware of the general compatability of his theory of "morphologic" organ inferiority with the work of the pathoanatomical psychiatrists. Thus, in discussing a disease of the central nervous system like epilepsy, he duly noted that "the anomalies of form in the brain emphasized by Meynert and others coincide with [his own conception of] morphologic inferiorities" (1970c, p. 18; 1907d, p. 13).

When Adler tied his notion of an inferior organ to manifest inadequacies in the organ's actual functioning, on the other hand, he was implicitly resorting to a criterion of pathology that typified theories of "functional disease." These theories were collectively informed by the assumption that certain clinical syndromes could involve changes in nervous system functioning unaccompanied by structural alterations in the brain (Levin, 1978, pp. 36n, 40–41). Adler, once more, dealt with clinical material that took him well beyond the parameters of brain lesions and nervous system functioning per se, but his adherence to a general theory of "functional" organ inferiority conformed with the viewpoint of the adherents of the theory of functional disease: certain types of organ inferiorities do not point to observable morphologic inferiorities in the organ, but are identified by the manifestly deficient level of functioning that characterizes the organ's performance.

Significantly, it is this "functional" criterion of organ inferiority that predominated in Adler's clinical conceptualizations of specific "inferiorities." Morphologic signs might provide useful confirmatory evidence of an inferior organ, but they were by themselves neither necessary nor sufficient to determine

---

[3]On pathoanatomical psychiatry in the late nineteenth century, see Levin (1978, pp. 16–41).

that an organ inferiority in fact existed. There seems to be an implicit reason why Adler retreated from a ''morphologic'' to a ''functional'' perspective on organ inferiority in his clinical work. Despite his aspiration to making a scientific contribution to clinical medicine, his theory of organ inferiority was in the final analysis the vehicle for developing certain psychological ideas, and it was only from the standpoint of functional organ deficiencies that the psychological assumptions underlying his ostensibly ''medical'' concerns could gain expression.

Thus, the most significant implication that emerges from Adler's doctrine of organ inferiority is veiled behind his opening statement of the functional dimension of the inferiority: the inferior organ is unable to perform work that is sufficient ''to satisfy a standard of required effectiveness'' (1907c, p. 10; 1907d, p. 6). The standard against which inferiority was to be gauged, in other words, was not an intrinsic level of performance formulated according to a conventional ''medical'' criterion, but a ''required'' standard forcibly brought to bear on the organ from the outside environment. In the *Study*, it was not until the sixth chapter that Adler bluntly restated what he meant—that the inferior organ was less able to meet the demands of culture, that by virtue of its inferiority ''the participation of the organ and its activity in the demands of culture (*die verlangte Kultur*) remain behind'' (1907c, p. 64; 1907d, p. 58). By invoking the cultural referent, Adler continued to incorporate into his clinical perspective his earlier concern with community medicine.

In a 1907 lecture on the theory of organ inferiority delivered to the Philosophical Society of the University of Vienna, he was more direct about the relationship between community standards and his governing clinical idea. Although an inferior organ could be inherited, Adler noted, the actual outbreak of illness represented a convergence between the organ's congenital vulnerability and the outer demands made on it. This formulation did not merely mean that cultural demands *triggered* the organ's demonstrable inferiority; it was rather a question of actually *defining* organ inferiority in terms of variable cultural demands. Such external demands were related to the developmental potentialities of the organ along with the ''psychological superstructure'' that built up around it, and they actually ''condition the relative inferiority of an organ when their requirements exceed a certain measure'' (1907a, p. 12; Ansbacher, p. 25).

II.

From the standpoint of clinical practice, Adler's ultimate reliance on a functional definition of organ inferiority incorporates a relativism that underscores the underlying psychosocial meaning of his theory. Apart from the cultural demands that demonstrated an organ's deficient level of functioning, Adler conceded that the attribution of inferiority was a hypothetical inference without any real therapeutic significance. To be sure, he made the inference of inferiority inductively from a knowledge of the manifest inferiorities present in a family tree, and he argued, without real explanation, that an inferiority could be demonstrated at the embryonic stage of development (1907a, p. 11). At this inductive level, however, Adler's inference about the presence of an inferiority lacked empirical content in the sense that it could never be falsified.[4]

---

[4]See Popper (1934, especially chapter 3). Significantly, Popper's "falsifiability" criterion of demarcation—i.e., his criterion for differentiating scientific from nonscientific theories—constitutes, in part, a reaction to his exposure to Adler and Individual Psychology following World War I. At that time, he came into contact with Adler to the point of "cooperat[ing] with him in his social work among the children and young people in the working-class districts of Vienna where he had established social guidance clinics." In 1919, following this experience, Popper arrived at the verdict that the principal weakness of Adler's theories (like Freud's) resided in the fact that they were necessarily confirmed by Adler's clinical work. Here are the two celebrated examples of human behavior that Popper invoked to make this point: "that of a man who pushes a child into the water with the intention of drowning it; and that of a man who sacrifices his life in an attempt to save the child. Each of these two cases can be explained with equal ease in Freudian and in Adlerian terms. According to Freud the first man suffered from repression (say, of some component of his Oedipus complex), while the second man had achieved sublimation. According to Adler the first man suffered from feelings of inferiority (producing perhaps the need to prove to himself that he dared to commit some crime), and so did the second man (whose need was to prove to himself that he dared to rescue the child). I could not think of any human behaviour which could not be interpreted in terms of either theory. It was precisely this fact—that they always fitted, that they were always confirmed—which in the eyes of their admirers constituted the strongest argument in favour of these theories. It began to dawn on me that this apparent strength was in fact their weakness." Adler's theories, like Freud's, "were simply nontestable, irrefutable. There was no conceivable human behaviour which could contradict them" (1963, pp. 33–34, 37).

In reaching this judgment, Popper was of course content to lump together Freud and Adler as the progenitors of two comparably "pseudoscientific" psychological theories. In recent years, the epistemological adequacy of Popper's falsifiability criterion of demarcation, particularly as a test of the scientific status of psychoanalytic theory, has been forcefully challenged by Adolf Gruenbaum (1977, 1979). Gruenbaum has undertaken to demonstrate that (1) psychoanalytic theory *does* generate hypotheses that are falsifiable and therefore "scientific" according to Popper's criterion of demarcation. But he goes on to contend that (2) psychoanalytic hypotheses have by and large failed to achieve scientific status according to the traditional canons of induction. Gruenbaum is thereby led to the conclusion that (3) the falsifiability criterion of demarcation is really less stringent—i.e., less capable of differentiating scientific from prescientific or pseudoscientific theories—than the inductivist criterion Popper intended it to supplant.

While a critical estimation of Gruenbaum's multifaceted critique of the falsifiability criterion is unnecessary here, I believe several observations relevant to my invocation of "falsifiability" vis-à-vis Adler's theory of organ inferiority are warranted. Initially, it should be borne in mind that Gruenbaum's case for the scientific *admissibility* of psychoanalytic theory from the standpoint of the falsifiability of psychoanalytic hypotheses takes the form of an attack on Popper's "slipshod" account of Freudian explanation; Adlerian explanation is never incorporated into his critique. Yet, Popper not only speaks of Freudian psychoanalysis *and* Adlerian Individual Psychology as two of the three theories that spurred him to develop the falsifiability criterion, but recounts that he had first-

In sum, the theory of organ inferiority embodies an ongoing tension between Adler's desire to provide an original explanation of organic disease that conforms with an understanding of inherited disorders and manifests itself at the level of morphologically inferior organs, and his knowledge that such a theory is necessarily reconstructive and of little value to the clinician. Stated somewhat differently, Adler wanted physicians to accept the fact that organs inferior from birth predetermined sickness and that inherited inferiorities frequently corresponded with inherited illness, but his scientific ambition of providing an *encompassing* explanation of disease never let his theory rest at this level of simple clinical convergence. In fact, the continual stress on the manifold clinical outcomes that could accrue from inferior organs served to undercut the predictive importance of those convergences between inferior organs and manifest illnesses that did occur. Thus, Adler argued that the appearance of sickness in one member of a family tree necessarily signified the existence of a comparable inferiority in the familial forebears and descendants even if these relations actually remained healthy (1907a, p. 13). The inference of organ inferiority on inductive hereditary grounds, in other words, was never tantamount to the claim that any of the "tainted" family members actually manifested a demonstrably inferior organ. At the level of modern genetics, then, the theory of organ inferiority had little predictive value, and Adler seemed to realize as much. He noted that the questions relating to the origins of organ inferiority were of deep biological significance, but added that the clinical importance of the theory did not hinge exclusively on the answer to these questions.

A year later, in a paper "On the Inheritance of Illnesses" (1908a), Adler addressed himself directly to the origins of organ inferiority, but his heuristic

---

hand experience only with Adler's theory at the time (1919) he arrived at the formulation (1963, pp. 34–35; 1974, p. 30). From the standpoint of Popper's own intellectual history, then, it appears that the Adlerian referent is considerably more relevant to the development of the falsifiability criterion than the Freudian—though neither, Popper cautions, is as important as Marxism (1974, pp. 27–28). Thus, even if the falsifiability criterion is actually satisfied by the hypotheses generated by *psychoanalytic* theory, it may remain unsatisfied by the relatively *less* falsifiable hypotheses of Adlerian psychology with which Popper came into personal contact. Popper, after all, believed that hypotheses were subject to "degrees" of testability based on subclass relations and considerations of dimensionality (1934, chapter 6). It may well be that Adlerian statements about "inferiorities" are more probable than Freudian statements about, say, castration anxiety, because they contain less empirical content and a lower degree of testability than the latter. Regrettably, neither Gruenbaum nor Popper himself has systematically compared Freudian and Adlerian hypotheses with respect to degrees of testability. Along related lines, I believe recent attempts to demonstrate the epistemological *inappropriateness* of falsifiability as a criterion for gauging the scientific character of psychoanalytic explanation (e.g., Rubinstein, 1975, 1978) can be granted without dismissing summarily the ability of Popper's criterion to pinpoint the empirical and predictive emptiness of more tautological Adlerian hypotheses.

construction was highly speculative and equally invulnerable to empirical refutation. His point was that organ inferiority could be triggered by any form of developmental, environmental, or chemical injury inflicted on an organ, even if the injury did not perceptibly harm the organ. According to Adler, the reason an inheritable organ inferiority could be inferred after such injuries was that the embryological material (*Keimstoff*) of the individual was far more vulnerable to injury than the finished organ. The embryological material was modifiable, moreover, in a way that was directly transmissible to offspring at the embryologic stage. Embryological damage was at the root of organ inferiority, in other words, even though the injury resulting in this damage need not cause manifest inferiority in the organ that sustained the injury.

The problem with the dichotomy between embryological damage and organ inferiority was that it removed to a new level, without really eliminating, the nonempirical dimension of Adler's speculations. This was because the built-in overcompensatory potential that characterized "mature" inferior organs was operative even at the embryological level at which the injury was transmitted. There was consequently no necessity for an empirically "inferior" outcome even when inferiority was implanted at the formative stage of development. While the transmitted injury could in fact promote incomplete development (*Entwicklungsstillstaende*) and malformations (*Fehlbildungen*) in the embryo, Adler noted that

> the list of embryological injuries, which, as harmless imprints, are recognized as "variations," is so diverse that the organ which can be traced to such injuries is by no means deficient or unfit. Rather, in many cases, such organs, due to their greater—because nearer to the embryo—energy for growth, are adapted to overcome resistances of a social nature. In the struggle for existence, such resistances might well bring the [healthy] parent organs to the point of breakdown [1908a, pp. 44–45].

The variable outcome of transmissible organ damage only reinforces the strictly pragmatic value of the theory of organ inferiority for clinical medicine. Adler suggested that the clinician need not wait until science could proceed inductively from manifest organ injury to the biological inference of congenital organ inferiority. In the meantime, he could make deductive use of the congenital vulnerability to organ inferiority to explain the different variations and alterations of organ functioning in clinical practice (1907a, p. 13). From this pragmatic standpoint, however, the functionally deficient organ could only be identified as the one that failed to perform the cultural work expected of it. Apart from the cultural requirements that condition the *relative* inferiority of an organ, attribution of inferiority to an organ is empiricially empty. The concept of inferiority can hardly possess meaningful therapeutic implications, it would seem, if Adler can contend in the first chapter of his *Study* that

> the inferiority of an organ does not need to reveal itself throughout a whole lifetime, or the expression may remain so insignificant that one scarcely thinks that one has an inferior organ before one, or else it expresses itself as a morphologic anomaly and even then at times so slightly that the condition of the individual is not brought into question [1907c, p. 16; 1907d, p. 11].

In Chapter 2, he goes on to admit that

> there are a great number of forms of inferiority which plainly injure neither health nor the duration of life. Such, in particular, are mild functional or peripherally situated inferiorities [1907c, p. 18; 1907d, p. 13].

And at the end of the same chapter,

> so the fact has to be acknowledged that in later life, under the influence of the manner of living, inferiority will not always be exposed or betrayed by illness. It happens perhaps just as frequently that in place of the expected inferiority we find nothing abnormal. Instead we may actually find an exaggerated peculiarity, even a superiority (*Ueberwertigkeit*) in its place [1907c, p. 26; 1907d, p. 20].[5]

From the virtually brazen irrefutability of the theory of organ inferiority, from Adler's total inability to correlate the notion of a physiological "inferiority" even probabilistically with demonstrable "inferiorities," we arrive once more at the realization that the clinical relevance of Adler's medical doctrine falls back on relative cultural requirements. It is these requirements that impose a standard of functional effectiveness on the organ that the "inferior" organ simply cannot meet. But why is this noteworthy? What are the implications of this latent cultural presupposition for our understanding of Adler's early "medical" theorizing?

The answer is obvious. The cultural referent for inferior organ performance points to the fact that Adler's prepsychiatric theory of organ inferiority veils important social psychological assumptions. To the extent that this is true, it further suggests that Adler's transition from social medicine to clinical medicine is partly misleading. Even within the arcane world of organ pathology, Adler

---

[5]For another good example of Adler's own recognition of the predictive emptiness of the concept of inferiority, see 1908a (p. 47).

retained his commitment to approaching human illness from the standpoint of the concerns of social medicine. Just as the illnesses besetting Austrian tailors had social significance as barometers of "occupational" disease, so the concept of organ inferiority had importance because of its implicit social meaning. It is only from this social vantage point, moreover, that we can comprehend what Adler meant when he spoke of the "compensation" and "overcompensation" that regularly accompanied organ inferiority. Adler did not formulate the concept of compensation as an afterthought, an ego-psychological formulation of what happened to the individual after an inferior organ became manifest. Rather, he introduced the idea of compensation as part of the initial definition of inferiority, intending to show how the tendency to rectify the inferiority functioned as a built-in part of the inferiority itself.

In the opening chapter of the *Study,* Adler referred to the "phenomena of vicariousness." He used this expression to characterize the following observation: "just the primary inferior organs seem predestined under certain conditions to take upon themselves for a shorter or longer time an increased functional activity." This, he suggested, was the customary criterion for the very diagnosis of organ inferiority. Even when "vicariousness" was lacking, Adler still contended that "partial compensation phenomena" occurred, and for the essential reason "that general inferiority of an organ or an apparatus represents a certain degree of incapacity to live (*Lebensunfaehigkeit*) which gives sufficient cause for premature death" (1907c, pp. 11, 13; 1907d, pp. 7, 8). This did not mean that the inferiority of an organ represented an "incapacity to live" by virtue of intrinsic biologic insufficiency. Instead, the incapacity derived from the organ's inability to satisfy the specific cultural requirements that were the preconditions of man's social life. While the organ consequently demonstrated its inferiority through the inability to meet the demands of culture, the inferiority was made manifest through the *effort* made to obtain this required level of functioning. Adler's claim was that the compensatory strivings (*Kompensationsbestrebungen*) that tended to overcome the inferiority were built into the very cell substance of the organ. These compensatory tendencies were responsible for producing new and potent varieties of organ functioning. Such compensatory organ functioning could actually result in a condition of heightened organ performance, moreover, because it issued from inferior organs which "have drawn their energy to grow from the overcoming of external requirements" (1907a, p. 14; cf. 1908a, p. 46).

In the initial biological formulation, the compensatory potential of the inferior organ lacked empirical content in the same way as the putative inferiority of the organ. The compensatory tendencies did not necessitate a specific kind of compensatory outcome, in other words, but rather provided the potential for an entire gamut of beneficial and debilitating accouterments to organ expression. In general, the compensation could either engender striking disturbance or, in more finished form, it could serve to obliterate the picture of organ inferiority altogether (1907a, p. 14). Adler presented much illustrative material in the *Study* to demonstrate the manifold outcomes of the interacting inferiority and compensatory tendencies of the organ. The convenient summary of these outcomes appears, once more, in the 1907 lecture. Inferior organs might yield any of the following outcomes, along with innumerable intermediate stages:

> inability to survive, anomaly of form, anomaly of function, lack of resistance and disposition to disease, compensation within the organ, compensation through a second organ, compensation through the psychological superstructure, and organic or psychological overcompensation. We find pure, compensated, and overcompensated inferiorities [1907a, p. 11; Ansbacher, p. 24].

III.

It was in discussing the different compensatory potentialities that could ensue from an inferior organ that Adler finally alluded to the important juncture at which his contribution to clinical medicine became a contribution to psychopathology. He postulated that organ inferiorities not only entailed organic compensations but could effect compensation through the agency of the organ's "psychological superstructure" as well. It is important to comprehend what exactly Adler had in mind when he made this interesting claim, because it is at this point that his theory provides a presumed basis for his collaboration with the Freudians. To this end, it is necessary to keep in mind psychological tenets that were first formulated not in Adler's work on organ inferiority, but in an important theoretical paper that chronologically accompanied the *Study*.

The paper in question is "The Aggressive Drive in Life and in Neurosis" published in the *Fortschritte der Medizin* in 1908. The title of Adler's paper is somewhat misleading. He did not follow Nietzsche in considering the aggressive drive as a historical vicissitude in the life of the "will to power," and he did not anticipate Freud's later treatment of aggression as a separate variety of instinctual activity. Instead, the point of Adler's paper was to redefine the concept of "drive" (*Trieb*) in terms of the individual organ and the characteristic "activity" that the organ pursued. The paper is therefore important because it provides key insights into the "instinctual" ramifications of organ inferiority at a new psychological level.

Adler equated normal organ activity with the "unobstructed functioning" (*ungehemmten Leistungen*) that satisfied the organ's own functional requirements. He proceeded to posit a psychological superstructure (*psychische Ueberbau*) for each organ that effectively brought the Freudian reality principle down to the level of the individual organ. For Adler, the psychological superstructure originated through cultural obstructions which restricted the pursuit of organ pleasure to certain narrowly prescribed channels. In order to ensure the pursuit of organ satisfaction in this culturally prescribed manner, the organ invoked the directive assistance of a superstructure to monitor and channel its activities.

Adler's remarks regarding the psychological superstructure represent another broad clinical application of the localization theory of psychic functioning that was prevalent in German psychiatric thought in the second half of the nineteenth century and was embodied in Vienna in the work of Theodore Meynert. Meynert and his disciples believed that different psychic functions could be localized in separate cerebral areas. Adler, in turn, accorded the psychological superstructure of each organ an anatomic substrate in the nerve fibers of the brain and equated each superstructure with additional modifications in the central nervous system. These neurological modifications were ultimately invoked to facilitate organ activity, but to ensure simultaneously that such activity occurred within the sanctioned cultural parameters. Adler observed that it was only the directive superstructure that enabled the organ to obtain functional satisfaction in the sanctioned way, and he added that the superstructure generally prospered to the extent that it satisfactorily served the drive of the organ. He noted, however, that the strength of the superstructure was not invariable, but rather corresponded directly with the drive strength (*Triebstaerke*) of the organ it served. The stronger the organ drive, the more exaggerated the development of the superstructure that had to provide for the needs of the organ. In the event of a heightened organ drive, Adler spoke of the "over-development" of the superstructure, indicating that such an abnormally heightened organ monitor could promote new struggles against the environment, induce repression, and cause compensatory disturbances. By the same token, the over-developed superstructure could implement new and more satisfying modes of drive activity by virtue of its heightened sensitivity to the needs of the drive it served.

This latter formulation seemed to modify what Adler intended to signify by the psychological superstructure of the organ in a very fundamental way. By correlating the strength of the superstructure with the drive strength of the organ, Adler made an important heuristic distinction between the relative "inferiority" of an organ and the drive strength vested in the organ. He formalized this distinction when he attributed any emergent struggles over the expression of organ activity not to simple "inferiority" of the organ, but to the joint convergence of the hereditary valence of an organ (*Organwertigkeit*) with the hereditary drive strength adhering to the organ. It was the struggle resulting from the superstructure's inability to mediate between the organ's hereditary valence and the strength of the drive which had to function through the organ that produced organ damage. This organ damage, in turn, modified the embryological condition of descendants in a way that corresponded to the organ damage that resulted from the initial imbalance.[6] The hereditary basis of both organ inferiority and the compensatory tendencies mitigating the inferiority, in other words, was not a direct ramification of the congenital inferiority of the organ. Instead, it was a ramification of *relative* inferiority made manifest through the organ's inability to serve as an adequate vehicle for the satisfaction of the instinctual drive vested in it.

What does Adler's distinction between organ valence and organ drive strength do to his concept of the inferior organ? In effect, it relativizes the concept in a second way. Having argued that organ inferiority only assumes empirical meaningfulness in relation to cultural requirements the organ cannot meet, he now added that the organ's failure to meet these cultural demands was a function not *merely* of the relative strength of the cultural demands themselves, but of the relative drive strength vested in the organ. The reason organ activity failed to meet cultural requirements was because the organ was invested with a drive endowment that exceeded the ability of the organ's cognitive-neurological imprint—the psychological superstructure—to find ample opportunities for culturally sanctioned drive satisfaction. Here, in 1908, Adler seems to have devised a tripartite formulation that parallels in certain respects the structural theory of id, ego, and superego that would emerge in Freud's writings after World War I, notably in *The Ego and the Id* (1923). For the ego, Adler posited, at a more delimited organizing level, the psychological superstructure of the individual organ; for the id, he posited the innate drive strength vested in the organ; and for the superego, he posited the transcendent cultural requirements that regulated the strategies the superstructure could pursue in the quest for drive satisfaction. As with the Freudian ego of the early structural theory, it was the psychological superstructure that had to mediate between the instinctual demands below it and the cultural requirements above it. From the Adlerian perspective, the congenital stamp of organ inferiority in a family tree no longer referred simply to the inherited predisposition of an organ to become manifestly inferior. It betokened, in addition, an actual ego failure: organ inferiority signified the injury an organ

---

[6]On the transmission of embryological damage to descendants, cf. Adler (1908a, pp. 44–45).

had absorbed through the superstructure's unsuccessful attempt to manage a quota of drive strength that exceeded its capacity to provide sanctioned organ activity.

In this way, Adler formulated a veritable conflict theory to account for the hereditary basis of organ inferiority. It was not the biological inferiority that was transmitted, but the traces of the struggle between the superstructure of the organ and the unmanageable drive strength attempting to gain expression through the organ. Adler made this new relativism of organ inferiority explicit in an important passage of the "Aggressive Drive" paper:

> Since, essentially, "relative" organ valence is determined by the tension between the organ material and the drive on one side, and the demands of the environment on the other, the greater damage in the pedigree (illness, overexertion, superfluity, deficiency) will make the organ inferior, inferior in the sense that traces of this struggle adhere to the organ to a considerable extent. I have investigated these traces and have shown them to affect organs in the following ways: a tendency to illness, signs of degeneration and the stigmata, hypoplastic and hyperplastic formations, childish defects and reflex anomalies.

He proceeded to assert that the investigation of organs constituted an important tool for the discovery of drive strength:

> The inferior eye has the greater drive to see, the inferior alimentary tract the greater drives to eat and drink, the inferior sexual organ the stronger sexual drive [1908b, p. 27].

In the paper on the "Aggressive Drive," then, Adler delineated in dynamic psychological terms the functional requirements that the organ's superstructure had to satisfy. Like the early theory of the Freudian ego, Adler's formulation made it plain that the superstructure's mediating activities only succeeded to the extent that they satisfied organ drives, and he characterized the superstructure's responsibility for the appropriation of techniques of organ activity consonant with culture as an adaptation proceeding from egoistical motives. Since only the superstructure could legitimize the quest for organ drive satisfaction, Adler said that the superstructure actually assumed a substitute function for the denied "primary activity" of the organ. He did not assume, however, that the degree of success with which the superstructure assumed its substitute function related merely to its organizing activities at the psychological level, and in this respect his formulation takes a biological turn away from the purely dynamic attributes of the Freudian ego. Already in the "Aggressive Drive" paper, he equated the psychological superstructure with potential neurophysiological changes occurring within the central nervous system (1908b, p. 26). Indeed, Adler felt that the varying degree to which compensatory potentialities were consolidated at the neurophysiological level would determine the outcome of compensation from a behavioral point of view.

At this juncture, we are back to the theory of organ inferiority proper, with its postulation of a built-in compensatory potential that accompanies the inferiority, but which cannot predict the likelihood of any specific compensatory outcome. Adler, we recall, said that the compensation for an inferior organ usually entailed striking damage, but could in its finished form obliterate the organ inferiority altogether. What he meant, in crediting the product of compensatory activity with this behavioral flexibility, was that compensation could only overcome the inferiority if it succeeded in inducing, neurologically, a heightened form of "brain activity."

Adler called this outcome "heightened brain performance" (*gesteigerter Hirnleistung*). He did not view elevated brain activity as the simple organic concomitant of all organ inferiorities, but rather as an index of the psychological achievement that had been effected through the superstructure's directive efforts. The extent to which the superstructure could effect neurological improvement, that is, hinged not on the characteristics of the inferiority per se, but was commensurate to the quality and intensity of the compensations that were psychologically undertaken.

In the lecture of 1907, Adler illustrated what he had in mind by referring to common children's defects (*Kinderfehler*) as the paradigmatic examples of functional anomalies that pointed to underlying organ inferiorities. With such defects—and Adler was referring to such things as developmental speech problems, stuttering, excessive blinking, thumbsucking—the normal growth of the superordinated nerve tracts generally sufficed to produce a "compensation through growth" that led to normal functioning. In these cases the organ anomaly, though not functionally manifest, was still present, and the physician could still detect remnants of it throughout the patient's life. As a slightly less optimal outcome, the defect could be satisfactorily overcome under normal conditions, but might reappear under situations that entailed elevated psychological tension. When this kind of periodic relapse occurred (i.e., when one tended to blink in bright light or stutter when excited), Adler said that the organ activity revealed a compensation that had been effected through an overperformance (*Mehrleistung*) and increased growth of the brain. The brain underwent actual organic growth, in other words, in order to accommodate as best it could the compensatory behaviors that the inferior organ strained to implement in order to satisfy the demands of culture. From this standpoint, Adler contended that the success of the psychological superstructure in muting expressions of organ inferiority revealed a direct relation between the strengthening of the superstructure and the "steady exercise" of the organ (1907a. p. 16).

This discussion of the compensation from the standpoint of the psychological superstructure provides the essential backdrop for evaluating the contribution to psychopathology Adler made in chapter 6 of his *Study*. The very title of the chapter—"The Part Played by the Central Nervous System in the Theory of Organ Inferiority: Psychogenesis and Foundations of Neuroses and Psychoneroses"—betrays at once the direction from which Adler approached the problem of neurotic conflict.

Adler paved the way for his theory of psychogenesis by linking the compensatory *efforts* of the psychological superstructure once more to organic changes in the central nervous system. He maintained a heuristic distinction between the protective initiatives undertaken by the superstructure and compensations grounded in neurological changes, but he simultaneously argued that *successful* compensation could only be consolidated through such neurological modifications. Indeed, Adler proceeded to characterize the superstructure as a derivative formation anchored in compensations that had been effected neurologically. Compensatory psychological behavior induced modifications in the central nervous system, that is, but was subsequently explained in terms of the organic compensation that consolidated such behavioral efforts. This seems to be the best way of deciphering the convoluted expression of compensatory dynamics with which Adler prefaced his explanation of the neuroses:

> Ordinarily the central nervous system will play the main part in this compensation, not only physically . . . but above all in a psychological manner. The reason [for the primacy of psychological compensation] is that a special interest seeks to protect the inferior organ and endeavors to ward off injury by constant attention, and the psyche, on a small scale, perhaps, gives the impulse to awaken the attention, to increase it, and to connect it with that organ [1907c, p. 62; 1907d, p. 57].

From the standpoint of this confluence of neurological and psychological compensation, then, how did Adler explain neurosis? At the outset of the chapter he characterized degeneration, neurosis, and genius as the results of the three "most important constellations" deriving from "organic and nerve inferiority" (1907c, p. 62; 1907d, p. 56). What, then, was the particular constellation from which neurosis proceeded? Adler answered this question, like Freud, by contrasting the initially undisciplined pursuit of pleasure characteristic of the organ activity of the child with the structured, acculturated pursuit of pleasure which the psychological superstructure imposed on the organ activity of the adult. He observed that "every free activity of the infant and child is connected with pleasure, or is calculated to obtain pleasure,'' adding that the ''accentuation of pleasure is often the cause of the intractableness of children's defects.'' He saw this observation as compatible with Freud's demonstration of the ''primary pleasure principle'' in the psychoanalysis of neuroses.

For Adler, the task of every organ subsequently became the subordination of ''its unrestricted, pleasure-seeking disposition to the compulsion of education.'' By this subordination, he meant that the superstructure of the organ had to modify the organ's pleasure-seeking activity, inducing it to undertake tasks ''which in the beginning are not easy, but which on the average undoubtedly succeed through the increase in the functional capability of the superstructure'' (1907c, p. 64; 1907d, p. 58). Adler noted that ''approximately normal organs'' could ''adjust themselves without delay to the requirements of surrounding culture.'' ''Increased external requirements,'' ''traumatic influences,'' and ''change of surroundings,'' on the other hand, could ''show up an organ and at the same its central superstructure as inferior.'' The superstructure failed in its mediating role because the organ's drive endowment exceeded the amount of satisfying organ activity that cultural requirements made available to the superstructure. This was tantamount to a strong reiteration of the dynamic cultural *definition* of the inferior organ which Adler finally developed at greater length:

> Thus the superior psychic realm is forced to do certain tasks, which in the beginning are not easy, but which on the average undoubtedly succeed by reason of the heightening of the functional capability. In the case of the inferiority of the organ, however, and the corresponding insufficiency of the related portions of the nervous system, the participation of the organ and its activity in the demands of culture remain behind. The function then does not follow the required cultural paths but is predominantly engaged in seeking pleasure (*Lustgewinn*). We accordingly find in the development of the normal organ a certain subordination of the pleasure component to the activities called forth by the environment—we would call them the ''moral'' activities—the final success of which ensures the child's cultural development. The harmony of physical and psychical functional capability, a psychophysical parallelism in the true sense of the word, characterizes the development of the normal child. In the inferior organ it is different. If there is a particular retardation of the development of the organs, as well as the related nerve tracts, all attempts at culture are unsuccessful and conditions such as idiocy and imbecility result. But in the milder cases also, the inferior organ turns spontaneously to gaining pleasure, averse to psychical interference, and therefore indulges itself all the more, the longer it has to wait for the moral redemption (*Abloesung*)—Freud's repression. Since in the meantime the organ has become accustomed to wanton (*spielerischen*) activity, it will now accomplish the later repression against greater organic opposition, and introduce a lasting struggle that will be felt as a torturing compulsion [1907c, p. 64; 1907d, p. 58].

Adler's distinction bears an interesting relation to the model of primary and secondary psychic processes that Freud initially presented in the *Project for a Scientific Psychology* of 1895 and elucidated further in *The Interpretation of Dreams* five years later. Just as Adler's clinical observations as a medical practitioner led him to postulate a "primary" form of organ activity, so Freud's early psychophysiological speculations in the *Project* led him to arrive at primary and secondary psychic processes that corresponded to different kinds of physiological energy discharge occurring in the nervous system. Freud's postulation of primary and secondary psychic processes in the *Project* followed from his attempt to apply Fechner's Constancy Principle to the nervous excitation that generated human behavior. His neurophysiological assumption, in this regard, was that behavior tended toward a reflexive discharge of excitation impinging on the receptor end of the nervous system, but that human development mandated certain strategies for circumventing such pure reflexive discharge when it did not serve adaptive needs. The reflexive discharge of excitation was useful in removing external sources of irritation, for example, but relatively useless in dealing with endogenous stimuli (such as hunger) from which the organism could not escape. In the neurophysiological model of normal psychic functioning outlined in Part I of the *Project,* the expression "psychical primary processes" characterized the primitive psychic modality governed by the reflex model: when a certain quantity of nervous excitation accumulated in the nervous system, it generated automatic neurophysiological discharge that took the form of hallucinations of previous experiences of satisfaction. Psychical secondary processes, on the other hand, signified a more mature level of neurological functioning in which a consolidated ego—which Freud conceptualized here as a body of permanently excited ("cathected") neurones—initiated inhibitory activity preventing the primary reflex response that eventuated in a strictly hallucinatory kind of satisfaction. In this way, the secondary processes promoted "true" experiences of satisfaction, i.e., they served to inhibit reflexive motor discharges until appropriately gratifying stimuli actually presented themselves in the environment (Freud, 1895, pp. 379–389).[7]

By the time Freud wrote *The Interpretation of Dreams,* he stopped short of defining the mental apparatus in terms of brain anatomy, but he retained the belief that mental activity could best be described through physiological processes (see Spehlmann, 1953, pp. 71–81). Thus, if Adler's understanding of primary mental activity derived from a clinical perspective on organ functioning,

---

[7]This material is insightfully interpreted by Fancher (1971) and Levin (1978, pp. 166–168). Cf. Sulloway (1979, pp. 116–117).

Freud's psychological conception of primary and secondary processes, as Spehlmann has shown, retained its original organic base: it was subsumed by the theory of brain physiology he had elaborated in the 1890s—particularly in the *Project*—in opposition to the prevalent localization theory of psychic functioning espoused by Meynert (1953, pp. 46–52).[8] In *The Interpretation of Dreams* (1900), Freud theorized on the assumption that all mental activity involved processes of energy discharge that *paralleled* energy transformations in the nervous system. He once again postulated a primary system aiming at the free discharge of quantities of excitation and originally modeled on the hallucinatory cathecting of a memory of satisfaction. The secondary system again served to inhibit excitatory discharge in order to facilitate the "exploratory thought-activity" that would permit satisfaction to be pursued in the culturally validated way. Elaborating in more psychological terms the neurophysiological model outlined in the *Project,* Freud held that the secondary process regulated the quest for satisfaction by "diverting the excitation arising from the need along a roundabout path which ultimately, by means of voluntary movement, altered the external world in such a way that it became possible to arrive at a real perception of the object of satisfaction" (p. 599).

Now, relative to the far-reaching implications of Freud's distinction, Adler was arguing on markedly delimited clinical grounds. His methodological starting point was not the fiction of a primitive psychical apparatus that functioned to avoid an accumulation of excitation, but the observable functional activity of the individual organ. Within the framework he adopted, however, Adler's distinction paralleled Freud's in important respects. The organ's initial pleasure-seeking activity became adaptively inadequate because it could not conform to the requirements of a maturing capability that promoted cultural development. When psychopathological formations arose, it was because the organ's "inferior" status had prevented it from transcending primary process "organ" functioning. When these primary modalities were finally undercut by the developmental imposition of repression, the organ's habitual recourse to the "wanton" primary activities provided a heightened "organic opposition" that precluded the success of repression. Because the inferior organ was by then committed to unstructured pleasure-seeking, the imposition of repression could only introduce a "lasting struggle" that betrayed itself as a "torturing compulsion." Analogously, Freud characterized the activity that led to hysterical symptoms (as well as dreams) as one that permitted thoughts which represented themselves as products of the

---

[8]On the medical prehistory of Freud's psychoanalysis, and especially on Freud's transition from neurophysiology to psychology, see also Dorer (1932), Bernfeld (1944, 1949, 1951), and Amacher (1965).

secondary thought-activity "to become subject to the primary psychical process" (1900, p. 603). This occurred when an unconscious wish in a state of repression received an "organic reinforcement" that permitted the "transference thoughts" embodying the wish to reach the Preconscious System. When this happened, Freud continued, the thoughts embodying the unconscious wish "force their way through in some form of compromise which is reached by the production of a symptom." The compromise, however, was a primary process phenomenon:

> But from the moment at which the repressed thoughts are strongly cathected by the unconscious wishful impulse and, on the other hand, abandoned by the preconscious cathexis, they become subject to the primary psychical process and their one aim is motor discharge or, if the path is open, hallucinatory revival of the desired perceptual identity [p. 605].

The analogy between Freud's neuropsychological "primary process" and Adler's psychobiological "primary organ activity" is significant, but it masks the crucial *redefinition* of neurosis that Adler accomplished in chapter 6 of his *Study*. If Adler saw the neurotic symptom as the product of a "lasting struggle" induced by the failure of repression to regulate organ activity, he unfailingly traced this struggle to the *organic* inadequacy of an organ that made excessive demands on the organ's superstructure. The neurotic conflict did not emerge as a compromise product embodying the simultaneous fulfillment of an unconscious wish arising from the primary process and an incompatible preconscious wish corresponding to the secondary mental process. For purposes of nosogenesis, Adler replaced the Freudian "wish" with biological organ activity as a heuristic psychophysiological goal. His conception of mental conflict related not to the incompatibility between unconscious and conscious wishes, but to the disjunction between the mode of organ activity that was most satisfying and the restrictive, reality-tested mode that the superstructure could authorize. The content of the "satisfaction" experienced by the organ was never in question. Indeed, "conflict" would never arise but for the fact that the drive endowment vested in a particular organ exceeded the capacity of the superstructure to structure organ activity.

Although the struggle between primary organ activity and the regulating efforts of the superstructure could occur outside of consciousness, Adler's conception of conflict never became a *function* of a system Ucs. whose primary "wishes" had to entail repression because their fulfillment "would be a contradiction of the purposive ideas of secondary thinking" (Freud, 1900, p. 604). Rather, Adler's sense of conflict was a social commentary on the status of an inferior organ. When conflict arose, it was the "inferior" organ's means of reaching its satisfaction that was at issue. It was never a question of "wishes" the fulfillment of which could not be uniformly satisfying given the divergent requirements of the different structures making up the mental apparatus. Instead, it was a question of an undifferentiated quota of organ "satisfaction" which either could or could not be obtained through the prescribed routes sanctioned by the superstructure.

This juxtaposition of Freudian and Adlerian "conflict" clarifies the important sense in which Adler's scheme never constituted a mere discourse on "neurotic disposition" that supplemented early psychoanalytic theory. Through his insights into the functioning of the inferior organ, Adler hoped to find an ordering concept which could make the symptomatic phenomena of psychoanalysis comprehensible within the framework of clinical medicine. Convinced that adequate organ functioning entailed the directing activities of the superstructure and further convinced that inferior organs were those least able to meet the demands of culture, he basically offered a position that was supportive of Freud's genetic perspective, but which translated the genetic phenomena Freud observed into the language of clinical medicine.

This translation ultimately fixed on the clinical meaning of the neurotic "symptom." Adler did not really buttress Freud's genetic account of the child's mental "symptoms" as the embodiment of neurotic conflict. Instead, he redefined the symptom from the vantage point of the theory of organ inferiority. Where Freud had seen the child's "symptoms," Adler saw "childish defects" that were "only the externally perceptible phenomena arising from the disturbed psyche and marking the lack of an adequate compensation in the psychomotor superstructure of the organ." When Adler proceeded to characterize these defects as "lines of direction from the life of the psyche" and "signals which indicate the peripheral and central inferiority has not yet been successfully overcome" (1907c, pp. 65, 67; 1907d, pp. 69, 61–62), he plainly meant to provide a clinical formulation that would encompass the entire question of "neurotic" symptomatology. He openly admitted as much in noting that his work

> aims to refer all phenomena of neuroses and psychoneuroses back to organ inferiority, to the degree and nature of the not completely successful central compensation and to compensatory disturbances which enter into the matter [1907c, p. 69; 1907d, p. 63].

Yet, Adler did not simply claim that all the phenomena of neuroses referred back to organ inferiority. He attempted to show, in considerable detail and with much illustrative material, how specific neurotic symptoms could be reinterpreted as motor discharges arising from "the motor portion of the compensating super-structure" (1907c, p. 70; 1907d, p. 64). By this analysis, all the motor symp-toms (like tic, different forms of paralysis, hysterical cramps, etc.) of neurosis became significant not merely as expressions of the original inferiority, but as expressions of the superstructure's compensatory attempts to energize the in-ferior organ by heightened activity.

Adler's final translation of psychoanalysis into the language of organ in-feriority revolved around Freud's putatively "sexual basis" of the neuroses. In an earlier chapter of the *Study* on "Manifold Organ Inferiorities," Adler had observed how adjoining organs frequently shared in the inferiority of an inferior organ. He noted, in this connection, that inferiority of the urinary apparatus was "regularly connected with inferiority of the sexual apparatus" (1907c, p. 57; 1907d, p. 51). In the chapter on psychogenesis, he broadened this connection and indicated that all inferior organs were "perhaps regularly accompanied by inferior sexual organs." Adler observed, furthermore, that the infantile anoma-lies to which Freud ascribed masturbatory properties (thumb-sucking, tickling the skin, etc.) actually represented "the wanton inclination aimed at obtaining pleasure which is peculiar to the inferior organ, the mouth, intestine, genitals." By proceeding in this way, he was ultimately able to contend that the sexual basis of the neuroses resolved itself into the concomitant expression of an inferior organ and a correspondingly inferior sexual organ. Their shared form of ex-pression was the free pleasure-seeking orientation of the inferior organ, and the specific kind of pleasure-seeking activity indulged in by both the inferior organ and the inferior sexual organ was infantile masturbation. Adler thereby arrived at an entirely new explanation for the "sexual" etiology of the neuroses, one that could explain sexual precocity from the standpoint of the general aim of *all* organ activity. Having cautioned in his 1907 lecture that childhood defects could be mistakenly related to sexual activity by virtue of the pleasure orientation of primitive organ activity (1907a, p. 16), he ended the *Study* by effecting a true translation of infantile sexuality into the language of organ inferiority. In so doing, he relegated sexual precocity itself to the status of a characteristic "child-ish defect." Hence,

> If we now remember that all inferior organs are perhaps regularly accompanied by inferior sexual organs, in which the inclination for pleasure (*Neigung nach Lustgewinn*) is likewise present in a marked degree, if we admit that almost all the children saddled with childish defects also engage in masturbatory touching of the genitals, then we must as a result of this consideration establish the fact that the possession of inferior organs can very easily lead to sexual precocity, to early masturbation [1907c, pp. 70–71; 1907d, p. 65].

This revealing passage is suggestive of the medical orientation Adler would bring to the study of infantile sexuality over the next four years. Adler never disputed the *manifest* importance of early sexual development, just as he never disputed the *manifest* etiological role of sexuality in the neuroses. It is for this reason, perhaps, that Wagner-Jauregg, in his negative assessment of Adler's work, mistakenly declared that sexuality played as central a role in Adler's clinical interpretations as in Freud's (Beckh-Widmanstetter, 1965, p. 187). But the fact is that Adler never accepted the etiological *authenticity* of sexual themes in his clinical work; he consistently maintained that sexual factors embodied a "manifest content" not to be taken at etiological face value. To borrow an important referent of Adler's later psychology, the sexual factors were always "fictional." By this, I mean that, for Adler, the sexual etiology of the neuroses, however obtrusive at the manifest level, was a necessarily disingenuous etiology; it achieved a borrowed significance as an instance of an ordering principle that transcended the sexual and, to that extent, accounted for the mental uses one made of one's sexuality. Here, in 1907, we see sexual precocity in early life reduced to an exemplification of "childish defects" derivative to inferior organs. Over the next four years, as Adler's thought was progressively freed of its biological moorings, his etiological devaluation of the sexual would be accomplished through an ordering principle that carried the latent psychological meaning of the theory of organ inferiority to a superordinate conceptual status. This is the principle of the masculine protest.

3

From Medicine to Psychiatry: The Foundations of Adlerian Theory, Part II

In his *Study of Organ Inferiority*, Adler presented a cultural-medical model of neurotic conflict that supplanted Freud's psychoanalytic explanation of neurotic symptoms. Although his theory succeeded in making the key connection between organ inferiority and psychiatry, it remained a skeletal conceptualization that provided a reductive explanation for isolated childhood symptoms on the basis of a simple one-to-one correlation between the "primary" activity of an organ and the "defect" embodied in the inability to forego that primary activity. The neatest example of this correlation, the paradigmatic example to which Adler returned again and again, concerned the cultural development of the excretory functions. Here, Adler claimed, we confront functions which, left to themselves, "go on purely wantonly in the infant and are consequently connected with sensory gratification as befits every instinctive organic function." While environmental influence sufficed "to place the function of the bladder and the rectum on a 'moral' basis in normal organs and in normal psychomotor superstructures," the "childhood defect" accrued to the child whose inferior organ could not relinquish the primary organ activity. In this case, "the psychomotor superstructure of the inferior organ leads a continual struggle against the pleasure activity and on behalf of the 'moral mission' of the organ" (1907c, p. 65; 1907d, p. 59).

Adler's formulation provided a clear explanation of "symptoms" dependent on specific organ functions that had to be acculturated during the course of childhood development. It did not suffice, however, to explain "adult" neuroses that extended beyond the residual deficits attached to specific organ activities. With this inherent limitation, we reach the end of one phase of Adler's theoretical development and the beginning of another. After 1908, Adler never disavowed the medical origins of his theory of organ inferiority. He did, however, turn his attention to supplementary psychological considerations that would broaden the range of psychological explanation embodied in his theory.

In this chapter, we shall follow chronologically Adler's attempt to elaborate theoretically these psychological considerations in the years immediately following the publication of the organ theory of inferiority. We shall see that by 1910 Adler's examination of the psychological assumptions that provided the basis for his "functional" viewpoint on organ inferiority effected a decisive shift of emphasis. Between 1908 and 1910, Adler's exploration of the psychological substrate of the theory of organ inferiority provided the basis for a broadened awareness of the determining role of "inferiority" in psychological development, and his increasing preoccupation with the psychological issue of "inferiority," in turn, relegated the inferior organ to a position of receding importance. By the time he wrote *The Nervous Character* in 1912, organ-based deficits were of secondary importance; they presented but one of several contributing substrata of early development that fueled inferiority feelings. Such inferiority feelings, moreover, were no longer reducible to, or understandable in terms of, inferior organs. Instead, organ performance itself was only accorded importance in childhood by feeding into a preexisting *psychological* paradigm that revolved around "inferiority" and "superiority" as intertwined developmental themes.

At the same time as this chapter charts Adler's gradual liberation from the restrictive framework of inferior organs, however, it will attempt to clarify the considerable extent to which Adler's transition from medicine to psychiatry was already embodied in the latent psychology of the theory of organ inferiority itself. In minimizing the explanatory importance of inferior organs after 1908, Adler was not abandoning but actually amplifying the latent social psychology that had informed his clinical perspective on inferior organs from the outset. Indeed, in positing the generative primacy of "inferiority feelings" and a "masculine protest" that ranged beyond the repercussions of inferior organs, Adler was doing no more than supplying a psychological rationale for the relative cultural criteria that had made the idea of inferior organs clinically meaningful in the first place.

Finally, we shall see how in 1910 Adler's developmental psychology provided the basis for clinical contributions to the *Zentralblatt fuer Psychoanalyse* that not only elaborated his reformulation of Freud's libido theory, but attempted to undercut Freud's libidinal explanation of certain recurring treatment phenomena. Writing as a "psychoanalyst" and utilizing the forum provided by a "psychoanalytic" journal, Adler argued that therapeutic resistance, the positive and negative transference, and the Oedipus complex itself all lacked genuine "erotic" significance, representing instead different forms of expression assumed by the masculine protest.

I.

The shift in emphasis in Adler's theorizing was initially tantamount to the admission that explained symptoms did not explain the underlying disposition of certain individuals to chronic neurotic suffering. They did not explain, in other words, what made a person neurotic. After 1908, Adler recognized this broader question as the ultimate testing ground for the theory of organ inferiority as a theory of psychopathology. It was, in fact, the question he pointedly addressed in 1909 in what is probably his most substantive contribution to psychoanalytic literature, "On the Neurotic Disposition: A Contribution both to the Etiology of Neurosis and the Question of the Choice of Neurosis." This little known and, to date, untranslated paper, is a crucial signpost of Adler's theoretical development: it bridges his transition from the subject matter of internal medicine to that of psychiatry proper.

The new psychophysiological concept that Adler invoked in this paper was called "oversensitivity" (*Ueberempfindlichkeit*). Adler labeled "psychical oversensitivity" the principal characteristic of the neurotic psyche. He defined psychical oversensitivity not from the standpoint of isolated neurotic symptoms, but in terms of the manifold expressions of heightened *vulnerability* that stemmed from the neurotic's self-deprecatory feelings.[1] Psychical oversensitivity signified the neurotic's morbid predisposition to capitalize on interpersonally threatening situations in a way that would confirm and even exacerbate the sense of inferiority. From the standpoint of the neurotic psyche, such situations came to assume a dualistic function. They represented both dreaded occasions to be avoided at any cost, and wish-fulfilling prophecies that confirmed the exactitude of the neurotic's low self-estimation and justified further recourse to

---

[1]Although I have followed the example of the Ansbachers in translating *Empfindlichkeit* as "sensitivity," Dr. Ernst Prelinger has reminded me that the root *empfindlich* does not share the conventional connotations of "sensitive" in the sense of being aware, impressionable, or sentient. Adler could have used the word *einfindsam* if he had this kind of sensitivity in mind. Rather, *empfindlich*, even without the prefix *ueber*, implies a kind of hypersensitivity, a vulnerability frequently applied to people who are unprotected and easily given to pain.

neurotic avoidance strategies. Thus, for Adler, the manifestations of oversensitivity ensued

> as soon as a situation arises in which the patient appears to be neglected, injured, small or dirty. In these instances, the patient is pushed to the conclusion that he must rely on his sense of insignificance (*Nebensaechlichkeiten*) and he will henceforth invent voluntarily situations that betray this insignificance. Often with the greatest acuteness he will try to give his perspective a logical repesentation that only the experienced psychotherapist can see through. In other cases the patient will adopt a delusional idea—as in paranoia but also in other neuroses—in order to make his inexplicable behavior seem comprehensible. In this context, one is always struck by the exaggerated frequency of the depreciations and humiliations to which such patients are subjected, until it is discovered how these patients seek out such humiliations [1909b, pp. 530–531].

With this opening statement of Adler's position, there is already a radical change in the mode of discourse from the *Study* of 1907. Adler wrote this paper when his prestige in Freud's psychoanalytic discussion group was at its height, and when his sympathetic identification with Freud's psychological methods was greatest. It seems likely that the weight of his psychoanalytic affiliation helped carry him from the psychology of inferior organs to the new psychology of the neurotic character. In accord with his new psychological sensibilities, Adler evaluated the "neurotic disposition" from the standpoint of an exaggerated *interpersonal* vulnerability that manifested itself in social situations and led to different kinds of interpersonal unhappiness. He used the idea of oversensitivity to characterize persons whose particular vulnerability drastically restricted the range of their interpersonal activity and thereby undercut their potential for interpersonal happiness:

> The lack of any joy of living, the constant expectation of bad luck, of being late, of unsuccessful undertakings and of setbacks—this expectation becomes recognizable in the attitude and the facial expression of the patient. Moreover, the superstitious fear of numbers, of unlucky days and of a telepathic tendency to surmise the worst, the mistrust in one's own energy that causes one to doubt everything alive, the mistrust in others which is socially destructive and dissolves every form of community—these attributes at times constitute the picture of oversensitive patients [1909b, p. 531].

How did Adler effect this change of discourse? He did so not by abandoning the presuppositions of his earlier medical work, but by amplifying the "organic" repercussions of the isolated "childhood defect" first explicated in the *Study of Organ Inferiority*. Adler submitted that the psychical oversensitivity that produced the neurotic character actually originated in the "organic" oversensitivity of the inferior organ. In this way, his previous emphasis on the deficient performance of the inferior organ was translated into a new emphasis on the more general kinds of "sensitivity" that accrued to the inferior organ. Adler enumerated as examples the same developmental deficits that he had formerly labeled "defects" (*fehler*), but he recast the import of these defects to accord with the new stress on the inferior organ's oversensitivity.

What was the result of this new stress? On the one hand, Adler could reaffirm and broaden his commitment to the organic basis of psychological disturbance by tracing "psychical" to "organic" oversensitivity as an hereditary expression of organ inferiority. This continuity, however, belies the significance of the new theory for Adler's status as a psychiatrist. By invoking the concept of oversensitivity to express the broadened psychological ramifications of organ inferiority, Adler correspondingly broadened the scope of the psychological compensations that were part of the inferiority. In the *Study,* these compensations were invoked to rectify deficient organ performance, to make organ activity conform with the prescribed ways of satisfying organ drives. By expanding the idea of organ inferiority beyond the bounds of individuated organ activity, Adler significantly redefined the nature of the compensations that could make good the inferiority.

The new conceptual schema for understanding the compensations generated by inferior organs related to the *aggression* associated with normal organ activity. To the extent that the organic oversensitivity of an inferior organ represented the inability of the organ to provide the energic release associated with normal organ activity, the compensation for the inferior organ came to entail a displaced release of the dammed up aggression that could not be released in the normal, acculturated way. Thus,

> We reach, in the course of psychoanalytic research, a phylogenetic factor which points back to the organic roots of neurosis and to the problem of heredity. Oversensitivity, together with its psychical substrate, causes the drive tendencies arising out of organs to remain unfulfilled. These drive tendencies are displaced on to the aggressive drive which is thereby left in a lasting state of stimulation. Heightened excitability, a violent temper, jealousy, defiance, and anxiety invariably appear and fill up the thought world of the child prematurely with an inner opposition to the compulsions of culture [1909b, p. 533].

This formulation of compensatory dynamics is an important modification of the viewpoint of the *Study,* but the presuppositions contained in it fall back, once more, on the critical "Aggressive Drive" paper of 1908. The timeworn criticisms of the Freudians (e.g., Jones, 1955, pp. 130–131) notwithstanding, this paper hardly constituted a protracted discourse on the aggressive drive from the vantage point of the masculine protest. Adler prefaced his presentation of the theory of "organ" drives by rejecting the idea of a reified theory of instinctual drives altogether. He argued instead that the concept of drive (*Trieb*) was from the beginning of life relative to the demands and restraints of the environment. The goal of a drive, on the other hand, could only be determined by the satisfaction of particular organ needs and by the cultural opportunities for satisfaction with which the environment provided the organ. Adler, as we have observed, proceeded to assign a separate drive to each organ, and he identified drive satisfaction with primary organ activity (1908b, pp. 23–25). Within this framework, "aggression" could only be abstracted as the energy field that potentiated individual organ performance. It was not an instinctual drive, but an aspect of the superstructure that directed organ activity. Adler called it "a superordinated psychological field connecting the drives" (*ein uebergeordnetes die Triebe verbindendes psychisches Feld*) (p. 28; Ansbacher, p. 34).

Adler's early conception of the aggressive drive seems broadly consonant with more recent developments in psychoanalytic theory. Since the mid-1940s, analysts like Heinz Hartmann (Hartmann, Kris, & Loewenstein, 1949), Beata Rank (1949), Willie Hoffer (1949, 1950a & b) and René Spitz (1953) have emphasized the extent to which aggressive behavior is an adaptive part of the ego's early organization. They have observed how, in infancy, aggression is expressed through increased motor activity, and they have elaborated how the infant's sensory organization, musculature, and motility all function as apparatuses for the discharge of aggression. Adler, however, was not content to view individual organs as mere "apparatuses" for the discharge of aggression. Rather, he defined aggressiveness in terms of the energic impetus that underlay all normal organ activity. For Adler, aggression *inhered* in organs, and any behavioral aggression existing apart from healthy organ activity was a secondary phenomenon; it resulted when an organ was frustrated and represented the unfinished excitation (*unerledigte Erregung*) that afflicted the individual when the organ drive was denied satisfaction. In this reactive sense, the strongest expressions of aggression normally corresponded to the incomplete activity of the strongest primary (organ) drives. Conversely, Adler claimed that the organ drives themselves were directly served by the excitation and discharge of the derivative aggressive drive (1908b, pp. 28–29; Ansbacher, pp. 34–35).[2]

In the paper on "Neurotic Disposition," Adler recast this analysis of aggression into the language of oversensitivity in order to provide an energic basis for

---

[2]I repeat this analysis of Adler's aggressive drive in another context in Stepansky (1977, pp. 161–164).

the neurotic character. He postulated once more that the inferior organ could not engage in satisfying organ activity, but he examined this incapacity from the vantage point of the aggressive release normally associated with organ activity. When the organic oversensitivity of the inferior organ prevented satisfying organ activity, the dammed up aggression associated with the activity was displaced to general behavior and released in (usually) antisocial and counterproductive ways. Unreleased organ aggression, in other words, became characterological aggression. This excited aggressive tendency in turn provided the organic foundation for the "psychical oversensitivity" that would result in neurosis, for it was this excited behavioral aggression that underminded the child's ability to comply with the cultural demands of his education (1909b, p. 533).

The aggressive behavioral ramifications of psychical oversensitivity represented but one dimension of the neurotic predisposition, however. This is because Adler's conception of psychical oversensitivity embodied not only the aggressive energy bottled up in the inferior organ, but the functional incapacity of the organ—its "inferiority" as well. Adler formulated this heuristic distinction in order to broaden further the clinical ground for which oversensitivity could be held accountable. In particular, he sought to encompass instances where the quality of oversensitivity was shaped simultaneously by the impact of an inferior organ and the external event of psychic impact that could channel the expression of "inferiority" in a definite direction. He spoke, for example, of the child's "emancipation" from his unregulated stool and urinary drives as effecting a comparable modification of his organ drives to see and smell; after toilet training, the child henceforth experienced a negative avoidance reaction to the smell and sight of filth.

By considering neurotic oversensitivity from the standpoint of both behavioral aggression and such passive avoidance reactions, Adler sought to demonstrate that the inferiority of an organ possessed transformational properties that explained the different sides of the neurotic character. To the extent that oversensitivity capitalized on the unrealized aggressive energy of the inferior organ, he pointed to the neurotically disposed child's hostile inclinations toward parents and siblings and active (oedipal) desire to displace the parent of the same sex. To the extent that the oversensitivity embodied a primitive psychological representation of the inferior organ elicited by outside demands, however, the behavioral reaction was one of avoidance motivated by fear, shame, and disgust. Taken together, these two directions enabled Adler to utilize his notion of oversensitivity to encompass the total affective condition (*Affektlagen*) radiating out of the wounded point of the neurotic psyche.

Regardless of the particular behavioral direction taken, Adler made it clear that the new perspective for gauging both organ inferiority and its variable outcomes hinged on the aggression affixed to the organ drive. He no longer emphasized the hereditary basis of the inferior organ. Instead, he isolated the hereditary transmission of an activated "aggressive drive" as a clear expression of the compensatory tendency deriving from the inferior organ. Correspondingly, he noted that one sign of an inborn organ inferiority was simple "physical weakness" as manifested in muscular insufficiency. Many of the "childhood defects" that had already been established as signs of organ inferiority, he added, could also be understood as expressions of the awkwardness (*Ungeschicklichkeit*) through which such organ-related physical weakness was manifested.

Once he had shown how psychical oversensitivity embodied the fear and confusion resulting from the "awkwardness" generated by an inferior organ, Adler found himself on the verge of the descriptive neurotic characterology that emerged full-blown in *The Nervous Character* three years later. Spurred by the organic deficiencies that made him awkward, the neurotically disposed child found that his psychical oversensitivity had increased to pathological dimensions that made interpersonal conflict inevitable. Originally the oversensitivity expressed itself as a general feeling of neglect stemming from the child's fearfulness and heightened need for affection, but this feeling was merely the starting point for an entire constellation of thoughts and fantasies that would come to dominate the child's life. Here, in the context of sketching the behavioral results of neurotic awkwardness and oversensitivity, Adler gave the first encapsulated formulation of the "masculine protest" that would become his clinical modus operandi within the next several years. The thoughts and fantasies that connected to the child's general sense of neglect, he characterized as

> alienation, an inclination towards mistrust and the burning ambition to do things before others, to be better than others, more attractive, stronger, bigger, and more intelligent. There is no question that these unbroken, enduring wishes create a powerful psychical impulse (*Antrieb*) and that they in fact help many of these children to a sense of superiority (*Ueberwertigkeit*) [1909b, p. 536].

The locus of the neurotic conflict was not simply the emergence of unrealistic ambitions rooted in the child's sense of neglect, but the incompatibility of these compensatory masculine goals with the fear of depreciation (*Herabsetzung*) and sense of wickedness (*Schlechtigkeit*) that underlay them. Always, with Adler, the neurotic potential rested in the intrinsically conflictive two-sidedness of the behavioral legacy of the inferior organ: on the one hand the aggressive fantasies that comprehended the child's compensatory reflections on his "inferiority" and led him away from it, on the other the sense of inadequacy and fear of humiliation that embodied the child's realization of his inferiority and served to mitigate the retaliatory fantasies that would set the matter right. So, in this case, it was the basic tension between the compensatory ambitions arising out of the "awkwardness" and the exaggerated fear of retribution for these "censored" ambitions that jointly accounted for the appearance of "oversensitivity" and produced the dynamic conflict in the child's psyche.

What particular developmental episodes heightened the "primary inner conflict"—the incompatibility of the child's aggressive-compensatory fantasies with the inferiority-based guilt that resulted from these fantasies—and simultaneously supplied the conflict with a definite content? Adler believed the child's initial contact with the sexual problem around the fifth year constituted such an episode. In pointing to the pathogenic potential of this episode, Adler was referring to the interpersonal dimension of early sexual awareness that isolated and ostracized the child in his ignorance. In this sense, he spoke of the first sexual knowledge that secretly came to the child as a serious injury to the child's oversensitivity. The taboo quality of sexual information, the fact that innocent curiosity was not rewarded with candid enlightenment, made the child feel deceived, teased, and excluded from a matter of common knowledge. Adler said the child gained the impression that a "comedy" was being enacted for his benefit and saw himself as a rank outsider facing an inaccessible "secret club."

The child's debasing inability to gain membership in the secret club guarding sexual knowledge was buttressed by his recognition of the physical inferiority of his own sexual organ. Jointly, the social exclusion and perception of sexual inferiority became traumatic for the child because they aggravated the available level of oversensitivity. On one hand, the child's first sexual knowledge provided new material for aggressive fantasies that earmarked the retaliatory vindication of his organ inferiority. On the other hand, the crippling interpersonal circumstances that accompanied the first insights into sexuality exacerbated the inhibitive avoidance component of the oversensitivity that led to heightened guilt and a conviction of sinfulness. The latter development proceeded not only from the interpersonal humiliation the child had experienced from the sexually knowledgeable adult world, but as a guilty reaction to the new aggressive fantasies that the awakening sexual drive made possible. In sum, when the demeaning reaction of the adult world to the child's sexual curiosity and the physical sexual inferiority of the child were teamed with the prematurely aroused sexual drive, the psychological result could be devastating:

The "sexual trauma," just like premature masturbation, comes of itself. More important, however, are the premature thoughts and fantasies which lead to incestuous aims and, for want of a more significant orientation, betray perverse traits or greatly strengthen the instability and doubt of the child. And beyond all the impulses of the child there now threatens the deepened consciousness of guilt, the suppression of every kind of aggression, the repentance and the expectation of punishment and an unhappy end. The period of masturbation produces similar processes. And it is a question of the fate of the individual . . . as to which of the enumerated manifestations of inferiority appear, and during which stage of development the neurosis is compelled to take shape [1909b, p. 539; cf. 1910a, p. 87 and 1910b, pp. 81–82].

II.

In the paper on "Neurotic Disposition," Adler laboriously effected his transition from a theory of organ inferiority with psychological ramifications to a theory of neurotic conflict rooted in the multifaceted behavioral *meaning* of the inferior organ. The offshoot of this transition was the psychological theory of character development contained in *The Nervous Character* of 1912. Still, it is important to note that the transition from organ-based psychopathology to inferiority-based psychology was not a conceptual shift effected in *The Nervous Character* itself. Instead, it is a maneuver that was fully rehearsed in the clinical papers of 1908 and 1909 that immediately followed publication of the *Study of Organ Inferiority*. In this respect, there is a certain degree of overlap in the chronological development of Adler's thought: at the same time as he made his transition from clinical medicine to organically based psychiatry, he was concurrently outlining the transition from organ psychiatry to developmental psychology.

In 1908, a year after the publication of the *Study of Organ Inferiority,* Adler published a short paper on the child's need for affection (*Zaertlichkeitsbeduerf-nis*). He submitted that this phenomenon was not a psychological attribute that could be localized in the brain, but a unique confluence (*Verschraenkung*) fed by separate components of the drives to touch, to look, and to listen. Adler claimed that a strong need for affection in the child betokened a strong instinct for life, and he proceeded to gauge the pathogenic potential of the need for affection in a manner reminiscent of the pathogenic potentialities afflicting the inferior organ beset with excessive drive strength and limited avenues of sanctioned organ activity.

Optimally, Adler saw the need for affection as a valuable educational lever that could be employed to facilitate the child's acculturation. He submitted that a large part of the child's development would depend on the proper guidance of this "affectional" drive complex. If the affectional impulses were selectively detoured in culturally suitable directions, the need for affection would become the basis for "derived and purified community feelings." Through the cultivation of such "community feelings" (*Gemeinschafsgefuehle*), the need for affection would transcend intense familial dependencies and form the basis for constructive human relationships. If, on the other hand, the child was spared the "detour via culture" and the affectional drive tendencies could not be directed onto substitute figures outside the family, the child could only obtain "satisfactions of a primitive kind without delay" whereby "his wishes will remain directed toward immediate, sensual pleasure" (1908c, p. 51; Ansbacher, p. 41). This verdict directly parallels the functional fate of the inferior organ, but the consequence of this affectional maladaptation is no longer described at the level of the organ-based "defects" characteristic of the *Study*. It anticipates, instead, the level of psychological explanation that would be employed in the paper on "Neurotic Disposition" of the following year.

In this short pedagogical essay, Adler was not concerned with using a mediating concept like "oversensitivity" to demonstrate how the psychological repercussions of organ inferiority could account for the neurotic character. This did not prevent him from positing at the level of developmental psychology the dichotomous neurotic character styles he would subsequently anchor in the "awkwardness" occasioned by oversensitivity. Thus, he maintained that when the need for affection was satisfied through undisciplined sensual pleasure, the child became oriented to the world in passive dependent ways. Such dependency undermined the development of initiative and self-sufficiency and facilitated the development of fearfulness, anxiety, and feminine traits. If, at the opposite extreme, the need for affection remained completely unsatisfied at both the primitive and acculturated levels, Adler foresaw the pathological predominance of different forms of self-love, the underdevelopment of social feelings (this time the German is *Sozialgefuehle*), and the potential arrival of the child at "a position of aggression":

> Every unsatisfied drive ultimately orients the organism toward aggression against the environment. The rough characters and the unbridled, incorrigible children can instruct us in the way the continuously unsatisfied drive for affection stimulates the paths of aggression [1908c, p. 52; Ansbacher, p. 42].

In "The Child's Need for Affection," Adler demonstrated how the two behavioral constellations typifying the neurotic style could be elaborated without recourse to the idea of organ inferiority. In 1910, a year after the important paper on "Neurotic Disposition," Adler published "Defiance and Obedience," a

noteworthy paper in which his increasing preoccupation with the neurotic character crystallized into a psychological discourse on the two polar attributes that
embodied this character: defiance (*Trotz*) and obedience (*Gehorsam*). Here,
Adler reiterated, almost pro forma, that all childhood peculiarities (*Eigenheiten*)
were directly connected to organ inferiorities and the sensitivity radiating out of
the inferiorities. His new concern, however, was less with the organ inferiority
itself than with the cultural-familial circumstances that made the inferiority operative at the level of personality formation. In making this change of discourse
explicit, Adler seemed to own up to the cultural relativism that was implicit in
the conception of organ inferiority from the outset. The developmental problem
posed in this paper was the same one encountered in the *Study* of 1907: to
accommodate the broadening needs for organ activity to the structuring requirements of the social environment. The new emphasis was not on the particular
status of the inferior organ itself, but on the inherent difficulty of any organ
system in adapting to the drive restrictions imposed by the family:

> Of the greatest importance are the influences of family life. They impose new
> restrictions on the expansion of drives, and the child's attitude about obtaining
> pleasure puts him in opposition with these influences. Here lie the roots of the
> customary, so to speak physiological, defiance of childhood. The child has to learn
> to fit himself into the working of culture (*Kulturbetrieb*) and to give up his childish
> inclination towards free organ activity [1910a, p. 85].

As in the "Aggressive Drive" paper, Adler invoked the concept of *Triebausbreitung*—an expansion or extension of the functional needs of an organ
drive—to characterize the developmental tendency of any organ drive to broaden
its sphere of pleasure-seeking activity without reference to cultural restrictions.
To the extent that the child found culturally prescribed substitutes for his broadened quest for drive satisfaction, he would be obedient. To the extent that he
resisted the restrictions on drive expression promoted by the family, he would be
defiant. Adler seemed to be reformulating from a new vantage point the "aggressive" character traits that, in the "Neurotic Disposition" paper, were depicted
as the displaced release of the aggressiveness associated with normal organ
activity. What was previously seen as an aggressiveness borrowed from thwarted
organ activity was now recast from the standpoint of the *social* relations that
imposed drive restrictions on the individual. The defiant child no longer adopted
aggressive character traits because his *organ* was functionally inferior, but because the child himself was unwilling to confine a natural *Triebausbreitung* of
his organs to the opportunities for organ activity that were culturally approved.
The argumentation ostensibly reverts to the categories of the 1907 *Study* in the

sense that the "defiant" character traits were inferred not on the basis of the inferior organ's functional incapacity, but by appealing to the administrative duties of a governing superstructure (in this case the "child" himself) whose incapacity revealed the fact of a "relative" inferiority.

There is a still more important shift embodied in "Defiance and Obedience." As congealed embodiments of the two neurotic coping styles, these traits were not traced back to organ inferiority alone, but to a more pervasive feeling of inferiority that transcended the psychological repercussions of inborn inferiorities. This crucial shift, fully elaborated in *The Nervous Character,* completed the movement from medicine to psychiatry begun in the 1907 *Study* and continued in the paper on "Neurotic Disposition." As a psychiatrist, Adler would not confine himself to the psychological implications of organ inferiority. He would enlarge his purview to the psychological momentousness of a "feeling of inferiority" that had organ inferiority as one of several determining substrata. In elucidating the fundamental conditions for the development of defiance in the child, Adler first presented

> Children who have an organ inferiority, who are weak, clumsy, sickly, retarded in growth, ugly or deformed, or who have retained childish defects. Such children are very prone to acquire through their relations to the environment a feeling of inferiority. This feeling rests heavily upon them, and they aim to overcome it by all means [1910a, p. 86; Ansbacher, p. 53].

Adler used this broadened starting point to dichotomize neurotic character traits in a way that conformed to his earlier elaboration of the "passive" and "active" strategies that resulted from the attempt to cope with organ-based oversensitivity. There were character traits grouped around the sense of inferiority and character traits grouped around the resulting aggression directed against the environment. The inferiority feelings accounted for an entire gamut of passive avoidance traits—timidity, insecurity, anxiety, submissive obedience. The compensatory attitude of defiance incorporated the "defensive and compensatory intent" that reacted against these self-deprecatory feelings. Adler claimed that the child's defiance was triggered by a constant and exaggerated feeling of being slighted (*Gefuehl der Zurueckgesetztheit*) which it sought to supplant "with its longing expectation of redemption and triumph." He further claimed that the father, the one "who is big, knows everything, and has everything," became the principal opponent in the child's quest for aggressive vindication and, consequently, the principal object of the child's defiance. The attitude of obedience also proceeded out of the debilitating sense of inferiority, but sought the "final triumph" through calculating forms of passivity and submission.

Adler characterized both groups of traits as "false attitudes" whose compensatory significance rested in "the annihilation of the inferiority feelings through a compensatory protest and through fantasies of greatness" (1910a, p. 88; Ansbacher, p. 54). He added that it generally was a question of mixed cases in which traits of obedience and defiance coexisted.

Adler did address his attention to an important reinforcing condition that paved the way for the development of neurotic defiance. He emphasized the "subjective uncertainty" of the young child regarding his sexual role. His concern, as in the paper on "Neurotic Disposition," was with the mistakes that accrued from the lack of sexual enlightenment that generally awaited the child. Such mistakes proceeded from the child's own ignorance of the genitals, but were unwittingly reinforced by parental activities like dressing small boys in girls' clothing (cf. Adler, 1910b, pp. 81–82). Under these conditions of sexual role confusion and uncertainty, Adler lambasted what he termed the "inveterate evil" of our culture—the excessive superiority attributed to manliness—as the catalytic ingredient that converted sexual uncertainty into defiance. This was because defiance was envisioned by the child as the prototypical "male" attribute, and all children suffering from sexual role confusion "exaggerate the traits which they consider masculine" (1910a, p. 89).

By tying the compensatory intention arising out of inferiority feelings to cultural judgments that defined the compensatory value of different kinds of attitudes, Adler found himself on the threshold of an evaluative psychology of the ego. At this crucial theoretical juncture, however, he was not abandoning the clinical program of his earlier research, but in effect supplying the cultural requirement of the theory of organ inferiority as he had formulated it in 1907. There he had made the "inferiority" of an organ, medically conceived, dependent on certain cultural requirements that provided the normative standards for organ activity. By the time he wrote "Defiance and Obedience" in 1910, he realized that the normative quality of organ functioning revolved around societal judgments about masculinity and the "active" character traits bound up in it. The "inferior" organ consequently had to be the one that could not perform in a way that was satisfactory from the standpoint of "active" masculine achievement. In the language of the "Neurotic Disposition" paper of 1909, the behavioral attitudes that embodied psychical oversensitivity were now to be judged from the standpoint of the cultural efficacy of these attitudes. Not merely the determinants of an organ's "inferiority," and, beyond that, of the general feeling of inferiority, but the criteria for adopting the attitude of "compensatory intent" that would make good the inferiority, were ascribed to the same set of evaluative guidelines. Thus, if the organ did not *perform* in a masculine way, and

THE FOUNDATIONS OF ADLERIAN THEORY, II

the individual could not perceive himself in a masculine way, he could at least adopt as a compensatory strategy a masculine trait that would operate, albeit neurotically, in accord with the prevailing cultural norms. This, then, was the interpretive vantage point from which the neurotic-prone child's recourse to defiance was elucidated:

> Obedience, submission, to be weak, small, stupid, passive—these things are all felt as female characteristics, because the father who remains the masculine rule of conduct, ordinarily manifests the opposite qualities. Victory is conceived as masculine, defeat as feminine, and an intense pressure towards, and search after, the masculine protest strengthens in prominent ways the attitude of defiance. It strengthens this attitude still more because henceforth, beyond the starting point provided by the feeling of inferiority, a special kind of inferiority feeling enters the picture—an inferiority feeling tied to the considered possibility of becoming like a woman. For these types of children, with their feeling of neglect and injury, to become a woman signifies an expectation of continual misery and suffering, of persecutions and defeats [1910a, p. 89].

Clearly, Adler was neither the first nor the last to invoke masculinity and femininity as the ordering principles behind psychological experience. Indeed, even within the context of his own turn-of-the-century Vienna, there were striking variations on this theme. Otto Weininger's *Sex and Character*, originally a philosophy dissertation that elicited Freud's sharp criticism for its "speculative" and "boldly deductive" method, had promulgated the basic Adlerian dichotomy in 1903. Weininger reduced psychological experience to the sexual types in terms even more strident than Adler's, for his argument was unquestionably fueled by severe sexual psychopathology that drove him to suicide several months after the book's appearance. He posited "femininity" as a principle of mere sexual consciousness that constituted the negation of human ethics. Woman, for Weininger, was thereby the "lack" of man. Man's self-mastery of his sexuality, conversely, was the key to his potential for ethical and intellectual experience, and masculinity came to represent consciousness, genius, logic, ego, and morality. To the extent that woman demanded emancipation from her traditional role, it was a function of the "maleness" in her.[3]

Karl Kraus, the social critic and satirist who, from 1899, charted the demise of Viennese moral sensibilities in the pages of his fortnightly *Die Fackel*, also popularized the idea of masculinity and femininity as psychological types during this time. Like Weininger, Kraus associated the "feminine idea" with a wanton

---

[3]See Weininger (1903, pp. 88–92, 100–102). On Weininger's theory of the sexual types, see H. Kohn (1962, pp. 30–46) and Abrahamsen (1946, pp. 104–122).

urge to sexual gratification that opposed the "masculine idea" of perfect rationality and creativity. Though he too believed all the positive achievements of human history derived from the masculine principle, Kraus's dichotomy was not as virulently depreciative as Weininger's. In his defense of prostitutes and homosexuals as persecuted minorities undertaken in 1902, Kraus was beneficial about the emotional composition of womanhood. Indeed, he exalted feminine sensibilities as a sort of tender fantasy that both civilized and nourished man in his creative work.[4]

Adler does not appear to have been influenced by either Weininger or Kraus,[5] but he brought to psychiatry the very dichotomy that Weininger and Kraus sought to impose on philosophy and social criticism. To be sure, Adler believed the "masculine" and "feminine" types were not timeless norms but the product of cultural judgments that were relative and therapeutically modifiable. Within the coordinates of present society, however, he believed these judgments to be so ubiquitous that the masculine-feminine principle represented the only paradigm in which to frame clinical diagnosis and treatment. He followed Weininger, moreover, in understanding the sexual types as ideal distinctions that did not exist in practice. In *Sex and Character* (1903), Weininger argued that each person represented some variable combination of masculinity and femininity (pp. 7–8, 79). In the paper of 1910 on "Defiance and Obedience," Adler comparably traced the recourse to "defiance" to an underlying feeling of hermaphroditism, adding that the implementation of a defiant strategy that sought to resolve psychic hermaphroditism in a "masculine" victory often occurred in the unconscious (p. 89, Ansbacher, p. 55). To the extent that education sought to mitigate the "unconscious and erroneous attitudes" of obedience and defiance, it had to remove the inferiority feelings that fueled these attitudes. Unlike Weininger, Adler therefore urged equalization of the status of women as a pedagogical goal that could prevent neurotic recourse to "false attitudes" by countering the exaggerated estimation of masculine character traits prevalent in our culture.

The offshoot of the adoption of masculinity and femininity as the evaluative criteria that measure inferiority was Adler's companion paper of 1910, "Psychi-

---

[4]See Janik & Toulmin (1973, pp. 68–81). On Kraus's conception of women, see also W. Iggers (1967, chapter 7). C Kohn (1963, pp. 45ff.) has argued that Kraus's conception of women was modeled on his early infatuation for the popular actress Annie Kalmar.

[5]As an educated Viennese, Adler was most certainly aware of Kraus's presence on the intellectual scene, but there is no evidence that he read *Die Fackel,* much less paid any special attention to Kraus's ideas about masculinity and femininity. Indeed, in a discussion of the Vienna Psychoanalytic Society of 12 January 1910 that followed Fritz Wittels' attack on Kraus in a presentation entitled "The 'Fackel'-Neurosis," Adler had very little to say on the subject. He professed no more than "an infinitesimal interest in the *Fackel*" (Nunberg & Federn, 1967, p. 388). Wittels' attack on Kraus is discussed in Szasz (1976, pp. 31–38) and Clark (1980, pp. 287–288).

cal Hermaphroditism in Life and in Neurosis.'' Here the cultural verdict of the theory of organ inferiority implicitly ceded in ''Defiance and Obedience'' was explicitly formulated at the level of psychology and psychotherapy. Adler arrived at his formulation by integrating the manifest presence of hermaphroditic traits in neurotics with his earlier views about the psychological effects of organ inferiority. Apart from the physical signs of the opposite sex present in neurotics, Adler discussed the presence of psychological attributes of the opposite sex that also entered the clinical picture. He supplied an explanation for this phenomenon by appealing to the same evaluative criteria that directed the child's recourse to defiance as a neurotic strategy. The ''objective phenomena'' of organ inferiority, he noted, gave rise to ''a subjective feeling of inferiority'' that hindered the independence of the child and increased his need for support and affection. Cognitively, however, Adler claimed that the child's subjective feeling of inferiority was tantamount to being

> in a role which appears to them as unmanly. All neurotics have a childhood behind them in which they were moved by doubt regarding the achievement of full masculinity. The renunciation of masculinity, however, appears to the child as synonymous with femininity, an opinion which holds not only for the child, but also for the greater part of our culture.

From this assessment of the inferior childish role, Adler posited the derivation of the classically ''Adlerian'' gamut of distorted childish value judgments:

> Accordingly, any form of uninhibited aggression, activity, potency, power, and the traits of being brave, free, rich, aggressive, or sadistic can be considered masculine. All inhibitions and deficiencies, as well as cowardliness, obedience, poverty, and similar traits, can be considered feminine [1910b, pp. 75–76; Ansbacher, p. 47].

It was the child's recourse to culturally derived equivalences which embodied both inferiority and repudiation of this inferiority that provided the explanation of psychological hermaphroditism. Behaviorally, this hermaphroditism was manifested in the child's propensity to play a double role. It was, in fact, the same double role embodied in the ambivalent posture adopted toward the inferior organ, the passive and active coping responses spurred by psychical oversensitivity, and the tactical fluctuations between the neurotic attitudes of defiance and obedience. Adler simply broadened the interpretive latitude of his earlier categories by linking the dualities to underlying cultural value judgments that victimized all children to one extent or another. On the basis of his hermaphroditic disposition, the child would invariably show tendencies of submission to parents and educators, but he would also harbor wishes and fantasies expressing "his striving for independence, a will of his own, and a sense of his own significance." Adler took the "inner disunion" of the child to be the "prototype and foundation of the most important psychological phenomena, especially neurosis, the splitting of consciousness, and indecision" (1910b, p. 76; Ansbacher, p. 47).

From here it was a short step indeed to the formal invocation of the "masculine protest" as the operative mechanism underlying neurosis. Adler termed the feminine tendencies of the neurotic the developmental imprint of the child's "feeling of weakness in the face of adults" as intensified by the "subjectively felt" legacy of organ inferiority. The structure of neurosis took these exaggerated feminine tendencies as both starting point and nemesis, and further

> shows the often ramified feminine traits carefully hidden by hypertrophied masculine wishes and efforts. This is the masculine protest. It follows necessarily as overcompensation, because the feminine tendency is evaluated as a childish defect and is retained only in sublimated form for external advantages [p. 77; Ansbacher, p. 48].

With the neurotic, the masculine protest was unable to relieve the full burden of felt inferiority. Adler said the neurosis broke out "when the masculine protest has failed in a main line (*Hauptlinie*)." Such failure did not mean that the masculine protest failed to operate, but only that it failed to achieve its goal of "felt" masculinity in normal constructive ways. The reason the "neurotic" masculine protest could not cope with the feeling of feminine inadequacy was that the same inferiority feelings that produced intolerable feminine traits also produced, as an overcompensatory shadow, a pathologically heightened need for masculine vindication. Here Adler once more picked up the theme implicit in the cultural definition of organ inferiority laid down in the *Study* of 1907. Just as the "inferiority" of an organ rested on the inability of the superstructure to cope with an organ drive, so neurosis betokened the inability of the individual to find strategies for obtaining masculine well-being that could satisfy an exaggerated need for continual masculine triumphs. While in the *Study* the inferiority of the organ was the result of the failure, Adler now theorized a broadened "feeling of inferiority" as the relevant factor that fueled the neurotic quest for the masculine. This feeling "whips along the drive life, intensifying wishes in their boundlessness, eliciting oversensitivity, and producing an eagerness for gratification" (1910b, p. 79).

In both cases the cultural demands remained the same. With the inferior organ, it was cultural limitations on the opportunities for permissible organ activity that rendered the amount of drive vested in the organ excessive. The inferior organ, ironically enough, was the organ whose "masculine" potential actually exceeded the cultural opportunities for organ activity. In the case of the neurotic character, on the other hand, it was the low cultural estimation of the manifestations of inferiority as "feminine" that was responsible for exaggerated masculine needs that could not be served through the normal workings of the "masculine protest." Through this analysis, Adler characterized the finished neurosis as the interactive combination of feminine traits and an hypertrophied masculine protest. This interaction resulted in the culminating two-sidedness that subsumed the two-sided legacy of the inferior organ and restated in broader psychological terms the two-sided response to oversensitivity that characterized the neurotic disposition. For the mature neurotic character, Adler wrote, the intensification of *feminine* traits led to the ineluctable exaggeration of the *masculine* protest. At the behavioral level, femininity invariably summoned its secondary masculine reaction (1910b, pp. 80–81).

With the presentation of psychological hermaphroditism firmly anchored in the evaluative criteria of "feminine" inferiority and "masculine" protest, Adler effectively completed the transition from medicine to psychiatry first announced in the *Study of Organ Inferiority*. It has been the express purpose of this chapter to underscore the considerable extent to which this "transition" was already embodied in the theory of organ inferiority itself. Here, in the guise of a contribution to clinical medicine, Adler implicitly invoked relative cultural criteria that would make the idea of the inferior organ clinically meaningful. To the extent that the *Study* made any contribution to clinical diagnosis and treatment, it was only by virtue of the latent social psychology that it necessarily incorporated. In the important papers leading up to *The Nervous Character* (1912), Adler's task was to elucidate in increasing detail, and with increasing reliance on autonomous psychological variables, the cultural requirements originally presumed by the theory of organ inferiority itself.

Adler's transition from medicine to psychiatry, then, was really no more than the transition from latent to manifest social psychology. "Defiance and Obedience" and "Psychical Hermaphroditism in Life and in Neurosis," the two important papers in which the transition was effected, do not represent bold theoretical departures, but perceptive elaborations of the defining cultural content of "inferiority" and "compensation" as these terms were originally used in 1907. Rather than supplanting the theory of organ inferiority, the contributions actually conferred a retrospective legitimacy on its implicit psychological presuppositions. They did so by invoking an evaluative "masculine" component that provides the underlying rationale for cultural judgments about the appropriateness of organ activity. To be sure, these papers significantly broadened the psychogenic foundations of Adler's original theory by claiming that the "masculine" component imposed judgments on much more than the simple adequacy of organ activity; that it in fact imposed judgments on what people did and said so ubiquitously and relentlessly that it was *the* relevant component for constructing a psychology of development above and beyond the functional status of specific organ systems. This broadening of the range of the "masculine" component is certainly significant, but it remains a broadening that is equally noteworthy for its delimited clinical origins: it completes the original program of the *Study of Organ Inferiority.*

III.

By the time Adler, along with Wilhelm Stekel, assumed the editorship of the *Zentralblatt fuer Psychoanalyse: Medizinische Monatsschrift fuer Seelenkunde* in 1910, his developmental psychology had already coalesced into a therapeutic perspective that was characteristically "Adlerian," i.e., antipsychoanalytic, in its tendency to refract clinical issues from the standpoint of the masculine protest. Thus, at the very point in his career when Adler achieved institutional prominence in the psychoanalytic community, he used a psychoanalytic forum to enunciate a clinical orientation that was fundamentally subversive of psychoanalysis.

In his contributions to the *Zentralblatt,* Adler was at pains to reinterpret Freud's clinical discoveries as instances of a masculine protest that derived from the version of "neurotic disposition" he had propounded over the preceding two years. Relegating the inferior organ to the status of an "infrequent complication" that could aggravate the behavioral manifestations of the neurotic disposition (1910c, p. 105n) or, alternatively, help provide the soil for subsequent neurotic development (1910d, p. 176n; 1910e, pp. 402–403; Radin, pp. 156–157), Adler attempted in these papers to show how the entire range of positive and negative transference developments that characterized psychoanalytic treatment fell back on the psychological dynamics of the masculine protest. Adler's assumption regarding treatment was that the clinical encounter was fundamentally confrontational in masculine-feminine terms, that patients were forever intent on manipulating their therapists, on "humbling" them in order to wind up "above" them in accord with the conscious and unconscious requirements of their masculine attitudes. Transference attitudes that emerged during therapy represented the twin poles of the patient's "psychic hermaphroditism" turned onto the physician. Thus, patients who postponed appointments did so out of a masculine protest directed against the physician (1910f, p. 214; Radin, p. 144). Those who lied to their therapists did so out of a "massive defiance" fueled by a neurotically activated aggressive drive (1910c, p. 104). Thus, a female patient who "invented" a dream for Adler to intrepret did so in order to "smear" Adler, to make him a woman in accord with her infantile masculine fantasy (p. 108). Correspondingly, the patient's praise and love for the physician derived from the complementary feminine side of the neurotic disposition. Such patients felt weak and depreciated alongside the physician; they resorted to passive feminine strategies in order to safeguard themselves against the threateningly masculine therapist. Accordingly, female patients who dreamt of having sexual relations with the analyst indulged in a "neurotic exaggeration" that safeguarded them against imagined sexual abuse at the hands of the therapist. Viewed in this way, the entire "love transference" (*Liebesuebertragung*) to the physician dissolved into elementary constituents of male manipulation and female victimization. Such a transference could have no genuinely "erotic" significance; it was, for Adler, sham (*unecht*), to be understood only as a "caricature" of true libido (1910f, pp. 217, 219; Radin, pp. 148, 151).

The psychological rationale for these "transference" interpretations was fully contained in the theoretical papers we have already considered, but the clinical contributions to the *Zentralblatt* are noteworthy for their more explicit consideration of the female neurotic's "sexuality" as disingenuous and "arranged," and for the more pointed statement they made on the explanatory status of Freud's Oedipus complex. Adler reiterated that the starting point of the neurotic disposition was the sex role confusion that typified early childhood teamed with the child's heightened (*verstaerkte*) tendency to play a masculine role through whatever means were available to it (1910d, p. 174). Female sexuality, according to Adler, only became implicated in neurotic development to the extent that it functioned as one dimension of a depreciated female sex role that was to be warded off for more general psychological reasons. The woman who was not strong enough to master her sexual drive, that is, did not become neurotic because of the specific conflicts surrounding the need for sexual gratification. Rather, her neurotic disposition derived from an exaggerated rejection of all feminine impulses; female eroticism fueled neurotic behavior to the extent that sexual needs were placed within this more encompassing framework. Female neurotics regarded their sexual needs as "evil" (*Feind*), Adler claimed, only because such needs underscored the weakness, submissiveness, and dependency that were equated with a depreciated female identity. To be unable to control one's sexual expressiveness was to live in a condition of heightened "female" vulnerability, subject to calumniation and mistreatment (*beschmutzen und miss-*

handeln), to sickness, to the pain of childbirth—to the status of a slave. To reject feminine sexual needs was therefore to reject all these unsavory accounterments of a female identity (1910f, p. 216; Radin, p. 147).

Because the female neurotic only became sensitized to the issue of sexuality through its association with the governing masculine protest, Adler ended up arguing that such "sexuality," like the transference love manifested in treatment, really constituted a "caricature of the sexual drive," one that elicited the same kind of "resistance" that neurotic women directed against all kinds of feminine expressiveness. Neurotic sexuality, in short, could only be a disingenous sexuality because it served a neurotically heightened masculine protest culminating in the rejection of all things feminine.

From this reinterpretation of the significance of sexuality in (female) neurotic behavior, Adler was but a short step from a direct reexamination of the Oedipus complex as it figured in psychoanalytic treatment. Adler undertook this task in the most significant of his *Zentralblatt* contributions, his "Contribution to the Theory of Resistance." Female neurotics became sensitized to their sexual needs and adopted all manner of contrived "arrangements" to avoid sexual encounters on behalf of a masculine protest that construed female sexual expressiveness as intolerably weak and degrading. Correspondingly, neurotically predisposed children who suffered from aggravated sex role confusion (*Unsicherheit der Geschlechtsrolle*) had to resort to sexual precocity and the Oedipus complex to "safeguard" themselves against the prospect of a demeaning female identity. Oedipal rivalry and jealousy in the young child did not point to an interpersonal configuration mandated by the requirements of normal sexual development. Instead, these emotions corresponded to the fact that, already in the first year of life, the infant operated in accord with a standard of masculine possessiveness that led him to seize hold of persons who satisfied his needs and to experience jealousy toward those who would frustrate this "desire to possess" (*Besitzenwollen*). The Oedipus complex did no more than mark the appearance of the child's safeguarding strategy in relation to his own parents. "The oedipal forms of experience," Adler wrote,

which Freud has described in the clearest and most unequivocal way, have in themselves no driving energy (*treibende Kraft*). They successfully function as a [developmental] landmark and they succeed in obtaining [clinical] recognition because they depict striking manifestations of the dynamics of neurosis, and furthermore because they can be construed without further consideration as a momento or a means of expression understood within the framework of the masculine protest [1910f, p. 218; the translation in Radin, p. 150 derives from a 1916 rewriting of the paper and does not correspond with the original German].

Having translated therapeutic resistance, the transference, and the Oedipus complex into the language of the masculine protest, it would seem that Adler's *Zentralblatt* papers of 1910 fully embody the Individual Psychological viewpoint that differentiates his psychological theories from those of Freud and psychoanalysis. Yet, the obvious paradox is that these preliminary distillations of "mature" Adlerian thought appear in a psychoanalytic journal that Freud personally directed and Adler coedited. Adler, moreover, seemed willing to accept the nominally "psychoanalytic" character of his clinical contributions. Even as he propounded psychological explanations that effectively supplanted the traditional categories of psychoanalytic explanation, he paid repeated lip service to Freud's priority as the clinical investigator who had discovered the very constellations that Adler felt obliged to refract from the standpoint of the masculine protest. Thus, he did not contest Freud's preeminence as the clinican who pointed to the existence of resistance, the transference, and the relationship between these two phenomena, and his reconsideration of these clinical issues was only prompted by his view that "the psychic relations pertaining to these two questions are occasionally misunderstood" (1910f, p. 214; the 1916 version in Radin, p. 145 is rewritten in a way that explicitly dissociates Adler's views from Freud's). If Adler's clinical observations demonstrated the depreciatory attitude toward men held by certain patients, it was the "psychoanalytic unraveling" (*psychoanalytische Verfolgung*) of such attitudes that regularly exposed the childhood pathogenic situation in which the patient, as a child, already wanted to be "above" his father and sought to achieve this goal through a variety of interpersonal behaviors. Adler continued:

> That in the course of psychic development the child must pursue this desire to be "above" through the Oedipus constellation, for the discovery of which we have Freud to thank, is an extremely secure finding (*ein ueberaus gesicherter Befund*). It does not seem any less certain to me that the neurotic character of the predisposed child, his exaggerated envy, ambition, desire to dominate, deepens and greatly stirs up this constellation [1910f, p. 217].

This same strategy of equivocation—the attempt to present a psychological theory that effectively supplants the categories of psychoanalytic explanation as a normative "clarification" of psychoanalysis—typifies the half-dozen book reviews Adler also contributed to the *Zentralblatt* in 1910. In all these reviews (e.g., 1910g, 1910h, 1910i, 1910j), Adler labored to do three things at once: to review the material at hand as a "psychoanalyst" intent on gauging its importance to "psychoanalysis," to append to his reviews encapsulated formulations of his own developmental psychology as supplementary "psychoanalytic" findings, and, more equivocally, to demonstrate how his own viewpoint could be used to reinterpret the clinical findings contained in the material under review.

Even when Adler reviewed authors who treated their subject matter entirely from the standpoint of Freud's libido theory, he casually assumed that the translatability of the psychoanalytic categories of explanation into the language of the masculine protest really meant the author under review was implicitly endorsing a "psychoanalysis" that conformed to the latent Adlerian frame of reference. His review of E. Wulffen's *The Sexual Criminal* plainly exemplifies this working assumption. Adler noted that Wulffen explicated criminal psychology strictly from the standpoint of the Freudian school; he observed that Wulffen equated criminal activity with repressed sexuality, that he cited Freud, Gross, and Stekel in attempting to classify criminal activity into different sexual categories according to the sadistic, masochistic, or homosexual sexual components that fueled it. Wulffen mentioned neither Adler nor the viewpoint on the sexual component instincts that Adler propounded in the review—i.e., that they were secondary *Triebverschraenkung* originating from other organ drives and an aggravated aggressive drive. The fact that this viewpoint was not incorporated into Wulffen's classificatory schema, however, did not prevent Adler from appraising *The Sexual Criminal* as a work that endorsed a psychoanalytic perspective revolving around his own developmental psychology:

> The perspective which he [Wulffen] presents to us strengthens us in our psychoanalytic worldview. Wulffen shows us in the criminal fellow creatures (*Mitmenschen*) who act under the compulsion of an unconscious attitude that is to be understood in terms of a whipped up (*aufgepeitschten*) masculine protest [1910h, p. 119].

In a review of Jung's important paper on "Psychic Conflicts in a Child"—the subject of Jung's paper was his five-year-old daughter Anna—Adler comparably used the format of the review to propound his own alternatives to the conventional psychoanalytic interpretations offered by the author. Thus, the "instinct to investigate" that Jung traced to his daughter's repressed sexual drive toward her father was reinterpreted from the standpoint of the masculine protest. Anna's instinct to investigate, Adler submitted, was activated only after she had witnessed the act of giving birth, equated the pain of childbirth with dying, and contemplated with anxiety her own future as a childbearer. It was Anna's "anxious expectation" regarding her future female role, for Adler, not her repressed sexual interest in her father, that fueled her subsequent investigatory zeal. Adler concluded his review of Jung's article with a statement that captured the essential ambiguity of his interpretive position as a "Freudian." He endorsed Jung's paper as a contribution to psychoanalysis, situated his own criticisms of Jung within the paradigm of psychoanalysis, but simultaneously enjoined Jung to consider the supplementary explanation he proposed in the review as an implicit counterpoise to the Freudian viewpoint:

> Analyses like Jung's represent precious gifts to psychoanalysis. The value of such an analysis resides not merely in the corroboration it offers of countless experiences, but in its communication and securing of the new perspectives. Perhaps the unraveling of his material relating to little Anna will also compel the author to consider the viewpoint I have presented above [1910j, p. 123].

Consideration of Adler's *Zentralblatt* papers and book reviews of 1910, rather than corroborating the distinctiveness of the "Individual Psychological" approach, ends on a note of seeming paradox: the very papers that signal the explanatory autonomy of Adler's theory of development and the ability of this theory to generate a nonpsychoanalytic theory of therapy are promulgated under a psychoanalytic banner and, still more paradoxically, are envisioned by Adler himself as emendations and elaborations of Freud's "secure" clinical findings. The obvious question presents itself: what role did Freud play in Adler's theoretical development by 1910 and, more relevantly, by what rationale could Adler construe his developmental theory of inferiority anchored in the masculine protest as "psychoanalytic"? Adler's early assumptions about social medicine, his concern with the psychological repercussions of inferior organs, his transmutation of the theory of organ inferiority into a theory of psychological "oversensitivity," and his interpretation of oversensitivity via a notion of psychic hermaphroditism that reduced to categories of feminine inferiority and masculine superiority—these signposts of his theoretical development all point to the radical disjunction between his psychological viewpoint and the early psychoanalytic perspective on neurotic conflict. If all the distinctive ingredients of Adler's Individual Psychology were present by 1910, how is it that Adler's papers of this year purport to be clarifications of Freud's doctrines?

To approach these difficult questions from the standpoint of Adler's intellectual biography, it will be necessary to retrace the path we have covered thus far and reevaluate Adler's theoretical development from the standpoint of his long involvement with Freud and the psychoanalytic circle. Chapters 4 and 5 of this study attend to this task by undertaking a chronological narrative of Adler's participation in the Vienna Psychoanalytic Society from 1906 to 1911.[6] But

---

[6]The founding of the Vienna Psychoanalytic Society (as the Psychological Wednesday Society) and Adler's participation in the group of course date back to 1903. Otto Rank's written minutes of the Society meetings begin in 1906, however, and the historical narrative charting the course of Adler's role in the group can only begin at this time.

narrative recapitulation of Adler's involvement with psychoanalysis will be preliminary to a more relevant task—a reassessment of Adler's subjective understanding of his collaboration with the Freudians and the important way in which his perspective on psychoanalysis belied Freud's own expectations toward his earliest group of coworkers. To put this differently, an adequate understanding of (1) the relationship between Adler's psychological theories and psychoanalysis and (2) the intense personal antipathy Adler and Freud came to feel toward one another cannot be derived from the historical record that charts the course of Adler's nominal "institutional" adherence to psychoanalysis. Instead, we must proceed to an evaluation of Adler's *sense* of his contributions to Freud's circle within the sociological framework of the early psychoanalytic movement. Only in this way can we meaningfully elaborate the circumstances in which Adler could gauge his ostensibly nonpsychoanalytic theory of development as a contribution to psychoanalytic science. In short, we must consider for the years 1906 to 1910 what Adler came to expect of Freud and the psychoanalytic forum Freud provided, and what Freud, in turn, came to expect of his "disciple" Adler.

4 Adler in Freud's Circle: I. The Vicissitudes of Discipleship

Disagreement between Freudians and Adlerians has not confined itself to rival assessments of the grounds of Adler's split from Freud's circle. It goes back to the initial status of Adler's membership in Freud's Wednesday evening discussion group. Both parties acknowledge that Adler was one of the original group of four colleagues to whom Freud addressed postcards in the autumn of 1902, extending an invitation to meet at his residence to discuss psychoanalysis.[1] It is comparably beyond dispute for both parties that Adler was a regular attendant at the weekly meetings of this original "Psychological Wednesday Society," that he was elected President of the successor Vienna Psychoanalytic Society in 1910, and that he left the Society with a group of sympathetic colleagues over his differences with Freud in 1911.

Beyond acceptance of the skeletal framework provided by these facts, the entire matter of Adler's "Freudian" collaboration has been the preserve of partisan polemics. In 1939, Adler's sympathetic biographer Phyllis Bottome claimed that Adler came to Freud's attention by replying to an editorial in the Viennese *Neue Freie Presse* that ridiculed Freud's *Interpretation of Dreams* (1900). Freud, her story goes, touched by Adler's defense of his work, subse-

---

[1]Freud sent out these invitations at the suggestion of one of the subsequent Society members, Wilhelm Stekel. Stekel had requested and received treatment from Freud some time earlier for psychological impotence. Stekel's eight sessions with Freud produced a cure, and his resulting enthusiasm for psychoanalysis led him to suggest the idea of the weekly discussion group to Freud. See Stekel (1950, pp. 107–108, 115–116).

quently asked him to join his discussion group not as a "pupil" but as an "equal"—"indeed as an asset, to its respectability and strength" (p. 57). Carl Furtmueller echoed Bottome's claim, adding that Adler published a still earlier report in a medical journal calling for an objective examination of Freud's new theories (1946, p. 336). Unfortunately, neither Ernest Jones (1955, p. 8) nor Henri Ellenberger (1970, p. 583) could confirm this traditional account of Adler's acquaintance with Freud, and Ellenberger's documentary investigation of the problem concluded that the *Neue Freie Presse* never even published a review of Freud's *Interpretation of Dreams*.

Adlerians, however, have explained Adler's entry into Freud's circle on the basis of this undocumented supposition. Furtmueller, who joined the psychoanalytic circle himself in 1909, characterized Adler at the time he entered Freud's discussion group as "an independent thinker on the way to important discoveries." There was, he added, no "emotional element" in Adler's attachment to the group, and Adler published nothing during the entire period of his collaboration "which would show him as a 'Freudian' in the narrow sense of a school" (1946, pp. 337–339).[2] A subsequent generation of Adler biographers and explicators has invariably seen fit to accept these presuppositions and to interpret Adler's period of Freudian collaboration accordingly. Unwilling to concede that Adler was ever a "pupil" of Freud's, they correspondingly choose to view the ill-fated course of Adler's psychoanalytic affiliation as a pejorative commentary on Freud's authoritarian control of his early discussion group. Adler, so this line of argument has it, was initially disinclined to join Freud's circle, was ill-suited to a "younger brother relationship," and was never able to accept Freud as the unquestionable paternal authority he sought to be (Orgler, 1939, p. 25; Furtmueller, 1946, pp. 342–352; Ansbacher, 1962; Rom, 1966, pp. 43–51; Sperber, 1970, pp. 33–45). Understandably, Adler himself became one of the most vociferous proponents of this position. Abraham Maslow, who dined with Adler in New York a year or two before Adler's death in 1937, records the psychologist's response to a question that implied his discipleship to Freud:

> He became very angry, flushed and talked loudly enough so that other people's attention was attracted. He said that this was a lie and a swindle for which he blamed Freud entirely, whom he then called names like swindler, sly, schemer, as nearly as I can recall. He said that he had never been a student of Freud, or a disciple or a follower. He had made it clear from the beginning that he didn't agree with Freud and that he had his own opinions.

---

[2] I would argue that there is one curious exception to this claim, Adler's "Two Dreams of a Prostitute" (1908d). This brief piece is a highly persuasive application of Freud's theory of dreams as wish fulfillments.

Freud suggested, he said, that they try to get together and perhaps they could come to agree eventually. When the disagreement remained and Adler left the group, Freud, according to Adler, spread the version of the break which has since been accepted by all, namely that Adler had been a disciple of Freud and had then broken away from him [Maslow, 1962, p. 127].

Freudian commentators, although willing to concede partially the sectarian character of the early psychoanalytic circle, adopt a circumstantial position that belies the relevance of Adler's indignation. They seek to disavow the imputation of theoretical equality between Adler and Freud by appealing to the duration and the quality of the collaboration that ensued once Adler joined the circle. On the one hand, they remind us that Adler came to Freud as an admitted "novice" interested in learning psychoanalysis, and they point to Adler's early status as one of Freud's "reigning favorites" as testimony to the conventional quality of his discipleship (Puner, 1947, p. 146; Stekel, 1950, pp. 116–117; E. Federn, 1963, pp. 80–81).[3] On the other hand, they emphasize the extent to which Adler, while officially embracing a nominally "Freudian" status, injected into the weekly discussions rigid theoretical preconceptions about "inferiority" that gradually eroded his standing with Freud. Although it is variously argued whether Freud was "constitutionally incapable" of absorbing Adler's ideas (Puner, 1947, pp. 157–158), or "did his utmost" to incorporate Adler's "master thought" into his teaching (Wittels, 1924, p. 148), the burden of the split is always lodged in the real incongruity of Adler's developing claims with the basic tenets of psychoanalysis as Freud established them. Adlerians cite Adler's inability to expound his theories within the framework of psychoanalysis to indict Freud's open-mindedness and scientific integrity, but Hanns Sachs (1944, pp. 53–57), Ernest Jones (1955, pp. 129–134), and Kurt Eissler (1971, pp. 139–142) all stress the fact that the early psychoanalytic group was never intended to be a forum for completely free scientific exchange, but rather a pedagogical study group operating within the theoretical preconceptions of Freud's psychoanalysis.[4] Within the context of the psychoanalytic meetings, Adler's own "ambition" is invoked to counter the complaint of Freud's scientific intolerance. Patience and goodwill are attributed to Freud, on the other

---

[3]The other "reigning favorite" was Stekel.

[4]Brome (1967, pp. 48–61) merely restates the different partisan viewpoints without any attempt at interpretation. Roazen's recent study (1975, pp. 202–213) adds nothing new to the discussion, besides the gratuitous contention that Freud's criticism of Adler is difficult to defend inasmuch as Adler's "heresy" has become the "orthodoxy" of today. Roazen similarly does little to illuminate the split in its historical context when he summarily dismisses the entire Freud-Adler controversy as "the narcissism of small differences" (p. 206).

hand, "who had put up with Adler as long as possible, trying hard to synthesize Adler's theories into psychoanalysis and paying him compliments even at the height of the debate with him" (Eissler, 1971, p. 142).

What these rival interpretations generally obscure is the duration of Adler's membership in Freud's circle. Intent on labeling summarily both the quality of Adler's participation and the quality of Freud's leadership of the discussion group, Adlerian and Freudian commentators make no allowance for the fact that Adler's affiliation with psychoanalysis has a nine-year history and that his evolving relationship to Freud during this long a period is inherently problematic. If Adler in fact entered Freud's circle as an "independent thinker on the way to important discoveries," it is difficult to understand why he retained an active nine-year membership (and even accepted the presidency) of a nonscientific organization whose "sectarian" character was clear from the outset. Adler clearly did not need nine years to size up Freud's control over the group, nor did he need nine years to gauge the restrictive quality of the weekly discussions that Freud monitored. If, on the other hand, Freud never intended the psychoanalytic discussion group to be a scientific forum to accommodate nonpsychoanalytic theories, it is hard to understand why he went to heroic lengths to "put up with Adler" for nine years, particularly given the clarity and the consistency with which Adler promulgated rival interpretations of psychoanalytic findings during the last five years of his membership in the Society. It is equally difficult to account for Adler's apparent leadership in an organization where his idiosyncratic contributions, according to the Freudians, consistently fell outside the range of discourse that typified the discussions.[5]

_____

[5]I should add that these historical issues are not addressed in recent "Freud" literature that falls outside the conventional Freudian and Adlerian camps. In *Freud: The Man and The Cause* (1980), for example, Ronald Clark ignores the chronology of Adler's affiliation and eventual split with Freud. His treatment of Adler in the context of the "First Defections" from psychoanalysis (pp. 305–315) posits that "Adler's theories were . . . in direct opposition to those of Freud," only to conclude that "Adler's resignation therefore became essential. Ensuring this was a task to which Freud devoted much skill" (p. 307). But why did Freud tolerate Adler for eight years before undertaking this task? Why did Adler remain in the Vienna Society for that long if his basic differences with Freud were clear from the outset and "simple enough to understand" (p. 307)? Clark does not undertake the kind of narrative reconstruction necessary to address such questions and, to this extent, he perpetuates a mythological depiction of the "split" that presumes a linear connection between Adler's "opposition" to Freud and Freud's concerted efforts to oust him from the Vienna Society. It is the express purpose of chapters 4 and 5 of this study to dispel this myth.

In *Freud, Biologist of the Mind* (1979), Frank Sulloway approaches the early dissidents from the standpoint of his general thesis about the determining influence of Freud's "crypto"-biological commitments on psychoanalytic theory. He is therefore content to equate the repudiation of Adler with Freud's strenuous resistance to "any attempt from the direction of biology to rob psychoanalysis of its independent disciplinary status" (p. 426). Sulloway specifically invokes the rival "so-

Clearly, there is more to the matter than Adlerian or Freudian commentators care to admit. Moreover, there is a key historical tool for unraveling the complicated course of Adler's status as a Freudian. Otto Rank, the Society's secretary from 1906 to 1915, recorded meticulous minutes of the weekly meetings for this entire period. Between 1962 and 1974, four volumes of these Minutes were published under the careful editorship of Herman Nunberg and Ernst Federn. The first three volumes chart the evolution of Freud's Vienna circle from 1906 through 1911, thereby encompassing the critical period of Adler's ascent and decline within the group. Although the Minutes have in the past been selectively cited to buttress preformed judgments about Adler, they have not been comprehensively examined for what they reveal about Adler's interaction with the Freudians and his evolving perspective on psychoanalysis from 1906 to 1911.

The offshoot of the partisan use of the Minutes has been the utter obscuring of the narrative context in which Adler's "split" from Freud must be situated. Beginning with Ernest Jones, a variety of commentators has assumed that the transactions of 1911 that culminated in Adler's resignation of the Vienna Society presidency in some way epitomize Freud's perspective on Adler for the duration of the collaborative relationship. Rather than examining the Minutes in toto as a record of the *evolving* course of Freud's estimation of Adler, these commentators

---

ciobiological framework'' comprised of Adler's theories of organ inferiority and bisexuality (i.e., psychic hermaphroditism) to account for Freud's ultimate rejection of him. In adopting this position, however, Sulloway overlooks entirely Freud's longstanding endorsement of Adler's "biology" as a supplemental viewpoint that enriched the perspective of psychoanalysis. Freud ultimately became disenchanted with Adler's biology, to be sure, but this disenchantment only became a substantive basis for questioning the advisability of Adler's continued affiliation with psychoanalysis in the course of 1910—after Adler had injected his biological viewpoint into the discussions of the Vienna Psychoanalytic Society for seven years. In short, Freud's estimation of Adler's biology has a complicated history of its own; the issue can only be unraveled in the context of a consideration of "Adler in Freud's Circle" which encompasses the various clinical, political, and sociological issues that figure in Freud's changing evaluation of Adler's work. The complicated chronology of Adler's collaboration with Freud's psychoanalytic circle belies the explanatory adequacy of Sulloway's verdict that Adler is merely one of a number of early "biological" analysts whose liberal use of biological assumptions was anathema to Freud (p. 428).

    Walter Kaufmann's recent consideration of "Adler's Break with Freud" in *Discovering the Mind, III: Freud versus Adler and Jung* (1980) is a debunking enterprise that sets out to vindicate Freud's interpretation of the split with Adler and, in the process, to vindicate Freud from the charge of "intolerant dogmatism" toward his followers. Kaufmann puts his finger on the relevant historical question—"what requires explanation is that Freud and Adler could have been as close as they were for ten years and not that eventually they parted ways" (p. 192)—but he too fails to examine this question historically, i.e., he does not undertake a narrative review of the course of Adler's eight-year collaboration with Freud and psychoanalysis. Instead, he is content to mediate between the rival interpretations of Adlerians and Freudians, always with a view to unmasking the Adlerian claim that Adler was "excommunicated" from the Vienna Psychoanalytic Society (see pp. 204–211).

take Freud's negative verdict on Adler's work in the winter of 1911 as emblematic of the verdict that Adler's work warranted right along—even if Freud was unwilling to deliver it sooner.

To a degree, this arbitrary use of the Minutes follows the chronology of historical disclosure about the Freud-Adler collaboration. Over a decade before the first volume of the Minutes was made public, Colby (1951), gaining access to the unpublished transcripts, provided a summary of the three Society meetings of 1911 that marked the culminating discussion of Adler's status in the Society. Characterizing Freud's negative critique of Adler's theories at this time as "a climax in their relationship" (p. 230), Colby's paper encouraged Ernest Jones and later Kurt Eissler to draw erroneous inferences about the character of Adler's discipleship over the eight-year course of his membership in the Vienna Society. Jones (1955), for example, immediately followed the assertion that "Freud took Adler's ideas very seriously and discussed their possibilities at length" with the claim that "other members of the Society . . . were more vehement in their criticism, or even denunciation." Citing Colby's paper in evidence, he pointed to the "full-dress debate" of 1911 as the direct expression of this collective disapproval (pp. 131–132). In thus conflating eight years of productive collaboration into the collective censure that issued from the debates of 1911, Jones effectively denied the chronological unfolding of the Adler-Freud relationship. The Minutes, we will see, confute both this implicit assumption and the judgment that Adler's split with Freud proceeded from the input of "other members" of the Society.

Eissler's (1971) commentary on Adler, which followed the publication of the first two volumes of Minutes but also relied on Colby for the record of the final developments of 1911, is equally unhistorical in its compression of eight years of collaboration into several pages of summary conclusions. In this account, Freud's "positive" comments on Adler's lectures to the group between 1906 and 1910 are passingly acknowledged, but not analyzed as substantively meaningful in charting the evolution of the relationship; these expressions of support are merely indicative of the good will and tolerance Eissler assigns to Freud as a priori attributes. Rather than examining Adler's rise to prominence within the psychoanalytic group as a sociological issue bearing on the needs and expectations of the Society members or as a political issue bearing on Freud's adroit strategies for welding his earliest group of followers into a unified psychoanalytic movement, Eissler is content to transmute Adler's relationship with psychoanalysis into a testimony to Freud's heroic forebearance with a disciple whose waywardness would have more quickly disabused a less beneficent mentor. Of Freud's initial endorsement of Adler's theory of organ inferiority, Eissler has only this to say: "Little did Freud seem to know, at that point, that organ inferiority would ultimately, in Adler's hands, devour the whole theory of childhood sexuality and of the repressed" (1971, p. 139). It follows that, regardless of what the Minutes from 1906 to 1911 may tell us, the significance of Adler's work is best adduced from the standpoint of Freud's harsh verdict of 1911. Thus, Adler's espousal of the theory of organ inferiority "may be regarded as the starting point of a way of thinking that was later to lead to Adler's leaving the Society" (p. 139).

The consideration of the Adler-Freud collaboration in Kanzer's 1971 account of Freud as "the first psychoanalytic group leader" is comparably polemical in its use of the Minutes to buttress a preformed estimation of Adler's role in the psychoanalytic movement. For Kanzer, Adler is from the outset "a counterclaimant for the leadership of the Vienna group," Freud's "archrival," "opponent," and "adversary." It follows that, like Eissler, he is more intent on circumscribing the nature of Freud's initial support of Adler's work than on accepting it as the starting point of a complex relationship that unfolds over time. Kanzer too implies that the ultimate outcome of Adler's involvement with Freud's circle is sufficient basis for viewing the documented record of Freud's strong support for Adler's contributions to the Society as substantially misleading. Thus, Freud's "cautiously favorable" attitude toward Adler's early presentations presumably begins to unravel as early as 1907, at which point "it became increasingly apparent . . . that Adler's use of analytic tools and inferences was very limited and that he took the leap from biological assumptions to social adjustments through a rarefied psychological atmosphere" (p. 43). Increasingly apparent to whom? one might ask. Kanzer offers no citations from the Minutes to support this conjecture; comparably, he does not draw on the Minutes to support the still harsher verdict that, beginning in 1907, few members of the Society responded favorably to Adler's psychobiological constructions because "the implication of the organic in all behavior, as construed by Adler, began to approach mysticism and yielded dogmatic obsessions rather than empirically derived conclusions" (p. 43). In reality, neither of these assertions is borne out by a chronological reading of the Minutes.

In gauging Freud's dissatisfaction with Adler's theorizing, Kanzer assumes, with Jones and Eissler, that a critique of Adler's theories that crystallized only in the fall of 1910 and winter of 1911 is essentially coterminous with the adumbration of these theories in Vienna Society meetings between 1906 and 1910. In this manner, Kanzer projects Freud's 1911 verdict on Adler's work back in time, effectively obscuring the sociological and political factors that contributed to Freud's changing estimation of Adler. In place of a detailed historical review of the Minutes designed to illuminate the vicissitudes of Freud's complicated rapport with Adler, we have a vague appeal to criticisms of Adler that are ostensibly "repeated over and over again" (p. 43).

In the most recent substantive contribution to the Adler-Freud controversy, the late Walter Kaufmann, for all his debunking ardor, is content to follow the lead of Jones, Eissler, and Kanzer. Rather than using the Minutes to chart the course of Adler's discipleship, he is content to pick up the thread with Adler's first summary lecture of 4 January 1911, at which time, he tells us, "Freud spelled out in detail how Adler's ideas seemed to him to differ radically from psychoanalysis" (1980, p. 206). Ronald Clark comparably neglects to use the Minutes as a basis for reconstructing the complex transactions that eventuated in Adler's departure from Freud's circle. After cursorily pointing to a single Society meeting of 1908 and a single meeting of 1909 when Adler's lectures elicited "criticism," he too proceeds directly to the culminating events of 1911 (1980, pp. 306–307).

Our task in this chapter differs substantially from these previous undertakings. Rather than scanning the Minutes for criticism that is summarily taken to anticipate Freud's harsh disavowal of Adler in 1911, we shall look to the Minutes to reconstruct the evolution of Adler's complex status as a Freudian. This strategy is tantamount to abstaining from preconceived notions about the significance of Adler's Freudian years that follow from our knowledge of the outcome of his collaborative relationship with Freud. We do not have to rely on Freud's retrospective judgment of Adler or Adler's retrospective judgment of Freud to orient our reading of the Minutes; as a rich mine of information about the early scientific, ideological, and institutional growth of psychoanalysis, the Minutes are entirely self-orienting. By letting the Minutes speak for themselves, we can document the historical evolution of Adler's status as a Freudian in a way that belies the simplistic caricature of Adler's collaboration that emerges from the extant accounts. In the following narrative, we approach Rank's weekly Minutes not as a chronicle of deviance that permits us to judge Adler as Freud judged him, but as an historical guide that permits us to evaluate sociologically his complex interactions with the Freudians between 1906 and 1911. Consideration of the Minutes as sociological documentation of Adler's status as a psychoanalytic "group member" provides the necessary context for a reevaluation of his subsequent departure from Freud. The protagonists who shaped this context were, beyond Freud and Adler themselves, the group of early Freudian disciples who attended the meetings of the Psychological Wednesday Society between 1906 and 1911. Federn, Hitschmann, Stekel, Reitler, and Rank were the discussants who reacted routinely to Adler's presentations, and it is their input that consequently supplies a vital frame of reference for evaluating Adler's status as a

"Freudian." With the exception of Rank, all of these participants were medical practitioners destined to become, through the stimulus of the weekly discussion group, members of the pioneer generation of psychoanalysts. Federn and Hitschmann remained loyal Freudians through their careers; Stekel left Freud in the immediate wake of Adler's departure while Rank went his own way after World War I.

I.
(1906–1908)

Adler's earliest recorded presentation before the Vienna Society, "On the Organic Bases of Neuroses," took place on 7 November 1906, and presented in summary form several of the main arguments of his organ inferiority monograph of 1907. He argued that childhood inferiorities constituted "the rule" with neurotics, and he added that such inferiorities prompted a continual pursuit of pleasure because of the demands of the inferior organ. In this manner, Adler saw overcompensation as causing the "supervalence" of the inferior organ and of its corresponding "psychomotor superstructure" (Nunberg & Federn, 1962, p. 42). In the ensuing discussion, Freud attributed "great importance" to Adler's work and noted that "much of what Adler said may be correct" (p. 42). In subsequent discussions of 31 January and 6 February 1907, Federn and Reitler seconded Adler's organic viewpoint by suggesting that infectious diseases were underlying etiologic factors in neurosis, hysteria, and dementia praecox (pp. 93, 94, 107). A week later, Otto Rank responded to a presentation on Frank Wedekind's play *Spring's Awakening* by contending that Wedekind was "a striking example of Adler's inferiority-overcompensation theory" (p. 115).

In his second recorded presentation of 6 March 1907, Adler offered one of his clinical case histories under the title "A Psychoanalysis." Here he discussed the compulsive symptoms of a Russian patient, and he attempted to relate these symptoms to a congenitally inferior alimentary tract. Although Freud did not feel that the case in question was fully in accord with Adler's own conceptualizations, he noted that Adler's inferiority doctrine nonetheless "added something to our knowledge of the organic basis of the neurosis." Jung, in attendance at the meeting as a guest, adjudged the organ inferiority doctrine "a brilliant idea which we are not justified in criticizing because we lack sufficient experience" (pp. 138–144).

Seven weeks later, Adler responded to Stekel's presentation on anxiety neurosis by submitting that anxiety neuroses were found in all conditions that showed physical impairments. The following week, in a discussion of degeneration in which Adler linked degenerative phenomena not to the individual as a whole but to single organs, Federn pronounced Adler the first to attempt a solution to the important problem of "which illnesses are already present in the germ cell and which illnesses appear only in the course of its development" (pp. 179, 188). Through the fall of 1907, Adler made continual reference to the organic inferiorities that underlay different kinds of psychic disturbance (pp. 207, 210, 274).

On 29 January 1908, Adler offered to the Vienna Society "A Contribution to the Problem of Paranoia." Here he submitted that the paranoiac's delusional ideas could be traced back to exhibitionistic impulses, adding that the delusions of being seen and heard emanated from "a psychic superstructure of the organs of seeing and hearing" based on the "inferiority" of these two organs. In accord with this formula, Adler reported observing occasional blinking, a high degree of myopia, and unequal refraction in the two eyes in paranoiacs. Freud proceeded to support Adler's contention that paranoid ideas of reference could be traced to a scoptophilic instinct while cautioning that Adler had gone too far in connecting delusions of persecution and megalomania with exhibitionism (pp. 291, 292, 295). Adler's trend of thought received additional support from Hitschmann who added that "defects of the eye and ear lead to great distrust" and submitted the following week that Adlerian "inferiorities" were involved in anesthetic women (p. 313).

In the spring of 1908, Adler momentarily shifted his attention from organ inferiority to repressed aggression in accord with the ideas expressed in his important paper of that year, "The Aggressive Drive in Life and in Neurosis" (see above, pp. 42ff.). In response to Stekel's presentation of 6 May on the genesis of psychic impotence, he argued that it was the repressed recollection of aggression associated with intercourse that underlay muscular inhibition. It was consequently the aggressive drive that had "the last word in the problem of psychic impotence." Freud proceeded to support Adler's contention that accidental factors combined with organic factors in the genesis of impotence, and he further agreed that the special case of psychic impotence "originates in an inhibition of the instinct of aggression." Freud disagreed, however, with Adler's general deduction that the neuroses had to be considered dependent upon the instinct because, for Freud, "all instincts are again found in all neuroses" (pp. 394–396).

When Adler formally presented his paper on the aggressive drive on 3 June, Hitschmann pronounced him quite correct in recognizing that "the new psychology has to proceed from the instinctual drives," and Stekel added that Adler's assumptions about aggression brought nothing new for practical purposes: "Everything is already contained in the Professor's writings.'' Freud, expressing full concurrence with Adler's earlier study of organ inferiority, registered agreement "with most of Adler's point," but for the definite reason that "what Adler calls aggressive drive is our libido.'' He criticized Adler only for confounding the aggressive drive and sadism, observing that "for the rest, Adler's description of the instinctual life contains many valuable and correct remarks and observations.'' It was Federn, not Freud, who stressed that it had not been Adler's intention to replace "aggressive drive" with "libido," and who submitted that "Adler was wrong to abandon so rashly the primary significance of the sexual drives" (pp. 406–407). Yet, three weeks later, when Adler linked hysterical pseudoepileptic attacks to the rage emanating from the aggressive drive, Freud reiterated that Adler's view "coincides in its essentials with his [Freud's] own" (Nunberg & Federn, 1967, p. 23).

These citations plainly establish the tenor of Adler's status in the psychoanalytic group through the fall of 1908. If Adler's varied interpretations of the organic basis of different kinds of psychological symptoms were occasionally disputed, his prerogative to inject this medical perspective into the discussions was wholly undisputed, and in terms of the open-ended, speculative quality of these early meetings, was in fact unexceptional. Adler's recourse to his "organ inferiority" doctrine was consequently accepted without a predisposed bias one way or the other. It was evaluated, instead, only in terms of the special case material under discussion at the moment. The fact that the group remained resistant to the splintering off of an actual "Adlerian" faction during this time provides important testimony to this open-minded state of affairs. Though Adler received consistent support from Hitschmann, the comments he elicited from Stekel, Federn, and, above all, Freud himself, embodied a fair admixture of support and criticism. The importance of the general idea of "organ inferiority," however, was universally acknowledged.

This situation is perhaps best captured by reviewing the minutes for 4 March 1908 which record one of the Society's meetings devoted to brief reviews of literature and case reports by all in attendance. On this occasion, Otto Rank attempted to prove that "inferiority" of Schiller's eyes (myopia, blinking, inflammation) "was one of the roots of his Tell figure by referring to the myth of the blind archer and to some characteristic passages in the Wilhelm Tell drama.'' Stekel, who would later befriend Adler in the discussions, reacted negatively to Rank's presentation, claiming that "the continuous recourse to the doctrine of inferiority" had "by now become painful.'' Even Hitschmann, Adler's regular supporter, found "Rank's explanation paradoxical and forced, and inferiority dragged in by the hair.'' Adler himself claimed that this opposition to the inferiority doctrine reflected the fact that it had not been understood: while erecting a compensatory superstructure for eye inferiority was not the driving motive of Schiller's drama, the dramatist's mental creation of a scene and subsequent visualization of it still pointed routinely to an inferior visual apparatus. Graf candidly admitted that he was not familiar with Adler's organ inferiority book, and simply cautioned "against the application of the theory where it does not belong." He conceded, nonetheless, the existence of some traces of "inferiority of the eye" in the Melchthal scene of Schiller's play and suggested that perhaps only second-rate poets had weak vision. Federn also objected to Rank's "Adlerian" explanation because the proofs for it were not conclusive. He admitted, however, that "it might very well be that the choice of the shot is connected with inferiority." Freud closed this phase of the discussion by emphasizing that from the standpoint of comparative mythology, on which Rank's interpretation was based, "a number of objections can be dismissed." He added that from a thematic standpoint, Rank's interpretation remained "a particularly beautiful mythological confirmation of Adler's principle and [is] secure as are few interpretations" (Nunberg & Federn, 1962, pp. 341–343).

II.
(1909)

The Society meetings of 1909 began on much the same tenor as those of the previous year had ended. At the second meeting of the year, Hitschmann spoke on "Neurosis and Toxicosis" in a distinctly Adlerian vein. He suggested that inferior organs could act as carriers in the transmission of hereditary taint in neurosis, and proposed that anxiety and neurasthenia be considered diseases of the endocrine glands which could be traced back to a diseased prostate in men and a diseased uterus in women (Nunberg & Federn, 1967, pp. 108–109).

   In his first presentation of the new year, Adler lectured on 3 February on "A Case of Compulsive Blushing (erythrophobia)." He concluded that his patient's condition was rooted in "the impossibility of impressing others, an impossibility that has led to a general inhibition of aggression and several ramifications." Freud did not take issue with Adler's emphasis on the "inhibition of aggression" as the immediate cause of neurosis, but merely indicated that Adler emphasized the second part of the expression while he chose to stress the first part (pp. 138–144). In his final observations, Adler made the first recorded acknowledgment of his difficulty with the "sexual factor":

Adler wishes to stress that the outbreak of an illness requires, in all cases of neurosis, a constellation of recent events, and that this constellation is the immediate triggering factor. As far as the sexual factor is concerned, Adler is well known to be a little in opposition to this view, because, in his opinion, sexual and other childhood defects intermingle; he believes that those other childhood defects are originally lacking in any sexual tinge, whereas the sexual does have the coloration of childhood defects [pp. 143–144].

Five weeks later, Adler supplemented his previous clinical presentations with a lecture ''On the Psychology of Marxism.'' Claiming that Marx's insight enabled him to see the primacy of instinctual life, Adler argued that the theory of class struggle was actually in harmony with the teachings on instincts. Marx's greatest achievement, for Adler, was his insight that the ''altruistic ideas'' of higher civilization were (in the language of psychoanalysis) reaction formations expressed as a form of sensitivity. Freud, in reply, indicated that his attitude toward such lectures ''can only be receptive,'' and that Adler's psychological critique of ''ideas'' seemed ''particularly valuable'' (pp. 173–175).

At the following meeting of 19 May, Adler returned to his circumscribed clinical interests in a way that highlighted his growing dependence on an increasingly personal clinical vocabulary. At this meeting, Freud presented a lecture ''On a Specific Type of Male Object-Choice.'' This lecture outlined the four prerequisites for a love relationship among certain men who suffered a libidinal fixation on the mother. Adler characterized the type of male Freud described as sharing a ''state of *sensitivity*'' manifested in a form that signified ''a return to the earliest condition under which their sensitivity was stimulated'' (p. 247). In elevating the conscious ''sensitivity'' of the ego to the status of a psychic phenomenon to which the libidinal factors owed their significance, however, Adler provided an amplification that invited criticism by Freud. In his concluding remarks, Freud noted that Adler had brought to attention

something quite worthy of note, which does not come to light in our presentations. We always follow up the sexual drives and their effect on the psyche; a complete description requires the relationship of the ego-instinct, and Adler demonstrates this part of the picture of behavior. This is the censorship that the ego exercised over the actual sexual situation; it is the real cause of repression.

On a single pregnant point, however, Freud could not agree with Adler:

Adler's view that the dynamic element is regularly furnished by the ego-instinct; this assumption seems not only arbitrary, but also to involve a grave underestimation of sexuality, which can just as well cathect certain forms with its energy [p. 249].

The Society meeting of 2 June 1909, following the two-week discussion of Freud's lecture on male object-choice, seemed to mark a turning point in Adler's status in the group. At this meeting, Adler presented a synthetic lecture on "The Oneness of the Neuroses" (pp. 259–265) that fused his heretofore separate remarks about organ inferiority, the aggressive drive, and "sensitivity" into a unified theory of the neuroses. He argued that neurotic disorder invariably reduced to the vicissitudes of these three variables. From the root fact of organ inferiority, he saw the potential not merely for "inhibitions of development in the psyche" but for "greater achievements of an organic and psychic nature" (p. 260). The aggressive drive represented the qualitative dimension through which "the psychic inhibitions of development become manifest." Transformations of the instinct of aggression led to a form of abnormally heightened sensitivity, and Adler called such oversensitivity "one of the most conspicuous characteristics of all neurotics" (p. 261).

Freud's reaction to Adler's presentation seemed to embody his first explicit recognition of the wider systemic implications of the clinical viewpoints that Adler had previously presented in piecemeal fashion. Freud found little to fault "in the details of Adler's unusually lucid and consistent train of thought." For himself, however, "he [Freud] has a different standpoint." Freud did not intend this remark as a depreciative characterization, however, and he still adhered to the supplemental nature of Adler's insights: "It is interesting to compare these standpoints with each other and thus to throw light on the problems from various sides." Thus, his most sweeping objection to Adler's presentation was still teamed with open acknowledgment of the corrective character of Adler's perspective:

> The most general objection is that Adler, almost as if by design, has eliminated the sexual factor, which cannot be omitted when one considers the oneness of the neuroses. Adler is essentially occupied with the psychology of consciousness and with that portion of psychology that he [Freud] has neglected; one might call it the psychology of the ego instincts. . . . The etiology of neuroses is on the whole sexual. As a complement to it, writing about the ego instincts and their behavior with regard to the sexual instincts that are to be warded off, is a matter of extraordinary importance; it is in fact indispensable. But one must oppose the view that the description of this part of psychology represents the characterization of the neuroses; it is the characterization of the ego [p. 266].

In addition to this objection, Freud attempted to undercut the ego-psychological framework from which Adler sought to unify the neuroses. He argued that the libido theory of psychoanalysis already provided a solid basis for the purported "oneness" of the neuroses; the "oneness" resided in the fact that all neuroses were substitutive formations for repressed libido (p. 268).

In all probability, it was Adler's lecture on the "Oneness of the Neuroses" that generated the first subterranean speculation about the compatibility of his work with Freud's and that prompted Freud himself to spectulate on the direction Adler's work was following. Ten days after Adler's lecture, Carl Gustav Jung, not yet Freud's designated successor but already his special confidant, wrote Freud that a patient had informed him that Adler "is moving away from you and going off on his own, in the opposite direction to you, even. Is there any truth in it?" (Freud/Jung Letters, p. 232). Freud's reply came a week later. It contained a measured acknowledgment that the story contained some truth, but that Adler still represented an unquestionable asset to the psychoanalytic movement:

> What brings Fraeulein E——[Jung's patient] to the subject of Adler? He has never heard of her. Yes, I believe there is truth in the story. He is a theorist, astute and original, but not attuned to psychology; he passes it by and concentrates on the biological aspect. A decent sort, though; he won't desert in the immediate future, but neither will he participate as we should like him to. We must hold him as long as possible [Freud/Jung Letters, p. 235].

Perhaps more noteworthy than the fact that this letter contains Freud's first admission of reserve about Adler's work is the specific quality of this reservation. Having previously given unqualified support to the supplemental importance of Adler's work on organ inferiority, Freud now decided that Adler's perspective was in fact "biological" and, as such, "not attuned to psychology." There is irony in the fact that Freud should reach this verdict through the immediate impetus of Adler's lecture on "The Oneness of the Neuroses," because this was the first substantive presentation in which Adler did not stop with deciphering the organic inferiorities behind neurotic symptoms but proceeded to adduce the uniform psychological characteristics of neurotics that rested on the biological substrate of organ inferiorities. In the six-page summary of Adler's lecture in the Minutes, only one paragraph concerned Adler's preliminary mention of organ inferiority as one of the bases of neurosis. The bulk of the lecture addressed itself to the psychological characteristics superimposed on this organic base. These characteristics, in turn, derived from Adler's assessment of the vicissitudes of the aggressive drive and manifestations of "oversensitivity."

In reality, then, Freud became pejoratively sensitized to Adler's "biological" perspective only at the point when Adler was no longer content with the role of medical consultant reminding analysts of the organic substrate underlying neurotic symptomatology, but sought instead to adduce his own psychology from his own biological foundations. As subsequent examination of the Minutes will reveal, Freud's new conclusion about Adler's biological perspective would soon develop into a veritable covering law to circumscribe and effectively undercut the validity of Adler's ego psychology.[6]

After Adler's June lecture on "The Oneness of the Neuroses," the remaining part of the year passed without major incident or confrontation. Adler was still very much a respected member of the circle. In November, Freud commented that the problem of why some anal character types only incompletely developed anal characteristics "could be pursued and answered in the spirit of certain Adlerian considerations" (Nunberg & Federn, 1967, p. 301). When Adler linked homosexuality to deficient sexual enlightenment that prevented the child from sexually distinguishing his father from his mother, the pediatrician Friedjung pronounced his remarks "of basic importance." When, on 17 November, Friedjung himself discussed the relationship of pediatrics to psychoanalytic research, Freud, in true Adlerian fashion, assigned to the pediatrician the task of finding "the relationship of congenital inferiorities to later developmental disturbances and functional defects" (p. 322). Echoing the basic Adlerian premise that psychoanalysis could be utilized as an adjunct to clinical medicine, Freud observed that "our task is not to take the place of organic pathology, but to trace the psychic contribution elsewhere" (p. 324). A month later, when Furtmueller ended the presentations of 1909 with a lecture on education, Freud expressed agreement with Adler's proposal that the child be educated by turning the need for affection to pedagogical advantage. Once education had functioned to support the organically determined repressions of childhood, Freud thought, "Adler's proposal will hold up—to educate the child by means of love, to wrest from him, in return for love, a part of his temperament" (p. 358).

Clearly, however, Freud's pragmatic endorsement of Adlerian recommendations did not fully blot out the qualms that had crystallized after the "Oneness of Neuroses" lecture. Four days after Furtmueller's final presentation of the year, in a letter of 19 December 1909, Freud confided to Jung that Adler did in fact have a "psychology," but one which ran the risk of neglecting the inference of "repressed libido" on which Freudian psychology itself centered:

---

[6]Here and in the following discussion, I use the expression "ego psychology" as a descriptive characterization of the content of Adler's early theories. In this respect, I follow Freud, whose references to Adler's ego psychology (*Ichpsychologie*) are found in the Minutes (Nunberg & Federn, 1974, p. 147) and in "On the History of the Psycho-Analytic Movement" (1914a, p. 52). My usage should not be confused with "ego psychology" as a technical development within classical psychoanalysis. In this latter sense, the expression is associated with the work of Anna Freud, Heinz Hartmann, Ernst Kris, and Rudolph Loewenstein.

Thus far, it is true, I have concentrated on the repressed material, because it is new and unknown; I have been a Cato championing the *causa victa:* I hope I have not forgotten that there is also a *victrix.* Adler's psychology takes account only of the repressive factor; consequently he describes "sensitivity," this attitude of the ego in opposition to the libido, as the fundamental condition of neurosis. And now I find you taking the same line and using almost the same word: i.e., by concentrating on the ego, which I have not adequately studied, you run the risk of neglecting the libido, to which I have done full justice [*Freud/Jung Letters*, pp. 277–278].

III.
(1910)

The central event of the winter of 1910 was Adler's lecture of 23 February on "Psychic Hermaphroditism." This lecture was a preliminary presentation of the paper on "Psychic Hermaphroditism in Life and in Neurosis" (1910b) that was published in the *Fortschritte der Medizin* later that year. Adler contended that the tendency to be like the opposite sex constituted a "component" of the sexual instinct that was usually atrophied or sublimated in the course of development. He stated that neurotics understood as "feminine" almost anything inferior, and he traced the "disposition to neurosis" to the feeling of inferiority that stemmed from the child's earliest encounter with the problem of sexuality. Neurosis itself arose only after the "masculine protest" had failed, and all neurotic compromise formations derived from the battle between a feminine foundation and the masculine protest (Nunberg & Federn, 1967, pp. 423–428).

Adler's presentation represented a new level of clinical concreteness. Going beyond assumptions about the organic inferiorities that underlay neurosis, or the behavioral manifestations of neurosis in its generic "oneness," he presented here an evaluative psychology of neurosis that could supply specific etiologies and anchor them in childhood development. In accord with Adler's new level of clinical specificity, the criticism he encountered became more pointed and less perspectivistic—more pointed in the sense that other Society members could draw on their own therapeutic experience to contest Adler's claims and less perspectivistic in the sense that they were less concerned with the "organic" presuppositions of Adler's argument than with the content of the new "Adlerian" psychology. Several discussants questioned the source of Adler's criterion of "masculine" and "feminine," claiming that he was erroneously equating a cultural value judgment with the issue of biological constitution (pp. 428–431).

Freud's response to Adler's presentation went well beyond the delimited critiques of his colleagues. He commented at the outset that one faced Adler's expositions

with a certain feeling of alienation, because Adler subjects the psychological material too soon to biological points of view, thus arriving at conclusions that are not
yet warranted by the psychological material [p. 432].

To date, Freud had not objected in principle to Adler's vigorous espousal of the
"organic" substrate of neuroses when it was a question of designating a neutral
kind of "inferiority." Once Adler reinterpreted his clinical foundation of "inferiority" in accord with his own psychological evaluation of masculinity and
femininity, however, Freud's criticism moved to a new level: Adler was no
longer supplementing psychoanalytic insight in a productive way, but prematurely "subjecting" psychological material to "biological points of view."
In pursuing this line of criticism, Freud echoed the contention of other discussants that in the area of psychology "we do not know what we should call
masculine and what feminine."

It is true that in the woman one does find in neurosis repressed masculinity, but in
the man one finds only repression of "masculine" impulses and not of "feminine"
ones. Neurosis always has a "feminine" character. But the concepts of "masculine" and "feminine" are of no use in psychology and we do better, in view of
the findings of the psychology of the neuroses, to employ the concepts of libido and
repression. Whatever is of the libido has a masculine character, and whatever is
repression is of a feminine character. Psychologically, we can present only the
character of activity and passivity [p. 432].

This passage reveals the new priority Freud assigned to the terminological
differences between himself and Adler by 1910. In Adler's initial explication of
the aggressive drive in June, 1908, Freud expressed agreement with most of
Adler's points for the simple reason that "what Adler calls aggressive drive is
our libido" (Nunberg & Federn, 1962, p. 432). Now, more than a year and a half
later, he professed "alienation" from Adler's standpoint, although Adler had in
reality done nothing more than shift the psychoanalytic "masculine" valuation
of the libido concept into the ego-psychological area of the neurotic's goal-
oriented strivings. What Adler called the masculine goal of the neurotic, Freud
could have stressed, was really nothing more than the ego's representation of the
active "masculine" libido that fueled neurotic conflict at the unconscious level.
Indeed, when Freud conceded that "whatever is of the libido has a masculine
character," he seemed to undercut the initial basis of his criticism that Adler had
prematurely subjected psychological material to "biological points of view" and
to recognize implicitly that his major dispute with Adler simply concerned the
terminological priority of the libido concept in explaining neurotic conflict.

Adler himself recognized that Freud's "masculinization" of the libido represented a cultural valuation no less than his own "masculine" characterization of neurotic strivings, and he made this point in his concluding remarks (Nunberg & Federn, 1967, p. 434).

Through the spring of 1910, Adler continued to discuss clinical case material along the lines of the evaluative masculine-feminine psychology broached in the "Psychic Hermaphroditism" lecture, and Freud reiterated his mounting antipathy for Adler's premature "biological" point of view. On 4 May, when Adler interpreted a child's obsessional idea in terms of a "feminine phobia," Freud reinterpreted the obsession according to the Oedipus complex, adding that the case "nicely demonstrated" the difference between "the sexual-biological view that Adler has expressed and the purely psychoanalytic view" (pp. 513–515; cf. p. 454). Yet, the following week, Freud returned to his traditionally supportive perspective on Adler's biological orientation. In reply to a suggestion of a participant that a bronchial affliction was necessary for the later development of asthma, Freud commented (as summarized by Rank) that

> According to the theory initiated by Freud and continued by Adler, in these phenomena are involved organs that inherently have a specific disposition, the nature of which could be imagined as follows. They are organs that greatly exaggerate their erotogenic function, alongside of their other biological functions. One must assume that all organs originally carry with them such erotogenic capabilities, in addition to their physiological ones. During the course of life, however, they are more and more forced to restrict their erotogenic function, and that can cause a great many disturbances, if it does not proceed smoothly. Adler's extensions [of Freud's theory] have brought to it a certain degree of penetrating illumination. These organs, for which Adler uses the very unfortunate term "inferior," would be completely sufficient for the disposition. For instance, in the case of stuttering, this is quite plausible, as is shown by the case of a stammering patient whose son at ten years of age suffers from bronchial asthma [pp. 526–527].

This revealing passage illustrates the opposite pole of Freud's fluctuating assessment of Adler that characterized the discussions of 1910. Having construed Adler's terminological liberties as the elaboration of a distinct "sexual-biological" viewpoint the previous week, Freud here reverted to his original perspective on organ inferiority as a valuable extension of Freudian theory, an extension obscured but not seriously jeopardized by Adler's recourse to the "unfortunate term" "inferior." Indeed, Freud seemed intent on minimizing the seeming disjunction he had previously drawn between his own work and Adler's when he linked organ inferiority to "the theory initiated by Freud and continued by Adler." If this latter remark represented a gratuitously generous characterization, it was one abetted by the fact that this was one of the very few Society meetings up to this time from which Adler was absent.

This conciliatory respite proved shortlived. The following week Adler returned to the group and restated the psychology of the ego that he believed to be the logical product of his biology of inferiority. In response to Stekel's presentation ''On the Feeling of Strangeness in Dream and in Life,'' Adler submitted that the feeling of strangeness always reduced to the patient's ''fear of degradation and the individual's painful feeling that he will not be able to fulfill his ambitious desires'' (p. 536). When Freud reinterpreted this symptom in terms of the withdrawal of ''libido'' from objects, he admonished that

> Adler can never do justice to the psychoanalytic facts, because his interest is focused on the ego and the conscious processes; psychoanalysis, however, takes hold of matters on the basis of the unconscious and the libido, which are indeed, what produce a neurosis [p. 538].

After this direct criticism, Freud muted any general pejorative references to Adler's psychology of consciousness for the remaining spring sessions of 1910. For the three weeks beginning 25 May, the Society was preoccupied with a freewheeling discussion on the alleged harmfulness of masturbation. The discussion proved quite amenable to Adler, dwelling as it did on the organic changes produced by increased masturbation. Adler generally argued that masturbation should not be viewed as an independent activity with unique pathogenic consequences, but as a tool utilized by neurotics for distinct interpersonal gains, i.e., as one form of the masculine protest (pp. 550, 567–569). The Society was generally receptive to Adler's comments, and when Stekel restated the timeworn objection that Adler ''falls into the error of applying his (certainly significant) principle to everything,'' Tausk quickly replied ''that the reproach to Adler remains unjustified, so long as it has not been proven that man-woman is not the central problem of neurosis'' (p. 569). Freud generally listened to Adler's remarks without direct rejoinder. It was only when Adler parenthetically stressed his priority in asserting the ''psychogenic unity of all neuroses'' (p. 560) that Freud entered the discussion. He restated his inability to see any advantage ''in postulating the oneness of the neuroses, since the libido, which is at the basis of all neuroses, itself established their oneness'' (p. 560).

The final meeting before the 1910 summer recess appeared to confirm further the fact that Freud's recurring attention to the limitations of Adler's biological viewpoint had not seriously undermined his respected standing in the Society. After Sadger's presentation ''On Urethal Erotism,'' Federn, perhaps Adler's most critical listener next to Freud, urged Sadger to refer to the essential works of Freud and Adler that preceded him. The latter did call attention to the significance of pharyngeal reflexes, the relationship of hyper- and hyposensitivity, and, in particular, heredity and the psychic superstructure [p. 577].

Four days after this meeting, Freud reported to Jung that Adler's theories presented a problem in the Society meetings, but he reiterated his firm intent to retain Adler's affiliation with psychoanalysis. The context of this revelation was Adler's desire to make the Vienna Society an official organization by registering it with the Viennese public authorities. In the immediate aftermath of the Nuremberg Congress of 1910, Adler had been elected president of the Vienna Psychoanalytic Society. He took his new administrative responsibilities seriously, and sought to implement the formal registration of the Vienna Psychoanalytic Society with the public authorities.[7] To submit its statutes to the public authorities, however, the Vienna Society needed to include those of the parent International Psychoanalytic Association. To this end, Adler repeatedly wrote Jung during the spring of 1910 requesting the needed information. On behalf of his Viennese colleagues, Adler further requested information about the implementation of decisions reached at the Nuremberg Congress: the payment of dues and the publication of a bulletin. He also solicited Jung's collaboration in the publication of the Vienna-based *Zentralblatt fuer Psychoanalyse* which Freud had authorized as a further concession to his Viennese colleagues. Jung, who had become president of the newly created International Psychoanalytic Association at the Nuremberg Congress, needlessly procrastinated in supplying this organizational information, to the mounting irritation of Vienna analysts already sensitized to Freud's growing preference for his Swiss follower. Freud subsequently wrote Jung on 19 June 1910, impressing upon him the increasing extent of Adler's disenchantment and urging his prompt compliance with the requests of the Vienna Society in the interests of institutional peace. He confided to Jung that

Adler is hypersensitive and deeply embittered because I consistently reject his theories. So it looks as if a secession were going to be attempted in Vienna, as though he would call on other members to take a step that implied calling the authority of the chairman into question. This I luckily managed to avoid. If you yourself agree to the *modus vivendi* suggested by Adler, then the entire difference is formal and meaningless [*Freud/Jung Letters*, p. 331].

Freud's revealing remarks underline his ongoing commitment to retain Adler's institutional affiliation apart from the allegedly nonpsychoanalytic char-

---

[7]On the Nuremberg Congress and Freud's subsequent decision to make Adler president of the Vienna Society, see below, pp. 110–111.

acter of his "theories." When the Society meetings resumed the following October, Adler's contributions were not maligned, and Freud's (by now customary) criticisms always presupposed Adler's accepted status within the Vienna group. During the first sessions, favorable references to Adler's ego psychology were made by Hitschmann, Furtmueller, and Stekel (Nunberg & Federn, 1974, pp. 10, 12, 14).

October 19 marked Adler's last formal presentation to the Society prior to the summary lectures that eventuated in his resignation. His "Small Contribution to the Subject of Hysterical Lying" made the point that behind every lie occurring during psychoanalytic treatment there existed the patient's concealed intention of humbling the physician and rising above him via the "masculine protest" (pp. 18–19). The ensuing discussion produced explicit acknowledgments that Adler's approach differed from Freud's, but it generally viewed the difference as a constructive, supplemental interplay. Stekel argued that Adler's contention that every dream revealed the masculine protest was an abuse of his "quite valuable concept." Hitschmann observed that "Adler's approach is very different from ours" and added that the character traits that Adler associated with neuroses were not always causes, but rather "their consequences, or phenomena that run parallel to them." Rank, though doubting that every dream embodied the masculine protest, nonetheless reported a dream that appeared "like a translation of Adler's theories into dream language." Federn used the opportunity provided by Adler's presentation "to speak about the position of Adler's system [in relation] to Freud's teachings" (pp. 19, 21–22). Freud's comments conceded Adler his own area of expertise and indicated that Adler's presentation was not antithetical to, but merely required the supplemental interpretations of, psychoanalysis. Freud acknowledged that "Adler, with his usual masterly skill, has shown the pedagogical and social settings of the case; on the other hand, his expositions require, as usual, psychoanalytic filling-out" (p. 22).

A week later, Freud once more thanked Adler "for his supplementations of a biological and genetic character" (p. 34), and as the Society moved into its November meetings, other members echoed Freud's positive verdict on Adler's "supplementations." In a presentation on "The Choice of a Profession and Neurosis" on 2 November, Stekel spoke of a "criminal layer" underlying the sexual layer of a neurosis, and added that "it is also the instinct of aggression in Adler's sense, that finds expression in this way" (p. 37). A week later, Hitschmann commented that it was understandable

> that when one deals with a topic which has to do with character, Adlerian conceptions force themselves into the forefront, since in the choice of a profession it is not only sexuality but also the other instincts that play an important role [p. 53].

The following week, on 16 November, Hitschmann offered the seemingly innocuous proposal that launched the heated reappraisal of Adler's doctrines that would culminate in his resignation from the Society. He moved

> that Adler's theories be for once thoroughly discussed in their interconnections, with particular attention to their divergence from Freud's doctrine, so that there may be achieved, if possible, a fusion of the two views, or at least a clarification of the differences between them [p. 59].

After Adler expressed "his readiness to discuss the question," Freud modified the proposal to the effect that only one aspect of Adler's views be discussed—the relationship of the masculine protest to the theory of repression. Freud's proposal was carried, and Adler declared "his readiness to name, within a week, a theme that will offer the opportunity for shedding light on the contrast" (p. 59).

The remaining fall meetings of 1910 consisted of brief reviews and clinical reports made by all members in attendance. As in the meetings prior to Hitschmann's proposal, these discussions incorporated an open-minded appropriation of Adler's theories as a supplemental viewpoint that, in its anchorage in the medical facts of organ inferiority, contributed much to the understanding of neurosis. When Adler reiterated on 23 November his thesis that the neuroses were connected with deficient developments of the sex organ, it was his frequent critic Federn who strongly seconded this view, adding that the main precondition for the childhood sexual abnormalities that resulted in neurosis was "a preceding abnormal organ-development." Federn proceeded to itemize the signficance of organ inferiority by linking it to the following developments:

1. that it brings about the same psychological attitude toward men and women;
2. that it produces extremely strong sexual urges which are hard to satisfy;
3. that it involves unusual sensations; and
4. anachronistic [age-inappropriate] development [p. 69].

When Hitschmann, one of Adler's regular advocates, protested that Federn's comments on organ inferiority could only be accepted when supported by "a large number of instances" and cautioned that "the connection between the doctrine of organ inferiority and neurosis is still very far from clear," Stekel jumped to Adler's defense. He declared he could

> fully confirm the validity of the psychological aspect of Adler's findings. Nor can he see in them any contradiction to what has been discovered up to now by Freud [p. 70].

Freud closed the discussion with a final reiteration of the terminological issue:

> A simplification of the entire train of thought would result if the individual's striving for self-assertion was not called ''masculine protest,'' but instead grouped among the ego instincts [p. 73].

IV.

This detailed review of Adler's participation in the Vienna Society discussions from 1906 to 1910 helps dispel several longstanding misconceptions about the preliminary dissension that preceded Adler's split with Freud in 1911. In addition, the review serves to focus attention on the relevant sociological dimension of the psychoanalytic ''group'' that illuminates the complex relationship between Adler and Freud within a framework of group dynamics. Both Freudian and Adlerian commentators have assumed that Adler's break with Freud was implicit in the quality of his interaction with Freud from the start.[8] Analysis of the Minutes shows this traditional perspective to be entirely inadequate. It does justice neither to the sheer duration of Adler's affiliation with the Freudian circle, to his willingness to accept the presidency of the Society in 1910, nor to the quality of his weekly interaction with the Freudians through 1910.

In our review of the first two recorded years of Adler's involvement with the Vienna Society, we saw how fully approving Freud was of the ''biological'' viewpoint that Adler brought to the psychoanalytic discussions. The meetings of this period were extremely speculative and wide ranging, and Adler's insistent emphasis on the psychological repercussions of organ inferiority was neither exceptional nor controversial. Indeed, in a discussion group that was fairly dominated by full-time medical practitioners (Reitler, Friedjung, Hitschmann, Federn), Adler's contributions were generally welcomed for the clarifying connections they provided between clinical medicine and psychoanalysis.

The Minutes suggest that the quality and tenor of Adler's contributions after 1909 were substantially the same as his earlier presentations. They suggest, further, the absence of any onerous crystallization of rival Freudian and Adlerian

---

[8]Bottome's (1939, p. 57) simplification is perhaps the most poignant: ''Adler was already working upon his idea of a psychical compensation for organic imperfection, and although Freud took little or no interest in this theory, Adler hoped to win him over to it, as no doubt Freud also hoped to make a more thorough-going advocate for his own ideas out of Adler. Both men were—in the nature of things—doomed to disappointment.'' Cf. Jones (1955, p. 131): ''Adler's scientific differences with Freud were so fundamental that I can only wonder . . . at Freud's patience in managing to work with him for so long.''

factions during this time. What they do reveal, on the other hand, are the erratic fluctuations that characterized Freud's hesitant reassessment of the import of Adler's doctrines. Foremost among these fluctuations was Freud's changing estimation of the implications of Adler's terminology on his status as a "psycho-analyst." When Adler presented his paper on the aggressive drive on 3 June 1907, Freud was pleased to express concurrence "with most of Adler's points," because what Adler called the aggressive drive "is our libido" (Nunberg & Federn, 1962, p. 408). By the middle of 1909, when Adler offered his concep-tion of the "oneness" of the neuroses, however, Freud criticized Adler's ego-psychological formulations because they merely paralleled without formally yielding place to the superordinate conceptual status "of our libido." When Adler presented his paper on "Psychic Hermaphroditism" on 23 February 1910, Freud proceeded to disavow Adler's formulation of the "masculine" impulses operative in neurosis formation. He rejected Adler's invocation of an evaluative "masculine protest" because of the explanatory power of the libido concept with its own "masculine character" (Nunberg & Federn, 1967, p. 432). Similarly, when Adler stressed his priority in asserting the psychogenic unity of all neuroses on 1 June 1910, Freud rejected his claim "since the libido, which is at the basis of all neuroses, itself establishes their oneness" (p. 560).

    In the course of these changing evaluations, both the theoretical content and the language of Adler's presentations remained basically the same. It was rather Freud's estimation of the theoretical position that informed Adler's language that changed. In 1907, Freud accepted Adler's formulations precisely because they paralleled psychoanalytic formulations that covered the same clinical material. By 1910, however, Freud became disenchanted with the language of the "mas-culine protest" for the very reason that it *merely* paralleled without adding anything new to the explanatory range of the psychoanalytic concept of "li-bido." In short, Freud became disenchanted with Adler at the time he began to take Adler's language at theoretical face value and not as a gratuitously cryptic approximation of the language of psychoanalysis.

    The middle of 1909 further marked the inception of Freud's reappraisal of Adler's "biological" perspective. When Adler made his earliest recorded pre-sentation to the Vienna Society in the fall of 1906 on the "Organic Bases of Neuroses," Freud pronounced his work of "great importance" (Nunberg & Federn, 1962, p. 42), and when Adler presented "A Psycho-Analysis" on 6 March 1907 that related neurosis to organic disorder in a specific case history, Freud submitted that Adler's work "added something to our knowledge of the organic basis of the neurosis" (p. 142). Yet, 16 days after Adler's 2 June presentation on the "Oneness of the Neuroses," Freud communicated to Jung serious reservations about Adler's concentration "on the biological aspect" (*Freud/Jung Letters,* p. 235), and after Adler's 23 February 1910 presentation on "Psychic Hermaphroditism," he professed an actual "feeling of alienation" toward Adler's "premature" subjection of psychological material "to biological points of view" (Nunberg & Federn, 1967, p. 432). This alienation did not prevent Freud from shifting back to a supportive perspective on Adler's biological views on 11 May 1910 when, in Adler's absence, he referred to the conception of simultaneous erotogenic and physiological capabilities in organs as "the theory initiated by Freud, and continued by Adler." It was on this occasion, moreover, that Freud generously added that Adler's extensions of Freudian theory actually brought to it "a certain degree of penetrating illumination" (p. 527).

What this suggestive chain of comments veils is the very substantial "backlash" effect that characterized Freud's exchanges with Adler during the 1909–1910 period. In this respect, the time intervals between Freud's negative criticisms of Adler's theories are highly revealing. After a critical exchange with Adler over the accuracy or completeness of his presentation, Freud appeared to overcompensate for his direct confrontation with Adler by making positive reference to the "Adlerian" perspective in ensuing meetings. After Freud's critical comments on Adler's "Oneness" presentation of 2 June 1909, for example, he avoided any negative reference to Adler's theories for the remainder of the year, and he made positive reference to the value of certain "Adlerian considerations" at the concluding fall meetings of 3 November, 17 November, and 15 December, 1909. It was only in the letter to Jung of 19 December 1909 that Freud restated the criticism that had been implanted by the "Oneness" presentation six months earlier—that Adler's psychology focused on the "repressive factor" and thus ran the risk of "neglecting the libido" (*Freud/Jung Letters,* pp. 277–278). Similarly, after Freud's direct negative reaction to Adler's "Psychic Hermaphroditism" presentation of 23 February 1910, he immediately rebounded and offered a long supportive endorsement of Adler's biological views (albeit in Adler's absence) on 11 May 1910. Though Freud did make a brief criticism of Adler's exclusive focus on the ego the following week (18 May 1910), he withheld any further pejorative characterizations of Adler's theories for the entire latter half of the year. Clearly, Freud's maneuvering reflected his unwillingness to jeopardize Adler's membership in the Vienna Society, and it was this sentiment that informed his revealing letter to Jung of 19 June 1910. Here, we recall, Freud reported Adler "embittered," but acknowledged his own good luck in averting any attempted "secession" (*Freud/Jung Letters,* p. 331).

When the Society meetings resumed in the fall of 1910, both Freud and the other Society members recognized the distinctiveness of Adler's views, but they readily conceded a constructive, supplemental character to them. Adlerian considerations were beneficially utilized to help explicate Sadger's and Friedjung's presentation "On the Psychology of the only Child" (5 October 1910) and Stekel's presentation on "The Choice of a Profession and Neurosis" (2 November 1910). When Adler lectured on "Hysterical Lying" on 19 October, Freud referred to Adler's "masterly skill" in presenting the pedagogical and social settings of his case, and observed that his expositions merely required "psychoanalytic filling-out" (Nunberg & Federn, 1974, p. 22).

The net effect of this chronology sheds considerable new light on the perspective from which Adler offered the summary presentations that culminated in his resignation from the Vienna Society in 1911. Up until 1911, Adler had very good reason for regarding Freud's criticisms as a limiting critique that circumscribed without actually refuting his clinical interpretations. The quality of this criticism was perhaps most plainly embodied in the reaction to the "Psychic Hermaphroditism" presentation of 23 February 1910. In his discussion of this lecture, Freud never disputed the accuracy of Adler's contention that the failure of the "masculine protest" constituted the precondition of neurosis. He opted, however, for a more encompassing formulation of this observation under the rubric of a repressed "masculine" libido (Nunberg & Federn, 1967, p. 432). Freud obviously felt at this juncture that the theoretical difference was substantive, but he did not characterize Adler's formulation as incompatible with his own, and he did not imply that Adler's lecture fell outside the parameters of psychoanalytic discourse altogether.

For the psychoanalysts, Freud's discreet criticism of Adler has been ascribed entirely to his "patience and tolerance" toward the dissenting viewpoints of his disciples (e.g., Wittels, 1924, p. 148; Jones, 1955, p. 131; Nunberg, 1959, p. xxiv; Eissler, 1971, pp. 142, 147–151). The Minutes, however, permit a more general sociological explanation of this seeming discretion; this explanation is formulated in the language of exchange structuralism.[9]

Following the pioneering contributions of George Homans and Peter Blau, sociologists have learned to approach social behavior from the standpoint of the exchange transactions that typify all social associations. In the most basic sense, an "exchange" obtains whenever the activity of each of two or more parties to a social transaction reinforces or punishes the activity of the other party or parties. According to exchange structuralism, the power relationships that ensue within groups can be conceptualized in terms of the variable outcome of exchange transactions for the different parties to the exchange. "Social power" accrues from the ability of certain group members to impose their will on other group

---

[9]My summary remarks on exchange structuralism, along with the ensuing attempt to illuminate Adler's interaction with Freud from the standpoint of this theory, rely on Homans (1974) and Blau (1964).

members by virtue of the particular "rewards" they are capable of either supplying or withholding. Self-evidently, the rewards at the disposal of group members with social power will be highly valued by other members of the group. Authority, as construed by exchange structuralism, is tantamount to the persuasiveness which follows from the assumption that one's advice, if followed, will lead to rewarding results. Authority may of course develop into power inasmuch as advice that leads to significant rewards may itself become rewarding.

Exchange structuralism is a useful tool for explicating group process by virtue of its ability to account for both the differentiation of power in groups and the types of reciprocity that maintain the distribution of power among different group members. The fact that different parties to exchange transactions profit from exchanges in different ways and to varying degrees means that reciprocity in these transactions may perpetuate an imbalance of dependence and power between different group members. By adopting the viewpoint of exchange structuralism, we can elucidate the structure of social rewards that generates such imbalances of power and proceed to illuminate how these imbalances are maintained via the "equilibrium" that results from a particular network of reciprocal exchanges.

Returning to Adler's evolving status in Freud's circle, the Minutes suggest that by 1910 Freud's rapport with Adler reached a condition of social equilibrium that reflected a condition of relatively equal power between the two men. This development actually typifies a general feature of small group behavior—the tendency for "power" to equalize in exchange relations that are repeated over time (Homans, 1974, p. 76). In the case of the psychoanalytic "group," Freud's social power resided in his status as the founder of psychoanalysis and the official "group leader" of the Wednesday discussion group. Freud's authoritative direction of the Vienna Society was tempered, however, by his perception of the official disrepute of psychoanalysis within German academic medicine.[10] This conviction undercut Freud's authority by substantially enlarging the range of discourse he felt obliged to permit and even to encourage at the weekly meetings of the Vienna Society. Sensitized to the low credibility of psychoanalysis in official circles, Freud's governing preoccupation was with securing the formal membership of reputable medical men whose affiliation with psychoanalysis would help garner vital recognition from the medical establishment. It

---

[10]It has fallen to the historian Hannah Decker (1977, Part I) to demonstrate the considerable degree to which Freud's perception did *not* correspond with reality, i.e., the early response to psychoanalysis in the German medical community was much more complex and ambivalent than Freud (and subsequent historians of psychoanalysis) made it out to be. See also Sulloway (1979, pp. 448–467), whose interpretation is entirely in the spirit of Decker.

was this preoccupation, in all probability, that induced Freud to dilute the demands for doctrinal purity among his earliest group of disciples.

The priority attached to the political institutionalization of psychoanalysis during these years is the critical factor that is routinely ignored in the polemical accounts of Adlerians and Freudians, but that ultimately provides a viable basis for integrating these rival perspectives. Freudians claim the Vienna Society was from the start a structured study group working within the confines of Freud's theoretical views. Adlerians, in turn, see the Society as an open "seminar" formally led by Freud, but incorporating the varying theoretical viewpoints of the different discussants. Each of these perspectives represents a partial truth. The Vienna Society was certainly established as a "Freudian" discussion group to elaborate and expound, under Freud's guidance, the basic tenets of psychoanalysis. Freud's own ulterior investment in the formal unity of the Society as the institutional embodiment of psychoanalysis, however, substantially diluted this formal intent. Concerned from the beginning of the weekly meetings with the institutional stature of his movement, Freud was unwilling to alienate any nominal adherent who would lend strength to his cause, and this unwillingness seems to have altered the quality of the weekly discussions from the start in the direction of the open "seminar" envisioned by the Adlerians. Freud became tolerant because, in his own mind, the need for an externally unified psychoanalytic movement was greater than the need for an internally purified psychoanalytic discussion group.[11] In this way, Freud's intensified commitment to the priority of a unified professional organization served to make him dependent on the voluntary affiliation of the reputable medical men who attended the weekly Society meetings. It was the ongoing affiliation of men like Adler, Federn, and Hitschmann that would impart crucial institutional leverage to the besieged psychoanalytic movement.[12]

---

[11]Dr. Ernst Prelinger has suggested to me an additional explanation for Freud's apparent tolerance within the Vienna Society. The fact that Freud conducted so much of the indoctrination of the incoming group members informally and personally might have strengthened his willingness to conduct the weekly meetings of the Society as an "open" seminar. This line of argument seems plausible, but it cannot be derived from the content of the Minutes.

[12]Freud's preoccupation with eliminating his official disrepute in the eyes of the German medical community is a constant theme in his correspondence with Jung. Indeed, Freud's close attachment to Jung followed the latter's published defenses of Freud's theory of hysteria against severe attacks that occurred at German psychiatric conventions in 1906 and 1907. Furthermore, it was Freud's preoccupation with winning adherents who were prominent within the mainstream of official psychiatry that led him to solicit unsuccessfully the support of a prominent psychiatrist who professed grave doubts about psychoanalysis. This was Jung's chief Eugen Bleuler. See Stepansky (1976, pp. 217, 220, 235–237). Decker (1971, 1977) simultaneously explores and delimits the reasons the German medical establishment was hostile to Freud.

Freud's simultaneous control over, and dependence upon, his earliest group of disciples, represent the relevant social context for appraising what sociologists would designate his "exchange transactions" with Adler. Despite Freud's authority in the Society meetings, his exclusive dependence on the Society for the institutionalization of his discoveries significantly undercut his prerogative to exercise this authority, thereby weakening his social independence as a group leader. In his evaluation of the work of all his early disciples, and of Adler's theories in particular, Freud's conduct thus incorporated an intrapersonal conflict between his desire to win social approval as a tolerant group leader, and his desire to gain instrumental advantage in pressing the superiority of his own theoretical views. This tension is clearly reflected in the discrepancy between his tolerant approval of Adler's ideas in the Society meetings, and his disparaging characterization of these same ideas in private correspondence with Jung. When Freud admitted to Jung that Adler had to be retained for the psychoanalytic movement despite the nonpsychoanalytic import of this theories, he implicitly admitted that the "social rewards" he received from the perpetuation of a unified Vienna Psychoanalytic Society were greater than the personal rewards he would derive from the satisfaction of passing definitive judgment on the incompatability of Adler's theories with psychoanalysis.[13]

This situation was at the heart of Adler's own social power within the Vienna Society. Between 1906 and 1910, Adler emerged as a genuine group leader second only to Freud, and his powerful role in the Society meetings emerged in conjunction with Freud's perpetual anxiety about the institutional future of psychoanalysis. Nineteen ten, the year when the distinctiveness of the "Adlerian" viewpoint crystallized for all members of the Society, was also the year of the Nuremberg Congress, where Freud's anxiety about the future of psychoanalysis induced him to anger his entire Viennese following by placing the presidency of the newborn International Psychoanalytic Association in the hands of Jung, the Zurich gentile best able to "form ties in the world of general science." Freud, who had naively overlooked the rebuff to the Viennese that this decision entailed, was still anxious enough to placate Adler, deviant theories and all, to offer him both the presidency of the local Vienna Psychoanalytic Society and the coeditorship with Stekel of a newly founded psychoanalytic journal.[14]

For Freud, Adler achieved social power because of the high regard in which

---

[13]On the concept of "social rewards," see Homans (1974, chapters 3 & 4).

[14]Freud's defense of Jung as the analyst best able to improve the official standing of psychoanalysis came at a protest meeting that had been organized by his wounded Viennese disciples. The protest meeting and Freud's speech are recounted by Wittels (1924, p. 140). For compatible reminiscences of the event, see Stekel (1950, pp. 128–129) and Jones (1959, pp. 215–216). The incident is interpreted in the context of Freud's relationship to Jung in Stepansky (1976, pp. 237–239).

he was held by the Vienna "group," and because a decision on Adler's part to resign his membership in the Society would unquestionably influence others in that direction (as it did). For his Viennese colleagues, however, Adler achieved social power by virtue of the originality of his ideas, and the forcefulness and consistency with which he offered counter-psychoanalytic interpretations of clinical material. Among this membership of the Vienna Society, Adler was hardly a renegade, and the Minutes give little indication of a genuine bifurcation into Adlerian and Freudian factions before 1911. Indeed, the muted quality of Freud's criticisms of Adler probably had much to do with the high status of Adler's theories with his colleagues. Through the end of 1910, Adler's associates generally reacted to his views on a presentation-by-presentation basis; both their advocacy and their criticisms were delimited and confined to the clinical material at hand. In fact, the very discussants who had the most to say about the "Adlerian viewpoint" were the very members who alternated on practically a weekly basis between positive endorsement and cautious criticism of Adler's theories— Hitschmann, Stekel, and Federn. Adler's theories were always discussed seriously, and it seems that the social rewards Adler received by way of this serious group consideration of his clinical perspectives more than compensated for Freud's belated reservations about his biology and his ego psychology.

In light of this state of affairs, there is every reason to assume that Adler accepted Hitschmann's proposal for a summary presentation of his views on 16 November 1910 not as a threat or challenge, but as an honest invitation to reconsider the common ground between his views and Freud's. Not only did the proposal come from a frequent advocate of Adler's organ theory of inferiority, but the proposal came during a period in which the topics discussed (e.g., masturbation) lent themselves to explanation in terms of Adler's theories, and during this time Adler's theories in fact elicited routinely favorable comments. In the general discussion that occurred the week after Hitschmann's proposal, it is interesting to note that it was not Adler or a future Adlerian like Furtmueller who declared "preceding abnormal organ-development" the main precondition of neurosis and systematically listed the significant offshoots of organ inferiority for the benefit of his colleagues. It was instead the loyal Freudian Paul Federn, the analyst who presided over society meetings in Freud's absence and has even been characterized as the "St. Peter of the movement" (Kardiner, 1977, p. 85).

The import of Federn's respectful attentiveness to Adler's theory dramatically highlights what the Minutes demonstrate: that the decision to consider anew the relation of Adler's theories to psychoanalysis did not reflect the pejorative distrust about Adler that Freud had already reached in private. It was rather a tribute to Adler from respectful colleagues who believed that his ego psychology merited formal comparison with the authoritative pronouncements of Freud.

5 Adler in Freud's Circle: II. The Anatomy of Dissension

Freudians, no less than Adlerians, have polemicized about Adler's departure from the Vienna Society to the point of utter caricature. One of the more recent (and restrained) Freudian accounts summarizes the sequence of events following Adler's assumption of the Society presidency in 1910 in the following terms:

> As for Adler, once the reins of power were in his hands, he abandoned caution and quickly gave scope to views that carried him increasingly away from the Freudian school. The members of the society, educated by Freud and chastened by their guilt toward the rightful leader, found this departure intolerable, and Adler was forced to resign after a few months in office [Kanzer, 1971, p. 45].

Evaluation of the Society Minutes from 1906 to 1909 provides no basis whatever for this kind of gratuitous reconstruction. Adler's theory of organ inferiority and his derivative ego psychology had been fully elaborated for his colleagues well before 1910. The views that allegedly "carried him away" from the Freudian school in 1910, moreover, were the same views that had enriched the Society discussions for five years and elevated Adler to a position of group leadership second only to Freud's at the beginning of 1911.

Analysis of the Minutes clearly calls for a new interpretation of the circumstances surrounding Adler's final "split" with the Freudians. The respectful colleagues who asked Adler to clarify the relationship between his ideas and Freud's in the fall of 1910 were paying tribute to a constructive viewpoint that figured prominently in the earlier discussions. These colleagues would have had

112

no reason to solicit a new exegesis of Adlerian theory if they had already decided that Adler's ideas were incompatible with Freud's. Moreover, the circumstances under which the Vienna Society invited Adler to present summary lectures in the winter of 1911 hardly point to a membership "chastened by their guilt toward the rightful leader" and intent on forcing Adler's resignation. Instead, Adler's final lectures to the Vienna Society merely provided the occasion for Freud to promulgate publicly the devastating reassessment of Adler's theories that he had confided privately to Jung during the preceding year. Everything in Adler's summary presentations followed necessarily and inevitably from his informal expositions of the preceding two years. Correspondingly, Freud's criticism of Adler's presentations did no more than restate and elaborate the reservations he had cautiously raised during this same period of time. The only new ingredient that entered the final exchange was the sudden significance Freud attributed to these longstanding reservations for Adler's future affiliation with psychoanalysis.

In order to evaluate the quality of Freud's final disavowal of Adler's theories, it is first necessary to examine in some detail the explanatory psychology that Adler confidently expounded to his colleagues in 1911. Although his final lectures did not add any new content to the psychology that had emerged in the Society discussions of 1909–1910, they were distinctive in the way that the Society membership had invited them to be distinctive: they explicitly demonstrated the considerable degree to which ego psychology could supplant psychoanalysis in evaluating and treating the neuroses.

I.

Adler's presentation of 4 January 1911 on "The Role of Sexuality in Neurosis" constituted a denial neither of the "existence" of childhood sexuality nor of the putative "role" of sexuality in the neuroses. It argued, however, that the masculine protest should be accorded explanatory priority as the primary developmental challenge that provided the rationale for the intrusion of sexuality in the neuroses. Adler took as the starting point of his argument the claim originally made in his "Aggressionstrieb" paper of 1908 that a biologically meaningful conception of drive (*Trieb*) had to take as its referent a particular organ and particular organ functions. By denying that organ satisfaction per se entailed an intrinsic sexual component, Adler redefined the question that was to be asked in assessing the "role" sexuality could play in the neuroses. He opened his lecture by claiming that the very question of whether a neurosis was possible without the inclusion of the sexual drive was idle (*muessig*) because sexuality had a similarly great significance for everyone. What had to be determined, instead, was "whether the beginning and the end and all the symptom formations of the neuroses are to be found in the fate of the sexual drive" (1911a, p. 94; Ansbacher, pp. 56–57). Adler's basic reliance on a functional conception of "organ satisfaction" meant that he was implicitly answering this question in the negative; sexuality played a significant role in the neuroses, but its "fate" in psychopathological formations was mediated through its service to different organs and the distinct functional requirements of these organs.

In this fashion, Adler was able to situate the intrusion of childhood sexuality precisely where he had left it in the 1907 study of organ inferiority: in the "overcompensatory" requirements of the inferior organ. For Adler, only the sexual organ itself could promote the development of genuine sexuality in life. If sexuality assumed a broader connection with the individual's drive life, this was because a different inferior organ could utilize the sexual factor in establishing its own psychical compensation. It was not that the inferior organ was tantamount to Havelock Ellis's "erogenous zone" or that, as Freud claimed, the child was by disposition "polymorphous perverse" in the expression of sexuality. Rather, Adler claimed that the sexual constitution represented a malleable potential that could be cultivated in response to the compensatory needs of different kinds of organ inferiorities.

Adler's assumption of the prevalence and the importance of early organ inferiorities allowed him to address the same developmental problems as Freud did, but without invoking the sexual drive per se as the beginning and end of neurotic symptom formation. In his lecture, Adler, like Freud, looked at the year-old child who was stubborn on the toilet and and examined the developmental issue at stake. Whereas Freud traced the child's defiance (*Trotz*) to the genuine feeling of sexual pleasure (*sexuelle Lustgefuehle*) experienced during bowel retention, Adler argued that it was the defiance itself that was significant as a "psychical compensation" for the child's organ-generated (i.e., intestinal) insecurity (1911a, p. 95; Ansbacher, pp. 58–59). This line of explanation did not prevent Adler from acknowledging that pleasurable sensations experienced during bowel retention would contribute to a later preference for this way of expressing defiance, but it did undermine his faith in "libidinal quantities" (*Libidogroessen*) as the best way to explain the defiant behavior itself. How can we take Freud's conceptual framework seriously, he asked, if defiant children whose activated "libido" prompts them to retain their bowel movements frequently "produce the feces before or after they have been brought to the toilet or right next to the toilet . . ." (pp. 95–96; Ansbacher, p. 59).

It was at this juncture in his argument, and with developmental incidents like this one in mind, that Adler invoked his primary ordering concept—the masculine protest. Adler had recourse to the masculine protest because it provided an evaluative paradigm for understanding the kind of compensatory psychic needs that could be occasioned by any inferior organ. It simultaneously constituted the key referent against which the *interpersonal* significance of childhood sexuality could be appraised. For Adler, we might say, the interpersonal context implicated in the 'polymorphous' expressions of the infantile sexual drive belied the putatively 'sexual' status of infantile sexuality:

> I have seen a thirteen-month-old boy who had barely learned to stand and to walk. If we sat him down he got up; if we told him, "sit down," he remained standing and looked mischievous. His six-year-old sister said on one such occasion, "keep standing," and the child sat down. There are the beginnings of the masculine protest. The sexuality which is meanwhile budding is continuously exposed to its impact and urges [p. 96; Ansbacher, p. 59].

Although Adler contended that the esteem for the "masculine" was a normal fact of childhood development, he submitted that only the exaggerated masculine protest occasioned by a pronounced organ inferiority predisposed the child to neurosis. The early stimulation of sexuality functioned as a part of the neurosis because it represented the cultivation of a type of safeguard or security device (*Sicherung*) through which the neurotic child could mitigate his feeling of inferiority. Adler envisioned this development according to a predetermined sequence of events. The "organ-inferior" child became precociously "libidinal" because only this type of anxious child needed to achieve a compensatory level of masculine security. The "inferior" child's quest for a new level of masculine assurance, according to Adler, promoted a compensatory thirst for knowledge (*Wissbegierde*). This thirst for knowledge eventually issued in a premature knowledge about sexuality and subsequent fantasies about sexual activity. With reference to the organ-inferior, neurotically predisposed child, Adler put the sequence in these terms:

> Their thirst for knowledge is a compensatory product of their insecurity and reaches at an early age toward questions about birth and sex differences. This strained and continous fantasy activity must be understood as a stimulus (*Reiz*) for the sex drive as soon as the primitive knowledge of sex processes has been achieved. Here, as well, their goal is to prove their masculinity [p. 97; Ansbacher, p. 59].

Adler added that the sexual organ itself could also be inferior, and that such "sexual inferiority" frequently promoted a heightened sensitization to pleasure (*Lustempfindung*) that resulted in sexual precocity. When the masculine protest and heightened sensitization converged in the genital region, premature masturbation and premature sexual fantasies were the result. Adler insisted, however, that "when neurotic birth fantasies and castration anxieties emerge, they reflect neither genuine 'wishes' nor repressed fantasies, but symbolically produced fears to be overcome" (p. 97). These sexual fantasies and anxieties were "symbolically produced" because they simultaneously embodied and served the child's preexisting estimation of the relative value of "masculinity" and "femininity." Early "libidinal" activities were equally symbolic because they represented compensatory expressions of the desire to obtain the same symbolic goal of masculinity. When Adler questioned whether the libido of the neurotic was actually authentic (*echt*), then, he meant to stress both the interpersonal context out of which libidinal activities arose and the ulterior interpersonal aims that these libidinal activities served:

> Is what the neurotic presents to us as libido to be taken as authentic? His sexual precocity is forced. His compulsion to masturbate serves his defiance and as a safeguard against the demon woman, and his love-passion (*Liebesleidenschaft*) only aims at victory. His love-bondage (*Liebeshoerigkeit*) is a game which aims at not submitting to the "right" partner, and his perverted fantasies, even his active perversions, serve him only in the sense that they keep him away from actual love. They naturally serve him as a substitute (*Ersatz*), but only because he wants to play his hero role and because he is afraid of getting caught under the wheels if he goes the normal way. The so-called core problem of the neurosis, the incest fantasy, usually nourishes the belief in one's own overpowering (*uebermaechtige*) libido and therefore avoids as much as possible any "real" danger [pp. 97–98; Ansbacher, pp. 59–60].

In his illustrative case history, Adler presented a prototypical instance of "arranged" libido masking interpersonal insecurities. The patient in question was a man whose inferiorities made him fearful of women and anxious about the consequences of intercourse. In order to "safeguard" himself against these apprehensions, he decided early in life that his supply of libido was excessive to the point of being uncontrollable. He used this rationalization to justify, concurrently, his unmanageable arousal in the presence of women, his inability to enjoy the companionship of women, and his eventual recourse to excessive masturbation. When, in later years, the patient was on the verge of marriage, he developed serious "libidinal disturbances"—massive pollutions, premature ejaculations, and impotence. For Adler, these disturbances were not the result of the patient's sexual practices, but an expression of his underlying wish to escape matrimony.

By recourse to this kind of clinical explanation, Adler was able to provide an answer to the question with which he initially framed his query. He concluded his lecture by arguing that sexuality was not at the source of neurosis, but represented the mask adopted by the masculine protest for purposes of the neurosis. This perspective by no means minimized the importance of sexuality in the clinical picture, but it effectively circumscribed the etiological scope of sexual impulses: they could never be causes, but were always worked-over material and a means of personal striving (*bearbeitetes Material und Mittel des persoenlichen Strebens*) (p. 102; Ansbacher, p. 60).

The immediate response of the Vienna Society to Adler's presentation of 4 January was discreet and respectful. The criticism that the lecture elicited was substantive but fairly delimited in scope. With the exception of remarks by Federn, the compatibility of Adler's views with the basic tenets of psychoanalysis was not questioned, and the appropriateness of the Vienna Society as a forum for the explication of Adler's theories was implicitly conceded. The ground rules governing this reaction seemed in full accord with Adler's expectations at the time. At the outset of his lecture, he had stressed that the ground for his examination of the problems of psychoanalysis "was prepared by Freud's work, which made it possible even to discuss them." Later in the discussion, he reiterated that his explanation of neurotic symptoms merely enlarged upon psychological factors to which Freud himself had had recourse (Nunberg & Federn, 1974, pp. 104, 107, 111).

Federn offered the only lengthy reply to Adler's presentation at this initial meeting. Although concerned that Adler's assumption that all organisms were "inferior" in relation to their environment extended the inferiority concept "so far that its specific character is lost," he submitted that Adler's new approach to the erogenous zones presented "no basic opposition to Freud's view." With reference to Adler's main thesis, Federn argued that the Adlerian conception of neurosis as the embodiment of fears rather than repressed sexual wishes

> does not differ essentially from Freud's because it is merely a question of whether one proceeds from the unconscious, the repressed, or from consciousness, which rejects sexuality. If one proceeds from consciousness, it must be possible to present the process as something against which the patient safeguards himself: otherwise, of course, he would not have repressed it [p. 106].

In this way, Federn concluded that Adler's "safeguarding tendency" had actually been known for a long time as Freud's "secondary function." Federn felt that Adler's viewpoint contained only a single "real danger." By contending that an activated aggressive drive awakened sexuality, Adler had reversed the true relation between aggression and sexuality, and had, for Federn, "done retrogressive work and aligned himself with the opponents of Freud's teachings" [p. 107].

After Federn's lengthy critique, Reitler, Hitschmann, and Tausk added brief, critical remarks directed to specific parts of Adler's lecture.

II.

Three weeks later, on 1 February 1911, Adler delivered the concluding part of his summary presentation to the Vienna Society. He entitled his second lecture "Repression and 'Masculine Protest': Their Role and Significance for the Dynamism of Neurosis." Adler's intent once again was to locate deficiencies in psychoanalytic theory that justified the reformulation of the "question" to be answered. The topic was the role of "repression" in neurosis, and Adler began by berating the Freudian reliance on repression as an explanatory dead end. By attempting to explain the causes of repression via unproven ancillary constructs (*Hilfsvorstellungen*) borrowed from physics and chemistry, the analysts, Adler claimed, really explained nothing. Likewise, they explained nothing when they traced repression back to "sexual constitution" and when they invoked "organic" repression as an "emergency exit" to account for changes in instinctual activity. In all these instances, Adler submitted, the analysts merely repeated the same idea in different words. In the process, they failed to account for the difference between successful and unsuccessful repression. For Adler, the relevant clinical perspective was one that could account for the interpersonal origins of repression from the standpoint of developmental ego needs. Thus, he formulated the relevant question in these terms: "Is the driving factor in the neurosis the repression, or is it . . . the deviating, irritated psyche, through the examination of which repression can also be found? (1911b, p. 104; Ansbacher, p. 61).

Adler clearly opted for the second formulation posed in the question. To do so, however, he had to ascribe to the ego instincts a new dynamic content that could account for a "deviating, irritated psyche" in early life. Freud's early clinical studies had presupposed the existence of an "ego" which entered into conflict with the sexual instinct, but had left the concept vague and undefined. It was not until 1910 that Freud formally invoked the notion of "ego instincts," identifying them with the instinctual aim of self-preservation and the repressive function (1910a, pp. 214, 216).[1] For Adler, this characterization was not sufficient. He rejected the psychoanalytic concept of ego instincts as redundant and empty (*pleonastisch und inhaltslos*), arguing that these instincts should not be

---

[1] On Freud's early neglect of the ego instincts, see Bibring (1934, pp. 103, 107).

viewed as rigidified and discrete, but as parts of an expansive outlook (*Einstellung*) directed toward the environment.[2] Adler claimed that this dynamic conception of the ego instincts was tantamount to a striving for significance (*Geltenwollen*), a striving for power (*Streben nach Macht*), for dominance (*Herrschaft*) and for being "above" (*oben*) (1911b, pp. 104–105; Ansbacher, pp. 61–62, 64).

To characterize more concretely the expansive "striving" orientation of the ego, Adler juxtaposed it with the supremely constant factor that set the parameters within which the ego could strive: *die Kultur*. Given the obdurate molding quality of society and its institutions, Adler submitted that instinctual drives, from the very beginning of life, were merely direction-giving means (*richtunggebendes Mittel*) that initiated prospective satisfactions along guidelines established by culture. Adler's argument here was the original argument of his organ inferiority study of 1907. He contended that the "organ systems" of the individual quickly learned to forego primitive methods of deriving satisfaction and to utilize the ego's anticipatory knowledge [Adler called it "presensitivity" (*Vorempfindlichkeit*)] to gauge the socially prescribed way of obtaining organ satisfaction. Because Adler saw the social regulation of organ drives as coterminous with the very appearance of these drives, he argued that socially aggravated tensions (*erhoehte Anspannungen*) were as significant in determining drive expressions as Freudian repressions (*Verdraengungen*). By this, Adler meant that the development of the ego—which he equated with the recourse to a system of protective safeguards—occurred in obedience to the structuring requirements of social pressures, not according to the requirements of an endogenous kind of "organic repression" (p. 105, Ansbacher, pp. 64–65).

At this point, Adler's provocative tour de force was ostensibly complete, and its verdict was clearly more threatening to Freud's psychoanalysis than his earlier translation of the "libido" into the language of the masculine protest. Adler's reworking of the repression concept had clinical implications that simultaneously ramified in several directions. To anchor the necessity for the ego's system of safeguards in the very conditions of psychic development, Adler had to claim that social pressures shaped the expression of inborn organ drives from the first day of infancy, so that "the adaptation of the child directs and modifies the

---

[2]In his attempt to supplant the conceptual focus on discrete ego instincts with a notion of the ego as part of an expansive, "striving" orientation directed toward the environment, Adler is a significant forebear of Heinz Kohut, whose psychoanalytic "self psychology" comparably supplants the focus on ego instincts operating inside a mental apparatus with the striving orientation of an assertive and expansive "self" (see Kohut, 1977). Elsewhere (Stepansky, 1983), I explore more fully the striking comparabilities between Adler's perspective of 1911 and Kohut's at the time of his death in 1981.

drives until he has adjusted himself in some way to the environment'' (p. 105; Ansbacher, pp. 64–65).[3] In making this claim, Adler was not merely crediting the infant with cognitive tools that permitted a seemingly instantaneous regulation of innate organic drives; he was also relativizing the concept of an instinctual drive altogether. In a spirit strikingly reminiscent of Marx's argument in Part I of *The German Ideology,* Adler expressly stated that it was useless even to discuss the issue of drives qua drives:

> If we consider the varied manner and tempo in which the satisfaction of drives has asserted itself everywhere and at all times, and how much it has depended on social institutions and economic conditions, we arrive at a conclusion which is analogous to the above, namely, that drive satisfaction, and consequently the quality and strength of the drive, are at all times variable and therefore not measurable [p. 105; Ansbacher, pp. 64–65].

Was Adler directly influenced by Marx in appealing to the role of ''social institutions and economic conditions'' in shaping drive satisfactions? We lack the evidence to answer this question definitively, but it is worth pointing out that Adler's lecture to the Vienna Society of 10 March 1909, ''On the Psychology of Marxism,'' is broadly supportive of this possibility. Although Otto Rank's cryptic summary of the lecture makes it virtually impossible to decipher Adler's argumentation, it is clear that Adler apprehended Marx as the theorist whose economic studies subserved an enlarged appreciation of instinctual life. Specifi-

---

[3]Adler's argument here is only superficially akin to the ''object relations'' perspective on instinctual development that has been propounded by the analyst Hans Loewald (1960, 1971, 1978). Building on D. W. Winnicott's observation that the instinctual development of the infant cannot be divorced from considerations of early ego development (1956, p. 305; 1960, p. 49), Loewald has stressed the way in which the early environment (particularly as mediated by the mother) shapes the organization and expression of the infant's drives. For Loewald, drives are constituted through interactions with objects, specifically, ''through interactions within the mother-child psychic field'' (1971, pp. 129–131). In conceptualizing the drives—and psychic-structure formation in general (1978)—as the product of interactions between the infant and its human environment, Loewald begins with the assumption that ''both recognition and fulfillment of a need are at first beyond the ability of the infant'' (1960, p. 237). It is only the mother's ''gathering mediation of structure and direction . . . in her caring activities'' (p. 238) that puts the recognition and satisfaction of the drives within the grasp of the growing infant. For Adler, of course, it is not that organized drive activity is *beyond* the infant's ability, but rather that such drive activity is from the beginning of life *subject* to ''social pressures'' from the outside. Adler never expatiated on the psychological meaning of these ''pressures'' in other than naive adultomorphic terms, and there is certainly no reason to believe he understood them at the level of a mother-infant matrix. In fact, Adler's belief that from the outset of life, the infant possessed cognitive equipment that yielded a seemingly instantaneous *prerogative* to regulate the drives is diametrically opposed to Loewald's argument that drives only emerge out of the mediating activities of the mother as a representative of the environment.

cally, Adler observed that Marx's "insight into natural and social processes enabled him, as did his psychological [capacity] for the intensive penetration of his field, to see clearly what is, through [our study of] analytic psychology, beginning to dawn on us with increasing clarity: *the primacy of instinctual life.*" Moreover, Marx comprehended economics itself "as a study of the forms in which the convergence of the instinctual life and tendencies toward gratification finds expression. The gratification is achieved only by a detour of aggression, which encompasses the conditions of production" (1909a, p. 173).

In the second summary lecture of 1911, it was the socioeconomically determined "detour of aggression" that enabled Adler to relativize the very concept of instinctual drive. The explicit relativization of the instinctual drive into a mere "direction-giving tendency" meant that Adler's entire psychology of childhood development had to become, perforce, a psychology of the ego. Adler hardly needed a challenge from the Vienna Society in 1911 to discourse on the early preeminence of the ego's "masculine" goals. In fact, this conclusion followed the dominant direction of all his "psychoanalytic" articles between 1908 and 1910. The central characteristics of this ego psychology had been fully spelled out in the papers Adler published as a member of Freud's circle. Only in the summary lectures of 1911, however, did Adler make a direct attempt to *supplant* Freud's perspective on early "libidinal" development with his own conviction of the primacy of ego development. In the second lecture of February 1, he tied childhood psychopathology to the quality of the child's adaptation (*Anpassung*) to his family environment, and he in turn related the quality of adaptation to the success with which family education shaped the child's "direction-giving" tendencies. He spoke in this connection of the affective values (*Gefuehlswerte*) that the child's first adaptations to the persons of its environment occasioned. When these values were negative, when the child's feelings towards those around him reflected insecurity, timidity, and defiance instead of security and love, Adler claimed that the child would resort to neurotic safeguards (*Sicherungen*) to ward off his resulting sense of unhappiness.

Adler's concentration on "safeguarding tendencies" as the key expression of incipient neurosis all came directly out of his important "Neurotic Disposition" paper of 1909. Yet, in the summary lecture of 1911, he seemed to refer less to specific ego defenses than to a more encompassing kind of "character armor" (Reich) that established the very style through which the ego's defensive strategies could be formulated. Defiance and obedience, *Trotz* and *Gehorsam*, here as in the 1910 paper of that title, represented the two basic routes that the neurotic safeguarding tendencies could follow. When appropriated by the insecure child who had been victimized by educational errors, these two tendencies blossomed into protective, compensatory strategies designed to "modify, change, suppress, or excite every drive impulse to such an extent that anything that manifests itself as a veritable drive can be understood only from this point of view" (1911b, p. 106; Ansbacher, p. 66).

Adler spoke here entirely from the standpoint of the ego and his understanding of "drive modification" referred exclusively to the interpersonal valuation of behavior from the standpoint of the ego's protective strategies. Thus, he characterized "defiant" children not as innately aggressive children, but as children whose insecurities induced them to be rationally manipulative:

> What the opponent loves will be hated, and what others discard will be highly valued. What culture prohibits, what parents and educators oppose, precisely that will be chosen as the most ardently desired goal. An object or a person will attain value only if others will suffer in consequence [pp. 106–107; Ansbacher, p. 66].

In a sentence that strikingly anticipates the later work of the neo-Freudian Karen Horney, Adler further observed: "The interpersonal tension is so excessively great with the neurotic, his drive desire (*Triebbegehren*) is so intensified, that he perpetually chases after his triumph" (p. 107; Ansbacher, p. 66).[4] Under the rubric of this "defiant" neurotic strategy for conquest, Adler grouped childhood disorders (thumbsucking, enuresis, stuttering) and manifestations of sexual precocity (early masturbation). These safeguarding symptoms were utilized and retained not for any direct libidinal satisfaction they might provide, but for the mediated interpersonal leverage they promoted: it was in the struggle with the opponent that they were retained, not because they were inherently pleasurable (*lustvoll*) but because they were valuable (*wertvoll*) (p. 107; Ansbacher, p. 67).

In the remaining part of his final presentation, Adler delineated the full-blown characterology of the neurotic that emerged from his propositions about childhood ego development. Although he briefly linked this characterology to the two foci of development that had preoccupied him earlier—the feeling of inferiority deriving from inferior organs and the fear of playing a feminine role—he quickly moved on to a new level of synthesis. In the presentation of 1 February Adler was more concerned with elucidating the neurotic character structure as the outgrowth of the system of ego safeguards than with enumerating the organic constituents of the feeling of inferiority that elicited neurotic reliance on safeguards in the first place.

---

[4]In 1950, Horney would explicate the neurotic process as a "search for glory" that included, among its principal constituents, the drive toward a vindictive triumph. She observed, in this connection, that "Alfred Adler was the first psychoanalyst to see the search for glory as a comprehensive phenomenon, and to point out its crucial significance in neurosis" (p. 28).

Adler described the emergent neurotic character as a collective representation of neurotic strategies directed toward neurotic interpersonal goals. Long before the arrival of Karen Horney and the neo-Freudians, he stressed the degree to which the neurotic's preoccupation with obtainable goals falsified his life of feeling (*Gefehlsleben verfaelscht*) and led to a morbid preoccupation with an imaginary (*vermeintlichen*) triumph in the future (p. 107; Ansbacher, p. 108). Adler did not contend that the neurotic character was incapable of altruistic behavior, but he did argue that such behavior only became manifest when it could be incorporated into the neurotic's "search for significance" (*Sucht zu gelten*)—when it served to promote interpersonal superiority in contexts where the display of overt ambition would be a liability. In this sense, the "neurosis" was not embodied in the negative character traits (jealousy, ambition, hatefulness) that safeguarded neurotic egoism, but rather in the underlying preoccupation with the estimation (*Wertschaetzung*) in which one was held by others. Thus the neurotic's interpersonal flexibility and willingness to disguise fundamental character traits as the situation required. Despite the tactical mobility the neurotic routinely employed in the quest for superiority, Adler always returned to the core sense of "masculine" inadequacy that fueled this tactical maneuvering (1911b, pp. 111–112).

By demonstrating the full range of behaviors that the anxious neurotic could adopt, Adler believed he had broadened the significance of the masculine protest to the point where it could answer the temporal question of when a "neurosis" actually appeared. He submitted that any situation of occurrence that provided the pretext for a feeling of disparagement (or simply the expectation of such a feeling) produced a neurotic "attack" in a suitably predisposed individual. Subsequent drive-repressions (*Triebverdraengungen*) that followed the neurotic attack were not causally important, but only incidental phenomena (*Begleiterscheinungen*) absorbed into a preexisting neurotic character structure. This structure was composed of the interpersonal strategies grouped around the striving for significance, the masculine protest, and the safeguarding tendencies (p. 110; Ansbacher, p. 67).

Adler did not believe that the childhood memory of feminine "inferiority" potentiated by a neurotic attack had to be forgotten or repressed. Such memories were merely divested of psychological significance until a contemporary event of equivalent *relational* import triggered the same kind of depreciative relational perception that characterized the childhood precursor. Thus, Adler made the point that a male child, threatened and emasculated by a domineering "masculine" mother, might become neurotic only when the child grew up and became engaged to an assertive woman who revitalized the past memory by conjuring up a comparable specter of feminine victimization (pp. 111–112). When such men sought to escape neurotically perceived enslavement through the regular depreciation of all women, Adler claimed they had recourse to a "neurotic" strategy that was *wertvoll;* the depreciation of women precluded any further injury to their masculine sensitivity and simultaneously served as a protective safeguarding tendency.

At this point in his argument, Adler mentioned the most dramatic example of this neurotic posturing that Freud would later cite as the reductio ad absurdum of Adlerian theory. I refer to his attempt to understand the neurotic's libidinal stirring as a vicissitude of the masculine protest. In the neurotic, Adler said, the tendencies to depreciate women and to have intercourse with women were closely related, and the neurotic's attitude clearly expressed the wish to depreciate women via sexual intercourse. Adler claimed that the depreciation of the sexual partner through intercourse served the masculine protest by enabling the neurotic to abandon his devalued sexual partners and turn his attention to new opportunities for conquest. He termed this kind of behavior the "Don Juan" characteristic of the neurotic (p. 113; Ansbacher, p. 68).

In explicating these interpersonal dynamics underlying neurosis, Adler did not explicitly deny the operation of the "libido" as Freud conceived it. He only claimed that the libido did not represent the relevant perspective from which to gauge the neurotic process as it presented itself in therapy; the degree to which the libido was implicated in neurosis was simply immaterial (*gleichgueltig*). This conclusion, however, had been reached well before the 1911 summary lectures. It followed directly from all Adler's "psychoanalytic" publications from 1908–1910 and from the ego-psychological viewpoint Adler consistently injected into the Vienna Society discussions. In the second summary lecture of 1911, Adler followed his "Contribution to the Theory of Resistance" of the preceding year in extending this verdict to the principal crystallized constellation of libidinal energies—the Oedipus complex. He argued that mere recognition of the libidinal component of the Oedipus complex frequently did not lead to therapeutic improvement. It was only when the Oedipus complex was understood as "a small part of the overpowering neurotic dynamic, a stage of the masculine protest" that it became "instructive in its context" (p. 114; Ansbacher, p. 69).

III.

Fritz Wittels, Freud's earliest biographer and a later member of the Vienna Society, relied on the participant recollections of Wilhelm Stekel to reconstruct the most widely accepted account of the Society discussions that followed Adler's lecture of 1 February. The "Freudian adepts," he wrote,

> made a mass attack on Adler, an attack almost unexampled for its ferocity even in the fiercely contested field of psychoanalytical controversy. . . . Freud had a sheaf of notes before him, and with gloomy mien seemed prepared to annihilate his adversary [1924, pp. 150–151].

In his autobiography, Stekel himself recounted the "very tense" atmosphere in which "one Freudian after another got up and denounced, in well-prepared speeches, the new concepts of Adler" (1950, p. 141). Three weeks after Adler's final presentation, Freud himself wrote Karl Abraham of the "intense debates" (*starke Debatten*) over Adler's theories that had occupied the Vienna Society (*Freud/Abraham Briefe*, p. 106; *Freud/Abraham Letters*, p. 101). Though Rank's condensed account in the Minutes conveys little of the emotional atmosphere that colored these discussions, it clearly demonstrates that Adler's 1 February presentation was the occasion for Freud's first sustained attack on the content of Adler's theories.

Adler's two summary lectures added little to the ego psychology he had forcefully espoused in the Society discussions for the last four years. They achieved distinction, however, through the explicit comparison they presented between ego psychology and "libidinal" psychology. Only in the summary lectures, that is, did Adler finally articulate what had been his implicit working premise—and Freud's latent presentiment—for at least four years: that his ego psychology was actually a rival perspective that could contest and even supplant psychoanalytic explanations. These lectures publicly confirmed what Freud had privately confided to Jung since 1910, and Freud consequently used the occasion of Adler's lectures to transform his earlier reservations into a full-scale indictment of the incompatibility of Adler's theories with the content of psychoanalysis. He initially vented irritation that Adler had for some time been talking about the same things as himself "but without designating them by the same terms they already had, and without making any effort to establish any relationship between his new terms and the old ones." He further contested Adler's claim that "within psychoanalysis leave must be given for every individuality to express itself." Freud then proceeded to the two specific tendencies disclosed in Adler's writings and restated in his final lectures: the antisexual tendency and the tendency "directed against the value of detail and against the phenomenology of the neurosis" (Nunberg & Federn, 1974, pp. 145–146). In these sweeping criticisms, Freud clearly added nothing to his earlier misgivings about Adler's work. The point is that these misgivings were no longer "reservations" appended to a supportive acknowledgment of Adler's "supplemental" viewpoint, but frontal attacks on the illicit incursion of Adler's viewpoint into the domain of psychoanalytic explanation. Moreover, Freud was prepared to avow to his colleagues the damaging political implications of Adler's "new terms" for the ongoing propagation of psychoanalysis:

> by adopting the new terms, we would have to suffer the loss of those terms that indicate our program and which have established our connection with the great cultural circles. The [concepts of] *suppression of instinct* and *overcoming resistance* have aroused the interest of all alert and educated people [p. 147, emphasis in the original].

Freud's apprehension of Adler's "biology" was comparably politicized in accord with the institutional requirements of the psychoanalytic movement.[5] Freud criticized Adler because the very attractiveness and accessibility of his "biologized" views exacerbated the resistance of those who were hostile to the psychology of the libido. He claimed that Adlerian doctrine had "a reactionary and retrogressive character" by virtue of the increased number of "pleasure premiums" it offered to its adherents. Bolstered by the weight of these political considerations, Freud finally articulated to the Society the verdict about Adler's "biology" that he had long since confided to Jung. Adler's recourse to biology was no longer indifferent to psychoanalysis, but actively antithetical to it by virtue of the antipsychoanalytic "surface psychology" that the biological infrastructure was made to support:

> Instead of psychology, it presents, in large part, biology; instead of the psychology of the unconscious, it presents surface ego psychology. Lastly, instead of the

---

[5]Frank Sulloway, in his treatment of the early psychoanalytic dissidents (1979, pp. 425ff.), presents a perspective that complements mine but still differs in certain noteworthy respects. In stressing that biological theory "turned out to be a double-edged sword for Freud and his movement" (p. 425), Sulloway seeks to illuminate the "rational, biological sources of the movement's schisms" (p. 427) as synchronous phenomena that are the obverse side of Freud's own continuing "crypto-biological" commitments. Sulloway assumes, in other words, that Freud's repudiation of *all* the early schismatics (Adler, Jung, Stekel, etc.) was essentially coterminous with the articulation of rival biological frameworks that (1) challenged Freud's own crypto-biology while (2) nominally attempting to "rob psychoanalysis of its independent disciplinary status" (p. 426)—however greatly this independent status was belied by Freud's cryptobiological assumptions. My restrictive treatment of Adler, on the other hand, stresses the chronological unfolding of Freud's attitude toward Adler's "biology" in the context of the changing character of Freud's expectations toward Adler vis-à-vis the psychoanalytic movement. Put differently, Sulloway wants to make the host of political and ideological issues that impinge on the question of discipleship derivative to a paradigmatic notion of Freud as "biologist of the mind." My more intensive treatment of Adler actually takes the opposite tack: I believe the *vicissitudes* of Freud's estimation of Adler's biology are determined by political and ideological imperatives that transcend the import of Freud's biological assumptions per se.

psychology of the libido, of sexuality, it offers general psychology. It will, therefore, make use of the latent resistances that are still alive in every psychoanalyst, in order to make its influence felt. Consequently, this doctrine will at first do harm to the development of psychoanalysis; on the other hand, as far as psychoanalytic findings are concerned, it will remain sterile [p. 147].

To these specific criticisms of Adler's theories, Freud appended three "general and fundamental objections": (1) that Adler subjected psychology to biological and physiological viewpoints while psychoanalysis strove "precisely to keep psychology pure, free from any dependence"; (2) that Adler's conceptions embodied a "considerable overvaluation" of the child's intellect (via the early doubts about the sex role that Adler imputed to the child); and (3) that Adler's entire representation of the neurosis "is seen from the standpoint of the ego and thought about from the standpoint of the ego, as the neurosis appears to the ego. This is ego psychology, deepened by the knowledge of the psychology of the unconscious" (p. 147).

Freud considered the last general objection the most important one, and it was this objection that he linked most directly to his final assessment of Adler's two summary lectures. By evaluating neurosis from the standpoint of the ego, Adler had produced a characterization of the neurotic that was excellent "in some respects" but "one-sided" in others. By pursuing this approach beyond the bounds of mere character description, however, Adler had mistakenly inferred that the ego motives of the masculine protest explained the origins and varied forms of the neurosis. For Freud, however, the ego motivation of the neurosis "cannot replace the other and more interesting motivation," and he reiterated his belief that "the core of the neurosis is the ego's fear of the libido." Freud thereby traced to the original fear of the libido the kind of primary "arrangements" that Adler believed to characterize the deployment of libidinal energies from the start. The imputation of such fear was psychologically justifiable inasmuch as "the libido is just as great as are its disturbing effects" (pp. 148–149).

After Freud's lengthy criticism, Adler made a brief reply, arguing that his conception of neurosis did not deny sexual relations, but rather sought to reveal "far more important relationships" behind the sexual. Stekel closed the session of 1 February with mixed remarks about Adler's work. Although astonished that Adler sought to abandon the "viewpoint of repression" and unconvinced of the causal importance of the masculine protest, it was Stekel who reiterated "that much of what Adler has to say is new and valuable" (pp. 150–151).

At the meeting of the following week, the Society resumed its discussion of Adler's two lectures with lengthy remarks by Rosenstein and Hitschmann. Both discussants had voiced considerable support for Adler's work in the past, but both saw fit on this occasion to continue the criticism along the new lines established by Freud the preceding week. This meant that their favorable comments on the value of Adler's presentations were largely undercut by acceptance of Freud's attack on the inability of the Adlerian perspective to explain neurosis. Rosenstein reiterated that behind Adler's concepts of ambition, the masculine protest, and the safeguard "are concepts of Freud's." Having made this admission, however, he added that

> In addition to [presenting an] excellent characterology, Adler has told us much about the causes of repression. He has given a close description of the ego drives, has set down the desire to "be someone," and has shown that the fear of debasement—the fear of the feeling of inferiority—may perhaps also be a cause of repression [pp. 153–154].

Hitschmann, a consistent advocate of the Adlerian assessment of organ inferiority, comparably placed new stress on Adler's elimination of "the sexual element." By denying a prominent place to the role of sexuality in his psychology, Hitschmann said, Adler had overlooked the very factor that accounted for neurosis. Having reechoed the kernel of Freud's complaint, however, Hitschmann went on to observe:

> One must acknowledge what Adler has done for characterology by considering the matter from a totally different angle. However, he has not clarified the problem of neurosis, but has merely offered a most valuable description of what a neurosis looks like. Some of his ideas have great value for pedagogy and also for therapy [p. 156].

After brief pro-Adler remarks by Furtmueller, Adler made his concluding remarks. Apart from responding to some individual objections of Rosenstein and Hitschmann, he emphasized the "steadily progressing development" of his theories, beginning with the study of inferior organs. He further emphasized that it was not his aim

> to devalue Freud's conception of the neurosis and its mechanisms, but merely to obey the practical and theoretical necessity of placing it on a broader basis and giving weight to a developmental standpoint that he believes Freud has already left behind him [p. 158].

In many ways, the final discussion of Adler's presentations of 22 February was anticlimactic. By the time of this meeting, Freud had already categorically opposed Adler's viewpoint to his own, and the majority of his disciples had accepted this new assessment of Adler's theories. Freud consequently became more circumspect and benign in his characterization of Adler. According to Rank's Minutes,

> Prof. Freud considers Adler's doctrines to be wrong and, as far as the development of psychoanalysis is concerned, dangerous. But these are scientific errors, brought on by the use of the wrong methods (by drawing in social and biological viewpoints); and they are errors that do great credit to their creator. Even though one rejects the contents of Adler's views, one can nevertheless appreciate their consistency and their logic [p. 172].

This patronizing and plainly double-edged tribute evoked what was clearly the most indignant and unequivocal defense of Adler during the entire discussion. The respondent was Stekel and the claim he disputed was that everything contributed by Adler was already present in Freud's work. This, he submitted, was "unscientific."

> Adler's views constitute a deeper understanding and a further elaboration of the facts that we have discovered up to now; they are not incompatible with those facts, but simply a structure built on Freud's foundation. The really great advance made by Adler lies in the psychological sphere and shows how the character of the neurotic has to develop from certain attitudes [pp. 172–173].

Freud immediately responded to Stekel by restating the drastically qualified nature of Adler's characterological "advances." He restated the kernel of his initial objections of 1 February:

> No one has disputed that the things Adler speaks of are to be found; but they are not where Adler has placed them. Adler seeks things from the standpoint of the ego . . . For this way of thinking we have the term "rationalization": the ego believes everything to be its conscious doing and overlooks the unconscious motives [p. 173].

This final estimation at the hands of Freud seemed to have had a cathartic effect on Adler. After Freud's virulent dismissal of Stekel's defense, the end point of the discussion became apparent and the tenor of Adler's remaining rejoinders altered perceptibly. In his final reply to Freud, Adler observed that

> His writings have been perceived by Freud and some colleagues as constituting a provocation; but they would not have been possible if Freud had not been his teacher. It is his own scientific and personal situation that he sees being somewhat

threatened, and he will not hestitate to draw the necessary conclusions in order to call a halt, in the interest of the psychoanalytic movement, to further development of such a state of affairs [p. 174].

After some mollifying comments by Federn, and summary remarks by Steiner and Adler, the meeting drew to a close. At the end of the Minutes for this session, Rank appended the following notification:

At the following committee meeting, Adler resigns his position as chairman of the society because of the incompatibility of his scientific attitude with his position in the society, and Stekel declares himself in complete agreement with him, to the extent of resigning his position as deputy chairman [p. 177].

With this brief concluding entry, the major signpost of Adler's "break" with Freud was entered into the record. Though he would remain a silent attender at most of the Society meetings through 24 May 1911, Adler's resignation of the presidency marked the effective termination of his attempts at active collaboration with Freud's circle. Adler's continuing attendance at Society meetings through the spring of 1911 and his recorded willingness, at the meeting of 24 May, to accept the resolution of a Society plenary session that his "scientific viewpoint . . . was not in any way in contradiction to the findings of other authors, especially those of Freud" (p. 268), belie the contention that he was actually "excommunicated" from the psychoanalytic circle (see Kaufmann, 1980, pp. 207–209). But this fact is relatively unimportant. It was Freud's dramatic reversal of his longstanding assessment of Adler's role in the Vienna Society in February, 1911 that not only undermined Adler's ability to retain administrative leadership of the psychoanalytic group, but eroded his personal standing with a majority of the Society members. Freud was too adroit to excommunicate Adler outright, but there can be little doubt that he undertook the animated refutation of the psychoanalytic admissibility of Adler's views in the express hope of bringing the latter's affiliation with the movement to an end. Writing Jung a month after the vituperative exchanges on Adler's theories had drawn to a close, Freud confessed his impatience to be rid of both Adler and Stekel once and for all: "Naturally I am only waiting for an occasion to throw them both out, but they know it and are being very cautious and conciliatory, so there is nothing I can do for the present. Of course I am watching them more closely, but they put up with it. In my heart I am through with them" (*Freud/ Jung Letters*, letter of 14 March 1911, p. 403).

Fortunately for Freud, the predictable denouement to his harsh reassessment of Adler's theories was not long in coming. Adler himself resigned his membership in the Society sometime after the final spring meeting of 31 May 1911 (Nunberg & Federn, 1974, p. 281). When the Society reconvened with a special plenary session on 11 October 1911, Freud immediately confronted the remaining "Adlerians" with an ultimatum to resign from either the Vienna Society or Adler's rival "Society for Free Psychoanalytic Research"; dual membership in the two groups was henceforth unacceptable given the "hostile competition" between them (p. 281). Freud's resolution was debated by the membership and subsequently put to a vote by open ballot; it was approved by a count of 11 to five. The inevitable resignations followed. It was with obvious satisfaction that Freud informed Abraham, three weeks later, of the departure of the remaining Adlerians: "I have completed the purge of the society and sent Adler's seven followers packing after him" (*Freud/Abraham Letters*, letter of 2 November 1911, p. 110).

IV.

The psychological dynamics that underlay Freud's dramatic reevaluation of Adler's theories will be explored in the following chapter. It is important, however, to pause at this point and clarify the basic area of disagreement that emerged in the heated discussions of 1, 8, and 22 February 1911. The key elements of Freud's final rejection of Adler's theories were contained in the important summary he formulated immediately after the second of Adler's two presentations on 1 February 1911. Freud said,

> Instead of psychology, it presents, in large part, biology; instead of the psychology of the unconscious, it presents surface ego psychology. Lastly, instead of the psychology of the libido, of sexuality, it offers general psychology (Nunberg & Federn, 1974, p. 147].

Instead of psychology, it presents, in large part, biology. Here Freud reiterated again his objection to the starting point of all Adler's theorizing. His apparent objection was that the physical substrate of "inferiority feelings" no longer provided a supplementary backdrop for neurotic symptoms as the embodiment of unconscious mental conflict. It constituted instead the basis for a new "surface ego psychology" that proceeded to redefine neurotic symptoms from the standpoint of the ego's conscious evaluation of biological inferiority. Freud claimed that Adler presented "biology" instead of "psychology" because his psychology was anchored in the conscious repercussions of deficiencies that generally had organic roots.

Instead of the psychology of the unconscious, it presents surface ego psychology. Adler's formulations were premised on the ego's cognitive awareness of its relative inferiority. By virtue of this awareness, the ego could consciously devise conative interpersonal strategies that enabled it to ''safeguard'' itself against the full debilitating impact of the feeling of inferiority. By proceeding in this direction, Adler had, for Freud, presented ''surface ego psychology.'' This meant that Adler represented neurosis solely from the ''standpoint'' of the ego, because the explanatory insights through which Adler accounted for neurotic conflict were restricted to evaluative perceptions that were available to the ego at the time it fell victim to neurosis. Adler did not deny that the neurotic life plan might exist in the unconscious, but he did not attribute any systemic discontinuities to such ''unconsciousness.'' For Adler, that is, unconsciousness was itself an ''artifice'' (*Kunstgriff*) adopted by the psyche to achieve conscious goals. When a neurotic ''guiding idea'' was consigned to the unconscious, this was because conscious superiority strivings could operate more effectively if the patient was ''safeguarded'' from the feeling of inferiority that fueled his tendency to depreciate others. The unconsciousness of the idea was merely a tactical ploy serving conscious neurotic ambitions, and Adler claimed that neurotic activity had to be regarded ''as though it were obeying a conscious goal'' (1913a, pp. 165; Radin, pp. 231, 234). In this sense, Adler described neurosis as it ''appeared'' to the ego.

Adler's major mistake, according to Freud, occurred when he confused this perspectivistic description with neurotic conflict as it impinged *on* the ego. Freud believed that Adler necessarily rejected the psychic autonomy of unconscious wishes by reducing them to ''artifices'' invoked to preserve the integrity of an ego-syntonic life style. His predictable rejoinder, therefore, was that Adler's explanation of the ''ego motivation of neurosis'' could not replace ''the other and more interesting motivation''—that stemming from repressed motives that were alien to the ego. Because Adler's presentations systematically overlooked these unconscious wishes, Freud characterized his doctrine as a ''theory of character'' that constituted the ''denial of the unconscious'' (Nunberg & Federn, 1974, pp. 147–149, 173).

Instead of the psychology of the libido, of sexuality, it offers general psychology. Inasmuch as the unconscious motives of neurosis ignored by Adler focused on the ego's fear of being overwhelmed by libido, Freud naturally claimed that Adlerian psychology could not be a psychology ''of the libido.'' He meant that Adler's theories did not attribute to sexuality a preeminent role in accounting for the neurotic *victimization* of the ego. Adler claimed that the individual became neurotic because the ego failed to implement its ''safeguarding'' strategies with an adequate degree of protective efficiency. Freud replied that the reason the ego could not "safeguard" itself was that it was bombarded with instinctual libidinal energies it could not consciously master. It was from this standpoint that Freud attacked Adler's designation of neurotic libido as a secondary "arranged" entity. Freud claimed that the primacy of the "unarranged" libido was directly deducible from the extent of its "disturbing effects" as manifested in the neurosis (p. 149).

Adler's defense of his formulations reasserted the clinical premises from which he began to theorize; his claim was that of therapeutic relevance. At the very outset of his first lecture on "The Role of Sexuality in Neurosis," he rejected the formulation of his problem in terms of the mere inclusion of sexuality in neurosis, claiming the question was idle because sexuality had a similarly great significance for everyone. In the second part of his presentation on "Repression and Masculine Protest," he never denied the existence of libido qua libido; he simply argued that an explanation formulated in terms of libidinal dynamics was immaterial (*gleichgueltig*) for an understanding of neurotic conflict that was therapeutically meaningful. By this, Adler meant that libidinal aims in themselves were not inherently conflictual to the extent of overwhelming the ego and evoking repression. Correspondingly, he argued that therapeutic progress was not commensurate with the simple uncovering of libidinal fantasies— "I have seen plenty of patients who are sufficiently knowledgeable about their Oedipus complexes without feeling any better" (1911b, pp. 113–114). When Adler alluded to the "arranged" or "falsified" libido of the neurotic, he did not mean to deny the existence of "primary" libido altogether. He only claimed that for purposes of therapeutic progress, it was *more* beneficial to evaluate expressions of libido as if they were instances of a more encompassing interpretive concept. He ended his second presentation by subsuming oedipal wishes and fantasies under the rubric of the masculine protest because it was the explanatory framework provided by the masculine protest that falsified the apparent *significance* of the libido within the therapeutic encounter. This falsification of libido was never tantamount to an outright denial of libido altogether. As he stated in the Society discussion of 8 February

> With regard to the falsified libido, what we could call libido *is simply not involved,* but rather manifestations of the desire to "count for something" [Nunberg & Federn, 1974, p. 157; my emphasis].

Adler could write of the "falsified" libido without denying the putative reality of libido because he originally defined instinctual drive in terms of the satisfaction associated with specific organ systems. At the same time, Adler had insisted as far back as the organ inferiority study of 1907 that "libidinal" energy was mobile enough to serve the compensatory needs of different organ systems. Although only the sexual organ itself could promote the development of genuine sexuality, Adler consistently argued that the role of sexuality in neurosis pertained not to its expression as genuine instinct, but to the way sexuality became implicated in the functioning of different inferior organs. When psychopathology appeared, in other words, it was not a function of "healthy" sexuality impinging on the ego, but "prematurely aroused" sexuality entering into relations with the drive requirements of a different organ system. More specifically, Adler meant that the appearance of premature sexuality signified that a particular inferior organ was able to utilize the sexual factor in the establishment of its psychical compensation (1911a, p. 95). Adler formulated this conception at the beginning of his first lecture, but he did not return to it when discussing the "arranged" neurotic libido in his second lecture, and the point did not come up in the ensuing Society discussions. Only a single comment during the final discussion of 22 February 1911 seemed to acknowledge the distinction that Adler originally had in mind. Klemperer, a minor participant, noted that for Adler

> the fear of being "underneath" would probably never have the strength to suppress a natural instinct such as sexuality. In Adler's thinking, however, these instinctual impulses are not natural, but have come into being as a result of this fear [Nunberg & Federn, 1974, p. 171].

The libidinal component that was capable of arrangement by the ego, in other words, was not the natural sexual instinct serving the specific "organ" needs of the genitals; it was a sexual "component" that had been called into premature action by a different inferior organ system.

It became increasingly clear as the Society discussion progressed that Freud's rejection of Adler's arranged libido proceeded from core assumptions about instinctuality that were incompatible with Adler's entire distinction between different "organ" instincts. Unfortunately, the discussions never dealt with the clinical and theoretical adequacy of Adler's conception of "organ" instinct from the standpoint of Adler's own *biological* presuppositions. Freud never really went beyond the simple accusation that Adler had "replaced" psychology with biology.

Given Freud's earlier receptivity to Adler's biological considerations, and his own continuing attention to the biological roots of psychoanalysis,[6] this criticism

---

[6]For a brilliant exposition of the sources, nature, and pervasive influence of the biological assumptions that informed Freud's psychoanalytic theories, scholars are indebted to Sulloway (1979).

proves less than convincing. In the important metapsychological essay "On Narcissism" written early in 1914, Freud expressly admitted that his basic hypothesis of sexual and ego instincts rested "scarcely at all upon a psychological basis, but derives its principal support from biology" (1914b, p. 79). In the essay on "Instincts and Their Vicissitudes" written a year later, Freud reiterated his belief in the two classes of instinct, but admitted he was "altogether doubtful whether any decisive pointers for the differentiation and classification of the instincts can be arrived at on the basis of working over the psychological material" (1915, p. 124). He added that it would be desirable if the basic assumptions about instinctual life could be transferred to psychology from some other branch of knowledge, and specified once more the supportive contribution that biology made to his distinction between sexual and ego instincts. A page later, he characterized the sexual instincts as emanating from "a great variety of organic sources" that initially acted independently of one another. Each of these instincts, he noted, strove for the attainment of "organ pleasure" (pp. 125–126).

In the important set of introductory lectures he delivered in 1917, Freud was still more emphatic in equating instinctual pleasure with the activity of different organ systems. He repeated that the plurality of sexual instincts referred to the fact that different organs represented independent sites of bodily pleasure. He confessed, furthermore, that the infant's "polymorphous perverse" quest for different kinds of organ pleasure was labeled "sexual" only because adult sexuality itself could not be defined as more than "organ pleasure"—usually, but not invariably, focusing on one pair of organs (1916–1917, pp. 320–324).

In short, Freud's own long-range commitment to providing a biological basis for the instincts, and his willingness to equate infantile sexuality with independent sites of "organ pleasure," reveal the polemical quality of his rejection of Adler's "biology" in 1911. From the standpoint of Adler's publications and informal Society lectures, the very criticisms that Freud delivered in February, 1911 could have been formulated any time between 1907 and 1910. The "biology" that informed Adler's 1911 summary lectures was the same "biology" that had earned him Freud's praise in the 1907 organ inferiority study. The basis for constructing an ego psychology on this type of "biology" was hardly broached in the course of these final presentations. The rationale behind Adler's psychology was fully contained in the key chapter of the organ inferiority monograph on "The Part Played by the Central Nervous System in the Theory of Organ Inferiority—Psychogenesis and Foundations of Neuroses and Psychoneuroses." Adler had further exemplified for Freud how his "biology" generated "psychology" in the important "Neurotic Disposition" paper of 1909. Every criticism that Freud directed at Adler in the winter of 1911 fully applied to this revealing "psychoanalytic" publication. Yet, Freud had confined his negative assessment of Adler's emphasis on the neurotic ego's conscious "oversensitivity" to his letter of 19 December 1909 to Jung (*Freud/Jung Letters*, pp. 277–278). Correspondingly, his judgment of Adler's 1910 "Psychical Hermaphroditism" paper as "heretical" was broached only to Jung three weeks before it was delivered at the Nuremberg Congress (*Freud/Jung Letters*, p. 301).

Freud's hostile reaction to Adler came only after the summary presentations of 1911 because it was a political maneuver of the first order. It was not the theoretical inadmissibility of Adler's views, but the increasing political preoccupation with forging a unified psychoanalytic movement that impelled Freud to reinterpret the status of his own prior reservations about Adler's theories with a view to ending Adler's active collaboration. From this standpoint, Freud's critique of Adler's work was exceptional precisely because it added nothing to the past reservations about Adler that he had repeatedly brought to the attention of the Society membership for two years.

Freud's critique of Adler's "biology" could have achieved new significance only if Adler's assumptions had for once been challenged at their conceptual starting point. To do this, Freud would have been compelled to go back to the core propositions of the organ inferiority study that he had let pass for four years. It would have meant challenging Adler's assumptions about the way the inferiority of a specific organ could implicate the central nervous system and thereby entail a "psychic compensation" that implicated different organ systems. In the language of Adler's 1909 paper on "Neurotic Disposition," Freud would have had to contest the notion that "organic oversensitivity" could provide the foundation for a "psychic oversensitivity" able to appropriate different organ systems in order to erect safeguards. As it was, Freud did not challenge Adler so much as argue at cross-purposes with him, choosing once again to dismiss Adler's clinical assumptions as "biology" rather than evaluate in any detail the adequacy of the very idea of "organ inferiority" from the standpoint of Adler's own biological findings.

The symptomatic level of Freud's objection is additionally reflected in the manner in which he responded to Adler's reevaluation of the libido. At the initial discussion of 1 February 1911, Freud claimed that Adler's preoccupation with the "ego motivation of neurosis" led him to "scientifically unsound judgments":

> In thus denying the reality of the libido, Adler behaves exactly as the neurotic ego does. Of course, the libido is not real: its strength lies entirely elsewhere; only one ought not to forget about the "neurotic currency." One has to judge the libido according to its consequences; it is in the inhibitions that its magnitude manifests

itself. If one says of the libido that it is not *real,* that is correct; but to say that it is *false* is totally arbitrary and an unscientific conception. The same thing applies to everything that Adler calls "neurotic swindle" [Nunberg & Federn, 1974, pp. 148–149].[7]

In offering this judgment, Freud set in motion a process of conceptual reification that had far-reaching consequences. The "truth" of the libido rested on its demonstrable clinical consequences; its "magnitude" was manifested in the "inhibitions" that were revealed during psychoanalysis; its "reality" was a function of its clinical truth-value. Although one might claim that the libido was not "real" on restrictive empirical grounds, Freud contended, it was "unscientific" and "totally arbitrary" to reject the reality of libido as a construct that possessed explanatory usefulness in evaluating the type of fantasies uncovered in psychoanalysis. In denying the truth of the libido in this operational sense, Adler behaved "exactly as the neurotic ego does."

What Freud plainly ignored was the fact that Adler could concede the "reality" of the libido and still impute relative "falsity" to it in evaluating neurotic symptomatology. This is because Adler found that that the libido tied up in such symptomatology was not "natural" genital libido, but a "falsified" derived libido, one prematurely mobilized for the compensatory purpose it had to serve. Adler even went beyond this: he never argued that "genuine" libido could not enter into neurosis, but merely observed that the relative infusion of libido was irrelevant for symptom formation because it subserved a neurotic character structure that had already crystallized along different dynamic lines. Adler may very well have been wrong in this supposition, but his argument could not be refuted along the lines Freud adopted. This is basically because Adler had recourse to the same implicit explanatory principle that Freud did: therapeutic relevance.[8] Freud

---

[7]Cf. Freud to Jung, 14 March 1911: "Adler's ego behaves as the ego always behaves, like the clown in the circus who keeps grimacing to assure the audience that he has planned everything that is going on. The poor fool!" (*Freud/Jung Letters,* p. 404).

[8]In observing that Adler and Freud *both* had recourse to a common principle of therapeutic relevance in defending their theoretical perspectives, I am alluding to the wealth of data from controlled treatment outcome studies suggesting that the ameliorative impact of *any* type of psychotherapeutic intervention is due not to the theoretical orientation of the therapist, but to a host of incidental (i.e., nonspecific) factors centering around the personal characteristics of the therapist and the quality of his interpersonal relationship with the patient. Gruenbaum (1980, pp. 343ff.) reviews this literature in the context of a searching consideration of the "placebogenic character" of psychoanalytic outcome success. He approvingly cites (p. 346) a remark by the analyst Judd Marmor that provides a particularly telling commentary on the disagreement between Adler and Freud. Confining himself to rival schools of psychoanalytic treatment, Marmor argued in 1962 that "interpretations that put the patient's material within one frame of reference seem to be just as effective for the patient as interpretations that put it within another frame of reference" (p. 290). Why should this be the

claimed that libido was "genuine" because it manifested itself in significant inhibitions that psychoanalysis invariably traced back to libido. Adler, however, claimed that the interpretive strategy of psychoanalysis was not the best way to evaluate psychic inhibitions because insight into the libidinal basis of the inhibitions did not yield clinical advances that were commensurate with the alleged psychoanalytic primacy of the insight: "I have seen plenty of patients who are sufficiently knowledgeable about their Oedipus complexes without feeling any better."

It seems that Freud's criticisms would have been more effective had he addressed himself to the technique of psychoanalysis, perhaps discussing the precise relation of insight to symptomatic relief and stressing the difference between intellectual apprehension and full emotional acceptance of the Oedipus complex. These arguments could have undercut the centrality of Adler's opposing therapeutic claims. Instead, Freud merely reasserted a fact that Adler had never intended to deny: the simple fact that the "libido" exists.

V.

To demonstrate the strikingly polemical nature of Freud's calculated reevaluation of Adler in 1911 is to pose a central question: given the continuity of Adler's views between 1907 and 1911, why did Freud finally decide to disown him when he did?

The answer to this question has much to do with Freud's deepening frustration with the quality of his entire Vienna circle during this time, a frustration that was admitted more freely after he had designated his gifted convert from Zurich, Carl Gustav Jung, the leader on whom the institutional victories of psychoanalysis would depend. As Freud's certainty grew that the institutional future of psychoanalysis depended on Jung, the political urgency of maintaining a united Viennese front that could accommodate even an "Adlerian" viewpoint diminished. More specifically, Freud's readiness to depreciate the contributions of the entire Viennese contingent accompanied his growing confidence throughout 1910 that Jung, and to a lesser extent Karl Abraham, would ultimately prevail in transforming what would otherwise have been construed as a parochial "Jewish

---

case? For Marmor, it follows from the inherently relativistic character of psychotherapeutic insight: "But what *is* insight? To a Freudian it means one thing, to a Jungian another, and to a Rankian, a Horneyite, an Adlerian or a Sullivanian, still another. Each school gives its own particular brand of insight. Whose are the correct insights? The fact is that patients treated by analysts of all these schools may not only respond favorably, but also believe strongly in the insights which they have been given" (p. 289).

science'' into an international political movement with secure anchorage in the medical and academic establishments of Europe and America. Beyond the leadership roles assumed by Jung and Abraham, Freud was bolstered in this hope by the enthusiastic dissemination of his work during 1910 by converts for whom the basic tenets of psychoanalysis were never in doubt. Chief among them were the Boston neurologist James Jackson Putnam, whose supportive publications endeared him to Freud (*Freud/Jung Letters*, pp. 286–287, 357, 376), and Ernest Jones, whose aggressive but civil propagandizing in the American psychological literature earned him Freud's "heartfelt gratitude" (*Freud/Jung Letters*, p. 399; cf. pp. 306, 310, 314, 317, 342, 347). Of somewhat reduced stature but equal dedication to the cause was A. A. Brill, a "thoroughly honest soul" whose translations of Freud's works into English and enthusiastic dissemination of psychoanalysis in the New York area made him responsible, with Jones, for the "extraordinary" gains registered by the movement in America (*Freud/Jung Letters*, pp. 206, 289).

A major political coup for the movement, occurring just days before Adler's summary lectures before the Vienna Society, involved Eugen Bleuler, the ranking Swiss psychiatrist whose high standing within the official world of European psychiatry induced Freud, Jung, and Abraham to make repeated efforts to win his allegiance to psychoanalysis.[9] During the Christmas holiday of 1910, following a correspondence he characterized as both "copious" and "exhausting," Freud journeyed to Munich for two days of talks with the equivocating Burghoelzli chief and was able to report, as the positive outcome of his "diplomatic undertaking," a "complete understanding" and "good personal relationship" with him.[10] Bleuler's shortlived reconciliation with Freud was accompanied by the publication of an apologia of psychoanalysis in the *Jahrbuch* that Freud deemed "enormously helpful," and on 18 January 1911, two weeks after Adler's first summary lecture on his theories, Jung wrote Freud with obvious satisfaction that Bleuler had finally thrown in his lot and joined the Zurich Psychoanalytic Society.[11]

From these developments, there followed a political reevaluation with two necessary consequences: by 1910 it was clear that the Viennese group was not

---

[9]The course of the negotiations with Bleuler is reviewed briefly in Stepansky (1976, pp. 235–237). For Freud's correspondence with Bleuler, see Alexander & Selesnick (1965).

[10]For Freud's perspective on the forthcoming visit with Bleuler, see *Freud/Jung Letters*, pp. 360, 365, 372. On the favorable outcome of the meeting, see Freud to Ferenczi, 29 December 1910, in Jones (1955, p. 140) and *Freud/Abraham Letters*, p. 98.

[11]On Bleuler's "apologia," see *Freud/Jung Letters*, p. 281 and *Freud/Abraham Letters*, pp. 95–96, 97. Bleuler's joining of the Zurich branch society is reported by Jung in *Freud/Jung Letters*, p. 384.

destined to play a decisive role in the international propagation of psychoanalysis and equally clear that dissident disciples like Adler need no longer be tolerated when staunch defenders of the creed like Jung, Abraham, Jones, and Brill, as well as ranking institutional adherents like Putnam and Bleuler, were to be found. As early as 22 January 1909, Freud confessed to Jung a closer affinity to his foreign "pseudostudents" than to his Viennese students *sensu strictiori* (*Freud/Jung Letters*, p. 201). After the mantle had been officially passed to Jung at the Nuremberg Congress, Freud's attitude toward his Viennese following became frankly opportunistic; thus the decision to placate the Viennese by ceding the presidency of the Vienna branch society to Adler. Speaking of this concession to wounded Viennese pride, Freud wrote Jung that "the Viennese have no manners, but they know a good deal and can still do good work for the movement" (p. 306). Freud's depreciatory attitude toward the Viennese remained equally strident 19 months later. When he reminisced to Abraham in the fall of 1911 about the successful Weimar Congress of that year, he bemoaned the fact that Vienna provided no adequate institutional base where he could locate present assistants and train new ones: "But Vienna is not soil in which anything can be undertaken" (*Freud/Abraham Letters*, pp. 109–110).

If Freud's decision to reassess Adler's theories in the winter of 1911 reflects his changed estimation of the significance of his Viennese following for the future development of psychoanalysis, the depreciation of the Viennese, in turn, can be fully understood only in the context of the institutional outcome of the Nuremberg Congress of March, 1910. By focusing on the sociological implications of the institutional growth that followed Nuremberg, the remaining portion of this chapter will attempt to provide an explanation of the timing of Freud's rupture with Adler.

The Nuremberg Congress, progenitor of the International Psychoanalytic Association and symbol of Jung's official enthronement as Freud's successor, represents a decisive watershed in the history of psychoanalysis. Several days after the Congress adjourned, on 3 April 1910, Freud confided this verdict to Ferenczi: "With the Nuremberg *Reichstag* closes the childhood of our movement; that is my impression. I hope now for a rich and fair time of youth" (quoted in Jones, 1955, pp. 70–71). In thus characterizing the Congress as a *Reichstag*, Freud invoked a metaphor that suggested more than the mildly facetious analogy between a legislative assembly and a structured professional convention; it conveyed, in addition, the very terms in which Freud himself envisioned the historic break signified by Nuremberg. By referring to the Nuremberg Congress as if to a session of the Austrian parliament, Freud gave testimony to the political footing of psychoanalysis that was the crucial outcome of the Nuremberg deliberations.

In the pre-Nuremberg period, the psychoanalytic "movement" had been a matter of informal recruitment, of persuasion, of defense against critics by what Ferenczi, in his proposal for the formation of the International Association, termed "guerilla warfare"[12]; in the aftermath of Nuremberg, however, it would become a campaign of systematic propagation and aggressive vindication orchestrated by a cohesive political organization.

This transformation was hardly surprising to Freud. From the outset, he had conceived of the Nuremberg Congress less as a forum for the explication of psychoanalysis than an occasion for institutional consolidation spearheaded by Jung (cf. Clark, 1980, pp. 295–299). In marked contrast to the Salzburg Congress of 1908, which Freud had willingly construed, with Abraham, as a pedagogical forum for highlighting the primacy of the libido concept in psychoanalytic theory, the Nuremberg Congress was to concern itself "primarily" with "questions of principle and organization" (*Freud/Abraham Letters*, pp. 25, 26, 85). To Jung, Freud pointed out in January, 1910 that whereas the Salzburg Congress had taken as its task the didactic communication of "how much there was to say and how much work there was to be done," this didactic function had, from 1909, been safely lodged in the *Jahrbuch fuer psychoanalytische und psychopathologische Forschungen*. As for the Nuremberg gathering, Freud continued, it "can be devoted to other tasks such as organization and the discussion of certain matters of fundamental importance." A few "specially chosen lectures" might be given, but Freud prescribed "more attention to practical questions concerning the present and immediate future" (*Freud/Jung Letters*, p. 282). In accord with these organizational priorities, Freud planned the Congress around major addresses concentrating on the politicization of the movement. Jung was directed to speak on the development of analysis in America, Ferenczi on "organization and propaganda," while Freud himself would lecture on the future prospects of psychoanalysis (pp. 292, 301).

Predictably, the Congress evidenced the institutional gain that corresponded with Freud's organizing intent: following Ferenczi's proposal, the International Psychoanalytic Association was founded under Jung's presidency. The Association was to provide an "official" organizational framework for the heretofore independent psychoanalytic societies of Zurich, Berlin, and Vienna. According to the statutes submitted by Ferenczi and subsequently amended and approved by the Nuremberg participants, the stated purpose of the Association entailed both the "cultivation and promotion of the psychoanalytic science as inaugurated by

---

[12]See Ferenczi's proposal for the formation of the International Association, reprinted as "On the Organization of the Psycho-Analytic Movement" (1911).

Freud," and the provision of "mutual assistance among members in their endeavours to acquire and foster psychoanalytic knowledge." A Central Office was instituted consisting of a president and secretary elected by the Congress for a two-year term. The statutes directed the Central Office to convene future Congresses at no more than two-year intervals and, in addition, to edit and distribute a monthly Bulletin, the *Correspondenzblatt der Internationaler Psychoanalytischen Vereinigung,* that would maintain contact between the Central Office and the members, publish "scientific and personal news relating to psychoanalysis," and report "on the most important events in the branch societies and on new literature concerned with psychoanalysis." Membership in the International Association was formally restricted to regular members of the branch societies on payment of annual membership dues of 10 frs. Members of the Association were entitled to attend meetings of any branch society, to receive the Bulletin regularly, and to participate in future Congresses at which they might vote and stand for election.[13]

From the conclusion of the Nuremberg Congress to the final split with Adler in 1911, Freud's correspondence with both Abraham and Jung bespeaks an intensifying preoccupation with the institutionalization of psychoanalysis under the aegis of the International Association. During this period, Freud demonstrated an active interest in the administrative and political issues that arose as his two adherents organized the branch societies of their respective cities.[14] He encouraged both men to attend the meetings of hostile psychiatric associations throughout Germany, Austria, and Switzerland, and he freely exchanged demeaning characterizations of the "enemies" encountered by his lieutenants in the context of an ongoing dialogue about the various tactics to be employed in defending "the cause." Throughout 1910, Freud exchanged vitriolic remarks with Abraham on the poor reception granted his Berlin disciple by German psychiatrists like Oppenheim (*Freud/Abraham Letters,* pp. 72, 93) and Ziehen (pp. 81, 84, 91, 104) whereas with Jung he engaged in patronizing diatribes against detractors like Isserlin (*Freud/Jung Letters,* pp. 300, 307–308, 309) and Friedlaender (pp. 309, 322–324, 325). With both men, but especially with Jung, there were more anguished ruminations about the kind of compromises that might be proffered to win the allegiance of the recalcitrant Bleuler (*Freud/Jung Letters,* pp. 311, 320, 354, 357, 360–361, 371, 374, 403).

Freud's correspondence with Jung during this period indicates an equally intense involvement with the *internal* politicization of psychoanalysis as man-

[13]The statutes of the International Psychoanalytic Association are included as an appendix to the *Freud/Jung Letters,* pp. 568–570.

[14]Jones (1955, p. 73) records that Freud took a "week-to-week interest" in the early progress of the branch societies.

dated by the statutes of the International Association. He chided Jung repeatedly for a complacent attitude toward his "official functions" (*Freud/Jung Letters*, pp. 330, 343) and urged him, as president of the International Association, to inject an official presence into the local Viennese scene by influencing the content of the new Vienna-based *Zentralblatt fuer Psychoanalyse* (pp. 362, 366–367). Unfailingly attentive to all the technical conditions of organization mandated by the statutes, Freud reacted with clear anger when Jung informed him in June, 1910 that the statutes of the Zurich branch society made the weekly meetings open to nonmembers of the society. Several months later, he expressed comparable displeasure at Jung's suggestion that everything in the Bulletin "might just as well be published in the *Zentralblatt*" and that the Bulletin could therefore be dispensed with altogether (pp. 329, 331, 363, 367). In a long and revealing letter of 31 October 1910, Freud pedantically enjoined Jung to embrace fully his administrative obligations as president of the International Association and, as part of his official responsibilities, to overcome his dislike of the "Viennese colleagues" and their new journal. On behalf of his efforts to sensitize Jung anew to the various projects that required his continuing involvement and occasional mediation, Freud took it upon himself to "patiently consider" on Jung's behalf the specific roles assigned to the *Zentralblatt* and the Bulletin by the statutes of the International Association (pp. 365–368).

In conjunction with his serious concern over the implementation of the statutes of the International Association, Freud repeatedly urged upon Jung, as a requirement for the successful propagation of analysis, the need to adopt and promulgate publicly a unified policy regarding the attacks of outsiders. In a letter of 23 October 1910, Freud expressed "amusement" at the "blows" Jung had meted out in the pages of the Bulletin, but wondered "if we oughtn't to go about it more systematically, and if so, in which of our organs." He proceeded to suggest that Jung publish a "manifesto" in a future issue of the Bulletin that would present the "official viewpoint," i.e., a statement that would address itself to "defining and justifying the attitude you propose to take toward enemies, or presenting such an attitude to the other members" (*Freud/Jung Letters*, pp. 361, 362). A week later, after Jung had confessed plain distaste for such a policy of confrontation (p. 364), Freud, reiterating his belief that an organized psychoanalytic movement mandated tactics that might offend the sensibilities of individual psychoanalysts, offered the following striking rejoinder:

> And now to politics and the right of self-defence! You speak after my own heart. If I had been alone, my tactics would have been to wait for our adversaries to destroy each other. But now we have become a little band, we have assumed responsibilities towards our supporters, we have a cause to defend before the public. And so we must do violence to our own nature, show that we are capable of adapting

ourselves to reality, and do what has to be done as intelligently as possible. For the President of the International Association and his mentor (!) the right of self-defence is no longer appropriate; it is time for the witches "Politics" and "Diplomacy" and the changeling "Compromise" to take a hand. But we can make it up to ourselves with humour when we talk about these "farts" together one day. Of course there must be limits. Cases can easily arise in which the diplomatic approach would be unwise and we must give our nature free rein. Then I am prepared to sally forth arm in arm with you and challenge the century. I have become neither timid nor dishonest, I am merely trying to be impersonal [*Freud/Jung Letters,* pp. 365–366].

Consideration of the significant signposts of institutionalization that accompanied the growth of psychoanalysis during 1910, particularly as it highlights Freud's heightened attentiveness to the politics of organized propagation, suggests a sociological perspective that aids considerably in understanding why Freud postponed his official reassessment of Adler's theories until the winter of 1911. I am referring to the sociology of group conflict, especially as it has been explicated in the pioneering work of Ralf Dahrendorf (1958, 1959, chapters 5 & 6). Dahrendorf has clarified the structural conditions of the organization of "conflict groups" in a way that is directly relevant to Freud's relationship to Adler.[15] In explaining how conflict groups arise within social organizations, Dahrendorf observes that only the realization of various technical, political, and social conditions of organization can transform "quasi-groups" that share certain latent interests into organized "conflict groups," i.e., groups capable of systematic social conflict over the distribution of power and authority within a social organization (1959, pp. 179–184). From the vantage point of Dahrendorf's analysis, it can be argued that only with the founding of the International Psychoanalytic Association in 1910 did the psychoanalytic movement undergo the kind of institutional growth that provided a structural foundation for the crystallization of rival "Freudian" and "Adlerian" conflict groups within the Viennese psychoanalytic community. Only when the manifest interests of the psychoanalytic movement were codified through the technical conditions of organization provided by the statutes of the International Association—a charter, administrative officers, membership dues, biannual Congresses, an "official" ideology binding members—could an "Adlerian viewpoint" become the locus of a rival conflict group that threatened not only to subvert the existing distribu-

---

[15]Dahrendorf's formulation of the structural conditions of the organization of conflict groups draws on Malinowski (1944). For a critique of Dahrendorf's perspective on conflict, incidental to the application of his work here, see Van Den Berghe (1963).

tion of authority within the psychoanalytic movement, but to confound political goals openly identified with the movement's progress.

Seen against the backdrop of the crystallized authority structure that emerged in 1910, the severity of Freud's reassessment of Adler's theories in the winter meetings of 1911 acquires a sociological import that transcends the bounds of his mounting personal displeasure with Adler's idiosyncratic clinical categories. Dahrendorf has suggested, as a general proposition of group conflict, a close positive correlation between the intensity of conflicts within a social organization and the degree to which different conflicts are superimposed on one another (1959, p. 215). Correspondingly, Freud's repudiation of Adler following the summary lectures of 1911 proceeded from a coalescence of two separate areas of conflict that only became possible after the institutional consolidation of the preceding year. It was only in 1911, in the wake of new political concerns that accompanied the birth of an International Association headed by Jung, that Freud's antipathy for Adler intensified to the point of repudiation because only at this juncture in the history of the psychoanalytic movement was Freud's conflict regarding the theoretical status of Adler's theories superimposed on the purely instrumental conflict involving the implications of the ''Adlerian viewpoint'' for the organized propagation of psychoanalysis. We have observed Freud's readiness to confide to Jung his unhappiness with the direction of Adler's theorizing as early as June, 1909. It was only in December, 1910, however, that Freud related to Jung a genuine concern that Adler's concentration on the ''masculine ego current'' and minimization of the sexual drive would provide the opponents of psychoanalysis with new and damaging leverage: ''our opponents will soon be able to speak of an experienced psychoanalyst whose conclusions are radically different from ours'' (*Freud/Jung Letters*, p. 376). Four months later, in the aftermath of the Vienna Society debates on Adler, it was this same preoccupation that induced Freud to reiterate to Jung the pressing need of the psychoanalytic circle to reach a final decision about Adler ''before he is held up to us by outsiders'' (p. 409).

In 1911, as in 1909, the advisability of Adler's continued affiliation with analysis was broached only from the standpoint of political considerations co-alescing around the issue of unity, but during this critical interval Freud's perspective on exactly how Adler impacted on the unity of the psychoanalytic movement underwent a formal change. An affiliation that had been viewed as an asset in the pre-Nuremberg period of informal recruitment became a liability fraught with damaging implications in the post-Nuremberg period of institutional consolidation. In June, 1909, still attentive to the fragile credibility of the psychoanalytic enterprise within organized medicine, Freud advised Jung of the need to retain the allegiance of an "astute and original" theorist like Adler "as long as possible" (p. 235). By December, 1910, however, when the institutional gains following Nuremberg permitted Freud's political priorities to veer sharply in the direction of organized propagation and systematic attack, his perspective on Adler underwent a corresponding change: Adler was henceforth a renegade, the "experienced psychoanalyst" whose minimization of the sexual drive jeopardized the boundary line of the movement and would likely fuel the attack of the movement's opponents (p. 376).

If Freud's abrupt disavowal of Adler in the winter of 1911 is intertwined with the intensification of political goals that followed the Nuremberg Congress, it remains to be seen why the majority of Adler's generally supportive colleagues were willing to rally around Freud and reassess their own positions in a way that lent support to Freud's critique. Freud's correspondence with Jung, after all, vividly corroborates what the Minutes suggest: that Adler's alienation from the Vienna group was hardly precipitated by a general consensus on the irreconcilability of his views with the level of discourse that typified the group discussions, indicating instead that his resignation of the Society presidency and subsequent departure from the group was the product of a premeditated assault engineered entirely by Freud.

It is surely reasonable to suggest that ultimate deference to Freud and Freud's prerogative to pass summary judgment on the work of his disciples induced colleagues who had formerly accepted Adler's role in the group discussions to respond to the summary lectures in the spirit of Freud's attack, and that this willingness to accept Freud's prerogative retrospectively gave the distorted impression of a coordinated mass attack on Adler. But this obvious explanation, once more, can be supplemented by considering the sociological factors that may have predisposed the Vienna Society membership to follow Freud at precisely this juncture in the group's history. Once again, consideration of the structural dimension of the Vienna Society's readiness to reassess Adler's theories in 1911 points to the importance of the transformation of the psychoanalytic movement into an institutionalized "conflict group" in the aftermath of the Nuremberg Congress. Given the originally open-ended nature of the dialogue within the Vienna Society (see chapter 4), it can be argued that Freud's reservations about Adler in the Society meetings remained muted through 1910 on behalf of the *kind* of unity that was of paramount importance in the pre-Nuremberg period; Freud's acceptance and frequent endorsement of Adler's contributions were part of a strategy of systematic tolerance that prevented the original Wednesday evening discussion group from fragmenting prematurely under the impetus of conflicting viewpoints. Freud, to repeat, was unwilling to alienate any nominal adherent whose identification with psychoanalysis lent strength to his cause in the pre-Nuremberg period and, in this context, it seems that his circumscribed misgivings about the limitations of Adler's biology and "ego psychology" through 1910 actually exemplify what Georg Simmel characterizes as the "group-binding" character of social conflict. Specifically, Freud's willingness to tolerate a "dissident" Adlerian viewpoint for as long as he did served to "maintain relations under conditions of stress," thereby preserving a semblance of group unity among the original participating clinicians.[16]

Until the Nuremberg Congress and the birth of the International Association, moreover, Freud's policy of systematic tolerance seems to have complemented the consensus of the Vienna Society membership about the purpose of the weekly discussions, thereby helping it to relegate Freud's differences with Adler to a position of secondary importance. The assumption that the commitment to psychoanalysis must be a total and virtually exclusionistic one—the assumption that informs all Freud's correspondence with confidants like Jung and Abraham and enthusiastic converts like Putnam and Prister—hardly typifies the mentality of the original participants in the Vienna Society. From its inception in 1903 as the Psychological Wednesday Society until its formalization under the statutes of the International Association, the Vienna Society retained its identity as an informal psychoanalytic discussion group receptive to occasional attenders and guests and requiring no more than a "segmental" type of commitment (See Simmel, 1923, pp. 43–45) from the full-time clinicians who were the weekly discussants. Affiliation with the Society began only as one professional activity among many for physicians who were interested in Freud's methods and clinical discoveries, but were themselves internists with primary professional commitments to clinical medicine. The four colleagues to whom Freud addressed postcards in the fall of 1902—Adler, Wilhelm Stekel, Max Kahane, and Rudolph Reitler—all came to the discussion group as clinicians whose interest in psychological medicine subserved their work as practicing internists. Of the four, only Kahane held an institutional appointment that brought him into regular contact with neurotics (see Stekel, 1950, p. 104). Paul Federn and Eduard Hitschmann, the first two major additions to the circle—and two regular contributors to the ongoing dialogue about Adler's work—also approached psychoanalysis from the standpoint of clinical medicine. Federn, who entered the group in 1903 after seven years of residency training in internal medicine at Vienna's *Allgemeines Krankhaus*, re-

---

[16]Here, and in what follows, I am adopting the sociological perspective of Simmel (1923) as elaborated and refined by Coser (1956, chapter 3).

ceived his introduction to Freud from Hermann Nothnagel, the ranking internist who, almost alone among the Vienna medical faculty, supported Freud. Edoardo Weiss, who entered analysis with Federn in 1909, recalls that Federn was still practicing internal medicine at the time (1966, pp. 142, 144). Hitschmann, who joined the group two years later at the introduction of Federn, was also a thriving internist when he met Freud (P. Becker, 1966, pp. 160–168).[17] These men did not come to Freud as clinical psychiatrists, much less as neophyte "psychoanalysts," and they hardly relinquished their medical identities on entering the Psychological Wednesday Society. It is interesting to note, in this connection, that as late as 1908, one of the original and regular attenders of the weekly meetings, Max Kahane, retained a sufficiently medical orientation in his work to edit the *Medizinisches Handlexikon fuer praktische Arzte*—a Medical Dictionary for the Practicing Physician—that was published by the well-known medical firm of Urban & Schwarzenberg. An additional Society member, Alfred Adler, was one of the 15 medical specialists from whom Kahane solicited contributions. It is indisputable that Reitler, Stekel, Federn, and Hitschmann all became psychoanalysts under the impetus of their exposure to Freud, but the collective assumption of new psychotherapeutic identities was a gradual process linked not only to the slowly increasing availability of psychoanalytic patients, but to the professionalization of psychoanalysis within the medical establishment.

In alluding to the relationship between the professionalization of psychoanalysis and the nature of the commitment expected of those physicians identifying themselves as psychoanalysts, we return once more to the matter of institutionalization and, more especially, to the crucial developments of 1910. The Nuremberg Congress stands as a watershed not only of the institutionalization of psychoanalysis, but of the deepened identification with psychoanalytic theory that Freud came to expect of his adherents at this juncture in the movement's history. As the institutionalization of psychoanalysis advanced in the aftermath of Nuremberg via the conditions of group organization spelled out in the statutes of the International Association, it can reasonably be inferred that the commitment of the members of the Vienna Society to analysis intensified at the expense of their medical identities. By 1911, the politicization of psychoanalysis in its struggle against the outside, teamed with the internal institutionalization of the Vienna Society—its formal registration with the Viennese public authorities, the publication of the Vienna-based *Zentralblatt fuer Psychoanalyse,* the collection of dues, and, perhaps most importantly, the growing extent to which Society members of 1911 were earning their livelihoods through the practice of psycho-

---

[17]Becker recalls Hitschmann as "a proud physician and an experienced internist" (1966, p. 167).

analysis—made participation in the Vienna Society less segmental than it had been in the years preceding Nuremberg and fostered a new sense of unity among the current members.[18] It is the heightened professional and political solidarity that emerged in the wake of Nuremberg that helps account for the intensification of hostility toward Adler by colleagues who had supported his role in the group dialogue up to the winter meetings of 1911. It seems incontestable, moreover, that Freud's personal actions at the Nuremberg Congress lent further impetus to the new cohesiveness between analysts that was the natural sequel to the founding of the International Association. By protesting the status of analysis as a beleaguered ideology beset with the attacks of a hostile psychiatric establishment, Freud not only promoted the consensus of his following, but helped redefine the group structure of the Vienna Society in a way that fostered its readiness to reassess the meaning of the internal dissension with Adler. Freud's severe criticism of Adler's summary lectures in the winter of 1911 only became a coup de grace by virtue of the Society membership's willingness to accept Freud's prerogative to reverse direction and recast the import of Adler's contributions to the group in a decisively negative way.

---

[18]In arguing that the orientation of Freud's original circle was basically medical, I am taking issue with the traditional characterization of the group as a heterogeneous collection of intellectuals who shared nothing beyond a common interest in psychoanalysis. Herman Nunberg, for example, in his "Introduction" to the Minutes (1959), describes the original circle as a body of "physicians, educators, writers, and others" who represented "a cross-section of the intellectuals at the beginning of the century" (p. xx; cf. 1969, p. 101). There is no question that the group was, from the outset, receptive to the participation of intellectuals outside of medicine and that by 1908 the contributions of men like David Bach, Max Graf, Hugo Heller, and Otto Rank lent a distinctly interdisciplinary flavor to some of the weekly meetings. With the exception of Rank, however, the nonmedical members were occasional attenders whose affiliation with the group was temporary. The fact remains that the original members of 1903 were all internists, as were the principal additions of the next five years: Paul Federn, Eduard Hitschmann, Isidor Sadger, and Fritz Wittels. It was the medical orientation of the *principal* members of the Vienna Society, not the relatively modest input of the rotating, nonmedical participants, that shaped the weekly discussions and provided the framework in which Adler's contributions were situated and assessed through 1910.

6

Adler in Freud's Circle: III. *The Nervous Character* and its Critic

Freud's orchestration of the Vienna Society discussions that resulted in Adler's resignation did not mark the end of his harsh reevaluation of Adler's "deviations." In many ways, the emotional denouement that transpired behind the Society's closed doors represented a beginning more than an end. Freud's published indictment of Adler's ego psychology emerged as a clear sequel to the Society discussions of February, 1911, and it was an indictment that mimicked his earlier disavowal of Adler's "biology" in its selective disregard of the epistemological and clinical bases of Adler's notion of the "nervous character." Before proceeding to Freud's polemical critique of Adler, however, it is important to underscore the considerable disparity between what Adler was saying and what Freud was to end up criticizing in his published writings. To this end, it is helpful to consider, by way of prologue to Freud's repudiation of Adler, two related topics: (1) the programmatic statement of his psychological theory that Adler wrote in the immediate aftermath of his departure from the Vienna Society in 1911 and (2) the substantive critique of Adler's theory found in the diary entries of Lou Andreas-Salomé, the only psychoanalyst to think seriously about Adler's work in the immediate aftermath of his departure from the Freudians.

There is a clear rationale for this two-part strategy. Analysis of *The Nervous Character* provides the necessary backdrop for a reappraisal of Adler's split from Freud because this book supplements Adler's clinical papers of the preceding years in a crucial way—it contains epistemological and sociological assumptions that are merely implicit in the articles of 1909–1911, thereby highlighting basic vulnerabilities of Adler's position that Freud chose to ignore. My own sociological interpretation of Adler's modal "neurotic character" attempts to elucidate the nonpsychoanalytic character of Adler's social theory of neurosis. By exposing the hidden sociologist that lurks beneath the manifest psychologist of *The Nervous Character*, we catch a preliminary glimpse of the Adler whose psychological theory would entirely subserve his call for a revitalized sense of community, for *Gemeinschaftsgefuehl*, in the years following World War I. Lou Andreas-Salomé's probing consideration of the epistemological vulnerabilities of Adler's theory represents a complementary reading that points up how a psychoanalyst might critically address the self-limiting character of any theory of neurosis that restricts itself to social-interactional referents. Her severe, yet ultimately fair-minded, critique of Adler's assumptions is not only a fitting place to end the formal exposition of early Adlerian theory; it further highlights the polemical selectivity of the written appraisal of Adler that would ultimately issue from Freud's own pen.

I.

At first glance, *Ueber den Nervoesen Charakter: Grundzuege einer vergleichenden Individual-Psychologie und Psychotherapie* (1912a) seems to restate in extended, albeit circular fashion, the clinical and theoretical content of the important papers published between 1907 and 1911 in which Adler spelled out the clinical role of inferiority feelings and the compensatory masculine protest in psychopathology. At the level of clinical explanation, the book offers little, beyond a wealth of clinical vignettes, that is not contained in "The Neurotic Disposition" (1909b), "Defiance and Obedience" (1910a), and "Psychic Hermaphroditism in Life and Neurosis" (1910b). But the ostensible predictability of Adler's arguments in *The Nervous Character* belies the significant change of discourse effected in this work. Adler was no longer concerned with explaining neurotic symptoms at the level of *Kinderfehler* or expanding the ramifications of organ inferiority to account for the "oversensitivity" that fueled the neurotic disposition. Having previously elucidated in his "psychoanalytic" publications the medical basis of neurotic discomfort, he turned to the neurosis itself as a finalized psychological product. In so doing, he sought to broaden his theoretical formula to the point of comprehending the self-propelling "nervous character" not as an assemblage of compartmentalized psychophysical vulnerabilities, but as the maintenance of a coherent life style (*Lebenstil*). Henceforth, neurotic discomfort would be viewed as the concomitant expression of an elective interpersonal strategy designed to minimize feelings of "feminine" inferiority and to maximize the opposing sense of masculine ego feeling (*Persoenlichkeitsgefuehl*) on behalf of the life style.

But what made a particular life style "neurotic"? Here we confront one of the subtle paradoxes that partially confounded Adler's therapeutic intent. *The Nervous Character* is less about the neurotic character itself than the neurotic potential that informs character development per se. This fact derived from Adler's conscious attempt to convert the clinical substrate of the *Minderwertigkeitslehre,* the theory of inferiority, into a self-sufficient developmental psychology, into, as he stated in the book's subtitle, a comparative psychology of the individual. To accomplish this aim, Adler had to broaden his psychological sense of "inferiority" well beyond the parameters of the localized inferiorities he had formerly explored. He had to effect this broadening, moreover, in a way that preserved the explicit admission that any "inferiority" was to be understood relative to particular cultural judgments and culturally conditioned expectations, that inferiority feelings "must always be understood in a relative sense, as growing out of the individual's relations to his environment or to his goals" (1912a, p. 14; 1912b, p. 13).

For Adler, it is incontestable that all children at all times and in all places perceive themselves as essentially inferior to all adults. In thus seizing on a social-interactional perspective that derives from an "adult" representational world, Adler undercuts at once the possibility of a genuinely developmental psychology, i.e., a psychology that can elucidate, both epigenetically and structurally, *how* a child comes to perceive himself as inferior to an adult, and what the child *understands* by such "inferiority" at successive stages of development. In his approach to the experiential meaning of inferiority, then, Adler is hardly an epistemological constructionist like Piaget, who believes that the infant must actively construct his world by assimilating it to the rudimentary schemas that are cognitively available at given points in development (see Flavell, 1963, p. 71 and Furth, 1969). Correspondingly, he is not disposed to consider the infant's inferiority as a judgmental commentary on an object world whose very formation is a graduated cognitive task (see Piaget, 1937 and Flavell, 1963, p. 62). Instead, Adler is content to ascribe a normative inferiority to the "infantile situation" writ large, and to construe this inferiority as experientially continuous with the inferiorities of later life. In the second chapter of his book, he pleaded the irresistibility of his paradigm in terms of the endemic "uncertainty in childhood, the great distance that separates the child from the potency (*Machtentfaltung*), the preeminence, and the privileges of the man, qualities of which the child has both presentiments and certain assurances" (1912a, p. 24; 1912b, p. 37). This contention was hardly tantamount to a retraction of the repeated claim that the neurotic character could be viewed as the product of a compensated inferior organ (1912a, pp. 10, 47; 1912b, pp. 3, 92–93), but it did permit Adler to abstract the quality of "inferiority" from the deficient organ and to identify the psychological task presented by the deficient organ with the more general strategic task implicit in childhood development per se.

The offshoot of the qualitative comparability of the developmental tasks presented to all children was a further theoretical relativism. Adler began *The Nervous Character* with the candid admission that the concept of inferiority feelings only took on clinical relevance when understood in a "relative sense." By the time he concluded the opening theoretical section of the book, however, he had extended the relativistic criteria of meaningfulness to the idea of psychopathology itself. It was not merely that the neurotic fell ill because he could not use his organs in a satisfactory way *relative* to cultural requirements of organ performance, but that he coped with the felt burden of his developmental inferiorities less effectively than others confronted with similar developmental deficits. He became neurotic not through the quality or even the intensity of his inferiorities, that is, but because his coping strategies were inappropriate and extreme *relative* to the more moderated compensatory life styles that sufficed for other.

In this way, Adler was able to break down the distinction between neurosis and mental health every bit as fully as Freud, and to do so by invoking, like Freud, the weight of culture. For Adler, however, the breakdown of the distinction did not hinge on a universal task of repression imposed by culture; it depended instead on the common need to arrive at an adequate degree of masculine self-esteem despite the universal burden of inferiority that accrued from interpersonal comparisons deriving from cultural standards. The Adlerian "neurotic" differed from his "normal" counterpart not in the nature of the interpersonal task he had to perform, nor even in the kinds of tactically compensatory traits he might adopt in undertaking it. The difference was rather one of degree, a difference hinging solely on the relative rigidity of the coping defenses adopted and the relative overestimation of the common end to which the defenses were directed.

Adler's transition from explicating the psychology of specific (organ) inferiorities to charting the role of inferiorities in developmental psychology is crucially highlighted by his recourse to the pragmatist Hans Vaihinger's neo-Kantian concept of the "fiction." Adler used the interchangeable notions of the "guiding fiction" (*leitende Fiktion*) and the "guiding principle" (*Leitlinie*) to characterize the cognitive dimension of the attempt to escape felt inferiority and achieve the idealized goal of masculine ego feeling. The guiding fiction laid out the fantasized route by which felt superiority was to be obtained. It provided a directive schema through which the child could behave—once more following Vaihinger—"as if" he had achieved a masculine superiority over his victimizing environment.

Adler's recourse to the "as if" philosophy of Vaihinger bespeaks an intellectual indebtedness that is confirmed by two letters from Adler to Vaihinger recently uncovered in the archives of the University of Bremen.[1] The letters indicate that Adler was in regular correspondence with Vaihinger at the time he was writing *The Nervous Character*. A letter of 5 June 1912 suggests that Adler and Vaihinger were actually exchanging publications through the mail; Adler expressed regret that his book (i.e., *The Nervous Character*) had still not been released, so that he could not reply to Vaihinger's "friendly letter" by sending a copy of the work. After advising the philosopher that he would receive a copy of Furtmueller's *Psychoanalysis and Ethics* (1912) before Adler's own book became available, he expressed the hope that the Individual Psychology society would be permitted to continue to exchange material with Vaihinger in the future, since the pragmatist was "the one philosopher who has brought greater clarity to our understanding of the 'as if' of healthy and sick mental life" (Adler to Vaihinger, 5 June 1912, Universitaet Bremen Bibliothek, Autogr. XXI, 1:C, Nr. 2). In a letter of 22 January 1913, Adler informed Vaihinger that a coworker (Schrecker) would be journeying to Halle the following April "and will personally express our dependence on you." Enjoining Vaihinger to take a hand, if only indirectly, in propagating the psychotherapeutic version of the "as if" philosophy, Adler added: "Perhaps you could make it possible for him to deliver a lecture, perhaps on 'The Fiction Theory in Psychotherapy'—a request that he himself still plans to present to you" (Adler to Vaihinger, 22 January 1913, Universitaet Bremen Bibliothek, Autogr. XXI, 1:C, Nr. 1).[2]

How exactly did Adler incorporate Vaihinger's concepts into his developmental psychology? He did so by construing the patterns of obtained infantile grati-

---

[1] I am grateful to Peter Swales for bringing these two letters to my attention.

[2] A letter from Freud to Vaihinger also uncovered in the archives of the University of Bremen reveals that the philosopher continued to hold Adler in high esteem as late as 1925. In an otherwise appreciative acknowledgment of an article sent by Vaihinger that dealt with certain philosophers (e.g., Schopenhauer and Nietzsche) who anticipated the insights of psychoanalysis, Freud gently chided Vaihinger for including Adler among the researchers who had guided psychoanalysis forward: "His [Adler's] theory is, on the contrary, a complete disavowal of psychoanalysis, a defiant reaction against it, so to speak" (Freud to Vaihinger, 27 January 1925 Universitaet Bremen Bibliothek, Autogr. XXI, 8:R, Nr. 2). Clearly, a substantive treatment of Adler's relationship to Vaihinger must await further archival discoveries, but the material in the three cited letters at least demonstrates that there is indeed a relationship to be uncovered.

fication as the model for the content and subsequent strengthening of the child's "guiding fiction" (1912a, p. 16; 1912b, p. 17). The child's fictionalized path to masculine ego feeling, in other words, amplified the behavioral patterns through which he had successfully manipulated his environment in securing drive gratification in the past. Once implanted in the psyche, the guiding fiction proceeded to shape apperception and memory on behalf of the posited ideal, and Adler credited it with the ability to organize "psychic preparations (*Bereitschaften*) toward the goal of security, among which the neurotic character as well as the functional neurosis are brought into relief as characteristic devices" (1912a, pp. 22, 45; 1912b, pp. 34, 87).

At the beginning of his chapter on "Psychic Compensation and its Preparation," Adler stated that the child's recourse to his fictional scheme conformed to the tendency of human understanding "to reduce that which is chaotic, fluid and intangible in life to measurable entities by means of the assumption of fictions." In this respect, recourse to the fiction was analogous to the division of the globe by means of meridional and parallel lines, "for only thus do we preserve fixed points which we can place in relation with each other." Adler proceeded to designate the presentation of the "fiction" conception based on the psychological study of neuroses and psychoses "the main object of this book," and he viewed this intent as a supportive elaboration of Vaihinger's contention that the fiction manifested itself in all scientific concepts:

> From whatever angle we observe the psychic development of a healthy or a nervous person he is always found ensnared in the meshes of his fictitious schema; a fiction from which the neurotic is unable to find his way back to reality and in which he believes while the healthy person utilizes it in order to reach the real goal. . . . And in this regard I wish to supplement the claims of the learned Vaihinger to the effect that the tendency toward security that compels us all—especially the neurotic and the child—to abandon the accessible path of induction and deduction and to make use of such devices as the schematic fiction, originates out of the feeling of uncertainty. The final purpose of this tendency aims at freedom from the feeling of inferiority in order to ascend to the full height of ego feeling, to complete manliness, to attain the ideal of being above (*zum Ideal des Obenseins*) [1912a, p. 24; 1912b, pp. 36–37].

Here, in Adler's emendation of Vaihinger's "as if" philosophy, we reach the nexus of the therapeutic ambiguity that breaks down the distinction between neurosis and mental health and bridges Adler's transition to a normal psychology based on the imputation of universal inferiority feelings. From the standpoint of Vaihinger's *Philosophy of 'As If'* (1911) and from the standpoint of the ineluctable developmental burden of inferiority, the "guiding fiction" was not specific to neurosis, but rather a pragmatic requirement of all adaptive goal-directed functioning. In *The Nervous Character,* Adler admitted as much, repeatedly. To the extent that any child carried out purposeful action, to the extent that he projected any "uniformity of conduct" into the outer world, Adler claimed it was necessary to assume that the child had discovered a "unified fixed point" existing outside his own personality. The child constructed a guiding fiction to facilitate his orientation to the environment and in the hope "of obtaining grati- fication of his needs, of avoiding pain, and of attaining his goal of pleasure" (1912a, p. 30; 1912b, p. 52). Unlike Vaihinger, Adler was not concerned with elucidating the detailed phenomenology of different categories of "guiding fic- tions" according to their content; he merely took the erection of the guiding fiction to be a heuristic psychological necessity and then proceeded to put all character traits and emotional predispositions at the service of the fiction.

Given the elastic adaptive potential of the "guiding fiction," it does not make sense to invoke this general notion to account for the particular kind of goal- directed strivings that typify the "neurotic" life style. Adler realized as much, and, accordingly, entitled the third chapter of his theoretical exposition the "heightened" or "accentuated" (*verstaerkte*) fiction as the guiding idea in neurosis. In invoking the "heightened fiction" as the primary *explanans* to account for neurotic character, however, Adler merely shifted his relativistic exegesis to a more rarified level without supplying his model of the "nervous character" with any new empirical content. For what, after all, makes a guiding fiction "heightened"?

Adler tried to attack this question by emphasizing the peculiar quality of neurotic apperception. In the incipient neurotic, the burden of inferiority was so oppressive, and the compensatory struggle to achieve superiority was so great, that he perceptually dichotomized his world in accord with the two abstracted variables that governed his emotional well-being. Adler said that the neurotic "always apperceives after the analogy of a contrast (*der Analogie eines Gegen- satzes*)," and that he usually "only recognizes and gives value to relations of contrast (*gegensaetzliche Beziehungen*)." All memories, feelings, and actions were subsequently arranged according to the primitive bipolar antithesis defined by the feeling of inferiority and the compensatory elevation of conscious ego feeling (1912a, pp. 18–19; 1912b, pp. 24–25). Adler later added that this abstract process of apperception grouped experiences according to a scheme "which has the form of an absolute antithesis, something like the debits and credits in bookkeeping, where no transactions are possible." It was this process that accounted for the "splitting of consciousness" which typified neurotic thought. Through his abstracted relationship to the world, the neurotic "becomes alienated from concrete reality." He no longer employed a guiding fiction on his own behalf, but was rather activated by the fiction on its behalf. This activation resulted in neurotic behavior, because "to find one's way back to concrete reality an elasticity and not a rigidity of the psyche is required, a utilization of abstraction, but not an adoration of the abstraction as the deified final purpose of existence" (1912a, p. 27; 1912b, pp. 45–46).

Adler's answer to the distinctive quality of the neurotic's peculiarly "heightened" guiding fiction thus revolved around the scope of the life processes governed by the fiction and the accessibility of the fiction to the ego's moderating influence. The distinction might well be between the "guiding" fiction of the healthy individual and the "driving" fiction of the neurotic. The former was willfully employed on behalf of discrete reality-tested goals; the latter posited the pursuit of masculine ego feeling as the material of an unrealizable quest. Adler spelled out the distinction between the "normal" and the "neurotic" guiding fiction in several suggestive passages (1912a, pp. 20–21, 31, 36, 54; 1912b, pp. 29–30, 54–55, 66–67, 109), but the basic message was always the same. The healthy guiding fiction was superimposed on the ego, was electively maintained as an orienting expedient, but was voluntarily discarded on behalf of reality-tested decision making and activity. The neurotic guiding fiction, conversely, became a reified value to be implemented in the world.

This is an interesting distinction, but hardly one that derives from Vaihinger's concept of the fiction in *The Philosophy of 'As If.'* In fact, Adler's construction of a neurotic guiding fiction divorced from reality was in glaring contradiction to the very philosophical tradition of which Vaihinger was part. If we pause now to offer a brief sketch of this tradition in German scholarship, particularly as it illuminates the roots of Vaihinger's thought, it is because of Vaihinger's putative importance to Adler's presentation. Adler, after all, construed his exposition of the guiding fiction as supplementing the claims of "the learned Vaihinger"; Vaihinger was the one philosopher able to impart clarity to Adler's "understanding of the 'as if' of healthy and sick mental life" (Adler to Vaihinger, 5 June 1912, Universitaet Bremen Bibliothek). In view of this conscious indebtedness to Vaihinger, it is indeed important to clarify the basic incommensurability between Adler's psychological fiction and the fiction of the pragmatists. Such clarification advances us toward a final estimation of *The Nervous Character* by underscoring the way in which Adler's philosophical pretentions in his book mask his underlying sociological commitments. In the present instance, Adler's uncomprehending treatment of Vaihinger points to the need to invoke a more relevant sociological referent to make sense of his curious distinction between the neurotic and healthy guiding fiction.

From his early theological studies at the University of Tuebingen in the 1870s, Vaihinger's two-fold commitment had been to the supremacy of practical reason in Kant and to the evolutionary development of thought grounded in organic service to the "will" found in Schopenhauer. Though unpublished until 1911, *The Philosophy of 'as If'* was completed in 1877. It consequently fell squarely within the neo-Kantian movement that had been a dominant force in German philosophy since the mid-1860s. In particular, Vaihinger's work was rooted in the "Baden School," a wing of the neo-Kantian movement which, under the leadership of Wilhelm Windelband, elaborated a philosophy of values and expounded the role of values in the cultural sciences during this time.

Windelband, along with his successor Heinrich Rickert, emphasized the centrality of a value-positing consciousness that lay behind empirical consciousness and generated the normative values that guided all logical and ethical thought. Windelband further regarded the existence of a supersensible divine reality (God) as a nonempirical "postulate" that permitted the recognition and affirmation of these absolute values. Only through the invocation of a "fictitious" God that enabled man to affirm objective values, in other words, could man acquire a metaphysical foundation on which logical and ethical judgments could be based. For Windelband, this kind of "postulate" was nonempirical, but it was much more than simply "useful." It fell to two other neo-Kantians, F. A. Lange and Hans Vaihinger, to develop fully a pragmatist interpretation of Kant's postulate-theory that reduced the transcendent value-affirming "postulates" of Windelband and Rickert to mere "useful fictions."[3]

In *The Philosophy of 'As If,'* Vaihinger did not juxtapose the "fiction" to a fictionless reality; he argued in the spirit of Kant's *Critique of Practical Reason* (1787) that the fiction was a false hypothesis with adaptive utility that served as a precondition of cognition. In invoking the explanatory necessity of the "fiction," Vaihinger made the preliminary philosophical statement of an interpretive position that would be elaborated by two influential European physicists and philosophers of science at the turn of the century, Henri Poincaré and Ernst Mach. Both these men stressed the degree to which thinking occurred in terms of the convenient fiction and the commensurate extent to which the very notion of science represented a mere conventional hypothesis (see Hughes, 1961, pp. 106–112).[4]

---

[3]For helpful discussions of the neo-Kantian movement, especially the Baden School, see Copleston (1963, pp. 361–373) and G. Iggers (1968, pp. 144–159).

[4]It is possible that Adler was influenced by Mach, who taught in Vienna from 1895 to 1902, a period covering the early years of Adler's medical career preceding his collaboration with Freud. Adler was certainly acquainted with Mach's work; he mentions Mach's *Contributions to the Analysis of Sensations* (1897) in a letter to Lou Andreas-Salomé of 16 August 1913 (see Andreas-Salomé, 1912–1913, p. 160).

Despite the Kantian basis of Vaihinger's theory, the catalytic agent that provided the epistemological basis for the "fiction" was the pessimistic philosophy of Schopenhauer. Schopenhauer's popularity in nineteenth-century Germany had dramatically increased in the decades following Hegel's death and the unsuccessful revolution of 1848, and Vaihinger's work was very much a reflection of this revival. In his reminiscences, Vaihinger pronounced the influence of Schopenhauer not as "extensive," but much more "intensive" than that of Kant, and he added that Schopenhauer's "pessimism" became in him "a fundamental and lasting state of consciousness, and all the more because of my own sad and difficult experiences" (1923, pp. 188–189). For Vaihinger, the significance of Schopenhauer resided in his comprehension of the irrational, and the most illuminating dimension of Schopenhauer's doctrine was the demonstration that "thought" originated in obedient service to the "will" and only emancipated itself and became an end-in-itself (*Selbstzweck*) in the course of development. It was this argument, he later recollected, that "rounded out for me Kant's doctrine that human thought is bound by definite limits and is incapable of reaching metaphysical knowledge" (p. 191).

In *The Philosophy of 'As If,'* Vaihinger followed this methodological starting point of Schopenhauer's *The World as Will and Representation* (1819) and pronounced "thought" the original servant of a "will to life" that fulfilled a purposive organic function. In breaking away from its organic base, however, thought proceeded to pose problems to which it was not equal and for which it had not been developed. The "as if" stratagem evolved as a utilitarian value that permitted man to gain cognitive access to a "reality" that was inaccessible to human "thought." The "fiction" was not adopted as a strategic device for circumventing the status conferred on one *by* reality; it represented instead an artificial thought-construct that permitted man's practical *management* of reality to continue, a construct adopted "in order to overcome difficulties of thought . . . and reach the goal of thought by roundabout ways and bypaths" (1911, p. xlvii). Only by means of the mediating fiction could man know anything of reality because, for Vaihinger, the correctness of thought lay in practice and only through the fiction could thoughts be embraced that promoted practical mastery of the environment. Rather than being superimposed on thought, then, the fiction actually fulfilled the purpose of thought. This purpose, for Vaihinger, was ". . . the elaboration and adjustment of the material of sensation for the attainment of a richer and fuller sensational life of experience" (p. 6). The world of ideas did not "portray" reality, but it provided man with the best perspective on reality he could hope to acquire, one that provided him with an "instrument for finding our way about more easily in this world" (p. 15).

It follows, then, that Adler's entire distinction between the healthy and neurotic guiding fiction is really not explicable within the framework of Vaihinger's "as if" philosophy. As soon as Adler pronounced the healthy individual capable of freeing himself from the fiction in order to cope with reality, he abandoned the Schopenhauerian presupposition that led Vaihinger to invoke the fiction as an epistemological necessity in the first place. Adler's insistence on situating the "nervous character" within the jurisdiction of a peculiarly "neurotic" guiding fiction must therefore be explained at the level of the latent presuppositions and "guiding principles" in *The Nervous Character* itself. What did Adler really seek to accomplish in his distinction between the healthy and neurotic guiding fiction? What is the content of the "reality" which, for the healthy individual, existed above and beyond the perspectivistic contours of the guiding fiction?

The most suggestive clues for answering these questions are scattered amid the rambling clinical illustrations of the fiction paradigm found in the lengthy "Practical Part" of *The Nervous Character*. Adler observed here that the neurotic's heightened feeling of uncertainty and inferiority hinders him in the proper estimation of his fiction" (1912a, p. 79; 1912b, p. 171). He proceeded to spell out in elaborate, repetitive detail the interpersonal ramifications of such "improper" estimation of the fictitious construct: major social disruption. The sociological verdict is not elucidated programmatically, but it constitutes the implicit sociopathic dimension contained in the many case histories Adler utilized to illustrate the range of coping strategies at the disposal of the neurotic character. The patients who formed the clinical base for Adler's theoretical generalizations embodied levels of psychopathology that push the descriptive "neurotic" appellation to the border of clinical meaningfulness. In part, this fact may stem from the demographic characteristics of Adler's clientele. We know that his socioeconomically depressed patient population included a substantial percentage of the poor, and it has been plausibly suggested that sexual questions were much less important and less anxiety-inducing for such patients than the problems of material existence (see Wasserman, 1958 and Ansbacher, 1959).

This conjecture seems compatible with the clinical material contained in *The Nervous Character*. Adler's patients do not appear to be neurotic; they are maladjusted sociopaths whose conscious unhappiness with life is so great that they frequently retreat from social life altogether. Adler, for example, repeatedly described severe depressives who were usually suicidal (1912a, pp. 64, 68, 99–100, 126, 174; 1912b, pp. 130, 140, 220, 284, 395). In doing so, he pointed to a serious *social* problem that had reached alarming proportions in Vienna only two years before the publication of his book. Suicides, especially among the young, witnessed a striking resurgence in Germany and Austria in 1910. Indeed, the public outcry in Vienna was substantial enough to induce the Vienna Psychoanalytic Society to conduct, and subsequently publish, a lengthy symposium on the topic in that same year.[5] In his own contribution to this symposium, Adler traced the idea of suicide to the same evaluative circumstances that precipitated "neurosis." He jointly categorized suicide and neurosis as "attempts of the overburdened psyche to escape the recognition of this feeling of inferiority." They were attempts, moreover, that could occasionally appear "in a social form" (quoted in Friedman, 1967, p. 120).

In *The Nervous Character,* the social context of the neurosis actually became the determining content, and when Adler described patients with more circumscribed forms of symptomatology, he still gauged the severity of the "neurosis" by referring to the general intrafamilial unhappiness caused by the symptom and to the patient's inability to assume any social responsibilities as a result of the symptomatic suffering. Thus, his repeated description of psychosomatic migraine sufferers whose calculating use of migraine attacks "serve to place the whole household at the service of the sufferer," permit the patient "to withdraw completely from society," and were accompanied by a general "disinclination for life and work" (1912a, pp. 140, 184, 149; 1912b, pp. 317, 421, 338).

The extent to which Adler's patients succumbed to a generalized withdrawal from all social and familial obligations draws attention to a fundamental difference between the conceptions of neurotic suffering held by Adler and Freud. In accord with psychoanalytic theory as it existed in 1913, Freud's "neurotic" could suffer in relative silence; he was the victim of intrapsychic conflict, his symptoms the product of the unruly vicissitudes of endogenous libidinal endowment. To the extent that neurotic misery was social, it was due to "social" parameters imposed on endogenous drive activity and to the social configurations that were phylogenetically built into the unfolding schema of instinctual maturation (e.g., the Oedipus complex). Adler, on the other hand, like the French sociologist Durkheim but unlike Freud, saw the essence of sociality as residing in the phenomena of social interaction. He consequently contended that the dynamic conflict producing neurosis was not an intrapsychic conflict embodying the tension between drive endowment and internalized social norms (i.e., the content of the superego), but an extrapsychic conflict embodying the variable social value assigned to different kinds of social interaction. Thus, for Adler, neurosis

---

[5]The symposium has been edited and reissued by Friedman as *On Suicide, With Particular Reference to Suicide Among Young Students* (1967).

was, per se, social neurosis, and individual symptomatic distress always found its *raison d'être* and its conscious realization in the collective unhappiness the neurosis generated for the surrounding milieu.[6]

Adler articulated his sense of the ''social whole'' in a circumscribed concern for the impact of neurotic suffering on family life, but the referents of his argument range beyond the family proper and, as such, take on a strikingly Durkheimian complexion. Did Adler borrow directly from the French sociologist? His published writings provide no evidence of such borrowing although, in the absence of archival sources chronicling Adler's intellectual development, we have very little notion of just who *did* influence him at this juncture in his career, beyond Vaihinger. In the following attempt to elaborate the surprising extent to which Adler's social theory of neurosis fits into the framework of Durkheim's sociology, I am *not* claiming that Durkheim ''influenced'' Adler, although the striking convergences I will outline should at least leave open the possibility that Adler was acquainted with Durkheim's work. Rather, I wish to restate the principal verdict of *The Nervous Character* in Durkheimian terminology because the transposition is interpretively useful at this point in my presentation: the language of the *conscience collective* enables me to demonstrate the considerable extent to which Adler's early conception of neurosis already incorporated fundamental assumptions about the therapeutic meaning of ''community feeling.'' These assumptions, in turn, underscore the preeminently sociological status of the theory of neurosis that Adler propounded in the aftermath of his departure from Freud's circle.

It is indeed curious that Adler's conception of neurosis should rely on the Continental estimation of social life that was principally represented at the turn of the century by Durkheim's ''sociologistic school,'' to borrow Sorokin's (1928, pp. 434ff.) expression. Durkheim, along with Marcel Mauss, Levy Bruhl, and other collaborators gathered around the journal, *L'Année Sociologique,* explicated the notion of the *conscience collective* at this time. By invoking the concept of a collective conscience that transcended individual moral codes, they were able to trace the logic of social life to a system of transcendent ''collective representations'' that ordered individual existence in society. The collective representations initially derived from the social relations between individuals, but they subsequently achieved a self-sustaining moral meaning that simul-

---

[6]Cf. the Freudian Schilder (1938), for whom social neurosis identifies a variant of a ''classical'' neurosis in which the symptomatic picture ''is dominated by suffering in social contacts'' (p. 161). For Schilder, social neurosis is a subspecies of neurosis; for Adler, social neurosis is coterminous with neurosis.

taneously transcended and regulated the social life of the individual (Durkheim, 1898).[7]

Adler's conception of neurosis embodied Durkheim's fundamental conclusion about the determinative moral character of collective social life. Durkheim (1911), operating within the framework of his "sociologistic" epistemology, equated "value judgments" with objective statements of value that were naturalistically rooted in collective life and thereby independent of the subjective states of individuals. Adler, in turn, operating within the framework of his pragmatic therapeutics, placed comparably "objective" social value judgments at the heart of his theory of neurosis. It was the collective conscience that appraised the adaptive adequacy of an individual's guiding fiction and imparted the "neurotic" appellation to the guiding fiction gone astray. The neurotic sufferer, that is, suffered precisely because he was subject to the constraining valuations of the collective conscience; his magnified feeling of inferiority reflected the impact of social judgments and beliefs on his evolving social identity. To the extent that he lacked an identity that was adequate in terms of the "masculine" standards of the defining social group, he lacked a viable personal identity altogether. Thus, for the Adlerian neurotic, the consequence of the inferior self-perception was so significant that it induced him to ignore willfully the binding solidarities that tied him to his "familial" whole. He was neurotic precisely to the extent that elaboration of a fantasized "masculine" identity ignored the integration and meaning that familial society imparted to his behavior. Thus, for Adler, the etiological kernel of the neurosis could never be mere intrapsychic conflict; instead, it was embodied in the adoption of a "guiding principle" that was neurotic precisely to the degree that it presupposed social conflict, i.e., to the extent that it sought a solution to the problem of inferiority without regard for the requirements of the *conscience collective*. The antisocial solution was adopted, in turn, because the neurotic's insecurity was so great that the only compensatory "masculine" strategies that could make good the magnified sense of inferiority were those extreme demonstrations of "superiority" that entailed the antisocial victimization of others. Social judgments about adequately "masculine" behavior thereby operate at two levels for Adler; they are constitutive of that degree of inferiority that cannot be remedied through normal superiority strivings, and they assign the "neurotic" appellation to the maladaptive strategies to which the individual with heightened inferiority feelings must, of necessity, resort.

---

[7]For general interpretations of Durkheim's thought and the influence of his school, see Sorokin (1928, pp. 463ff.), Maus (1962, pp. 79ff.), and Mitchell (1968, pp. 72ff.).

Adler observed that such "neurotic" traits were always accessible to the guiding fiction and even played a limited developmental role in the case of the healthy child. Only when a degree of inferiority commensurate with neurosis eventuated, however, were these traits deployed as a compulsory strategy for regaining ego feeling. From this vantage point, it was reasonable for Adler to argue, as he did, that the outbreak of neurosis was really no more than a strengthening of those "psychic preparations" that had been elicited during developmental periods characterized by heightened uncertainty. The neurosis drew on these psychic preparations to mobilize the kind of antisocial traits that would have maximum effectiveness in controlling a heightened feeling of inferiority (1912a, pp. 20, 22; 1912b, pp. 29, 34). The "strength" of the particular preparations invoked by the neurosis, in turn, rested in the broadened social dimension over which the compensatory "superiority" could assert itself. Defensive preparations became neurotic preparations precisely to the extent that they yielded strategies of interpersonal control that were socially malignant, i.e., that sacrificed the health of the social whole to the untempered requirements of the feeling of inferiority. The requirements of the feeling of inferiority became untempered, correspondingly, to the degree that the individual was unaffected by the social unhappiness that was an integral consequence of his "neurotic" guiding fiction.

By examining the implicit sociological assumptions underlying Adler's theory of neurosis, we see the crucial way in which a supposition about the therapeutic significance of "community feeling" filtered into Adler's exposition of the neurotic character well before he became formally preoccupied with the idea of *Gemeinschaftsgefuehl* in the aftermath of World War I. Adler did not directly anchor the neurotic character in a putative lack of community feeling. He did, however, implicitly differentiate between the healthy and neurotic guiding fictions on the basis of the degree to which "collective representations" (in the sense of Durkheim) restricted the range of social activity over which the fiction could lead the individual to the goal of imagined superiority. Both fictions aspired to the same unreachable height, but the inferiority that fueled the healthy fiction was never so great as to allow the individual to remain selectively inattentive to the social repercussions of the strategy by which superiority was sought.

Adler seemed to come closest to articulating this implicit working assumption when he invoked the idea of a "counter-fiction" (*Gegenfiktion*) to express one of the circuitous routes by which the guiding fiction could lead to mastery over others without damaging the "establishment of relations" (*die Anknuepfung von Beziehungen*) on which the individual was dependent. We must acknowledge, of course, that Adler posited the counter-fiction as a tactical disguise that a neurotic fiction could adopt to gain its ends. Yet, even in the guise of the neurotic strategy, the counter-fiction conformed with the real demands of the social environment in a way that inescapably led the neurotic back to the social responsibilities that temper the quest for superiority. It was a neurotic strategy that plotted a course which, ironically, paralleled genuine health. It did so by promoting a therapeutic balance between the demands of society and the superiority strivings:

> This concealment takes place through the arrangement of a counter-fiction. This counter-fiction first of all directs visible conduct, and through the impetus provided by the counter-fiction reality is approached and the recognition of the effective energies (*wirksamen Kraefte*) of reality is effected. This counter-fiction, always bearing the character of contemporary, corrective courts of justice, effects a change in the form of the guiding fiction. It does so by pressing for consideration its claim for the recognition of social and ethical demands (*soziale, ethische Zukunftsforderungen*) at their true value, thereby assuring the reasonableness (*Vernuenftigkeit*) of thought and behavior. It is the security coefficient of the guiding line to power and the harmony of the two fictions, their mutual compatibility, which is the sign of mental health. Practical experiences, intellectual information, social and cultural rules and the traditions of society all reside in the counter-fiction [1912a, p. 42; 1912b, pp. 80–81].[8]

The counter-fiction, though instigated neurotically, subsequently functioned as a healthy corrective to the guiding fiction that carried the individual back towards *Gemeinschaftsgefuehl*. At the level of clinical psychiatry, Adler made the action of therapy hinge on the educability of the patient to the insights embodied in the counter-fiction. He found the "chief therapeutic hope" in the "fictive basis" of the feeling of inferiority that was unnecessarily exaggerated to correspond to the neurotic's equally exaggerated need for security. He proceeded to equate the task of therapy with the unmasking to the patient of "the superficiality of his attempts at orientation, to tear apart these attempts in their fictiveness, and thereby to weaken the feeling of inferiority that drives the patient frantically in accord with these [neurotic] lines of direction" (1912a, pp. 34, 36; 1912b, pp. 60–65). In the "Practical Part" of his study, Adler listed the three levers that the therapist had at his disposal in treating neurosis: the destruction of the "false perspective" that issued in neurotic apperception, the damming up of the "fictive influxes leading to the masculine protest," and the therapeutic "understanding of the superstitious belief in an abstract guiding line" to which

---

[8]In the fourth edition of the book (1928), Adler actually used the word *Gemeinschaftsgefuehl* to designate the corrective nature of the counter-fiction (1912c, pp. 47–48).

the neurotic mistakenly adhered (1912a, pp. 103, 195; 1912b, pp. 227–228, 446).

II.

Our prologue to Freud's repudiation of Adler remains incomplete as long as it is confined to the text of *The Nervous Character* itself. New insight is obtained by considering the single critic in the psychoanalytic camp who scrutinized the epistemological foundations of Adler's neurotic character in considerable detail at the time the book appeared, and who underlined the key vulnerabilities of Adler's system that called for psychoanalytic correctives. The critic in question is Lou Andreas-Salomé, and the value of her reflections on Adler gains from the unusual circumstances in which they were conceived: for a short time she sought to do simultaneous justice to the ideas of Freud and Adler and, in the process, unwittingly played the awkward part of an Adlerian Freudian (or vice versa). The "Adlerian" qualifier was subsequently dropped, but the Freudian critique of Adler's doctrine that she proceeded to formulate in her diary entries is important precisely because it took Adler's epistemology and psychology seriously, thereby providing a psychoanalytic rejoinder to Adlerian theory that operated at the level of Adler's own internal preconceptions.

Salomé journeyed to Vienna in the fall of 1912, a neophyte student of psychoanalysis committed to Freud but sympathetic to the recent Adlerian critique of Freudian doctrine promulgated in *The Nervous Character*. Her initiation into psychoanalysis came in her fifty-first year, well after her publicized affairs with Nietzsche and Rilke had given her a decided notoriety as one of the feminist "free spirits" of the fin de siècle. Salomé's introduction to Freud had come by way of Poul Bjerre, the Swedish psychotherapist who was her lover from 1911 to 1913. Salomé accompanied Bjerre to the Weimar Congress of the International Psychoanalytic Association in September, 1911 where she bemused Freud with her "vehemently expressed desire to study psychoanalysis" (Andreas-Salomé, quoted in Peters, 1962, p. 273).[9] Deeply impressed with the importance of Freud's discoveries, she began a serious study of psychoanalysis and subsequently requested and received Freud's permission to come to Vienna to place herself under his formal tutelage. Her enthusiasm for Freud initially spilled over to Adler as well. She had corresponded with Adler prior to her arrival in Vienna, and in a letter dated 6 August 1912, Adler indicated that he shared her apprecia-

---

[9]For the biographical context of Andreas-Salomé's initiation into psychoanalysis, see Binion (1968, pp. 305–331).

tion of Freud's scientific significance "up to the point at which I further and further parted company with him" (Adler, quoted in Andreas-Salomé, 1912–1913, p. 33). Three days after her arrival in Vienna, she paid Adler a friendly visit, pronounced him "charming and very intelligent," and recorded the following mixed judgment:

> What I liked best in Adler was the mobility of his mind, whereby many divergent things could be woven together; the trouble is that it is superficial and unreliable, *skipping* about when it should pace off the distances [1912–1913, pp. 34–35; emphasis in the original].

If Salomé came to Vienna in broad sympathy with certain elements of Adler's critique of Freud, it is equally clear that there was no interval of her stay when she suppressed a pointed skepticism about certain sacred assumptions of the Adlerian system. In the diary entry recording her first visit to Adler, she considered it "unproductive" that Adler's evaluative schema should always attribute to the "feminine" a "negative sign." Two days later she recorded a discussion in which she took issue with Paul Federn's defense of Adler's theory of inferiority, contending that Adler's theory failed "in its principal implication that specific psychic events are based on specific organic defects" (1912–1913, pp. 34–35, 37–38). These substantive reservations did not dampen her interest in pursuing Adler's theories, however, and did not prevent her from confiding to Freud on 3 November the extent to which Adler's book "stimulated and confirmed" her in work outside the scope of psychoanalysis proper. Apparently unaware of the strong emotional animus that fueled Adler's separation from Freud, she naively appended to her letter a reference to Adler's invitation to her to attend his Thursday evening discussions (*Freud/Andreas-Salomé Letters,* p. 7). In a response written the following day, Freud undertook to enlighten her as to "this disagreeable state of affairs":

> The relationship between the two groups is not such as ought to result from analogous, even if divergent endeavours. They frequently carry on something else besides psychoanalysis. We found ourselves obliged to break off all contact between Adler's splinter group and our own, and even our medical guests are asked to choose between one or the other. That is not pleasant, but the personal behaviour of those who have left our ranks left us no choice [*Freud/Andreas-Salomé Letters,* p. 8].

In the case of Salomé, Freud gallantly chose to lift this restriction. He could not forego the request, however, that she "make no reference to your contact with us when with them, and vice versa" (p. 8).

Years later, Salomé recollected that this initial stipulation accounted for the duration of her uncomfortable participation in the two rival study groups. The requirement was so well satisfied, she mused, "that Freud only effected my separation from Adler's circle after months" (1951, p. 209). Yet, no sooner was this permission wrested from Freud than Salomé's perspective on Adler took a decidedly negative turn. In this case, immediate exposure to Adler yielded important insights that sensitized her to the limitations of Adler's ego psychology. Three days after Freud's letter of permission, on 7 November, she recorded learning of Adler's development as a student of Marx. She noted that this piece of information attuned her to the social comparisons from which Adlerian personality ideals arose and in which the Freudian unconscious could play no role (Andreas-Salomé, 1912–1913, pp. 42–43). Two days later, she wrote Freud that Adler's "symbolic interpretation of sexuality" was "very convincing," but only on condition that it be understood as a "reciprocal process, i.e., an identical procedure from the standpoint of sexuality as from that of the ego-ideal." Adler's claim that sexuality symbolized the compensatory claims of the ego was suggestive, that is, but no more suggestive than the Freudian rejoinder that ego claims themselves could also be sexual symbols. The following day Salomé received a letter from Freud expressing satisfaction that her absence from his lecture the preceding day "was not occasioned by a visit to the camp of the masculine protest" (*Freud/Andreas-Salomé Letters,* pp. 8–11; Andreas-Salomé, 1912–1913, p. 44).

Salomé would in fact continue to frequent the camp of the masculine protest, but the question of her loyalty was no longer in serious doubt. The key factor that quickly precipitated her departure from the Adlerian camp was Adler's recourse to the neurotic "arrangement" (i.e., via the "guiding fiction") in the explanation of neurotic conflict and suffering. She did not deny the explanatory utility of the "arrangement" outright; she merely resented Adler's unwillingness to consider alternative formulations and to explore the "inferiority" that prompted the arrangement from a broader vantage point than that provided by the masculine protest. On 12 November 1912, she complained that Adler "just cannot be pinned down," adding that expressions of pain could indeed be "arranged," but could also be traced to many other causes. The decision to end her participation in Adler's study group was recorded in the diary entry nine days later. Here Salomé summarized the verdict she had reached after attendance at her final Adler discussion group. Adler suceeded in reducing Freud's "facts" to psychic fictions, she observed, "only in that he hides epistemologically behind the illusoriness of events, the 'as if' . . . in the present state of affairs it is plain that I shall have to drop out of Adler's evening discussions" (1912–1913, pp. 44–45; 53–54).

This decision to leave Adler's circle did not close Salomé's mind to the critical issues raised by Adler's theories, and in the aftermath of her decision she added to her diary several illuminating passages that clarified what she felt to be the critical flaws in the Adlerian approach. In an entry following a Vienna Society discussion in early December that she characterized as "practically a debate on Adler," for example, she complained that, for Adler,

> an "arrangement" is manifest where compensation for a physical inferiority through ambition is "arranged" to ward off invidious comparison with others. But it is impossible to bring to consciousness the fact that such an exaggeration of self-esteem might have its roots in a disturbed sexual attitude toward others—*simply because it is itself one of the arrangements of consciousness*. This forcible self-isolation from real life which Adler, too, sees as so characteristic of all neurotics, has become a property of his own ideas. He turns realities into allegories . . . but in this process he treats the "arranger," the personality in question, as itself a fiction; it has no independent existence and can be involved with itself only through the "as if" of arrangements. The plane whence the personality arises to become ego, from whose unconscious layers the personality derives the broad reality underlying its conscious interpretations—this plane of Freud's real achievement is ignored and bypassed [1912–1913, pp. 62–63; emphasis in the original].

Five days later, Salomé reflected on a two-hour talk she had with Adler. Her theme was once more the basic inability of the Adlerian "arrangement" to comprehend the full two-sidedness of sexuality: the "ego" perception of sexuality and physical reality of the sexual drive itself. It was at the figurative point of intersection between these two perspectives, for Salomé, that "all mental disorders and neuroses meet," and she chided Adler for failing to apprehend the "intersectional" character of the neurotic's suffering: "But only Freud has appropriated the word 'compromise' for this, and only he has done justice to the double character of the process, even though he has predominantly emphasized the sexual role" (pp. 67–68). On 25 January 1913, she professed a fuller comprehension of the equal significance of the ego and sex in neurosis. This equality permitted the possibility of a "sublimation" that would allow the ego instinct to rearrange sexuality according to its own ends, but this insight was embodied in a formulation that transcended the Adlerian schema:

> Before this was clear Adler had, through misunderstanding, some justification for his notion, namely that the ego employs sexuality merely symbolically for its own guiding purpose. But now light is cast on the heart of the matter (which Adler reduces to a disembodied psychic game), namely the true mutuality of the psyche with the source of its conscious organization [p. 84].

Salomé recorded her final good-by to Adler in her diary entry of 21 March 1913. She recalled the organ inferiority study as his best written achievement, only to add that "organ feeling (in a medical sense) is outside the reach of any psychological consideration; it remains a sphere of its own and no substitute for the basis provided by Freud . . ." On the final week of her stay in Vienna, she reached her studied verdict: a temperate assessment that opted for Freud without denying or maligning the importance of Adler's limited contribution. Adler's theory of inferiority, she wrote on 2 April 1913, "unquestioningly has 'social significance' for the development of character as well as experience." While granting the mental import of a physical handicap, however, she disputed the typicality of such defects as causes of neuroses. To the large degree that neuroses occurred when the body was intact, she submitted that "the fundamental causes must be grasped then in those very depths of the psyche itself in which the psychic structure originates" (pp. 126–129). In her "Retrospect" of 6 April 1913, she reflected that Freud's modifications according the ego (*Ichfaktor*) a role of greater equality with that of sexuality betokened a discernible advance toward the position of the dissenting analysts—"all except Adler":

> Only Adler takes the stand not of emphasizing the ego, but of eliminating the role of sex, and hence of negating the two-sidedness of the relation. But here alone lies the crux of the matter, and thus Freud is right [p. 132].

The reflective assessment of Adler sprinkled through these diary entries of 1912–1913 has a significance that transcends its immediate relevance to the life history of Lou Andreas-Salomé: it embodies the dispassionate Freudian critique of Adler that Freud himself would never make. In her probing appraisal of the implications of the Adlerian "arrangement" for the very conception of a healthy ego, Salomé immediately put her finger on the interpretive heart of *The Nervous Character* in a way that Freud never would. Her concern was not with the "aggressive" instinctual content of the masculine protest, but with the epistemological implications of the "guiding fiction" as a strategy for understanding ego qua ego and as a clinical device for differentiating the healthy from the neurotic ego. She suggested that Adler's "guiding fiction" would, per se, reduce the very concept of personality to an "arranger" without independent existence apart from the fictitious "as if" strategies it adopted. More pointedly still, she questioned the potential falsifiability (to borrow the language of Karl Popper) of Adler's assumptions about the "arrangeability" of sexuality, given his circular a priori assumption that disturbed sexual object relations constituted an arrangement of consciousness in the first place (1912–1913, pp. 62–63).

Perceiving the dual character of Adler's theory as a psychological system with epistemological referents and a pragmatic foundation for psychotherapy, Salomé questioned the theoretical relevance of the former perspective to the latter. Thus her plaint that the epistemological illusoriness of all psychological events via Adler's "as if" strategem did not forestall the need for a "practical orientation" entailing the need "to make distinctions and separations within the illusoriness of such events, i.e., to again establish the categories of the 'psychic' and the 'real.' " To the extent that mental health was tantamount to a "guiding fiction" that maintained a valid orientation to the real world, Salomé maintained that Freud's therapeutic postulates supplanted Adler's even within the framework of Adler's own epistemology: "to pursue the psychic as far as possible with psychic means, that is, up to the point where only somatic signs are left to us" (p. 53, cf. p. 127).

In the diary entry of 21 March 1913 recording her farewell to Adler, Salomé returned one final time to the epistemological foundations of *The Nervous Character*. She questioned, as we have done, the legitimacy of Adler's derivation of the "guiding fiction" from Vaihinger's *Philosophy of 'As If'*, and she questioned further the extent to which Adler's formulation yielded a meaningful distinction between sickness and health. Speaking of Vaihinger, she observed that

> This philosophy speaks of purely auxiliary constructs of theoretical ideas, of "arrangements" which must on two accounts be absolutely differentiated from Adler's. In the first place they operate on a completely conscious basis; in the second place they exist quite beyond any value judgments . . . The fictitious goals posed by Adler's theory are the exact opposite of these, being effective only in that they are *un*conscious and perishing when they become conscious; in addition they constitute the genuine reservoirs of value, invulnerable to any criticism. It is also not to be overlooked that he does not regard the fictions as symptoms of disorder, but as the central mental manifestations of the healthy person, one might say as the only symptom of mental activity in Adler's model man. Hence it is quite impossible for him to discriminate in this area between the sick and the well [p. 128].

To this epistemological malaise, one that could be cleared up only by invoking Adler's latent presuppositions about the relative quality of community feeling that informed the neurotic and healthy guiding fictions, Salomé appended the Freudian rejoinder that the "healthy fiction" originated in a reality that was no fiction at all. For Adler to acknowledge this fact, she added, "would put him on the road back to Freud" (p. 128).

At the same time as Salomé presented a theoretical critique of Adler's epistemology that challenged the ability of the "guiding fiction" to discriminate between neurosis and mental health, she launched an important critique of Adler's practical therapeutic assumptions. Her remarks followed from one emergent component of the opposing Freudian epistemology: the metapsychology of narcissism. Anticipating and elaborating in essential respects Freud's own formulation of "primal narcissism" two years later, Salomé pointed out that the ego could not be credited with the ability to "arrange" sexuality from a detached vantage point given the initial interpenetration of sexual feeling and ego feeling in the prototypical narcissistic union of infancy (p. 68; cf. Freud, 1914b, p. 87).

At this point, Freudian metapsychology became infused with a philosophical imperative. For Salomé, narcissism in this initial form was not a stage to be transcended, but "the persistent accompaniment of all our deeper experience." The Adlerian ego of the masculine protest was inadequate in its denial of this vital fusion of ego and libido from which an enriched ego could aspire to its own creative goals (1912–1913, p. 110). In a letter written to Freud two years after these diary entries, Salomé actually proposed the theoretical discrimination between the "primal narcissism" in which sexual and ego energies could not be discriminated, and the ensuing "secondary" narcissism in which the ego consciously chose itself as object. The former embodied a holistic unity of personality rooted "in the deepest naïvete there can be." The latter embodied that split by which the fully formed ego recognized itself as a distinct object to be infused with self-admiration and vanity. She confided to Freud that this distinction, along with the ramifications of the Freudian concept of narcissism in general, constituted the "crux" on which her parting from Adler "really took place," and she proceeded to elaborate the flaws in the Adlerian ego that she had hinted at two years earlier:

> his [Adler's] power instinct is simply narcissism of the second type, the libidinal hypercathexis of the ego. And then it always seemed to me: as long as the concept of narcissism starts out from the priority of the ego, to which the libido is attached, one cannot allow Adler the right to assess the whole matter from the standpoint of the ego—as if the libido was something in the possession of the ego, which it can turn, utilize, adjust to its ego-aims as it likes [*Freud/Andreas-Salomé Letters*, pp. 23–24; cf. Andreas-Salomé, 1912–1913, p. 110].[10]

The point is telling, and it is one that Adler never directly confronted. To the extent that the ego was "eroticized" as a result of the initial condition of consciousness from which it was differentiated, Salomé was right to question the extent to which the ego could be credited with the ability to "arrange" a libido in which it had only a tactical interest. Indeed, once the libidinal infusion was incorporated into the developmental history of the ego, the adequacy of a strictly

---

[10]Binion (1968, pp. 340ff.) discourses at length on Salomé's personal affinity to "primal narcissism."

two-dimensional masculine protest as the embodiment of the ego's developmental mission was in serious jeopardy.

Salomé's critique of the Adlerian position incorporated a final point, one articulated from both epistemological and empirical premises. This part of the critique focused on the meaningfulness of Adler's organ concept, labeling it "his leap from the psychological into another realm of knowledge requiring other methods." In contrast to this means of representation, she opted once more for the Freudian conception of narcissism, holding that this idea provided an intrapsychic explanation of one's cathectic bearing to one's own body parts in a way that "hold[s] fast to psychology's right to its own media and methods." She reiterated this judgment after her farewell to Adler on 21 March 1913, adding that the futile attempt to discover a localized organic basis for psychic life was the "intellectual blind alley" that negated the useful idea of a psycho-physical parallelism. The point at issue was not the admissibility, but the therapeutic sterility, of Adler's governing assumptions. Organ feeling was "outside the reach of any psychological consideration." Even if the organic basis of psychic life was demonstrable, moreover, "it would not be for our eyes to see, since they would find it only the last refuge of the incomprehensible." This reservation was not merely conjectural; it proceeded from her conclusion about the limited extent to which clinical practice bore out Adler's assumptions. She admired the original organ inferiority study for its elucidation of the overcompensatory potential of blatantly "inferior" organs, but she felt from the beginning that Adler's work failed to bind "specific psychic events" to "specific organic defects" (1912–1913, pp. 111, 127, 138). She never disputed that the "somatic foundations of neuroses" existed; she merely contended that "no one knows anything about them." The futility of pursuing the matter, she added, stemmed from the "fundamentally philosophical" character of the distinction. By definition, we understand "physical" in the eliminative sense of that which is not psychically accessible. It is consequently self-explanatory "that the bodily processes equivalent to mental processes are hidden from use" (p. 54).

III.

Salomé's sweeping critique of Adler's theoretical and clinical premises, though generally persuasive, is not immune to criticism itself, and it is not offered here as a definitive "Freudian" statement on *The Nervous Character*. In terms of her serious reservations about the clinical meaningfulness of "organ feelings," for example, one could point to subsequent work that implicitly supports Adler's imputed relationship between "specific psychic events" and "specific organic defects" for one particular class of neuroses. In the case of classical "conversion" neuroses, the shape of a psychic event can indeed be determined by a specific organic defect; the defect takes the form of an organically predisposed organ that attracts the "stream of [psychic] impulses" (Schilder, 1950, p. 179). Thus observed Paul Schilder in his classic psychoanalytic study of *The Image and Appearance of the Human Body*. Schilder added that the question of "the choice of the organ" in conversion phenomena could indeed "justify an organic theory of the neurosis" and lead one to "consider especially the individuality of the organ in which the neurosis expresses itself." He believed this admission imparted a clearer meaning not only to Freud's concept of "somatic predisposition," but to what "Adler summarized in the rather vague connotation, 'organ inferiority' " (p. 185).

Schilder's para-Adlerian rejoinder to the problem of correlating psychic event with organic defect can be granted without mitigating the significance of Salomé's misgivings, for the point at issue is not the adequacy of her specific objections but the level of discourse embodied in her overall critique. Despite Adler's central role in the debates of the Vienna Psychoanalytic Society through 1911, his theories received scant attention in the psychoanalytic literature. Apart from Reitler's (1911) limited clinical assessment of the masculine protest, there are but two narrowly gauged commentaries of any interest: Rosenstein's (1910) perfunctory attempt to evaluate the theory of organ inferiority as an organic basis of the neuroses compatible with Freud's work and P. Federn's (1913) passing consideration of Adler's theory of aggression in his psychoanalytic exposition of sadism. Salomé, alone among the analysts, was not content to fragment Adler's work in order to criticize it. Instead, she integrated the complementary components of the emergent Adlerian system into a comprehensive epistemological framework, and she addressed herself to the theoretical and clinical limitations that inhered in the framework itself. In this way, her informal diary reflections not only transcend the restrictive clinical vantage point from which Adler's theories were discussed within the Vienna Psychoanalytic Society; they considerably transcend the limited parameters within which Freud himself would subsequently guage his own disaffection with Adler.

7

Adler in Freud's Circle: IV. The Psychology of Repudiation

It is one of the minor tragedies in the history of psychoanalysis that Freud's own published critique of Adler would never incorporate the substantive issues raised by Lou Andreas-Salomé in her diary entries of 1912–1913. In fact, Freud's critique of Adler never addressed itself to Adlerian psychology at all because Freud never conceded to Adler the stature of a veritable psychological theorist. With Adler, as with Jung, Freud managed to exercise an unwitting "selective inattention" that blinded him to the significance of theoretical divergence until the divergence became tantamount to intolerable incompatibility.[1] When confronted with the overt irreconcilability of his early disciples' work as a theoretical fait accompli, Freud accepted the inevitability of a "split," bitterly disowned the disciple in question, and maligned the character of the disciple in a way that retrospectively colored the quality of the collaboration from the outset.

To illustrate the operation of this sequence of events, and to provide deeper insight into the quality of Freud's critique of Adler, it is useful at this juncture to consider briefly the case of Jung, the Swiss disciple destined to inherit the mantle of the psychoanalytic movement during and immediately following the climax of the Adler episode. Such comparison is helpful because, for Jung, we have extensive correspondence plainly documenting the dynamics of his "discipleship" to Freud. In the case of Jung, moreover, Freud's heightened affective

---

[1] I borrow the expression "selective inattention" from Harry Stack Sullivan (1953, pp. 170, 246–247, 319–320, 374).

investment in a disciple dramatizes in explicit detail certain key expectations that figured in a more muted form in his rapport with Adler.[2]

I.

In his very first letter to Freud of 5 October 1906, Jung heuristically distinguished between Freud's "psychology" and his "sexual theory," submitting that the former was "the essential thing" while the latter involved only "delicate theoretical questions." He took further issue with Freud's claim that the genesis of hysteria relied on "exclusively" sexual factors (*Freud/Jung Letters,* pp. 4–5). In the letters that immediately followed, Jung voiced clear "alarm" at what he termed the "positivism" of Freud's presentation. He questioned, in this respect, whether certain borderline phenomena might be considered more appropriately in terms of "hunger" rather than sex, and he empirically qualified his advocacy of psychoanalysis in a tone that was deferent but explicit:

> If I confine myself to advocating the bare minimum, this is simply because I can advocate only as much as I myself have unquestionably experienced, and that, in comparison with your experience, is naturally very little. I am only beginning to understand many of your formulations and several of them are still beyond me, which does not mean by a long shot that I think you are wrong. I have gradually learnt to be cautious even in disbelief [*Freud/Jung Letters,* letter of 4 December 1906, pp. 10–11].

These theoretical reservations were clearly embodied in Jung's subsequent published endorsements of the psychoanalytic credo. In these papers, Jung de-

---

[2]Analytic commentators on the *Freud/Jung Letters* have perceptively probed the nature of Freud's "heightened affective investment" in Jung. Shengold (1976) and Loewald (1977) have addressed the oedipal dimension of Freud's investment in Jung, elaborating on Freud's contemporary perception of Jung as the "son and heir" who would carry forward the work of psychoanalysis. Gedo (1979a; 1983, Part IV), who has charted the chronology of the Freud/Jung relationship in greater detail, goes beyond the oedipal level of analysis in pointing to the more primitive fantasies of psychic merger with Jung that can be gleaned from Freud's letters. He believes these fantasies persisted until 1910, at which point Freud's expectations toward Jung significantly changed. In the following observations on the Freud/Jung relationship, I am not contesting the importance of exploring the psychological roots of the relationship. I do believe, however, that straightforward historical investigation of the relevant documents—in this case, the *Freud/Jung Letters* and Jung's publications of the time—does yield certain valid sociological conclusions with respect to Freud's *manifest* requirements of his early followers. I restrict myself to this type of sociological commentary on Freud's expectations toward Jung because I believe it represents the level of explanation that is most relevant to the story I am telling: that of Adler and *his* disaffection with Freud and psychoanalysis.

nied the existence of a "cut-and-dried theory of hysteria," challenged the om-
nipresence of the sexual factor, and injected irritating academic qualifications
that would have been anathema to the Freudian "convert" of the time (e.g.,
Jung, 1907, pp. 10, 18).[3] Despite these repeated indications of Jung's theoretical
position, Freud proceeded to designate him his heir apparent with an alacrity and
finality that cannot be objectively explained on the basis of Jung's published
"defenses" of psychoanalysis and his circumscribed research interests. In doing
so, Freud resorted to the wish-fulfilling prophecy that Jung's theoretical timidity
would inevitably yield to the input of additional clinical experience. In a reply to
Jung's first letter in October, 1906, Freud recognized that Jung's appreciation of
his psychology did not extend to all his views on hysteria and sexuality, but he
ventured to hope "that in the course of years you will come much closer to me
than you now think possible." Indeed, Freud proceeded to construe Jung's
substantive reservations about psychoanalysis as a veritable promise "to trust me
for the present in matters where your experience does not enable you to make up
your own mind" (*Freud/Jung Letters*, p. 5; cf. pp. 13, 140).

This wish-fulfilling inception established the keynote of Jung's six-year collaboration with the Freudians. It also represented the supportive and sympathetic
spirit in which Freud responded to Jung's progressive dissatisfaction with the
broadened psychoanalytic conception of sexuality and his gradual commitment
to a redefinition of the "libido" as general psychic energy. In the context of
Freud's supportive reliance on Jung as key ally in the propagation of psychoanalysis, these modifications, as initially communicated to Freud, did not have
the "deviant" status they would retroactively receive after the final split between
the two men had occurred. Indeed, it was precisely because Freud's wishful
adoption of Jung was prematurely effected at such an early stage in their relationship that Jung's empirical reservations could recede into the background for a
time, intellectually acknowledged by Freud but dissociated from his affective
sense of Jung's "chosen-ness."

Freud's prolonged unwillingness to accept Jung's empirical reservations at
doctrinal face value significantly mitigates Jung's own responsibility for the
"split" from Freud that eventuated. Jung hardly considered himself a derelict
Freudian during this period, and in terms of his cautious theoretical development, there is little reason why he should have felt obliged to do so. He had
openly articulated the empirical ground rules governing his loyalty to psychoanalytic doctrine as early as 1906, and in his subsequent work he really produced

---

[3]For additional documentation of this tendency in Jung's "psychoanalytic" writings, see Stepansky (1976, pp. 218–221).

nothing that betrayed them. Given Jung's original working assumption about the limited empirical content of psychoanalytic theory, he never had reason to doubt that his "empirical" modifications followed a sensible evolutionary logic and would ultimately be endorsed by Freud himself (see Stepansky, 1976).

This conclusion applies especially to *Wandlungen und Symbole der Libido* (1911–1912), the momentous study of the symbol-making collective unconscious that ostensibly confirmed Jung's "deviance" from the Freudian viewpoint. In reality, Freud had been an enthusiastic supporter of Jung's psychoanalytic exploration of mythology and archeology from the summer of 1909 onward, and in the spring of 1911 he fully endorsed Jung's developing preoccupation with the psychology of the occult.[4] When Jung saw fit to reformulate Freud's libido concept in terms of universal "psychic energy," he did not view the expanded field of application of libido as a dramatic "break" from Freud. Instead, he saw it as an evolutionary theoretical development anticipated in Freud's own writings. It is noteworthy, in this connection, that Jung's demonstration of the sense in which a psychogenic "withdrawal from reality" could not be equated with a withdrawal of "libidinal interest" in the narrow psychoanalytic sense relied not only on his own clinical investigation of dementia praecox, but on Freud's analysis of paranoia in the Schreber case history (Stepansky, 1976, pp. 221–226.

In a more muted form, the chronology of Freud's changing estimation of Jung pertains to Adler as well. Up to the point of Adler's culminating presentations before the Vienna Society in the winter of 1911, Freud's decided inclination was to depreciate the significance of Adler's ideas as *psychological* alternatives to psychoanalytic formulations. He accomplished this by appraising these ideas as the fruits of a "biology" that was at best complementary, and at worst irrelevant, to psychoanalysis. This perspective was already embodied in the limited basis of Freud's favorable attitude toward Adler's *Study of Organ Inferiority* of 1907. Here Freud was content to evaluate as a complementary attempt to provide the "organic substrate" of the neuroses a work that explicitly redefined the very concept of the neurotic symptom from the standpoint of the "childhood defects" (*Kinderfehler*) deriving from inferior organs (cf. Rosenstein [1910], which is in the spirit of Freud's original positive verdict on Adler). More specifically, Freud was selectively inattentive to the theoretical import of Adler's important chapter on "The Part Played by the Central Nervous System in the Theory of Organ Inferiority." Here, we may recall, the theory of organ inferiority was invoked

---

[4]See Freud to Jung, 12 May 1911: "I am aware that you are driven by innermost inclination to the study of the occult and I am sure you will return home richly laden. I cannot argue with that, it is always right to go where your impulses lead" (*Freud/Jung Letters*, p. 422).

not simply as a "substrate," but as the basis for a dynamic explanation of psychopathology qua psychopathology.

In the ensuing years of collaboration, Freud's original reaction to the theory of organ inferiority became the governing precedent. As Adler's presentations before the Vienna Society made increasingly explicit his commitment to a developmental system of psychopathology that merely used the theory of organ inferiority as one conceptual starting point, Freud's repeated response was to fall back on the organic substrate of the Adlerian psychology as a mitigating factor that forestalled detailed consideration of the psychology on its own explanatory terms. As we earlier demonstrated (chapter 5), Freud did not really consider the adequacy of Adler's biology as a basis for psychology; he merely invoked the biology to escape the need to inspect the psychology from the standpoint of Adler's own internal presuppositions. The more Adler talked psychology, the more Freud was content to dismiss it as biology. In the process, Freud not only maintained clinical distance from Adler's formulations, but retained his conviction that Adler's "biology," a bypath based on relatively inessential assumptions, would not preclude eventual acceptance of Freud's psychoanalysis by Adler himself. Thus with Adler, as with Jung, the avowed need to retain a disciple for the sake of the movement, even when the theoretical grounds of discipleship were in question, was long in evidence.

In considering Adler's participation in the discussions of the Vienna Society (chapter 4), we charted in some detail the series of adroit political maneuvers by which Freud sought to retain Adler's affiliation with institutional psychoanalysis. The mentality that informed these maneuvers was plainly broached to Jung shortly after Adler's "Oneness of the Neuroses" presentation of 12 June 1909. Freud, we recall, expressed open dissatisfaction at the time that Adler was concentrating on the "biological aspect" and bemoaned his inability to participate "as we should like him to." He qualified the import of these criticisms, however, by adding that Adler was to be retained "as long as possible." It was this latter commitment that induced Freud to cede the presidency of the Vienna Society to Adler after affronting his Viennese following by naming Jung his political successor at the Nuremberg Congress of 1910[5]; it was this same political intent that led Freud to urge Jung to accommodate Adler's post-Nuremberg

---

[5]Freud's political motivation was quite transparent in the supercilious tone in which he related this nominal transfer of power to Jung: "At last Wednesday's meeting of our Society I ceded the presidency to Adler. They all behaved very affectionately, so I promised to stay on as chairman of the scientific sessions. They are very much shaken, and for the present I am satisfied with the outcome of my statesmanship. . . . The Viennese have no manners, but they know a good deal and can still do good work for the movement" (*Freud/Jung Letters*, letter of 12 April 1910, p. 306).

attempt to implement the formal registration of the Vienna Society with the local public authorities. In the telling letter to Jung of 19 June 1910, Freud pronounced Adler "hypersensitive and deeply embittered because I consistently reject his theories." But he added that if Jung would only accommodate Adler's administrative requests, "then the entire difference is formal and meaningless" (*Freud/Jung Letters*, p. 331).

". . . then the entire difference is formal and meaningless." This was Freud's verdict on the potential implications of Adler's theories for his continuing affiliation with the psychoanalytic movement. This self-conscious attempt to retain Adler's institutional affiliation came in the middle of 1910, following the publication of "The Neurotic Disposition" (1909b), "Defiance and Obedience" (1910a), and the other clinical papers that are integral to the psychological theory of *The Nervous Character* (1912a & b). It followed Freud's candid realization that he "consistently rejected" Adler's theories. It is indeed a striking insight that even at this late date, the governing priority remained the nominal unity of the psychoanalytic movement and the concomitant need to avoid a secession at any cost.

The net impact of Freud's selective inattention to the significance of theoretical divergence thus showed itself to be double-edged. It not only forestalled serious consideration and refutation of a dissenting viewpoint during the period when it was formulated; it simultaneously justified tactical compromises to prevent a damaging secession by minimizing the import of the dissenting viewpoint within the psychoanalytic circle. Thus, at the same time as Freud was inattentive to the apparent incompatibility of Adler's theories with those of psychoanalysis, the very nature of this doctrinal inattentiveness sensitized him to the existence and seeming inappropriateness of Adler's personal discontent. "Adler is hypersensitive and deeply embittered because I consistently reject his theories." The implication, in the summer of 1910, was that Adler's disappointment was cumulative, that he reacted to every successive negative evaluation of his theories as a new and unexpected defeat from his colleagues. Freud might have mitigated Adler's bitterness by frankly confessing to him the irreconcilability, or at least the irrelevance, of the Adlerian perspective for the work of psychoanalysis. Instead, he made Adler president of the Vienna Society as a conciliatory gesture and disguised his theoretical appraisal of Adler's work by urging Jung to support the administrative initiatives Adler was undertaking. When, by the fall of 1910, it became clear that tactical compromises to facilitate Adler's activities as president of the Vienna Society would not soften his outspoken advocacy of his theories, Freud reverted to a subjective appraisal of Adler's personal discontent to rationalize Adler's ongoing refusal to cede interpretive priority to psychoanalytic formulations. In this way, he finally came to broach the only admissible standpoint from which Adler's split from the movement was to be contemplated. Adler was henceforth a "paranoid," and his theories were "almost unintelligible," or intelligible only to the degree that they put "new names" on Freud's own ideas. In this vein, Freud wrote Jung that

> Adler is a very decent and highly intelligent man, but he is paranoid; in the *Zentralblatt* he puts so much stress on his almost unintelligible theories that the readers must be utterly confused. He is always claiming priority, putting new names on everything, complaining that he is disappearing under my shadow, and forcing me into the unwelcome role of the aging despot who prevents young men from getting ahead. They [Adler and Stekel] are also rude to me personally, and I'd gladly get rid of them both. But it won't be possible. . . . They don't want a break and they can't change. And on top of it all, this absurd Viennese local pride and jealousy of you and Zurich! ΨA [psychoanalysis] has really made no change in these people [*Freud/Jung Letters,* letter of 25 November 1910, p. 373].

By the late fall of 1910, then, for Freud at least, the die was finally cast. But the powerful thrust of the new negative evaluation of Adler and Adler's theories cannot be taken at simple face value. It must be situated in the chronology of Freud's changing estimation of Adler during the preceding three years to be fully understood. As with Jung, so with Adler. Freud's realization that the magnitude of theoretical differences was so great as to preclude fruitful collaboration was just that—a relatively spontaneous ex post facto realization coming long after the full basis for theoretical inrreconcilability had been elaborated. In both cases, as well, Freud's negative judgment followed a long period in which the apparent recognition of serious dissension within his ranks was forestalled alternatively by denial and the recurrent hope that tactical compromises and patient reiteration of the psychoanalytic viewpoint would result in the conversion of the recalcitrant disciple.

In his wishful perspective on Adler's biology as a benign mediator that could be integrated with psychoanalysis, Freud was bolstered by the great faith, initially broached to Jung in the fall of 1906, that repeated clinical exposure to the subject matter and methods of psychoanalysis would ultimately permit a cautious follower to "come much closer to me than you now think possible" (*Freud/Jung Letters,* p. 5). For Adler, however this was never the case, and it can legitimately be questioned, as Adlerians invariably do, whether he was ever a full-fledged "disciple" of Freud's in any meaningful sense of the term. When Freud finally realized that Adler would never relinquish his theoretical perspective in the weeks preceding the culminating Vienna Society presentations of 1911, he disowned Adler with a finality that pejoratively recast the entire course of his past affiliation with psychoanalysis. There never seems to have been an interval when Freud dispassionately reconsidered the import of Adler's theories and concluded with relative intellectual detachment that Adler was not, and never had been, a psychoanalyst. He rather leaped from the wish-fulfilling assumption that Adler's biology was a diverting tributary that would eventually flow into the mainstream of psychoanalysis to the harsh denunciation of Adler that made any further consideration of the psychological outcome of the Adlerian biology unnecessary. With Adler, as with Jung, Freud's final realization of irreconcilable differences was accompanied by a personal judgment so harsh and uncompromising that it made dispassionate refutation of the "deviant" viewpoint irrelevant from that point on.

In both cases, as well, it was a personal judgment that reevaluated the predestined course of collaboration less from the standpoint of discipleship than patienthood. "After the disgraceful defection of Adler, a gifted thinker but a malicious paranoiac, I am now in trouble with our friend, Jung, who apparently has not outgrown his own neurosis" (Hale, 1971, p. 146). Freud wrote these words to the Harvard neurologist James Jackson Putnam in August of 1912, shortly after he perceived the first premonitory signs of Jung's "deviance." It is a telling testimony to the clinical vantage point from which Freud both characterized exdisciples and evaluated incipient deviance among his present followers. However genuine the psychopathology of Adler and Jung may have been, it is a limiting assessment which, in both cases, obscures a complicated chronology of collaboration that seemed ill-fated only in retrospect. For both Adler and Jung, Freud's retrospective equation of discipleship with patienthood thus has a negative consequence: it obscures the crucial sense in which these complicated discipleships provide meaningful commentaries on the social and political history of the early psychoanalytic movement.

II.

There remains the matter of Freud's published evaluation of Adler's theories. If Freud's written critique of Adlerian psychology did not incorporate the epistemological and clinical issues raised in 1913 by Lou Andreas-Salomé, of what did it consist? Basically, Freud's critique took the form of an attempted refutation of the empirical and clinical need to invoke an "aggressive instinct" that he saw as the chief instrumentality of the masculine protest. Ernest Jones, mimicking Freud's interpretive perspective on Adler, has provided the most encapsulated statement of this position. Adler's "whole theory," he has argued, was based on "the aggression arising from the 'masculine protest' " and, in addition, the tendency to compensate for feelings of inferiority was reinforced by an "innate aggressivity." Jones's statement is contained in a retrospective criticism of Adler that embodies the orthodox psychoanalytic attitude toward all his theorizing:

> Adler's view of the neuroses was seen from the side of the ego only and could be described as essentially a misinterpreted picture of the secondary defenses against the repressed and unconscious impulses [1955, p. 131].

Jones's position has long been accepted as the official psychoanalytic verdict on Adler. It is a verdict, however, that does not immediately derive from Freud's own written appraisal of Adler. Rather than confronting Adler as the perspectivistic psychologist of the ego, that is, Freud was repeatedly content to fix on Adler as the misguided theorist of aggression. We shall see that a combination of institutional and psychological factors predisposed Freud to misconstrue the meaning of Adler's "aggressive drive" and subsequently to criticize Adler's theory entirely from the standpoint of this misconception about the status of aggression in Adler's thought. We shall further see how this misconception is embodied in Freud's written critique of Adler, a critique that essentially takes the form of a long polemic on the perils of embracing Adler's forbidding "aggressive drive."

From the standpoint of the history of the psychoanalytic movement, it must first be noted that the real significance of Adler's work is less important than the context in which this work was received and judged by Freud. Adler was the earliest rebel provoking the first schism in the psychoanalytic movement. Freud was subsequently obliged to respond to the Adlerian "threat" in order to insure his prerogative both to equate psychoanalysis with his own theoretical presuppositions and to consolidate his political control over the emergent psychoanalytic movement. And if, as Jones tells us, the response to Adler was really not one of bitterness, it was clearly one of marked analytic condescension fueled by heightened affect. As Freud himself admitted in a letter to Ferenczi, Adler rekindled the constellation of troubled personal feelings that characterized his earlier turbulent relationship with the Berlin physician Wilhelm Fliess; Adler was in fact "a little Fliess come to life again," a degenerate theorist who was "rapidly developing backwards" and would soon end up "denying the existence of the unconscious" (letter of 6 April 1911, quoted in Jones, 1955, p. 130). In the ensuing attempt to repudiate Adler's improperly "psychoanalytic" pretensions, the issue of aggression, removed from its descriptive role within the framework of ego defense, would function as a convenient symbol of divergence and a ready source of written refutation.

There is considerable irony in this recourse to aggression, because the two lengthy presentations that epitomized Adler's disagreement with Freud and marked the termination of his participation in the discussions of the Vienna Psychoanalytic Society not only divorced the masculine protest from the issue of aggressive instinctuality, but proceeded to question the clinical utility of the notion of instinctual drives altogether. We earlier reviewed (chapter 5) how Adler used these presentations to enunciate an ego psychology reactively predicated on the growing child's need to "safeguard" himself against early experiences of insecurity. Such experiences stemmed from the helpless state of infancy, but were abetted by educational mistakes and a lack of affective concern on the part of the adult environment. As such, there are striking similarities between Adler's presentations of 1911 and the developmental systems of later theorists like Karen Horney and Harry Stack Sullivan. Sullivan's "self-system," for example, the "organization of educative experience" that strives to avoid incidents of anxiety, is rooted in the interpersonal encounter of infant and "anxious" mother (1953, pp. 73–75, 165–166). Comparably, Horney's view of the neurotic process as an (overcompensatory) quest for self-idealization is predicated on a notion of "basic anxiety" that is entirely reactive: insensitive caretakers "too wrapped up in their own neuroses to be able to love the child" undermine self-development and instill in the child a "profound insecurity and vague apprehensiveness" (1950, p. 18).

In his second summary lecture before the Vienna Society on "Repression and the Masculine Protest," Adler underscored the reactive quality of his psychology by dissociating the masculine protest from the notion of an aggressive instinct in the clearest possible manner. He argued that instinctual gratification depended on social institutions and economic conditions, and that instincts consequently had to be consigned to the status of mere direction-giving means (*richtunggebendes Mittel*) for initiating future satisfactions. Adler thereby countered the psychoanalytic reliance on a theory of instinctual drives with the imputation of classical sociological relativism, and within the framework of nineteenth-century social theory, his argument resonates with Marx's attempt to historicize human needs in *The German Ideology* (1846–1847, pp. 48–49) and Durkheim's attempt to provide a social definition of human needs in his momentous study of suicide (1897). Like these predecessors, Adler implied that we can never benefit from a discussion of instincts qua instincts, inasmuch as their expression is shaped from earliest infancy by the social and economic environment (1911b, pp. 105–106; Ansbacher, pp. 64–66). From the standpoint of this developmental premise,

Adler never proceeded to consider an innately "aggressive" or "cruel" child, but only a child whose healthy drive endowment had been pathologically shaped by defiance (*Trotz*) as a certain kind of direction-giving tendency. Such children received insufficient affection and comfort in their early years, found themselves subject to insecurity and unhappiness, and subsequently resorted to a character style that utilized defiance as a defensive attempt to achieve a degree of masculine mastery over the environment. The aggressive child, in other words, was nothing but the child who used aggression as an interpersonal safeguard (*Sicherung*) (1911b, pp. 106–107; Ansbacher, pp. 66–67).

Adler's thesis in these lectures plainly anticipated the verdict he would formalize shortly thereafter in *The Nervous Character*. In this work, Adler always intended aggression to be understood within the framework of a "psychological field" (cf. Lewin, 1935). The question of aggression was thereby a secondary consideration arising from a substratum of compensatory dynamics and the conditioned inevitability of the quest for superiority. Sadism and hate did not emanate from an "instinct," but represented character traits that aimed at elevating a feeling of worth by degrading others (1912a, pp. 16, 26; 1912b, pp. 19, 44).

From this standpoint, it becomes clear that Adler did not understand aggression as a willful "cruelty impulse" directed toward others, but rather as one coping response addressed to the feeling of inferiority. As such, it attained characterological preeminence only in conjunction with the quest to satisfy organic needs. Whereas the attitude of child to environment was initially "aggressive" in the sense that it constantly opposed the denial of gratification of certain organic functions, the generic quest for superiority in interpersonal relations remained multifaceted and capable of adopting different kinds of characterological masks. In fact, as Adler repeatedly insisted, both the child and the neurotic drew on two opposing strands to reach the situation of imagined superiority. Neurotic superiority hinged not only on activity but on caution as well, and juxtaposed with the control gained by direct expressions of rage, anger, and jealousy were conquests along the lines of "obedience, submissiveness, 'hysterical impressionability,' in order to chain people down through . . . weakness, anxiety, passivity, a need for affection" (1913b, p. 25; Radin, p. 36). The masculine protest, Adler pointed out again and again, could readily appropriate the feminine role to attain its own ends (1912a, pp. 21, 26, 33; 1912b, pp. 32, 43, 58).

Adler delivered his two final presentations to the Vienna Society in January and February, 1911. We have already examined the ensuing vitriolic debate that preoccupied the members for four weeks and culminated in Adler's resignation of his presidency on 22 February 1911. For purposes of the present discussion, one salient feature of this debate should be underscored: Freud's verbal rejection of Adler's theories at the time of these final presentations had nothing to do with the equation of the masculine protest with an aggressive instinct. Freud's general displeasure stemmed from his perception that Adler was talking about the same things as he was, but without designating them by the terms he had already assigned to them. Freud criticized the antisexual tendency in Adler's writings and Adler's tendency to minimize the value of a detailed phenomenology of the different neuroses by arguing for the unity (*Einheit*) of neuroses. To these criticisms, he appended three general reservations: that Adler had contaminated psychoanalysis by subjecting it to biological viewpoints, that he had overestimated the intellectual aspect of the child's early valuation of sex, and that he had represented neurosis only from the standpoint of the ego (Nunberg & Federn, 1974, pp. 145–147). These criticisms established the wide parameters that characterized the ensuing discussion. The resulting dissension crystallized around two broad issues implicit in Adler's developmental approach: the relative explanatory primacy of the libido versus the masculine protest and the relative merits and deficiencies of a theory of neurosis that restricted its purview to the psychology of the ego (Nunberg & Federn, 1974, pp. 102–111; 140–158; 168–177).

The wide-ranging discussions of the Vienna Society are noteworthy precisely because they highlight the paradoxical quality of Freud's subsequent published verdict on Adler. Despite his control of the debate that culminated in Adler's resignation of the Society presidency, Freud was unwilling to formulate his estimate of Adler's role in the history of psychoanalysis in accord with the broad referents that momentarily emerged in the Society discussions. Instead, his published attempts to appraise critically the status of Adler's ego-psychological approach generally faltered and yielded to a distorted reductionism by which Adler symbolized only the "aggression" arising from the masculine protest. Seemingly unconcerned with what aggression actually meant to Adler, Freud disowned him in writing by erroneously attacking the validity of aggression as a separate instinctual aim.

Interestingly enough, the first medium for the repudiation of Adlerian "aggression" was Freud's case history of "Little Hans" (1909). Paradoxically, the analysis of this case constituted, in large measure, an extended discourse on the manifest and latent aggressive dimension of Oedipal rivalry. Beginning with Little Hans' anxious need to be "coaxed" by his mother and subsequent fear of being "bitten" by horses (i.e., by his father), Freud's analysis proceeded to unravel the constellation of intertwined "aggressions" that underlay these anxieties. And although the resolution of Little Hans' phobia ultimately hinged on the resolution of a broader problem, specifically, the child's confused fantasies of birth and copulation, the emergent symptomatology still took as both its starting point and nexus a complementary array of decidedly "aggressive" propensities. Freud made constant reference not only to the conscious and unconscious substratum of hostility Little Hans directed toward his father (pp. 82–82, 90, 111, 123, 131, 134–135, 187), but to the "sadistic" dimension of his quest for his mother (pp. 81, 83, 130, 135) and the hostile death wishes he directed toward his infant sister Hanna (pp. 68–69, 72–73, 113–114, 128). At the time of this case history, Adler had not formally promulgated the masculine protest, but Freud was already skeptical about Adler's formulation in his paper on the aggressive drive (1908) that anxiety itself arose from the suppression of aggression. It was to this Adlerian contention that Freud at once juxtaposed the path that the analysis of Little Hans had taken. At an initial glance, he submitted, the facts of the case history appeared to be remarkably congruent with Adler's theoretic position in the aggression paper:

> As we have come to the conclusion that in our present case of phobia the anxiety is to be explained as being due to the repression of Hans's aggressive propensities (the hostile ones against his father and the sadistic ones against his mother), we seem to have produced a most striking piece of confirmation of Adler's view [p. 140].

Such ostensible agreements, however, belied a crucial conceptual difference. Whereas Adler (as Freud understood him) spoke of a special "aggressive instinct," Freud contended that all instincts were, a priori, "aggressive" in obtaining their ends. In 1915, he would characterize every instinct as a form of activity and would use the word "pressure" (*Drang*) to label offically this motor element, "the amount of force or the measure of the demand for work which it represents" (p. 122). If "aggression" designated a universal attribute of all instincts, it consequently became semantic nonsense to isolate one conceptually self-contained "aggressive instinct."

Freud further added that in the case of Little Hans the facts themselves did not require the assumption of a special aggressive instinct. This was because the libido theory itself posited an "aggressive" component impulse through which the etiology of Little Hans' phobia could be comprehended. In one sweeping statement, Freud thus formulated his rejection of Adler's interpretive position and reasserted his own control over the theoretic underpinnings of psychoanalysis:

> I cannot bring myself to assume the existence of a special aggressive instinct alongside of the familiar instincts of self-preservation and of sex, and on an equal footing with them. It appears to me that Adler has mistakenly promoted into a

special and self-subsisting instinct what is in reality a universal and indispensable attribute of *all* instincts—their instinctual and "pressing" character, what might be described as their capacity for initiating movement. Nothing would then remain of the other instincts but their relation to an aim, for their relation to the means of reaching that aim would have been taken over from them by the "aggressive instinct." In spite of all the uncertainty and obscurity of our theory of instincts I should prefer for the present to adhere to the usual view, which leaves each instinct its own power of becoming aggressive; and I should be inclined to recognize the two instincts which became repressed in Hans as familiar components of the sexual libido [1909, pp. 140–141].

Here, Freud forcefully echoed the response he had made to Adler's aggression paper when it had been presented at the Vienna Society a year earlier. Adler's analysis was right, but his conclusion wrong (or at least unnecessary); what he called the aggressive instinct "is our libido" (Nunberg & Federn, 1962, p. 408). Ironically, Freud's critical rejoinder that all instincts possessed their own "pressing" aggressive impetus captured more of the essential Adlerian position than the allegedly "Adlerian" aggressive instinct to which he juxtaposed it. What, after all, had Adler's 1908 aggressive instinct been if not, in Adler's own words, "a superordinated psychological field connecting the drives" (1908, p. 28; Ansbacher, p. 34), and hence characterizing from the standpoint of "field theory" what Freud called "a universal and indispensable attribute of *all* instincts" (1909, pp. 140–141). What the Freudians caricature as my "aggressive instinct," Adler could well have replied, is not Freud's "libido," but the pathological manifestations of a "defiant" resolution of the masculine protest.

Five years later, the renunciation of what Freud termed Adler's "misleading generalization" would warrant more than a laconic disavowal. In *On the History of the Psychoanalytic Movement* (1914a) it received more extended and emotionally charged treatment that corresponded with the events that had transpired by that time.

Taken together, the breaks with Adler in 1911 and Jung in 1913 shook Freud in a way that transcended the empirical limitations of the rival Adlerian and Jungian systems. However sensitive to the fact of "deviation" in and of itself, moreover, Freud's annoyance in 1914 was exacerbated by the stubborn persistence with which both Adler and Jung continued to call their work "psychoanalysis," causing, as Jones relates, "endless confusion in the minds of those outside the whole field" (1955, p. 362). It was primarily in response to this latter dilemma that Freud wrote his *History,* hoping it would serve as testimony to his continuing personal prerogative to direct the movement that his work had generated. Freud's professed reason for expounding the Adler and Jung episodes was thus limited and ostensibly justifiable:

I am not concerned with the truth that may be contained in the theories which I am rejecting, nor shall I attempt to refute them. . . . I wish merely to show that these theories controvert the fundamental principles of analysis . . . and that for this reason they should not be known by the name of analysis [1914a, pp. 49–50].

During the interval between the case history of Little Hans and the writing of the *History*, however, Freud's ultimate disenchantment with the course of Adler's discipleship was paralleled by the hardening of his subjective appraisal of the Adlerian system as the embodiment of a special "aggressive instinct." As early as 3 December 1910 he protested to Jung that Adler tried "to force the wonderful diversity of psychology into the narrow bed of a single aggressive 'masculine' ego current" and on 1 March 1911, a week after the conclusion of the protracted debate of Adler's theories in the Vienna Society, Freud informed Jung of his personal resumption of the chairmanship of the Vienna group with this proviso: "I now feel that I must avenge the offended goddess Libido, and I mean to be more careful from now on that heresy does not occupy too much space in the *Zentralblatt*" (*Freud/Jung Letters*, pp. 376, 400). Two days later he reiterated to Karl Abraham that

Adler's behaviour was no longer reconcilable with our psychoanalytical interests, he denies the importance of the libido, and traces everything back to aggression. The damaging effects of his publications will not take long to make themselves felt [*Freud/Abraham Letters*, p. 103].

Even more telling than either of these straightforward communications was the more impressionistic rendering of the "split" Freud had sent several days earlier to a more junior colleague, the psychoanalytically informed Swiss pastor Oskar Pfister. On 26 February 1911, only four days after Adler's resignation of the Society presidency, Freud informed Pfister that

Adler's theories were departing too far from the right path, and it was time to make a stand against them. He forgets the saying of the apostle Paul the exact words of which you know better than I: "And I know that ye have not love in you." He has created for himself a world system without love, and I am in the process of carrying out on him the revenge of the offended goddess Libido. I have always made it my principle to be tolerant and not to exercise authority, but in practice it does not always work. It is like cars and pedestrians. When I began going about by car I got just as angry at the carelessness of pedestrians as I used to be at the recklessness of drivers [*Freud/Pfister Letters*, 1963, p. 43].

It was this subjective valuation of Adler as a monistic theorist elevating man's aggressiveness to a new position of primacy that nullified Freud's moderated intent and enabled the critique formulated in his *History of the Psychoanalytic Movement* to branch into a sustained polemic. This polemic, in addition to demonstrating the irreconcilability of Adler's system with psychoanalysis, attempted to undermine the intellectual integrity from which his work had proceeded. Adler, we now learn, with his "particularly speculative disposition" and "striving for a place in the sun," had long resented standing in Freud's shadow, and had attacked him from motives of personal ambition (1914a, pp. 50–51).

In reality, Freud's personal indictment of Adler was strongly colored by the deprecatory psychiatric assessment that, we earlier observed, coincided with the decision in the fall of 1910 to abandon the conciliatory course designed to retain Adler for the movement and that proceeded, from that point in time, to consign Adler's ambition to the status of outright pathology. In the important letter of 25 November 1910 already cited, Freud complained to Jung of Adler's claims of priority, qualifying his plaint with the assertion that Adler was paranoid (*Freud/Jung Letters*, p. 373). In subsequent correspondence with Jung extending through June, 1911, Adler's alleged "paranoia" would function as a veritable leitmotif, one decreasingly circumscribed by any allusion to Adler's decency or intelligence (*Freud/Jung Letters*, pp. 373, 376, 387, 403, 422, 428). Shortly after Adler's resignation of the Society presidency, Freud also confided to Abraham his certainty about Adler's "fine paranoid traits" (*Freud/Abraham Letters*, p. 105), and in the original draft of the *History of the Psychoanalytic Movement* he specifically mentioned Adler's complaints of persecution.[6] Abraham, who read the unpublished manuscript, made the following suggestion:

> There is only one expression which I would like to have changed. You say about Adler how much he complained of your persecution (*Verfolgungen*), and I am afraid this word might cause harm. Adler will protest against being called paranoid. An expression with less pathological implications, such as hostility (*Anfeindungen*), would be preferable [*Freud/Abraham Briefe*, p. 165; *Freud/Abraham Letters*, p. 169].

Freud accepted the criticism, though with apparent misgivings:

> "Persecution" is the term used by Adler himself. I shall replace it in accordance with your suggestion, and instead of the "filthy" spirit (*"unsaubere" Geist*) of A. Hoche I shall insert "evil" spirit (*"bose Geist"*) [*Freud/Abraham Briefe*, pp. 166; *Freud/Abraham Letters*, p. 170].

---

[6]In a letter to Sabina Spielrein of 15 May 1914, Freud provided an explanation for Adler's complaints of persecution: "And your argument that I have not yet sent you any patients? Exactly the same thing happened with Adler, who pronounced himself persecuted because I had sent him no patients" (quoted in Carotenuto, 1982, p. 121).

In the published version of the *History,* Freud did not embellish his pejorative mention of Adler's ambition with the "paranoid" ascription, but he did proceed to make light of Adler's very comprehension of psychoanalysis. We hear that Adler had "never from the first shown any understanding of repression" (1914a, p. 56). His blanket denial of "libidinal trends" in favor of the "egoistic component" contained in them, moreover, was nothing more than a piece of rationalization which, in its unwitting concealment of unconscious motives, resembled dream material that had undergone "secondary elaboration":

> In Adler's case the place of dream-material is taken by the new material obtained through psychoanalytic studies; this is then viewed purely from the standpoint of the ego, reduced to the categories with which the ego is familiar, translated, twisted, and—exactly as happens in dream-formation—is misunderstood [p. 52].

In addition, Adler's now exalted masculine protest, the primary mode of self-preservation (as Freud perceived it), was in reality nothing else "but repression detached from its psychological mechanism and, moreover, sexualized in addition." In the important paper "On Narcissism" written that same year, Freud contended that psychoanalysis had always recognized the existence of a masculine protest, but, unlike Adler, had correctly viewed it "as narcissistic in nature and derived from the castration complex" (1914a, p. 54; 1914b, p. 92).[7]

More crucial for our purposes than the questionable validity of these criticisms was the reductionistic summary statement to which they led. Freud's last word on Adler followed the same law of condensation he discovered in the dream work and echoed his comments to Pfister and Jung three years earlier. From a condemnation of Adler's allegedly uncompromising belief that ultimately "everything alike is pressed into the service of the masculine protest, self-assertion and the aggrandizement of the personality," he offered the verdict that "the Adlerian system is founded exclusively on the aggressive instinct; there is no room in it for love" (1914, pp. 57–58).

III.

From this cross section of published material and personal correspondence, a fairly accurate reconstruction can be made of Freud's motives for rejecting Adler and the aggressive instinct he was made to represent.

---

[7]See the Appendix, "The Hidden Adler in Freud," for a discussion of the considerable extent to which Freud's formulation of "castration anxiety" merely begged the question that Adler raised.

The first explanatory strand, which has already been mentioned, concerns the political significance of Adler's "rebellion" in the context of the psychoanalytic movement itself. Despite Jones's (1955, pp. 127–128) strong protestations of Freud's receptivity to intellectual independence, subsequent research has circumscribed the "sectarian" character of the early development of psychoanalysis and established the resulting sense of urgency Freud attached to his personal direction of the movement (Fromm, 1959; Weisz, 1975; Stepansky, 1976; Sulloway, 1979, pp. 480–483). According to Freud's earliest biographer Fritz Wittels, himself an early participant in the Vienna Society discussions, Freud viewed his pupils as subjects owing "fealty" to him alone, and he sought able people who would merely systematize and amplify his own theoretic suppositions:

> Freud's design in the promotion of these [Wednesday evening] gatherings was to have his own thoughts passed through the filter of other trained intelligences. It did not matter if the intelligences were mediocre. Indeed, he had little desire that these associates should be persons of strong individuality, that they should be critical and ambitious collaborators. The realm of psychoanalysis was his idea and his will, and he welcomed anyone who accepted his views. What he wanted was to look into a kaleidoscope lined with mirrors that would multiply the images he introduced into it [1924, p. 134].[8]

---

[8]The Wittels biography in general, and the passage I have quoted in particular, are, it should be noted, matters of controversy. Eissler (1971, pp. 135–137), in his long refutation of Roazen's study of Freud and Tausk (1969), has challenged the accuracy of the "kaleidoscope" metaphor by referring to the retractions that Wittels himself (1933) subsequently published. Though Wittels did come to regard the book as a "youthful indiscretion," his retraction centered on his earlier attribution to Freud of a despotic "Jehovah complex" (1933, p. 362). This changed estimation of Freud is not, however, tantamount to a retraction of his characterization of the Wednesday evening discussion group, and in fact Wittels never made such a retraction. In modifying his assessment of Freud's personality and teaching following his readmission to Freud's circle, Wittels' basic point seems to have been that, as man and scientist, Freud was fully deserving of the supportive "mirroring" of his early disciples, not that such "mirroring" never occurred. Wittels never recinded his initial characterization of the demands Freud placed upon his disciples; he sought instead to mitigate the authoritarian connotations of these demands by appealing to Freud's own personal modesty and modest expectations as to the fate of psychoanalysis. This seems to be the sense of claims like "among all psychoanalysts, myself included, he [Freud] is perhaps the only one who is not intoxicated with the method [of psychoanalysis] and its results," and "if one speaks of his world renown, he answers not only with the wisdom of Solomon that this is vanity, but he reminds us that many an 'immortal' together with his theories, has been forgotten in an incredibly short time" (p. 363). These claims in turn pave the way for Wittels' verdict that "therefore it now seems to be that it is his disciples who bestow upon him a rank (*ipse dixit*) against which he does not defend himself because it is a matter of indifference to him" (p. 363). In a comparable way, Wittels does not claim that Freud openly tolerated deviation in the Wednesday evening discussion, but now submits that when "because he 'tolerates no deviation from his theory,' I called him a despot, I wronged him" (p. 364).

Moreover, there are other characterizations of the early Wednesday evening discussion group that substantiate Wittels' initial judgment and that come from reliable sources. Eissler does not mention

The most basic element of Freud's leadership involved his summary prerogative to determine the minimal prerequisites of what, by definition, constituted psychoanalysis (see Freud, 1914a, p. 16). By presenting a system of ego psychology that minimized several principal constituents of the theoretical structure of psychoanalysis, Adler clearly placed himself beyond the pale of even "healthy" dissent. Lou Andreas-Salomé, Adler's erstwhile friend and critic, accurately assessed his situation in the fall of 1912. Between Adler's "rationalis-

---

these sources, and it is perhaps important to cite them here in support of my acceptance of the Wittels passage in question. I am referring to Helene Deutsch (1940), who wrote that "Freud's need for an assentient echo from the outer world expresses itself particularly in his relationship to his first small group of pupils. In the fervor of his work, in the overcoming of his own doubts which he expresses so often and with such humility in his writings, he had to have peace in his scientific house. His pupils were to be above all passive understanding listeners; no 'yes men' but projection objects through whom he reviewed—sometimes to correct or to retract them—his own ideas. . . .

"As an inspired pathfinder he felt justified in regarding his co-workers as a means towards his own impersonal objective accomplishment; and with this end in mind, probably every impulse towards originality, when it subserved other than *objective* purposes, annoyed him and made him impatient. Freud was too far ahead of his time to leave much room for anything really new in his own generation. It seems to be characteristic of every discoverer of genius that his influence on contemporary thought is not only fructifying but inhibitory as well" (pp. 188–189, 191).

In addition to Deutsch's observations, we have the important reminiscences of Max Graf (1942). Graf, himself an early member of the Wednesday evening circle, subsequently left Freud but remained on good terms with him. He has recounted that at the early meetings "there was an atmosphere of the foundation of a religion in that room. Freud himself was its new prophet who made the theretofore prevailing methods of psychological investigation appear superficial. Freud's pupils—all inspired and convinced—were his apostles" (p. 471). Graf also felt that "good hearted and considerate though he was in private life, Freud was hard and relentless in the presentation of his ideas. When the question of his science came up, he would break with his most intimate and reliable friends. If we do consider him as a founder of a religion, we may think of him as a Moses full of wrath and unmoved by prayers, a Moses like the one Michael Angelo brought to life out of stone" (p. 472).

I quote the Wittels passage and these corroborative perceptions not to make any general claim about Freud's alleged "authoritarianism" but merely to indicate that the institutional history of the psychoanalytic movement does provide an important basis for understanding Freud's unwillingness to consider fully Adler's theories at the time they were formulated. In this respect, I would supplement Waelder's (1963) formulation that the whole reality behind the charge of Freud's authoritarianism actually boils down to the fact that "Freud was tolerant of his disciple's opinions but did not surrender his own views to him" (p. 636) by adding that Freud's "inner-directed" refusal to surrender to the influence of others could in the case of Adler—and I would argue for Jung as well— obstruct full comprehension of what the dissenting disciple was actually saying. This perspective does not deny that Freud had every reason for passing judgment on who could be a psychoanalyst, for, as Waelder observed, "it is not outlandish for the man who invented and named a thing to request the right to inspect the products offered by others under this name, and to judge whether they are correctly so labeled" (p. 633). It does suggest, however, that selective inattention to the complete theoretical grounds for deviance may be an unfortunate by-product of this justifiable prerogative, and it seems that just this kind of selective inattention typifies Freud's cursory written refutation of Adler's theories.

tic milieu therapy'' and his doctrine of organ inferiority based on physiology, she observed, ''the Freudian Ucs. falls to the ground—as it were between bodily defects and the formation of ideals'' (1912–1913, p. 42).

Salomé's verdict was accurate, and it reasonably abstained from any pejorative psychoanalytic commentary on the motives impelling Adler to theorize in his own way. Freud would hardly do as much. In his *Autobiographical Study* of 1925, he would relate the strength of both Adler's and Jung's movements not to their content, but to the temptation they presented of escaping the ''repellent'' findings of psychoanalysis without rejecting its ''actual material'' (1925a, p. 52). The assumption, forthrightly made by Jones, was that the competing systems formulated by dissenting analysts could not represent viable intellectual differences so much as ''lost insight'' to ''repellent'' findings generated by ''the recurring wave of resistance'' (1955, pp. 126–128). By 1925, Freud felt that Adler had

> entirely repudiated the importance of sexuality, traced back the formation both of character and of the neuroses solely to men's desire for power and to their need to compensate for their constitutional inferiorities, and threw all the psychological discoveries of psychoanalysis to the winds [p. 53].

In the attempt to repudiate Adler at the time his ''deviance'' first became clear, the issue of aggression was appropriated for several reasons. The first concerns its vulnerability to attack. The notion of instinctual aggression clearly existed outside the theoretical structure of psychoanalysis and, at the same time, could easily be subsumed by that structure. Freud, that is, could always explain clinically significant aggression in terms of the anal-sadistic organization and ''aggressive'' component instinct provided by the libido theory (see, e.g., Freud, 1911, 1918). The idea of aggressive instinctuality was thus operationally proximate to the observations of psychoanalytic theory, but conceptually distinguishable from the governing psychoanalytic assumptions. The issue of aggression was noteworthy, then, because it provided Freud with a judgmental latitude that could encompass his changing evaluation of Adler's relation to psychoanalysis.

Until the fall of 1910, the concentration on the issue of aggression permitted Freud to remain generally supportive of Adler's status within the movement; he was content with the knowledge that Adler had made valuable clinical observations conforming to those provided by psychoanalytic theory, with the terminological reservation that what Adler called the aggressive instinct ''is our libido.'' Freud could remain hopeful that Adler would eventually accept the orthodox psychoanalytic interpretation of aggression, however, as long as his clinical observation base was equivalent to that which supported the parallel psychoanalytic interpretations. Once Freud altered his prognosis of Adler's potential reconciliation with psychoanalysis, he simply shifted emphasis: the terminological difference was henceforth construed at the level of conceptualization. The principal issue was no longer the compatibility of Adler's clinical observations with those of psychoanalysis, but the conceptual disparity between Adler's interpretation of the facts of aggression and the interpretation provided by the psychoanalytic theory of sexual and ego instincts. From this new perspective, there simply was no *need* to speak of "aggression" apart from the "impulsive" energic quality intrinsic to all instincts, and Adler was theoretically misguided (and not merely terminologically eccentric) in his attempt to recast the "aggression" of instinctual behavior in any other way.

This negative evaluation further shades into the adjunct criticism that Adler's unorthodox perspective on aggression was tantamount to a denial of the explanatory primacy of the libido. Although Adler had consistently maintained since 1909 that libidinal expressions were "arranged," it was only after the 1911 lectures to the Vienna Society that Freud became retrospectively alerted to the catastrophic implications of this viewpoint for Adler's continued role in the movement. The plaint, from this time onward, was no longer that Adler's theories selectively focused on the attitude of the ego in opposition to the libido (*Freud/Jung Letters,* letter of 19 December 1909, pp. 277–278); it was rather that Adler's refusal to analyze the "aggressive" attitude of the ego itself from the standpoint of psychoanalytic instinct theory was tantamount to a denial of the importance of the libido in toto. This position, from the vantage point of Freud's changed estimation of Adler's importance to the movement, was henceforth construed as theoretically intolerable. "Even though our common ground is in the exercise of the method," Freud wrote Ludwig Binswanger on 5 March 1911, "the truth is that what unites us against the world is our conviction of the importance of the libido, from which view Adler has moved very far away" (letter of 5 March 1911, quoted in Binswanger, 1957, p. 30).

The point to be stressed here is that this judgment was a retrospective commentary following Adler's departure from the movement. The criticism could just as easily have been made on the basis of Adler's organ inferiority monograph of 1907. Yet, it was only after Adler's concluding presentations of 1911 that his dubious status as psychoanalyst became plainly incompatible with the sectarian requirements of a psychoanalytic movement that had to maintain a unified front "against the world" (see Weisz, 1975). Consequently, it was only at this time that Freud expressed to Jung his concern lest Adler's concentration on the masculine ego current and minimization of the sexual drive provide the opponents of analysis with damaging ammunition (*Freud/Jung Letters*, letters of 3 December 1910 and 25 March 1911, pp. 376, 409).

There is a second broad consideration involved in Freud's appropriation of the issue of aggression in repudiating Adler's work; it is the question of convenience. Despite his hasty synopsis of Adler's theory in *On the History of the Psychoanalytic Movement* and his repeated rationalization of the phenomena of the masculine protest whenever it appeared in his clinical work (e.g., 1911, p. 42; cf. 1914b, p. 92), Freud's published material never addressed the epistemological issues that Lou Andreas-Salomé had raised, and the analytic quality of his written critique hardly confirms Jones's contention that he took Adler's ideas "very seriously and discussed their possibilities at length" (1955, p. 132). More telling, and certainly from the Adlerian perspective closer to the truth, was Adler's plaint to Salomé during the summer of 1913:

> My position with respect to Freud's school has alas never had to reckon with its scientific arguments. All I ever see, all my friends ever see, is a busy-busy grabbing and pilfering and all the learned shenanigans of the kind Mach mentions in his *Analysis*. Why is it that that school attempts to treat our views as common property, whereas we have always insisted on the errors of *their* opinions? [letter of 16 August 1913, quoted in Andreas-Salomé, 1912–1913, p. 160].

Given this context and given Freud's enormous emotional investment in his leadership of the Vienna Society, it seems likely that, at least for purposes of written refutation, his reading of Adler was highly inaccurate and his appreciation of Adler's findings purposefully rudimentary. Only through such an intentionally vague sense of what the masculine protest was and what part it played in a system of ego psychology, that is, could Freud allow himself to associate Adler with nothing more than a mundane "aggressive instinct." This was hardly a fair association, however, for as a clinician Adler was not concerned with aggression per se, but with the general question of neurotic superiority and the entire gamut of active and passive means through which interpersonal control could be achieved. He designated the psyche simply "a name for the *life-potentiality of an inferior creature*," whereas the "aggressive instinct" that strove to realize this potentiality was no more than "the tendency toward expansion, and a reaching out for that which is more highly valued culturally—the male" (letter of 16 August 1913, quoted in Andreas-Salomé, 1912–1913, p. 161, emphasis in the original). It was simply not convenient for Freud consistently to underscore this distinction.

Yet, from the letters written to Jung, Abraham, and Pfister, it is clear that the political motives for attacking Adler through the issue of aggression coalesced and interacted with a more subjective personal reaction to the very possibility of aggressive instinctuality. Sixteen years after the attack on Adler in the *History of the Psychoanalytic Movement,* Freud admitted in *Civilization and its Discontents* (1930) the emotional resistance he originally displayed toward the existence of an aggressive instinct:

> I remember my own defensive attitude when the idea of an instinct of destruction first emerged in psychoanalytic literature, and how long it took before I became receptive to it [p. 120].

Clearly, Freud's emotional resistance was most dramatically exemplified in his reaction to Adler. Although receptive to the conception of sadism as one component instinct of sexuality ultimately subordinated to genitality, to a "cruelty impulse" that was harmlessly manifested in childhood, and to the existence of unconscious death wishes operative in dream life, Freud was apparently unable at this time to accept psychologically the ramifications of an aggressive instinct that was operationally "adult." This partly accounts for the vituperation that colored his account of the Adler episode in the *History.* Freud himself owned up to his hostile intent in a letter to Salomé (*Freud/Andreas-Salomé Letters,* letter of 29 June 1914, pp. 17–18), and even so loyal a defender as Jones admits that the last section of the essay "contains a few personal expressions that had been aroused by some painful experiences at the time" (1955, p. 363). What Freud's correspondence intimates, however, is that the "painful experiences" associated with this episode were directly related to the *content* of Adler's system. In creating a world system that was allegedly "without love," Adler had sinned against an "offended goddess Libido" to whom Freud revealed a relationship that clearly went beyond the clinical.

What was the source of this emotional reaction? Although the question cannot be answered definitively, an important hint is embodied in Freud's own perception of the affair: Adler was "a little Fliess come to life again" and, hence, probably evoked the same conflicted misgivings Freud felt toward his former confidant of the 1890s. That Freud should have perceived Adler in this way is hardly surprising, given the manifest similarities between Fliess's "sexual biology" (see Sulloway, 1979, pp. 135ff.) and certain essential aspects of Adler's ego psychology. Adler not only shared Fliess's belief in the essential bisexuality of all human beings (which he recast as a "psychic hermaphroditism"), but followed Fliess in embracing a sexualized theory of repression organized around the fact of bisexuality. It was Fliess, as Freud himself later recorded, who preceded Adler in propounding the notion that "The dominant sex of the person, that which is the more strongly developed, has repressed the mental representation of the subordinated sex into the unconscious. Therefore the nucleus of the unconscious (that is to say, the repressed) is in each human being that side of him which belongs to the opposite sex.'' Adler's later variant of this theory, Freud continued, was in agreement with Fliess's ''insofar as it too represents the struggle between the two sexes as being the decisive cause of repression'' (1919, pp. 200–201). In fact, Adler seemed to realize as much. In his paper of 1910 on ''Psychic Hermaphroditism in Life and in Neurosis,'' he acknowledged Fliess as the researcher who anticipated him in demonstrating that the male neurotic suppressed his feminine characteristics, the female neurotic her masculine characteristics (1910b, p. 74). In the *Zentralblatt* article on ''Syphilophobia'' of the same year, Fliess, along with Moebius and Weininger, is given credit for the ''scientific utilization'' of the struggle against the opposite sex in the psychology of the neuroses (1910e, pp. 403–404; Radin, p. 158). As late as 1918, in a lengthy review of Fliess's *Das Jahr im Lebendigen* written for the Berlin newspaper *Vossische Zeitung,* Adler even undertook a striking defense of the scientific admissibility of Fliess's research into human periodicity.[9]

---

[9]In this intriguing review, Adler is actually skeptical about certain of Fliess's periodical constructions. With respect to Fliess's contention about the periodicity of death dates within a given family tree, for example, Adler observes that a ''mathematical talent'' like Fliess's could find the same periodical expiration (*Ablauf*) in the dates of utterly unrelated men. He indicates at several points in the review that the nervous patients whom he has encountered *make* periodic connections responsible for all their sensations in order to disclaim any responsibility for them. In fact, Adler suggests, ''Fliess's exact method cannot give us any final proofs. Its adherents possess a greater amount of faith; its opponents a greater amount of skepticism'' (1981b, p. 2, col. 3). What Adler does defend, however, is the scientific credibility—and importance—of Fliess's undertaking:

''The silence of the exact, scientific schools in relation to [Fliess's] publications is not merely to be understood in terms of the generally known seclusion of professors and their disciples from nevertheless striking research. In the case of [their silence about] Fliess, it is provocatively loathesome that the official representatives of scholarship stand as though in a secret society which automatically blocks the door to gifted researchers. Fliess has his own original field of research; he does not work intuitively [and] concerns himself only with the demonstrative power of numbers. He attacks old teaching only in nonessential matters, [and] sets out trains of thought which, in the teaching of undulation (*Wellenbewegung*) in the life of woman, [and] in the old idea of masculine and feminine substance in men, have become scholarly common property. [Fliess's acceptance by others] is revealed by the generally practiced hushing-up tactic as well as by scholarly pillaging, [and by the fact that] in each of his books he has to take a position against conscious falsifications of his thoughts and against plagiarism. If he had not been excluded from the necessary stream of critical examination by an artificial isolation, [and] if a clarification of his positions had [as a result of scholarly contact] long since ensued, Fliess himself would have been able to set aside, in a fruitful exchange, the untenable parts [of his doctrines]. No living scholar works in a more exact way than he. Does [the] exact scholarship [of other scholars] fear its own exactness [in Fliess's work]? The reception of Fliessian thoughts, or their transformation, can be readily confirmed not only in Swoboda's *Periodenschieber* and in Weininger's *Hermaphroditismus,* but also in Freud's *Sexualphantomen* and Eicknack's [sp?] black magic (*Schwarzkunst*) and that of his adherents and those preceding him who could make little women out of little men, and vice versa'' (p. 2, col. 6).

It has fallen to Frank Sulloway (1979) to demonstrate "just how extensively Fliess's notion of bisexuality served to link Freud's psychoanalytic conception of human development to the biological theory championed by Fliess" (p. 182). He has stressed, in this connection, Freud's integral reliance on Fliess's theory of bisexuality in arriving at key constituents of the psychoanalytic theory of neurosis. Beyond its general contribution to Freud's understanding of repression, Fleiss's theory of bisexuality was significantly implicated in Freud's developmental theory of erotogenic zones (p. 197), in his ongoing attempts to resolve the problem of the choice of neurosis (p. 203), and, finally, in his conception of the relationship between perversions and neurotic symptoms (pp. 183–184). Yet at the same time as Fliess's bisexuality theory constituted a vital substratum of Freud's early psychological theorizing, it was the same issue of bisexuality that would become fatally implicated in the demise of his intellectual partnership with Fliess (see Mahony, 1979 and Swales, 1982). By the turn of the century, Sulloway recounts, the very theory of bisexuality that so fundamentally informed Freud's theorizing during the late 1890s offered a serious threat to his "quest for an independent psychoanalytic science of mind" (1979, pp. 222–223).[10]

And what of Adler, the "little Fliess come to life again"? In Freud's early endorsement of his organ theory of inferiority as a valuable attempt to elucidate the organic basis of neurosis, we see a clear echo of his prior eagerness to construe Fliess's bisexuality theory and "organological" approach to sexual function (Sulloway, 1979, pp. 173–175) as the infrastructure of his own science of mind. In Freud's subsequent unwillingness to cede priority to Adler's formulation of neurotic conflict in terms of "psychic hermaphroditism" in 1910 (see above, chapter 4, pp. 97–99), we see a clear echo of his unwillingness a decade earlier to cede priority to Fliess in the application of the bisexuality theory to the psyche (Sulloway, 1979, pp. 222ff.).[11] Little wonder, then, that Freud not

---

[10]Mahony (1979, pp. 78–89) and Swales (1982, pp. 6–10), in reviewing the complicated chronology of Freud's perspective on bisexuality in the context of the Fliess affair, have stressed Freud's tortured equivocation in acknowledging Fliess's clear priority in authoring and elaborating the idea. To wit: an ardently enthusiastic Freud listened to Fliess explicate his theory of bisexuality in Nuremberg in the spring of 1897, only to disclaim any interest in the topic in Breslau in the fall of 1897, and only to claim, three months later, that he had in fact arrived at the idea simultaneously with—and, by implication, independently of—Fliess during the very Breslau talks in which he had disclaimed interest (see Swales, 1982, p. 8).

[11]A letter to Ferenczi of 6 October 1910 betrays Freud's continuing preoccupation with the "traumatic" Fliess episode seven months after Adler's "psychic hermaphroditism" presentation before the Vienna Psychoanalytic Society (quoted in Jones, 1955, pp. 83–84). As if to bear out Freud's admission, Mahony (1979, pp. 87–88) has observed that Freud's interest in both Fliess and bisexuality intensified in 1910 and was reflected in his writings of the year: "1910 was a pivotal year with Fliess as a revenant, appearing with da Vinci in the spring, with Schreber from the summer into the winter, and then influencing Freud not to have a Christmas meeting with Bleuler in Innsbruck, associated as it was with 'horrid memories' of a private congress [with Fliess] in 1899."

only made the connection between Fliess and Adler explicit in two letters to Jung, but recognized the crucial affective analogy as well. "It is getting really bad with Adler," he confided to Jung on 3 December 1910. "You see a resemblance to Bleuler; in me he awakens the memory of Fliess, but an octave lower. The same paranoia" *(Freud/Jung Letters,* p. 376). Less than three weeks later he made a more pointed confession:

> I am very glad that you see Adler as I do. The only reason the affair upsets me so much is that it has opened up the wounds of the Fliess affair. It was the same feeling that disturbed the peace I otherwise enjoyed during my work on paranoia; this time I am not sure to what extent I have been able to exclude my own complexes, and shall be glad to accept criticism [p. 382].

A month later, in the midst of the Vienna Society debate on Adler's theories, Freud professed a fuller comprehension of Adler that tempered the affective residue of the Fliess affair: "Now that I understand him fully, I have become master of my affects. I shall treat him gently and temporize, though without hope of success" (p. 387).

In the language used in these three letters to Jung, Freud underscored the importance of the Adler episode in the context of his own continuing self-analysis, with particular reference to the recurring need to master affects associated with the Fliess relationship. What exactly were the recurring affects, the complexes that disturbed Freud's equilibrium during this time and permitted things with Adler to get "really bad"? In *Freud: Living and Dying* (1972), Max Schur has analyzed Freud's own continuing superstitious preoccupations as derivatives of the suppressed "hostile and cruel impulses" emanating from the Fliess episode. To do so, he borrows the analysis of superstition that Freud himself appended to the 1904 (second) edition of *The Psychopathology of Everyday Life:*

> It can be recognized most clearly in neurotics suffering from obsessional thinking or obsessional states—people who are often of high intelligence—that superstition derives from suppressed hostile and cruel impulses. Superstition is in large part the expectation of trouble; and a person who has harboured frequent evil wishes against others, but has been brought up to be good and has therefore repressed such wishes into the unconscious, will be especially ready to expect punishment for his unconscious wickedness in the form of trouble threatening him from without [1901, p. 260; quoted in Schur, 1972, p. 234].

On the basis of close textual analysis and investigation of Freud's correspondence, Schur sees Freud's "guilt" over his hostile wishes toward Fliess and superstitious anticipation of punishment for this "aggression" as operative years after the episode had been formally concluded. Although Freud's obsessive superstitions reached the intensity of a symptom in 1904, the year Fliess attacked him over the bisexuality theory in connection with the publication of Otto Weininger's *Sex and Character,*[12] Schur argues that Freud's preoccupation with the traumatic Fliess affair and the guilt resulting from his aggressive fantasies were still operative as late as 1913 in the analysis of ''neurotic superstitions'' in *Totem and Taboo* (1972, p. 279; cf. pp. 237, 256–257).

That Freud's estrangement from Fliess left in its wake a residue of ongoing hostility is clear beyond doubt. Even before the break, Freud's aggressive feelings toward his intimate companion are charted in a number of dream specimens in *The Interpretation of Dreams,* culminating in the associations surrounding the ''Non Vixit'' dream of 1898 (see Schur, 1972, pp. 153–171 and Stepansky, 1977, pp. 77–80).[13] In the aftermath of the Weininger-Swoboda affair, Freud's hostility toward Fliess intensified; for Sulloway, Freud's ''subsequent references to Fliess and the troublesome notion of bisexuality reveal a lingering animosity over the whole priority dispute'' (1979, p. 229). Moreover, ''Freud's disregard for his old friend's priorities reflected an unmistakable desire for revenge in the wake of Fliess's distressing desertion of both him and his psychoanalytic cause'' (p. 231). As the torch bearer of a Fliessian theory of bisexuality and as a colleague who, like Fliess, refused to cede priority to the psychoanalytic transformation of the bisexual theory of repression into the categories of ''masculine'' libido and ''feminine'' repression, Adler was well-suited indeed to become the target of Freud's animosity toward Fliess.

---

[12]Weininger's study took the form of a speculative philosophical exposition of bisexuality in man. Fliess correctly adduced that Weininger had arrived at his understanding of bisexuality through Hermann Swoboda, a onetime patient and student of Freud's. Fliess proceeded to accuse Freud of indiscreetly making his bisexuality theory available to Swoboda and, subsequently, of reading Weininger's completed manuscript without alerting him to the ''theft'' involved. Freud eventually acknowledged his responsibility for this unauthorized transmission of Fliess's ideas through Swoboda and apologized to Fliess for implicitly handing over his discoveries to Weininger. On the Weininger-Swoboda affair and its aftermath, see Sulloway (1979, pp. 223ff.).

[13]Swales (1982, pp. 12ff.), reconstructing Freud's final ''congress'' with Fliess at Achensee in August, 1900 on the basis of Fliess's reminiscences and Freud's disguised commentary on the meeting in *The Psychopathology of Everyday Life* (1901, pp. 143–144, 210–211), goes so far as to argue that Freud entertained serious fantasies of murdering Fliess at the time. Swales's inference in this respect is highly speculative, to say the least, but he is certainly persuasive in demonstrating the ongoing centrality of the fratricidal theme in Freud's relationship with Fliess. Moreover, Freud himself (1901, pp. 143–144) acknowledged that the Achensee meeting was the scene of a dispute over the priority of authorship of the bisexuality theory and, in particular, revolved around his inability at the time to recall Fliess's revelations about the idea two-and-a-half years earlier at Breslau. Swales reasonably conjectures that after Freud's denial of Fliess's earlier communication on this topic ''all of the animosity latent between the two men must have flared up openly'' (p. 12).

But what does the association between Fliess and Adler suggest about Freud's propensity to reduce Adler's work to a putative "aggressive instinct"? As the first vivid reincarnation of Fliess appearing at a time when the episode was still emotionally charged for Freud, Adler may well have aggravated certain aggressive fantasies that were the continuing legacy of the Fliess episode. From the standpoint of Freud's own psychology, then, it seems not unreasonable to suggest that Freud's summary rejection of Adler's aggressive instinct was associated with the suppression of his own hostility toward Fliess. Seen in this light, Freud's need to disavow Adler's aggressive instinct takes on an added dimension: to embrace the aggressive instinct would compel him to acknowledge the intruding immediacy of his own aggressive fantasies and would, at the same time, exacerbate the guilty superstitious "dread" that accompanied them. To deny the aggressive instinct, on the other hand, was to deny both the aggressive residue of the Fliess episode and the superstitious expectation of punishment that continued to plague him.

IV.

Freud's antipathy toward his first wayward collaborator persisted throughout his life. As late as 1922, he continued to dismiss Adler summarily as the follower too proud to live in the shadow of a giant (Kardiner, 1977, p. 70). When, in May, 1937, his correspondent Arnold Zweig confessed himself "moved" on learning of Adler's death in Scotland, Freud offered the following ungenerous reply: "I don't understand your sympathy for Adler. For a Jew boy out of a Viennese suburb a death in Aberdeen is an unheard-of career in itself and a proof of how far he had got on. The world really rewarded him richly for his service in having contradicted psychoanalysis" (letter of 22 June 1937, quoted in Jones, 1957, p. 208; cf. Eissler, 1971, pp. 299–300). But had Adler actually "contradicted psychoanalysis," or, in any event, contradicted it in the willful sense that Freud implied? Adler himself hardly thought so, at least in the period preceding and immediately following his alleged defection. Consider in this respect his prefatory remarks to Carl Furtmueller's *Psychoanalyse und Ethik* (1912d), the first monograph published under the auspices of his newly formed "Society for Free Psychoanalytic Research." Here Adler was at pains to depict the formation of his group as a necessary development within the psychoanalytic movement; it was predicated, he submitted, on the members' conviction of "the crucial importance of the psychoanalytic method of working and problem-solving orientation." Adler's rationale for the separation from Freud thereby revolved around

the assumption that one could do justice to psychoanalysis as a research procedure only by retaining the prerogative to contradict Freud. In this sense, it was
Freud and not Adler whose demands had become contradictory to the spirit of
free psychoanalytic research:

> The impulse for the founding of the ''Society for Free Psychoanalytic Research''
> came in June, 1911 from several members of the ''Vienna Psychoanalytic Society''
> that was under the direction of Professor Sigmund Freud. These members had
> occasion to point out that it was being undertaken to commit the members of the
> original Society scientifically to the entire range of Freud's assumptions and theo-
> ries. For these members, such a development not only seemed difficult to reconcile
> with the fundamental principles of scientific research, but particularly dangerous
> with a science as young as psychoanalysis. In their opinion, it would further place
> in question the value of the results that had already been achieved if members of the
> Society were prematurely bound to certain formulas and thereby obliged to give up
> the possibility of undertaking research directed toward new solutions [1912d, p.
> iii].

In accord with his conviction of the continuity of his work with a *psychoanalytic*
research tradition, Adler was quick to point out that it was the parent Vienna
Psychoanalytic Society which, in October, 1911, had proscribed joint membership in both groups. As a result, there was presently no connection between his
''Society for Free Psychoanalytic Research'' and the International Psychoanalytic Association. Adler was constrained to offer this clarification

> lest scientific criticism should attribute responsibility for our work to men with
> whom we differ in our conception of the basic preconceptions of free scientific
> work. In the same spirit, we would, for our part, claim the right to be judged only
> on the basis of our own contributions [and not the work of Freud's circle] [1912d,
> p. iii].

Whereas Adler, in accord with the name of his interim body, was intent on
underscoring the issue of *free* scientific work, hindsight suggests that the more
meaningful stress should be accorded his use of the term *scientific*. In protesting
his allegiance to psychoanalysis as a fruitful method of scientific research, Adler
betrayed his continuing unwillingness to accept psychoanalysis on terms that
were acceptable to Freud: as a body of scientific *theories* with explanatory power
adequate to the conceptualization of mental life. Adler mistakenly assumed, in
other words, that psychoanalysis had independent status as a superordinate research tradition that transcended the content of Freud's clinical theories. Here he
was sadly mistaken. In the period we are considering, psychoanalysis did not
entail methodological commitments that transcended the basic content of Freud's

early clinical discoveries; there was no possibility of studying psychopathology from the standpoint of a psychoanalytic "method" that could be dissociated from the content, say, of libido theory and the Oedipus complex.[14]

How could Adler be so misinformed in this respect? Our review of the Minutes indicates that Freud must bear a major share of the responsibility for Adler's ongoing misapprehension. Long appreciative and even admiring of Adler's biological "supplementations" to psychoanalytic theory and, until 1911, heroically discreet in pointing to the psychoanalytic "incompleteness" of Adler's psychological formulations, Freud's studied equivocation toward Adler resulted in what cognitive psychologists term "cognitive dissonance" with respect to the requirements for membership in the psychoanalytic circle. Prior to 1911, the Minutes suggest, Freud was more than willing to let Adler construe his perspectivistic contributions to the weekly meetings of the Society as the basis for an entirely viable adherence to psychoanalysis. It was only in his commentary on Adler's summary lectures of 1911 that Freud gave Adler reason to believe that a theoretically noncommittal identification with psychoanalysis as a research methodology was grossly inadequate to *Freud's* conception of discipleship. Prior to this abrupt disillusionment, Adler had good reason to believe that his dialogue with Freud and, in the context of this dialogue, his "Adlerian" commentary on psychoanalytic formulations, were sufficient basis for the adoption of a nominally psychoanalytic identity. Historically, we can see that Adler was deluded in this belief, but we are also in a position to appreciate the confluence of circumstances that rendered his assumption plausible at the time. On the one hand, we have commented on the degree to which the structure of the early weekly meetings and, in particular, the expectations and assumptions of the leading medical contributors to the discussions, lent credibility to Adler's minimalist notion of psychoanalytic affiliation (see chapter 5, pp. 147–148). But, again, we have also stressed the extent to which Freud's own behavior is systematically implicated in Adler's delusion of affiliation. Specifically, Freud could have enlightened Adler much sooner as to the verdict he began to confide to Jung as early as June, 1909: that Adler's theoretical perspective was inadmissible or, at the very least, irrelevant to the work of psychoanalysis.

Freud's unwillingness to disabuse Adler sooner, I have argued, is largely attributable to extratheoretical considerations that bear on the transformation of psychoanalysis into an organized political movement during the first decade of the century. In fact, Adler was a casualty of extrascientific issues on more than

---

[14]I make this point at greater length in a comparative analysis of Adler and Heinz Kohut as psychoanalytic "dissidents" (Stepansky, 1983).

one score. Lulled into a fallacious psychoanalytic identity by Freud's unwillingness to forego the idiosyncratic input of a Viennese internist who, until the Nuremberg Congress, represented a political asset to the cause, Adler's victimization was compounded by Freud's ultimate proclivity to identify him with Fliess. It is this identification that helps account for Freud's summary dismissal of the content of Adler's theories at the time of the split and, especially, for his persistent reduction of Adler's ego psychology to an ''aggressive instinct'' associated with the masculine protest. Between Freud's politically motivated accommodation of Adler's viewpoint within the Vienna Society discussions and his subsequent antipathy to Adler as a reincarnation of Fliess, we might say, Adler's psychological theories ultimately fell by the wayside. From a strategy of systematic tolerance, Freud proceeded posthaste to the expedient of total repudiation. It fell to Lou Andreas-Salomé, the enigmatic newcomer to the Viennese scene who, for a time, straddled with impunity the Vienna Psychoanalytic Society and the Society for Free Psychoanalytic Research, to offer the penetrating critique of Adler's ego psychology that Freud was constrained to forego.

It is regrettable indeed that we possess no collection of Adler's correspondence able to provide detailed documentation of the vicissitudes of Adler's estimation of Freud. But there can be little doubt that Adler's affiliation with the psychoanalytic movement was *never* tantamount to the profession of discipleship that, by 1910, was a veritable sine qua non for membership in the Vienna Psychoanalytic Society. In the remaining chapters of this study, we shall ratify this verdict by documenting the degree to which the stridently antipsychoanalytic resting place of Adler's later psychological thought revolves around the very assumptions he first articulated during the period of anomalous ''collaboration'' with Freud.

8

The Psychologist as Pedagogue: Adler and the Education of the Child

*To disturb people in order to be the centre of attention is very
cowardly. It is much braver to help other people. Are you brave
enough to try it?*

Alfred Adler
The Pattern of Life (1930b)

I.

In the aftermath of the departure from Freud, and especially in the phase of his career following World War I, pedagogy became the arena for the practical implementation of Adler's therapeutic imperatives. Once more, however, any seeming discontinuity between Adler's applied pedagogy and his earlier status as 'Individual Psychologist' is more apparent than real. The change in the mode of discourse belies the significant continuities that linked Adler's later role as educator and social reformer to his early one as internist and psychiatrist.

The central legacy of Adler's break with Freud, and certainly a central plank of the clinical argument in *The Nervous Character,* was the assumption that psychotherapy was concentrated education. To cure the neurotic, Adler argued, one had to educate him to the maladaptive quality of his style of life, the ''fictional'' quality of his neurotic goals, the needlessly exaggerated quality of his felt inferiorities. In the years following the break with Freud, Adler elaborated the range of these therapeutic assumptions by stressing the reversibility of his equation: if it was true that therapy was education, it was equally true that successful education was therapeutic. Failure at school, conversely, no longer denoted simple intellectual deficiency. It was a testimony, instead, to the student's underlying psychological deficiencies, a sign of psychological failure, an index of maladjustment gauged against the "socially average expectations" of school and environment (1930c, pp. 12–13; cf. 1914a, 485). The ongoing pedagogical challenge was to educate the child to "community feeling"—*Gemeinschaftsgefuehl,* to induce him to accept the desirability and the inevitability of the social ties that bound him to his school environment, and to cultivate in him "useful" (*nuetzliche*) kinds of superiority strivings.[1]

This summary statement of Adler's educational goals established at once the intriguing limitations of his pedagogical approach. As a pedagogue, Adler merely generalized without modifying or supplementing his earliest assumptions about the evaluative significance of child development. These assumptions, implicit in all of Adler's educational writings but explicitly spelled out in an early paper "On Child Psychology and the Study of Neurosis (1913c)," boiled down to the psychological comparability of the childish psyche and the neurotic psyche. Both child and neurotic confronted the environment from the same evaluative standpoint: both felt an exaggerated sense of inferiority, lacked independence, and relied on either helplessness (the child) or illness (the neurotic) to evade social responsibilities and manipulate the immediate familial environment. For Adler, the "adult" neurotic did no more than elaborate in his flawed life style the evaluative significance of childhood. Indeed, just as the circumstances of child development made every child temporarily neurotic, so the circumstances of neurotic development made every neurotic permanently a child (pp. 47–48; Radin, pp. 67–68).

Like his theory of neurosis, then, Adler's pedagogy was no more than a derivative reiteration of his perspective on the child. Educability was basically the positive side of neurotic malleability. The child was educable and susceptible to the moral guidance of the teacher because he felt inferior and was concerned for his future (1914b, p. 40; 1914c, pp. 9–10; Radin, pp. 13–14; cf. 1927a, p. 25; 1927b, p. 35). To the degree that education worked, it taught the child to find the solution to his personal inferiority in *Gemeinschaftsgefuehl* and helped the child channel his compensatory superiority strivings in socially useful directions. The child's entrance into school thus provided a "test" of the adequacy of his previous preparation for social intercourse (1930c, p. 166). As such, the school

---

[1]See *Problems of Neurosis: A Book of Case Histories* (1929a, especially chapters 1 & 9), for Adler's most protracted discourse on "useless" goals of superiority.

injected no new ingredients into the quality or range of the child's psychological goals; it was merely the new social arena where Adlerian assumptions about child development were confirmed and where Individual Psychological corrective measures could be applied.

This much, however, is clear: when Adler turned his therapeutic attention to the school he became, perforce, a social reformer. In calling upon the educator to accept the profound therapeutic potential of his role, Adler passed summary judgment on parents as inept psychologists unable to minimize childhood inferiority and channel the compensatory superiority strivings in useful adaptive directions. In an essay of 1914, he submitted that family life and the nursery were often poorly suited to the demands of community sense (*Gemeinsinn*) (1914a, p. 481), and in *Understanding Human Nature* (1927a & b), he claimed that contemporary education in the family did no more than abet ''the striving for power and the development of vanity.'' He in turn derived this power striving from a ''pathological family egoism'' (*ausartender Familienegoismus*) that, to varying degrees, ''play[ed] the chief role in the home education of today'' (1927a, pp. 226, 49–50; 1927b, pp. 279–280, 64–65). The offshoot of these criticisms rebounded on the educational primacy of the theory of Individual Psychology. ''We must acknowledge that making the majority of parents into good educators would be an endless and hopeless undertaking,'' Adler concluded in 1935. ''So we must turn to the school'' (1935, p. 10).

Adler's optimistic forecast of the positive psychological benefits to be derived from education was the obverse side of his pessimistic prognosis for those children who were deprived of pedagogical direction. Not only did the family fail to provide the educational direction the child needed, but the psychotherapist himself could not improve the situation as long as he confined his efforts to individual therapy. After World War I, the social crux of Adler's broadened therapeutic mission became prophylaxis, and he equated prophylaxis with the education of the educator. It was the teacher who became the new Adlerian disciple par excellence, and it was the teacher who was charged with implementing Individual Psychological imperatives to children on a daily basis. The injunction given to the teacher was the same Adlerian injunction that informed all therapeutic enterprises: correct the child's mistaken estimation of his own deficits, channel the ineluctable superiority strivings into areas of ''useful accomplishment'' that were ''normal'' but seldom obtainable without educational intervention (1930c, pp. 29, 41).

Adler's idea of the ''normal'' child was the ''courageous'' child, the child whose mature self-perception of his deficits did not undercut self-esteem, but rather spurred compensatory action in the direction of socially useful activity. Adler's pedagogic mandate thus revolved around the same relativistic presupposition that informed his perception of neurosis. He flatly rejected the belief that innate mental or emotional deficiencies undercut the child's educative potential. He premised the pedagogic mandate of Individual Psychology on the assumption that, educationally, "no child should be thought hopeless," and he further considered the resigned belief in the inheritance of abilities "perhaps the greatest mistake that is ever made in regard to the education of children" (1930c, pp. 179, 175; also 1914a, p. 477). "No educator who believes in the *educative* value of his work, who believes in education as the training of character," he wrote, "can consistently accept the doctrine of heredity" (1930c, p. 176; cf. p. 97). In his pedagogy, as in his psychotherapy, Adler supplanted heredity and inborn drives with the notion of educational error—*Erziehungsfehler* (1914a, p. 479). He took this extreme position because he steadfastly tied his own concept of "inferiority" to relative social judgments and simultaneously refused to attach it to any self-explanatory medical referent.

This is an important point to bear in mind in the consideration of all Adler's educational writings. Despite the genetic relation between psychological inferiority and organ inferiority, Adlerian "inferiority" was increasingly interpreted less as a biological fact than as a flexible social potentiality. It was not the *fact* of inferiority, but the child's socially conditioned evaluation of any biological deficit that determined the net psychological meaning of the inferiority (1930c, p. 29). Thus, if the interpretive estimation of a deficit could point in the direction of neurosis and sociopathy, it could also point, with proper educative direction, toward mental growth and productive overcompensations. The meaning of the inferiority, for Adler, could never be abstracted from the concrete judgments the child made *about* the inferiority. The import of the inferiority thus derived exclusively from the way the child incorporated his deficits into his own subjective goal-oriented behavior. Heightened inferiority feelings were not equivalent signs of, but subjective interpretations of, inborn and acquired inferiorities formulated in the context of a particular life style. Indeed, Adler saw the estimation of inferiority as so theoretically open-ended that he claimed his psychology was tantamount to a refutation, from the standpoint of personality theory, of the "theory of causality": "We know that the depth or character of the impression which the situation makes upon the child does not depend upon the objective fact or circumstance . . . but depends rather on how this child regards the fact (1930c, p. 29).

The putative refutation of causality in later Adlerian psychology rebounded on the primacy of the educational mission. Adler's pedagogical optimism did not only rely on his supposition about the malleability and reversibility of the child's ongoing estimations of his inferiorities and superiorities. It relied as well on the supposition that the teacher was the skilled professional ideally situated to influence the subjective way the child chose to interpret the facts of his interpersonal situation. This pedagogical prerogative encompassed not only the interpersonal judgments that had been formed in the home, but also the unfolding relations among classmates. Thus, it fell to the "wisdom of the teacher," Adler observed in 1935, to make the child understand "which of his schoolmates is a fellow-worker, which a malingerer and which asocial" (p. 11). In the context of Adlerian psychology, the psychopedagogical leverage accorded the teacher amounted to an optimistic reiteration of the open-ended educability of the child, the fact that the relevant variable in child development was the child's subjective and highly malleable perceptions of both self and object world.

Inasmuch as Adler summarily rejected both the child's inherited abilities and the weight of the environment as self-limiting factors, his entire theory of educa-tion ultimately fell back on the interpersonal theory of psychopathology delin-eated in *The Nervous Character*. The adaptive and maladaptive strategies the child brought to school were continuous with the evaluative self-perceptions he had created for himself within the home. Because these self-perceptions were emblematic not of intrapsychic conflict but of ongoing subjective evaluations that had been sustained by the home situation, however, they could be sup-planted once the home situation—and with it the child's evaluative understand-ing of his status in the home—were altered. Therein lay both the potential of education and the therapeutic mission of the psychologist-educator. Once the educator relinquished the role of judge and assumed that of comrade or doctor, he would achieve a powerful vantage point from which to convince the child that his maladaptive strategies were unnecessary and unprofitable (1930c, pp. 125–126; 1914a, p. 483). The proper word from the teacher, Adler observed, would suffice to "transfer the energies of the child from competitive to coopera-tive channels" (1930c, p. 173).

Yet, how was this transference to be effected? In answering this question Adler betrayed the political conservatism that belied the socialism of his early career and routinely diverted his later theorizing in the direction of abject social conformism. The years of the socialist school reforms in Vienna ironically marked the very period when Adler formally rejected any connection between socialism and Individual Psychology, and, from 1925, he actively disavowed Marxist Individual Psychologists like Alice and Otto Ruehle and Manès Sperber (see Sperber, 1970, pp. 129–131, 223). Adler's entire pedagogy embodied the core conservatism of his later years. Despite occasional positive references to Nietzsche's "will to power" at the ontogenetic level of the child's superiority strivings, Adler's conformist psychology was poles apart from Nietzsche, and never farther than in the manipulative persuasion he commended to the educator to instill community feeling in the child. Adler was no transvaluator of values, no

Zarathustra admonishing his disciples simultaneously to ignore and to transcend the banality of the "teachable." Instead, he reified *Gemeinschaftsgefuehl* into the ur-value of adult culture and urged the teacher to graft adult conformist sensibilities onto the self-perceptions of the child. This grafting process was manipulative because it fully relied on the unreflective dichotomy of childish value judgments without imparting any true insight into the content of *Gemeinschaftsgefuehl* at the level of the child's own understanding.

Thus Adler advised the teacher to indoctrinate the disobedient child into community feeling by convincing him that antisocial actions that ignored the responsibility of community feeling were in reality actions that betrayed the fear of appearing a "weakling" (1930c, p. 105). This pejorative characterization was typical of Adler, and it was the necessary obverse of the educator's attempt to "encourage" the child to equate "courage" with socially useful, i.e. conformist, activities. Through this two-pronged strategy, Adler believed, education afforded the child "compensation" for his insecurities "by schooling him in the technique of life, by giving him an educated understanding, and by furnishing him with a social feeling for his fellows" (1927a, p. 75; 1927b, p. 74). The point was that such schooling did not really "educate" the child, but rather used the child's immature "superiority" motive as a lever for regulating the conformist dimension of his behavior. After Adlerian schooling, as before it, the child could still harbor unrealistic inferiority feelings and a pathological overcompensatory need to be superior. Now, however, the child would be fully willing to accept the educator's verdict as to the *quality* of behavior that betrayed, respectively, inferiority and superiority. The child might not have outgrown his invidious "apperceptive schema," but he would at least have learned to enact his neurotic melodrama in a way that coincided with the Adlerian educator's requirements for "useful activity."[2]

Of course, we may legitimately question the extent to which such manipulative guidance toward *Gemeinschaftsgefuehl* actually accomplished the education of the child.

II.

The seemingly banal conformist goals of Adlerian education acquire additional meaning when placed in the context of the Viennese educational reforms that followed World War I. Following military defeat at the hands of the Allies,

---

[2]For one of many examples where Adler uses his patient's neurotic motive for praise as a lever when it issues in "useful" work, see 1930b (pp. 75–76).

Austria's Provisional Government of Social Democrats and Christian Socialists underwrote in 1918 a program of massive educational reforms designed to safeguard the new Austrian Republic and to inculcate in the Republic's citizens respect for the ideals of participatory democracy. Otto Gloeckel, a radical educator who joined the Social Democrats in his youth in revolt against the inequality of educational opportunity in Austria, spearheaded the reform movement. First as Undersecretary to Minister of Instruction Rafael Pacher, then as Secretary of Education, Gloeckel engineered the far-reaching reorganization of the Austrian school system that would both democratize the operation of the schools and systematically cultivate in students a root identification with the ideals and expectations of the community. Hans Fischl, one of Gloeckel's chief lieutenants, recounts how Austria's newfound preoccupation with the democratic cultural ideal redirected educational goals in accord with the revivified sense of community feeling that was to animate the Republic:

> From the beginning, however, the political founding and the politically conceived goals of the school reform were tightly connected with cultural intentions. Democracy imparted a new dimension to the formation of a cultural ideal: it furnished a new standard by which to determine the cultural elevation of the people. Also, it saw in the development of the personality toward the idea of a noble conception of humanity a task of the individual. It did not believe, however, that this task could be accomplished other than through a complete submission to a like-minded, cohesive community (*eine gleichstrebende Gemeinschaft*). Democracy, therefore, was not able to transform a thin upper strata into a cultural elite, but only to estimate the highest level of popular culture compatible with the cultural circumstances of the masses. From this standpoint, the democratization of the school was a cultural necessity of the first order. It was a national activity, begun with the wish to enter into the great cultural community (*die grosse Kulturgemeinschaft*) of the German people [1929, pp. 18–19].

How did this political preoccupation with democratic ideals translate into educational practice? Gloeckel's proposed reforms proceeded from the assumption that democratic education should be based on the child's experiential identification with the community and should enhance the child's appreciation of the degree to which useful knowledge was community knowledge. Administratively, it followed that the school could only point to an idealized community awareness if it was organized to transcend the class and economic distinctions of the real community. From this need proceeded Gloeckel's dedication to the governing idea of an *Enheitsschule*—a unified system of education that would extend the duration of common schooling before occupational preferences and intellectual aptitude steered students into different branches of the school system.[3] Prior to the educational reforms the Austrian school system bifurcated into a *Mittelschule* for the intellectually elite and a *Pflichtschule* (accompanied by a five-class *Volksschule* and a three-class *Buergerschule*) for the rest of the population. This separation, theoretically according to intellect, led in practice to a separation according to social status in which the higher schools became in actuality "class schools of the upper strata of society."[4] Gloeckel's endorsement of the *Einheitschule* was intended to eliminate such premature stratification, and it was to be implemented in particular via an *Allgemeine Mittelschule*—a general high school—that would forestall any educational divisions according to talent and occupational preference through the fourteenth year. To its partisans, this kind of general high school was envisioned as the crucial means for developing "general culture and national feelings" (Dottrens, 1930, pp. 41–42).

If the concepts of the *Einheitschule* and the *Allgemeine Mittelschule* were intended to provide the structural context for the democratization of the child, Gloeckel's reform program for classroom instruction went still further in this direction. The intent here was to democratize classroom activity by incorporating Dewey-like dicta designed to maximize the child's awareness of the integral relationship between community feeling and knowledge. The governing idea was the *Arbeitschule Methode*—education premised on the child's natural self-activity. This general principle yielded several specific instructional strategies. In advocating education based on *Bodenstaendigkeit* (i.e., on firmly established experience), Gloeckel and his associates endorsed a method of instruction deriving from the needs and issues presented by the child's immediate environment. Through advocacy of *Gesamtunterricht* (i.e., of total instruction), they endorsed an instructional approach that did not artificially break the school day into designated subjects, but rather focused exclusively on one classroom topic for intervals dictated by the interest of the class. Thus, for a period of days or even weeks, the entire school day would be devoted to the one central topic that stimulated and absorbed the energies of the students.[5] The community aims embodied in these teaching principles were succinctly enunciated in the *Leitsaetze* (guiding principles) promulgated by Hermann Raschke, the director of the reform division of Gloeckel's Ministry of Education, in 1920. The first of these principles, which paralleled the essential Adlerian presupposition, stated that the

---

[3] Papanek (1962, p. 5) translates *Einheitsschule* as "a universal single-ladder school."

[4] See Fischl (1950, pp. 29–30). This entire chapter of Fischl's comprehensive study ("Otto Gloeckel und die Schulreform 1919–1934") was first published as the postscript to Gloeckel's autobiography. See Gloeckel (1939, pp. 90–91).

[5] On these central planks of the school reforms, see Dottrens (1930, chapter 2), Siegl (1933, chapter 3), Fischl (1950, pp. 24–36), and Papanek (1962, chapter 3).

school must educate students toward community spirit. The remaining principles elaborated this mandate, adding that the school must be unified, that specialization of studies should begin as late as possible, and that compulsory course requirements should be minimized (Papenek, 1962, pp. 73–75).

Unfortunately, the ambitious program of educational reform embodied in these principles was not to materialize. Though experimental classes to test the workability of Gloeckel's innovative principles of instruction were conducted during the 1919–1920 school year, the possibility of restructuring Austrian education on a national scale disappeared when the coalition Socialist-Christian Social government collapsed in 1920. As the Social Democrats and Gloeckel left the Ministry of Education, the impetus for national school reform went with them. Fortunately, however, the reform program that Gloeckel and his associates laboriously constructed between 1918 and 1920 was not fated to remain on the drawing board. When the Social Democrats left office, Gloeckel moved on to Vienna. There he became Acting Second President of Vienna's own municipal Board of Education (the mayor being the nominal First President) and oversaw the implementation of his national reform program within Vienna. This all came to pass through a happy vicissitude of Austrian geography. After World War I, the shrunken Austrian state reorganized as a confederation of individual states, and, in 1922, the city of Vienna became the State of Vienna with administrative autonomy in the field of education.

With Gloeckel's relocation in Vienna, the stage was set for the regional implementation of the educational reforms. Between 1918 and 1934, the Social Democrats controlled both the municipal and state governments of Vienna. Moreover, the educational reforms themselves proved unexceptional within the context of the dramatically extended range of municipal activities that sought to revitalize Viennese life during the period of inflation and unemployment that followed the war. Gloeckel's reforms were subsequently realized as one part of the extensive social welfare program that aimed at securing the health of Viennese children. This program, which included social services covering pregnancy, birth, infant care, and a wide range of educational institutions for gifted, exceptional, and homeless children, was one important arm of Vienna's far-reaching experiment in municipal socialism during this period (see Dottrens, 1930, pp. 25ff. and Fischl, 1950, pp. 36–55).

Adler's Individual Psychology antedated the Viennese school reforms, but its own pedagogical program paralleled Gloeckel's system in essential respects. Adler's central idea of *Gemeinschaftsgefuehl* posited as the stuff of mental health what Gloeckel and his collaborators posited as the social and historical requirement of postwar Viennese education. In *The Education of Children* (1930c),

Individual Psychology in the School (1929d), *The Problem Child* (1930b), and other later works, Adler plainly enunciated pedagogical principles paralleling those embodied in the *Leitsaetze* of 1920. It is difficult to ascertain whether these suggestive parallels reflect any actual interaction between Gloeckel and Adler. Though Adler did not directly participate in the formulation of Gloeckel's reform program of 1918, his collaborator and long-time disciple Carl Furtmueller was one of the experts appointed by Gloeckel to the reform division of the Ministry of Education in 1920. Furtmueller subsequently followed Gloeckel to Vienna where he became a State Inspector for Vienna's experimental schools (Fischl, 1929, p. 43; Papanek, 1962, pp. 62–63). It seems reasonable to assume that Gloeckel was acquainted with Adler's ideas through his close working relationship with Furtmueller.[6]

Adler himself, along with Furtmueller, lectured at the Pedagogical Institute which the city established during this period. The activities of the Institute constituted one important plank of the teacher education reforms that accompanied the educational reforms. Affiliated with both the philosophical faculty of the University of Vienna and the Vienna "Psychological Institute" headed by Karl and Charlotte Buehler, the Institute devoted itself to the introduction of scientific educational theory (*Erziehungswissenschaft*) in teachers' training. To this end, it provided lectures and practical workshops directed to the "pedagogical improvement of the teaching profession" (Fischl, 1929, p. 75). In the mid 1920s, when the city lifted its hiring ban on teachers, the Institute expanded its offerings to include a two-year high school level program in teacher education to train elementary school teachers for city schools.[7]

Apart from lectures that Adler delivered at the Pedagogical Institute, there were two noteworthy areas of Adlerian involvement in the Viennese social reforms. The first was the organization of an experimental school based on Individual Psychology by an Adler disciple, Ferdinand Birnbaum, in 1925. This project was one of the numerous experimental schools authorized by Gloeckel and the Vienna School Board during this time. Under the aegis of the school board, an existing city school was transformed into an Individual Psychology workshop where the principles of the *Arbeitschule* could be enacted in a setting of intensified community awareness. In the Adlerian school, one eyewitness recounts, both activity and learning were ruled by the ranging idea of commu-

---

[6]Bottome (1939, p. 113) reports that Furtmueller brought Adler to Gloeckel's attention, and that Gloeckel subsequently "encouraged and allowed" Adler to affiliate his child guidance clinics with the Viennese schools.

[7]On the Pedagogical Institute, see Fischl (1929, pp. 35–37, 67, 75–78; 1950, pp. 49–50) and Papanek (1962, pp. 91–92).

nity; all facts of school life were subsumed by one of the multivarious dimensions of community experience, including the community of work (*Arbeitsgemeinschaft*), of government (*Verwaltungsgemeinschaft*), of discussion (*Aussprachegemeinschaft*), of mutual support (*Stuetzungsgemeinschaft*), and of common experience (*Erlebnisgemeinschaft*). The instructional orientation of the school correspondingly induced the pupil to understand his role in the class as a "community experience," and the teacher sought to instill the complementary ideals of autodidacticism and cooperation by presenting the child's "failures" as public rather than private matters that affected the entire class community.[8]

The most significant area of Adler's personal involvement, however, and the one through which the educational precepts of Individual Psychology directly penetrated the day to day operations of the Vienna schools, lay in the establishment of an entire network of educational guidance clinics (*Erziehungsberatungsstellen*). Adler organized the first of these clinics in 1920, staffing it with his collaborators and pupils.[9] As an adjunct to the city school system, the network of guidance clinics included both teacher and child guidance clinics. In the former, the first of which Adler himself conducted, Viennese teachers brought their problem pupils along with the pupils' parents and presented the cases for discussion and review. These clinics were envisioned as training schools in which the teachers of Vienna could be instructed in the rationale and strategies of Adlerian counseling; they operated on a strictly voluntary basis, with the teachers themselves deciding when certain pupils would benefit from educational counseling and bringing them to the Adlerian clinics only with the permission and participation of the parents. Regine Seidler, one of the early Adlerian educators involved with the guidance clinics, examined in 1935 the records of those cases brought before the clinics. She found, predictably enough, that the majority of "problems" of the problem students brought to the clinics involved school-related difficulties: the most frequent complaint heard at the clinics pertained to children who were unable to do their school work and obtained very poor grades. In order of decreasing frequency, these students were followed by children "who caused a continuous disturbance in the classroom by clowning, talking constantly, etc.," "slovenly" children, children "who had succumbed to lying or stealing," and, in equal numbers, children with an "uncontrolled desire for dominance," children with sexual problems, and children with phobias (Seidler, 1935, pp. 76–77).

---

[8]On the Adlerian experimental school, see Birnbaum (1935a), Ganz (1953, chapter 3), and Spiel (1956). On the typology of community forms that organized the classroom, see also Birnbaum (1935b).

[9]The number of teacher guidance clinics peaked at 11 in 1928, thereafter declining until 1934, when they were discontinued altogether (Seidler, 1935).

The clinic sessions were normally conducted in regular school classrooms according to the following format: the presenting teacher announced the nature of the pupil's problem and both child and parents were interviewed separately by the presiding Adlerian teacher or therapist. Following the interviews, the case was openly discussed (the teacher guidance clinics were open to the public), the child's particular "*misinterpretation* of life" was illuminated (see Seidler, 1935, p. 76), and therapeutic recommendations were offered to the child and parents. Seidler (p. 76) has recollected the "very comprehensive handling" of the cases brought before these clinics, with individual cases frequently taking two hours or more of clinic time. The child guidance clinics served as adjuncts to these teacher clinics. Here the problem students themselves were encouraged to come voluntarily as long as they felt the need for supportive counseling (see Seidler & Zilah, 1929 and Ganz, 1953, chapter 4).

III.

It was in Adler's educational guidance clinics that his psychological principles were fully translated into pedagogical practice. As an educator, Adler's own "guiding principle" remained community feeling. He took this concept not merely as the primary goal of psychotherapy, but as a philosophical requirement of human existence that was the crux of the didactic training of the child. In practical counseling terms, this meant that Adler used the idea of community feeling as the governing criterion for differentiating "useful" from "useless" superiority strivings (1930c, p. 61), and as the basis of his admonitory instructions to the "problem children" brought before him.

To effect therapeutic change in his young patients, however, Adler elected to enhance the judgmental impact of his diagnostic categories. To the extent that the child had recourse to "useless" antisocial behavior in order to achieve superiority, Adler accused him of escaping the responsibility of reconciling private impulses with community requirements and pronounced the child a coward (*Feigling*). Conversely, to the extent that the child channeled his superiority strivings in useful directions supportive of community feelings, Adler claimed that the child possessed "courage" (*Mut*). Courage, in this admonitory context, was not a descriptive characterization applying to a wide range of behavior, but an objective denotation of a life style that embraced the requirements of community feeling. "What we call interest in the community is only one aspect of the close bond with others," Adler observed, "what we call courage is the rhythm which an individual has within himself which enables him to feel that he is a part of the whole" (1930b, p. x). When Adler subsequently designated "community feeling'' and ''courage'' the two watchwords of Individual Psychology (1930c, p. 208), he was only referring to two complementary dimensions of one objective reality because, for him, ''courage is a social function. Only someone who considers himself a part of the whole can be courageous'' (1930b, p. 169; cf. p. 71).

Adler's educational counseling imparted ''courage'' to children; it strove to give them the courage to conform. He directly *told* his problem students that the antisocial striving for superiority that resulted from an exaggerated inferiority complex was really the easy way out. It achieved sham superiority while bypassing the only criterion for the ascription of genuine superiority—the standard of the community. Social adjustment was consequently at the core of Adler's educational goals (1930c, pp. 17–21, 119). ''Cowardice,'' correspondingly, was the characterological original sin of deviant children who displayed different kinds of antisocial behavior. Such children deviated not through intentional malice, but through lack of education: they had not been stimulated to embrace the imperative mandate to conform. Their deviant behavior was ''cowardly'' because it corresponded to privatized superiority needs that were neurotically overcompensatory, i.e., that embodied a quest for interpersonal control that was not a healthy reflection of adaptive ego growth and expansiveness, but a compulsory outgrowth of exaggerated feelings of inferiority. Rephrased somewhat differently, deviant behavior was cowardly because it reflected a self-perception so demeaning and disabling that the deviate was afraid to compete for self-esteem in the marketplace of human relations and social values. ''Cowardice,'' Adler observed, ''is a trait which always destroys human relations'' (1930c, p. 82).

By redefining deviant behavior as a variety of cowardly self-indulgence, Adler converted educational counseling into a form of didactic moral training. By choosing to explicate deviant behavior in a depreciatory phraseology that resonated with the child's own deviant ego ideal, he acquired the therapeutic leverage that could produce behavior modification. His counseling, therefore, was never tantamount to ''insight'' therapy. The child was given no genetic insight into his behavior beyond Adler's strict and abstractive insistence that the cowardly ''useless'' way had been chosen. More essentially, the child's self-knowledge became therapeutically meaningful only when it was catalyzed by the therapist's didactic admonitions; it was the counselor who had to gain understanding of the child's ''error'' in his life style, the constitutional or environmental basis for the exaggerated inferiority feelings that eventuated in antisocial superiority strivings. Insight became curative only when the counselor had achieved the moral leverage needed to persuade the child that he was ''making a mistake.''

Once the deviant child's life style was adequately exposed, therapeutic social conformity was assured via Adler's extraordinary therapeutic optimism:

> One often encounters the following objection: "What do you do when the individual has recognized his error and does not correct it?" If he actually recognizes his error—if he understands the connection and persists in his attitude despite the harmfulness involved—we can only say that he has not understood everything. I have not yet seen a case of this kind. *Really* to recognize an error and then not to modify it runs counter to human nature; it is opposed to the principle of the preservation of life. The objection concerns a pseudo-recognition of errors. It is not a fundamental recognition, where the social connection is actually realized [1930b, p. 3].

Adler plainly made the Socratic identity of virtue with knowledge the basis of his therapeutic optimism. If the delinquent child really *knew* the objective significance of his maladaptive interpersonal strategies, his "mistaken" life style would be undermined at its base. The obvious question concerns the clinical grounds for this extraordinary optimism. How could Adler, the educational counselor, invariably persuade the child of the "error" of his ways? He apparently did so by aggressively challenging the degree to which the child's deviant behavior proved successful within the child's *own* subjective goal-oriented frame of reference. In his counseling sessions, that is, Adler usually reformulated the child's activity in a way that made it clash with the child's own subjective ego ideal. He told children who lied, stole, and bragged that liars, thieves and braggarts were the *real* cowards of society who were weak and inferior in their indulgent social nonconformity. In this way, he undermined the vicarious ego gains derived from deviant activities by demeaning such behavior as useless and weak (1930b, pp. 7–8).[10]

Having undermined the subjective superiority gains tied to antisocial behavior, Adler proceeded to modify the child's behavior by proposing more realizable ways of fulfilling the subjective goal of superiority. The attempt at therapy was voiced, once more, within the teleological framework of the child's own subjec-

---

[10]Adler's counseling strategy bears striking resemblance to therapeutic techniques developed in the 1950s and 60s that rely on the use of "paradox" to alter pathological behavior. These techniques, which, in general, represent an outgrowth of Bateson's pioneering elucidation of the pathological "double bind" (Bateson et al., 1956, 1963), include the use of "reframing" as a type of therapeutic double bind capable of inducing behavioral changes. Reframing, of which Adler's reformulation of delinquent behavior as "weak" and "cowardly" certainly constitutes an example, "involves changing the entire meaning of a situation by altering both or either its conceptual and/or emotional context in such a manner that the entire situation is experienced as completely different, i.e., the situation has been placed in a new frame" (Soper & L'Abate, 1980, p. 371). On reframing in general, see the literature cited in Soper & L'Abate, especially Watzlawick et al. (1974).

tive preconceptions about inferior and superior behavior. As an educational counselor, then, Adler was no patron of strategies aiming at "optimal disillusionment" (Gedo & Goldberg, 1973, pp. 164–165; cf. Gedo, 1979b). He was unconcerned, in other words, that the delinquent should comprehend and ultimately relinquish those elements of illusional grandiosity which fueled the maladaptive superiority strivings. Rather, he attempted to do no more than domesticate the child's preexisting ego ideal, to make the child understand that real interpersonal power was not tantamount to simple domination, but to domination that was enacted within a framework of social obligations (e.g., 1930b, p. 90). The therapeutic appeal was partly Nietzschean: Adler wanted the child to understand that the "will to power" operated at different levels and that indulgent antisocial behavior generally embodied less "strength" than behavior powerful enough to win legitimate respect and esteem within the coordinates of social acceptability. In the *Genealogy of Morals* (1887), Nietzsche made this point to dramatize the enormous will to power vested in the renunciation and self-control of the ascetic who withdrew from society.[11] Adler of course made the appeal on behalf of conformist social adaptation. He broached the desirability of "useful" adaptive behavior in terms of the child's own inferiority-superiority imagery. In this way he was able to present socially compliant behavior as the kind of behavior that embodied a higher level of strength, power, and masculine ego feeling than the child's deviant strategies. Adler consequently made the child's neurotic "power" motivation fuel a new commitment to social conformity for the reason that the child's neurotic expectations were being met.[12]

This, then, was the new twist Adler gave to conventional "supportive" therapy. Just as the educator's most important task was the prevention of the child's "discouragement" at school (1930c, p. 84), so the therapist could not let the child become discouraged about the possibility of attaining his own subjective goal of interpersonal superiority. Adler never considered the phenomenological or epistemological status of "superiority" as a fully adequate characterization of ego strength, nor did he address himself to the phenomenology of different kinds of "superiorities" and the degree to which certain *perceptions* of superiority could be in and of themselves pathological. He never went beyond

---

[11]Nietzsche's point, of course, was that ascetic abnegation was actually affirmative: in the process of "willing" his self-denial, the ascetic actually affirmed life, inasmuch as "man would rather will nothingness than not will" (1887, p. 599). For amplification of Nietzsche's perception of the quantitative degrees of power adhering to various forms of behavior, see Kaufmann (1968, pp. 195–196, 218, 233, 250–251).

[12]See, for example, 1930b (pp. 74–75) for reference to neurotic expectations as a "lever" that can redirect the child to "useful" work.

the tautological contention that both superiority strivings and community feeling expressed a "root desire for confirmation" (1930c, p. 116). Despite the popular understanding of Adlerian psychology as a goal-directed teleological psychology, Adler has no comparative psychology addressing itself to the phenomenological or therapeutic status of human goals. He was consequently content, time and again, simply to reiterate the fact that there were "useful" and "useless" paths through which the goal of superiority could be pursued, however neurotically malformed or conflictive the very *understanding* of superiority might be.

In fact, Adler's genuine therapeutic concern was restricted to the social repercussions of behavioral patterns that were only intrasubjectively meaningful. Herein lay the important subjectivist element that confounded his scientific pretentions: despite his continual insistence that "strivings toward the creation of unity in human society" had to be evaluated "above all from the viewpoint of scientific truth" (1930b, p. ix), Adler's manipulative therapeutic strategems incorporated an important presupposition of subjectivist thought. I refer to his repeated claim that the unity, style, and goal of the individual personality "is not built upon objective reality, but upon the subjective view the individual takes of the facts of life" (1930c, p. 6).

Given this subjectivist assumption that informed Adler's understanding of personality development, it was inevitable that his educational counseling could never be more than mundane "encouragement" therapy (see, e.g., 1930b, pp. 13–14, 20, 27, 63, 70). Accept the intrasubjective autonomy of the child's own goals, he continually implied, merely try to mitigate the child's perception of his inferiorities to the point where the compensatory superiority strivings no longer require antisocial acting out, but can be adequately realized within the prescriptive boundaries of society. This change was to be effected by encouragement. Bolster the child's self-confidence and self-esteem to the point where he can achieve the level of superiority posited by his own subjective goal within the parameters of community standards. Clear a way to the "useful side of life," he enjoined, by imparting "courage." The goal of therapy, he protested, was simply "to make the child understand what we believe we ourselves understand"—that the quest for superiority is not incompatible with socially conformist behavior (1930b, p. 33).

The level of conceptualization employed here resonates with Adler's early medical theory of organ inferiority. As educational counselor, Adler accused the child of cowardly escape, of being driven by his inferiorities to seek so much superiority so quickly and so easily that he could not contain his superiority strivings within prescribed social channels. As internist, Adler had argued that the "inferior organ" was *socially* inferior by virtue of the reservoir of excessive drive endowment that inhered in the organ, a quantity that could not be fully channeled into the prescribed opportunities for organ activity by the organ's "psychological superstructure." And just as his earliest therapeutic strategy was to redirect the excess of organ drive toward "overcompensatory" socialized activities, so his later counseling strategy was to redirect the excessive "superiority" needs fueling delinquent behavior onto new competitive paths that were legitimized and regulated by community feeling.

IV.

The relative shallowness of Adler's counseling efforts is highlighted by comparison with the two Freudian analysts who did their own educational counseling with young delinquents and criminals during the same period as Adler. One of these analysts, August Aichhorn, was a fellow Viennese whose medicopedagogical efforts were also underwritten by the Austrian Social Democratic party in the years following World War I. Aichhorn became the director of a residential institution for delinquent Viennese children and resolved to apply psychoanalysis to the treatment of delinquent problems. About a decade after Aichhorn's work with Viennese children got under way, the Hungarian analyst Franz Alexander received foundation support to spend nine months analyzing offenders at the Judge Baker Guidance Center in Massachusetts. While practicing psychoanalysis in Berlin, Alexander coauthored with Hugo Staub in 1929 a pioneering work on psychoanalytic criminology, and it was this work that attracted the attention of William Healy of Boston, Director of the Judge Baker Foundation and pioneer of the American Child Guidance movement. Healy called on Alexander in Berlin and invited him to visit the United States to collaborate on a psychoanalytic study of American criminality. Alexander came to Healy's Guidance Center in 1931, and from his ensuing collaboration there emerged one of the classic attempts to apply psychoanalytic insight to the practical management of delinquent behavior, Alexander and Healy's *Roots of Crime*.[13]

Though neither Aichhorn nor Alexander was a student of Adler, both implicitly accepted, in a general sense, Adler's therapeutic framework for the treatment of delinquents and criminals. Yet, as psychoanalysts, both arrived at counseling strategies that were considerably deeper than Adler's moral instruc-

---

[13]On the course of Alexander's collaboration with Healy, see Alexander's autobiography, *The Western Mind in Transition* (1960, pp. 89, 92–94).

tion in viewing delinquent behavior as fully coterminous with neurotic symptoms at the level of psychoanalytic explanation. Like neurotic symptoms, that is, delinquent behavior embodied true intrapsychic conflict either between unconscious wishes and the conscious ego or between competing unconscious wishes.[14] For both Aichhorn and Alexander, this conceptualization meant that the counseling of deviants had to do more than simply challenge the social acceptability of the way the delinquent pursued his "goal." Instead, it meant that educational counseling had to be genuinely psychodynamic: it had to view the delinquent's own understanding of his delinquent "goal" as inadequate rationalization for which unconscious determinants were to be uncovered. In contradistinction to Adler's method, there was no moral valuation of the strategies by which the delinquent pursued his goal; there was only the neutral therapeutic insistence that the delinquent himself did not really understand his behavioral goals at the level of the unconscious determinants.

Aichhorn, a former grade teacher in the Viennese school system, began his counseling work in the immediate aftermath of World War I. In December, 1918, he and a group of colleagues assumed the administration of a home for delinquent boys established by the city of Vienna at the former refugee camp at Ober-Hollabrunn. Like Adler, Aichhorn subsequently organized and conducted for the city administration a network of child guidance clinics, eventually becoming chairman of the child guidance clinic of the Vienna Psychoanalytic Society (see Eissler, 1949; A. Freud, 1951). Compared to the later work of Alexander, Aichhorn's methods were the simpler in their applied model of Freudian explanation. He viewed antisocial behavior as fully analogous to neurotic symptoms in its immediate dependence on unconscious sexual wishes, and he located the primary causes of antisocial behavior in the "abnormal libidinal ties" of early childhood. Delinquency arose from this infantile base, according to Aichhorn, because the potential delinquent possessed "little capacity for repressing instinctual impulses and for directing energy away from primitive goals," and, furthermore, because the child's "unsatisfied need for tenderness and love" brought him into conflict with the ethical code of society (Aichhorn, 1925, p. 148).

---

[14]Friedlander's *The Psycho-Analytical Approach to Juvenile Delinquency* (1947) is entirely in the spirit of Aichhorn and Alexander's pioneering work. Citing Alexander and Healy's *Roots of Crime*, she contends "that there is no fundamental difference between unconscious conflicts underlying neurotic symptom formation and unconscious conflicts causing those delinquent actions which we might call 'delinquent symptoms' " (p. 116). For a more subtle differentiation of the respective roles of unconscious conflict in delinquency and in neurosis, one must turn to the work of Glover (1960, e.g., pp. 56–57).

Aichhorn's counseling strictures proceeded from the presupposition of libidinal conflict. "The cure of delinquency," he wrote, "is fundamentally a problem of libido." Successful treatment, he added, meant that the counselor had "influenced the later development of the libido in the direction of sublimation and compensation" (1925, pp. 153, 155). To achieve this redirection of libidinal energies, Aichhorn ascribed to the therapist the same positive pedagogical rapport that Adler espoused. For Aichhorn, however, it was a rapport that was established less for purposes of didactic moral training than to engender a libidinal responsiveness that would render the child suggestible. Like Adler, Aichhorn saw therapeutic redirection issuing from a vantage point of superior pedagogic authority, and he stated that effective counseling hinged on the counselor's ability to establish a "positive tranference" relationship with both the delinquent child and his parents.[15] Only under the "pressure of transference" could action "be forced into specific channels and conveniently used for the attainment of definite purposes" (1936, p. 104). In accordance with this reliance on the positive transference, Aichhorn contended that the counselor, as a libidinal object, had to become a parent to the delinquent, but without committing the parental mistakes that had facilitated delinquency (1925, pp. 122–123, 129). The counselor was to socialize the child's behavior not by preaching community feeling as a normative ideal, but by supplying in the therapeutic encounter the positive emotional correctives that could undercut the unconscious justification for the deviant behavior.

Admittedly, Aichhorn believed the counselor ultimately had to curb the delinquent's undisciplined instinctual gratification by inducing him to accept the desirability of instinctual renunciation. He submitted, however, that the counselor could only accomplish this if he initially compensated in his therapeutic rapport for the lack of instinctual gratification the child had experienced to date. Community feeling, in other words, was not an abstract social ideal to be instilled in the child, but a libidinal objective to be realized in the course of therapy. Thus, within certain prescribed limits, it could be assumed that "education will succeed in direct proportion to the love the child receives from his parents and educators" (1925, p. 196). With Adler, Aichhorn contended that a change in the delinquent's ego ideal had to be mediated by the authority of the

---

[15]See Aichhorn's paper "On the Technique of Child Guidance: The Process of Transference" (1936). Aichhorn's pioneering invocation of the transference relationship in the reeducation of delinquents was subsequently endorsed and refined by Glover (1960), who spoke of the multiplicity of transference stimuli—and hence "distributed transference"—to which the delinquent was subjected (pp. 102–104, 167, 306).

counselor with whom the child could retrieve his lost identification with his father (pp. 234–236). Against Adler, however, he argued that the basis of the retrieved identity was not the logic or "reasonableness" of the counselor's didactic pronouncements, but the fact that therapy itself created the positive libidinal bond between child and therapist that imparted authority to the pedagogical recommendations. It was as a "libidinally charged object for the pupil," that is, that the teacher "offers traits for identification that bring about a lasting change in the structure of the ego ideal" (p. 235). Only in this way did the counselor acquire the therapeutic leverage with which to accomplish the didactic Adlerian task: to imbue the delinquent's ego ideal with the necessary social qualities. This modification was the *product* of therapy, not, as for Adler, the *content* of therapy.

Historians of psychoanalysis have to date paid insufficient attention to the important Adlerian presuppositions that inform the work of Franz Alexander. Alexander was no follower of Adler and, despite the "Adlerian" direction of his therapeutic reforms, no friend of Adler. As a Freudian, he criticized Adler for dealing only with the "progressive forces" in man to the detriment of the "fundamental regressive trend," and he negatively assessed the import of Adler's "deviations" from the standpoint of traditional Freudian orthodoxy (1942, pp. 130, 167; 1960, p. 118). Apart from these general criticisms, Adler is never cited in his work. Yet, at every stage of his theoretical development, Alexander managed to elaborate psychoanalytic themes that paralleled and subsumed the therapeutic perspectives emphasized by Adler. Alexander was one of the first analysts to isolate the concept of a "neurotic character" from that of a symptomatic "neurosis" in order to describe patients in whom the unconscious did not use delimited neurotic "mechanisms" but functioned as a pervasive determinant of the overall life style (1923, 1930). Although he was most concerned to show how "neurotic character" formed under the pressure of the castration complex, Alexander also showed, at the clinical level, how the castration complex translated into exaggerated feelings of inferiority that the neurotic character "used" as the basis for self-punishment tendencies (1923, pp. 36–38).

The implicit Adlerian dimension carried over to Alexander's central theoretical work, *Psychoanalysis and the Total Personality,* a pioneering attempt of the mid-1920s to restate the mechanism of neurotic symptom-formation in the language of Freud's structural theory of id, ego, and superego. Alexander subtitled his work an "Application of Freud's Theory of the Ego to the Neuroses," and he proceeded to argue that every neurotic symptom could represent a substitutive expression of a repressed wish for the reason that the "suffering" caused by the symptom satisfied the punitive demands of the superego, thereby relieving the sense of guilt engendered by the illicit wish (1935, pp. 26–33).[16] Yet, in attempting to differentiate those disguised expressions of instinctual wishes that required expiatory "suffering" from those instinctual sublimations that did not, Alexander returned to a customary Adlerian premise. If both neurotic symptoms and healthy sublimations resulted from comparable instinctual restrictions, he asked, why did only the former cause the ego to inflict upon itself the threatened punishment of the superego? Because, he replied, sublimations entailed instinct modifications acceptable to the ego according to "the prejudices and connections of society." Sublimations did not offend the superego because gratification of the illicit wish was mitigated by the "social quality" accruing to the disguised wish fulfillment. This differentiation brought Alexander to a fundamentally Adlerian position. Though Alexander did not acknowledge Adler in this regard, he argued, with Adler, that neurosis was social neurosis because psychic conflict ultimately fell back on social judgments about the acceptability of the different vicissitudes of the life of instinct. For Adler, it was the "psychic superstructure" that determined what kinds of gratifying organ activity were acceptable; for Alexander, it was "social conscience" that watched over the sublimated impulses according to the requirements of social behavior (1935, pp. 125–127). Three years after propounding this Freudian variant of the social theory of neurosis, Alexander returned to another prototypical Adlerian theme in stressing the primacy of "inferiority feelings" as that emotional constellation which played "a permanent and central role in the dynamic explanations of psychopathological phenomena" (1938, p. 41). Acutely sensitive to the dynamic interplay between inferiority feelings that led to compensatory expressions of aggression and subsequent guilt feelings that inhibited this aggressiveness, Alexander maintained that the structure of many neuroses "consists precisely in the conflict in which the coexistence of strong inferiority and guilt feelings brings the patient" (p. 45).

In his later work at the Chicago Institute for Psychoanalysis, Alexander worked out the therapeutic requirements of his social theory of neurosis in a distinctly Adlerian direction. In the important text on *Psychoanalytic Therapy* (1946) he coauthored late in life with Thomas French, he defined psychoneurosis as "a failure to find socially acceptable gratification for subjective needs under given circumstances." From this definition, in turn, he deduced the need to

---

[16]"Corruptibility of the neurotic superego" was Alexander's (1935) phrase for characterizing the superego's "secret alliance" with the id whereby the expression of a repressed wish was permitted in exchange for the "suffering" caused by the illness.

reconceptualize psychoanalytic therapy as a "corrective emotional experience" that was integrally tied to the therapist's "guidance" of his patient's daily activities (pp. 19–22). In making this prescriptive recommendation, Alexander implicitly bowed to Adler's requirement that the therapist become a moral judge ready and willing to expose the "mistaken" dimension of a life style. Though his critique of traditional psychoanalytic practice was more refined and systematic than Adler's, he definitely made his case from the traditional Adlerian position. Just as Adler insistently caricatured psychoanalysis as a therapy for pampered children (e.g., 1931a, p. 97; 1933a, p. 140; 1933b, pp. 213–214; 1935, p. 10), so Alexander cautioned that daily psychoanalytic interviews aggravated the patient's dependent needs, and as such could "exercise a seductive influence on a patient's regressive and procrastinating tendencies." He countered that a skillful psychoanalytic treatment would minimize the time spent with regressive material, and that the nearer the analyst kept the patient to his "actual life problems," the more effective the treatment would be (Alexander & French, 1946, pp. 28, 30–34).

The overtly Adlerian dimension of Alexander's work seemed to rebound decisively on his applied work with delinquents in the 1930s. Like Aichhorn, he characterized his analytic work with criminals as "an etiological study of delinquency and crime" that sought to contribute to the prevention of delinquency by a genetic determination of where things went wrong for the young criminals under study (Alexander & Healy, 1935, p. 4). Unlike Aichhorn, however, Alexander never limited himself to a strictly libidinal perspective on delinquent behavior. Instead, he moved back toward Adler in the sense of evaluating criminal activity as a means of obtaining the compensatory "masculine" self-image the criminal otherwise lacked. At the conclusion of his study, Alexander articulated this conclusion in conjunction with a cultural verdict on the "heroic exhibitionistic evaluation of criminal deeds in America." "In spite of official condemnation," he wrote,

> not only instinctively but even consciously, the public views criminality with a sort of adolescent hero-worship. At the same time machine civilization with its mechanizing and leveling tendencies, strangulates individuality and compels the individual to become a part of the collective unit. Criminality remains one of those few outlets left through which the individual can express his spite against this pressure and emphasize his masculine sovereignty. . . . The tendency to display one's masculinity by showing disrespect for the law is a reaction to the restrictions of the instinctual life which lead to a deep sense of inferiority. This serves as a permanent stimulus to the wish to compensate for inner weakness by toughness and aggressiveness [Alexander & Healy, 1935, p. 283].

Alexander elaborated this ostensibly Adlerian viewpoint in the first case study in his book. Here he dealt at length with a 20-year-old thief whose stealing represented "the self-deceiving way in which he wants to get rid of the shame because of his dependence by assuming an external appearance of chivalry, toughness, and aggressiveness" (p. 34). For this patient, Alexander continued, psychoanalytic insight "spoils the significance of his criminality as a means of increasing his masculine vanity" (pp. 36–37).

Despite the Adlerian thrust of these statements, Alexander's perspective remained Freudian in a crucial respect: he deciphered the criminal's "masculine protest" not as a subjective goal incorporating predetermined cultural evaluations of "feminine" and "masculine" activity, but as an embodiment of ongoing psychic conflict between equally potent feminine and masculine attitudes. In the first case study, to be sure, he pronounced the criminal's stealing "a reaction to a strong sense of inferiority, giving him a feeling of bravado and toughness." He added, however, that the criminal's "sense of inferiority" was itself "a reaction to a strong dependent, receptive wish expressed in the attitude of obtaining things without working for them" (p. 67). In another case history, Alexander demonstrated the key sense in which the "sense of inferiority" did not embody the negative self-image the delinquent hoped to escape, but rather the "receptive dependent demanding attitudes" that were actively realized through the delinquent activity (pp. 236–237, 249–250). In recasting the psychological import of the "sense of inferiority" in this way, Alexander decisively departed from the Adlerian level of explanation. He viewed "dependent receptive wishes" not as indirect byroads to the goal of superiority, but as an autonomous dimension of psychic striving. In fact, he saw in such wishes the basis for propensities for "feminine" passivity that actively confounded the overcompensatory criminal activities at the level of the delinquent's unconscious wishes.

Given the Freudian "guiding line" of his reconstructions, Alexander's therapeutic task was not to educate the patient to embrace the social parameters within which "masculine" goals could be sought. It was rather to expose the unconscious conflict between masculine and feminine goals from which the delinquent behavior issued.[17] In all his case studies, Alexander paralleled the

---

[17]In the case of an adolescent female shoplifter, for example, Alexander asserted that the patient had a "masculinity complex" and stole out of "masculine" identification with her derelict father. At a deeper unconscious level, however, he found that the girl's criminal delinquency was motivated by the need to obtain a genuinely "feminine" self-image. The girl, he discovered, had a rich fantasy life centering on masochistic sexuality, and had actually been subjected to early seductive activity. As a result of this childhood experience, the patient developed "inferiority feelings" relating to the unconscious "feminine" deficiency in her personality structure. She subsequently stole feminine

general direction of Adler's pedagogical verdict, but with deepened therapeutic insight. This insight proceeded from the recognition that inferiority and superiority strivings themselves were complex behavioral endproducts and not ultimate categories of psychological explanation. Thus, Alexander imparted experiential substance to such strivings by subjecting them to a genetic consideration, by analyzing developmental issues that provided a framework for understanding the underlying wishes that coalesced in such strivings. By recognizing inferiority feelings not merely as the absence of superiority feelings, but as behavioral indices of competing ''wishes'' that were psychologically primary, Alexander was able to enlarge his perspective on delinquent behavior with the notion of unconscious mental conflict. The offshoot was a richer and infinitely more nuanced depiction of the delinquent than Adler ever accomplished. Thus, Alexander could implicitly agree with Adler that delinquent activity was an ''overcompensatory reaction to an internally felt weakness'' (p. 284), but he chose to analyze this reaction not at the level of cultural abstractions about superiority strivings. Instead, he viewed the reaction as conditioned by, and in continual conflict with, the genuine psychological claims of infantile dependence. This imputation of intrapsychic conflict was in striking contrast to Adler's dismissive verdict that the delinquent was simply the individual ''whose community feeling suffered shipwreck in childhood'' by virtue of a ''pampered life style'' (1935, p. 6).

To understand why young delinquents chose to enact their superiority strivings in deviant ways, Alexander did not rest content with the question that preoccupied Adler: why does the child feel so ''inferior'' that he lacks the ''courage'' to strive for superiority in the prescribed way? He pressed on to ask why, genetically, the claims of infantile dependence in certain individuals came to be so strong that they were not compatible with the competing claims of the independent adult ego, and subsequently mitigated against the delinquent patient's willingness to undertake the ''continuous and systematic efforts that are necessary in a self-supporting scheme of life'' (Alexander & Healy, 1935, pp. 284–286). In explicating the conflict between two active dimensions of personality, Alexander chose, with Aichhorn but contra Adler, to analyze delinquent and criminal activity not as behavior directed toward an intrasubjectively meaningful goal, but as an externalized counterpart of the ''Freudian'' neurotic symptom. Like the symptom, that is, delinquent behavior served the purpose of ''gratifying repressed urges and at the same time it is also a source of suffering

---

clothing, Alexander tells us, to become a ''new person,'' one, that is, who was ''successfully feminine'' (Alexander & Healy, 1935, pp. 115–116, 121).

which satisfies the claims of the guilty conscience" (p. 290). Here, once more, was the edifying insight that was at the core of Alexander's main contribution to psychoanalytic theory, *Psychoanalysis and the Total Personality.*

V.

In his readiness to construe therapeutic reeducation as moral education, Adler once again bears a striking affinity to the sociologist of the *conscience collective,* Emile Durkheim. We have already observed how Adler's social theory of neurosis incorporates an essentially Durkheimian estimation of the binding nature of community judgments on the assessment of individual behavior (see chapter 6, pp. 162ff.). Here, we will consider how closely Adler's identification of moral education with the requirements of community feeling parallels the argument of Durkheim's own contribution to pedagogical theory, *Moral Education* (1925). Like Adler, Durkheim construed morality as coterminous with social life (pp. 78–79). Durkheim said that society simultaneously produced morality and served as the end of morality, and he theorized in this work that the requirements of society accounted for the spirit of discipline and the attachment to the social group that are the two elements of moral behavior (pp. 86, 92, 98–99). Unlike Adler, however, Durkheim translated the pedagogical mandate embodied in the child's moral education into concrete pedagogical guidelines. The rationale for this was clear: if the child was to receive a moral education that equated moral behavior with socially useful behavior, there had to be concrete operational strategies for developing the elements of community feeling in the child.

This need for concrete pedagogical strategies was clearly embodied in Durkheim's treatment of the role of discipline in the school. If behavior animated by the *conscience collective* presupposed a spirit of discipline informed by the ideas of regularity and authority, Durkheim fully accepted the need to discipline as integral to the sense of collective life imparted by the school. When construed as an instrument of moral education, Durkheim observed, school discipline solidified the morality of the classroom and turned the class into a small society (p. 148). It did this by presenting the student with disciplinary rules of conduct that mimicked the rigorous morality of civil life. Punishment served the community of the classroom by reestablishing the authority of society's rules. Durkheim said that punishment could in fact make amends for offenses committed by demonstrating that, despite the appearance of a violation, the law "remains always itself, that it has lost none of its force or authority despite the act that repudiated it." Through this type of demonstration, punishment fulfilled its essential function—"not to make the guilty expiate his crime through suffering or to intimidate possible imitators through threats, but to buttress those consciences which violations of a rule can and must necessarily disturb in their faith" (p. 167).

Adler, on the other hand, never construed the pedagogical imperative of *Gemeinschaft* at the level of concrete pedagogical practice. He reiterated in his lectures the desirability of eliminating punishment in the classroom altogether,[18] but he had no substantive recommendations for transforming the viable community that would no longer require conventional forms of punishment. This is one crucial sense in which Adler's pedagogical perspective breaks down. He wanted the school to imbue the child with community feeling, but he had nothing to say about how the school itself could be transformed into the kind of community that would provide the experiential base for that "felt" *Gemeinschaftsgefuehl* that could animate the child. His sole prescriptive guideline was the therapeutic one that informed his educational counseling: objectify (reify) community feeling for the benefit of the child and present it to him with such compelling logic and such sympathetic authority that the child cannot help but admit the "mistaken" life style he has chosen.

Clearly, this insight was pedagogically inadequate. Adler consistently treated the child as a miniature adult for whom the logic of community feeling was as intellectually self-evident and compelling as it was for the teacher and psychologist. He refused to explore the phenomenological and psychological preconditions for community feeling in the classroom, giving no attention to teaching techniques, curriculum, or class government. Consequently, his therapeutic principle did no more than abstract and reify the goal that the proponents of the progressive "activity school" had tried to implement in the decades before World War I.

Durkheim, in *Moral Education,* ended his presentation by proposing specific strategies by which the school environment could be used to inculcate altruism and an appreciation of collective life in the child. It was the school, he noted, that "must give the child the clearest possible idea of the social groups to which he belongs. It is here that the role of the educator is most important" (p. 228). It was a role, however, that far transcended the didactic explication of community feeling that Adler recommended. The teacher, to Durkheim, had to shape the class's own sense of community if he was to impart to the child experientially the

---

[18]Adler's contention in this regard was that children who were delinquent were "only challenged to continue in their style of life by punishment" (1931a, p. 175). For additional statements to this effect, including Adler's blanket admonition to give up "the whole process of punishment," see 1930b (pp. 3, 89, 98).

"clearest possible idea" of his own social groups, and Durkheim provided concrete suggestions (e.g., the use of collective punishments and rewards) for enhancing the class's internal sense of community (pp. 243–249).

This brief comparison with Durkheim exemplifies the key divergence between Adler's pedagogy and the work of the progressive educators of the early twentieth century. We have already seen how Freudians like Aichhorn and Alexander developed modified psychoanalytic techniques that paralleled but ultimately transcended Adler's limited counseling strategies. A similar relationship obtains between Adler and progressive educators like Dewey, James, Baldwin, and Montessori. The progressive educators did not know Adler and did not cite Adler, but they consistently provided parallel formulations that impart deepened meaning to Adler's quest for *Gemeinschaft* in the classroom. In the remainder of this chapter, we evaluate Adler's educational philosophy alongside the work of the outstanding philosopher of progressive education (Dewey) and the outstanding psychologist of progressive education (Piaget). Though Dewey and Piaget did not refer to Adler in their contributions to pedagogy, such comparison remains important for two related reasons. It clarifies the wide range of organizational and instructional issues that invariably interpose between the teacher's appeal to *Gemeinschaft* and the student's ability to relate to this appeal in a way that is experientially and psychologically meaningful. By demonstrating what must actually occur in the classroom if Adler's chief dictum is to be taken seriously, such clarification in turn demonstrates the important sense in which Adler's simple call to community feeling, however laudable in intent, fails to provide the basis for a substantive educational psychology.

Adler, we have observed, believed community feeling to be a normative social ideal that the child could intellectually accept on the adult's own terms if it was presented with sufficient logic, clarity, and sympathy. The progressive educators believed, conversely, that the child would only embrace an ideal of community feeling when the school itself came to exemplify community feeling in both its administration and its instructional orientation. This insight certainly informed the early work of Maria Montessori, who saw her organization of infant schools in Rome's model tenements in 1907 as supplanting the individual home as the locus of community. By establishing "a school within the house," that is, she saw the school as communizing a "maternal function" for the benefit of working mothers who could not provide the basis for community feeling within their individual homes (1912, pp. 65–67). Really, though, it was only with the work of John Dewey that the goal of a community feeling in action received broad exemplification at the level of pedagogical practice. A year after the founding of The Laboratory School of the University of Chicago in 1896, Dewey drafted a ''Pedagogic Creed'' that elaborated the centrality of community feeling in education. ''The only true education,'' he wrote

> comes through the stimulation of the child's powers by the demands of the social situations in which he finds himself. Through these demands he is stimulated to act as a member of a unity, to emerge from his original narrowness of action and feeling, and to conceive of himself from the standpoint of the welfare of the group to which he belongs [1897, p. 443].

Dewey's appeal to the educational significance of community feeling was multidimensional. He defined the school as a social institution, ''that form of community life'' in which the agencies were concentrated that most effectively educated the child ''to use his own powers for social ends'' (p. 445). When he turned to the subject matter of education, he argued, comparably, that ''the social life of the child is the basis of concentration, or correlation, in all his training or growth. The social life gives the unconscious unity and the background of all his efforts and of all his attainments'' (p. 448; cf. 1899, pp. 91–92; 1902, pp. 61–62).

But Dewey departed from Adler in one key respect: he viewed education as ''a process of living and not a preparation for future living'' (1897, p. 445) and therefore believed that pedagogic initiation into community feeling could only be meaningful when it had a solid experiential base in the classroom. Dewey consequently went far beyond Adler in presenting a programmatic framework which would educate the child to realize his ''social heritage.'' Specifically, he endorsed the ''expressive'' or ''constructive'' activities as the formal route to community feeling in the schools. In manual activities like cooking, sewing, and carpentry, he believed he had located the ''fundamental forms of social activity,'' and he recommended that introduction to more formal subjects ''be through the medium of these activities'' (1897, p. 449).

This guiding concern for the pragmatic implementation of community feeling within a revitalized school community was at the heart of Dewey's early work, *The School and Society* (1899). Here he presented a persuasive defense of one key dimension of the modern school movement: manual (or vocational) training. He based his defense of manual training on the impossibility of inculcating community feeling in the formal educational activities of the school, for in the classroom ''the motive and the cement of social organization are alike wanting.'' Through manual work with wood and metal, through weaving, sewing, and cooking, on the other hand, school life could organize itself on a social basis. Such activities were to be conceived of in their social significance, as types of the processes by which society keeps itself going, as agencies for bringing home to the child some of the primal necessities of community life, and as ways in which these needs have been met by the growing insight and ingenuity of man; in short, as instrumentalities through which the school itself shall be made a genuine form of active community life, instead of a place set apart in which to learn lessons [1899, p. 14].

In his concrete recommendations for incorporating these "instrumentalities" into school life, Dewey boldly translated Adler's therapeutic injunction into the reformist mandate of progressive education: if the child was to be trained to embrace community feeling, the school itself could not simply "teach," but had to embody "an embryonic community life" in and of itself (1899, p. 29).

Concern with transforming the school into a community of felt experience was equally at the heart of Dewey's early critique of the traditional school curriculum. In *The Child and the Curriculum* (1902), he lambasted the contrived opposition between the integral life of the child and a school curriculum that artifically divided and fractionalized the unity of the child's personal and social interests (pp. 4–6). Instead, Dewey argued, the subject matter of education should be the potentialities of development inherent in the child. For the teacher, the principal pedagogical challenge was, accordingly, to make the subject matter of instruction resonate with the child's own experience.[19]

These specific instructional recommendations indicated how an initiation into the ways of *Gemeinschaftsgefuehl* could be achieved in practice. In theory, what imparted pedagogical substance to Dewey's program for community feeling that was missing from Adler's was this: Dewey's pedagogical strategies were always situated within an experiential philosophy of mind. For Dewey, that is, the appeal to community feeling was necessarily operationalized in the process of meeting the requirements of a philosophy that made the child's very educability hinge on the integral relationship between knowledge and lived experience. This connection became clearer in later works like *Democracy and Education* (1916). There Dewey viewed the "discernment of relationships" as the principal matter of education, and he submitted that relationships were not intellectually perceptible without experience (p. 169). Dewey's transformation of the school class into a viable community represented his attempt to expedite the experiential base from which "thought" emerged. Only in the school community, that is, did the

---

[19]With respect to teaching a science, for example, Dewey said the teacher's problem must be "that of inducing a vital and personal experiencing. Hence, what concerns him, as teacher, is the ways in which that subject may become a part of experience; what there is in the child's present that is usable with reference to it; how such elements are to be used; how his own knowledge of the subject-matter may assist in interpreting the child's needs and doings, and determine the medium in which the child should be placed in order that his growth may be properly directed" (1902, p. 23).

child find the experimental context in which experiences could be ordered and assessed on behalf of true intellectual growth. The task of the educator, in this connection, was to solidify and mold the tight linkage between experience and intellection. In his classroom format, the educator had to select and arrange the kinds of experiences that would have the greatest educative potential, i.e., those that would "live fruitfully and creatively in subsequent experiences" (1938, p. 508).

Dewey's philosophy of experience carried the appeal to community feeling from mere therapeutic exhortation to concrete pedagogical practice. Only in practice, he repeatedly enjoined, could the idea of community feeling become educationally meaningful. Despite his devotion to the idea of a felt community in the classroom, Dewey's philosophy of experience ultimately served to expose the rarefied level at which the Adlerian call to *Gemeinschaftsgefuehl* was actually sounded:

> The more definitely and sincerely it is held that education is a development within, by, and for experience, the more important it is that there shall be clear conceptions of what experience is. Unless experience is so conceived that the result is a plan for deciding upon subject-matter, upon methods of instruction and discipline, and upon material equipment and social organization of the school, it is wholly in the air. It is reduced to a form of words which may be emotionally stirring but for which any other set of words might equally well be substituted unless they indicate operations to be initiated and executed [1938, p. 509].

From the standpoint of progressive educational practice, Adler's appeal to community feeling was flawed in its failure to generate a concrete pedagogic program; from the standpoint of a progressive educational theory, it was equally flawed in its failure to consider the cognitive meaning of *Gemeinschaftsgefuehl* at the level of the child's own psychology. The most important corrective to Adler's facile optimism about the didactic potency of community as a normative idea is Piaget's momentous study, *The Moral Judgment of the Child* (1932). Piaget's general verdict was that "community feeling" could not be instilled into the child, that the pedagogical offshoot of didactic moral training could only be a morality of unilateral respect and adult constraint that was antithetical to the affective core of Adler's *Gemeinschaftsgefuehl*—cooperation and mutual respect. Piaget showed that the very capacity for "community feeling" was an emergent property programmed into the child's mental development. Although the child began to be socialized from the end of its first year, he observed,

> the very nature of the relation between child and adult places the child apart, so that his thought is isolated, and while he believes himself to be sharing the point of view of the world at large he is really still shut up in his own point of view. The social

bond itself, by which the child is held, close as it may seem when viewed from outside, thus implies an unconscious intellectual egocentrism which is further promoted by the spontaneous egocentrism peculiar to all primitive mentality [1932, p. 36].

Piaget's conclusion followed from his Adler-like presupposition about the great psychological gulf separating child from adult, but Piaget interpreted this gulf not from the standpoint of the child's resulting sense of "inferiority" but in terms of the qualitative cognitive impact that the adult's moral training could have on the child. He found that didactic moral training did not impart the psychological readiness for cooperation and mutual respect that constituted the core of an "adult" morality of autonomy and reciprocity. Instead, moral training that utilized the adult's authority to elicit the unilateral respect of the child issued in what Piaget termed "moral realism" and a correspondingly "objective" conception of responsibility. These concepts designated the young child's proclivity to evaluate actions only on the basis of "material damage" and to gauge material damage in accord with objective and unreflective obedience to the "rules" laid down by adults.

The second of Piaget's two moralities, a morality based on autonomy, cooperation, and mutuality—a morality embodying everything Adler imputed to *Gemeinschaftsgefuehl*—was not only qualitatively different from a morality based on unilateral respect for the rules of adults, but only emerged as the morality taught by the adult world was transcended and disavowed.

The body of *The Moral Judgment of the Child* impressively charted this transition. Piaget's most important insight was that the child arrived at a morality of autonomy and mutual respect (i.e., at a morality of community feeling) not as a product of moral instruction proper, but through interaction with other children. Community feeling, in other words, could have no therapeutic or even psychological meaning before it was experienced by the child in the child's *own* communities, i.e., in a way that resonated with the child's own experiential world. Thus did Piaget show the kind of democratic community into which Montessori, Dewey, Mead, and others sought to transform the school to be an emergent characteristic of the play activities among children themselves. In the first part of his study, he demonstrated how the child arrived at a general understanding of what Adler termed *Gemeinschaftsgefuehl* on the basis of a felt need for mutual understanding in playing the game of marbles (1932, pp. 42, 46). More importantly, Piaget proceeded to document how the child's emergent sense of justice was largely independent of parental influence, requiring only mutual respect and solidarity among children themselves.

In terms of the acquisition of an "adult" understanding of the idea of justice, Piaget showed that parental constraint and didactic instruction generated an unreflective acceptance of expiatory punishment. The passage from such expiatory punishment to a preference for punishments by reciprocity and, beyond that, the entire passage from belief in retributive to belief in equalitarian distributive justice, were developmental consequences of the child's reaction to other children. The more the child's notion of justice approximated the goals of a veritable community feeling, the more it necessarily opposed the didactic substance of the retributive justice that came from docile acceptance of adult authority. Thus Piaget's considered verdict:

> Equalitarian justice develops with age at the expense of submission to adult authority, and in correlation with solidarity between children. Equalitarianism would therefore seem to come from the habits of reciprocity peculiar to mutual respect rather than from the mechanism of duties that was founded upon unilateral respect [pp. 294–295].

Piaget's conclusion, elaborately documented in his book, seriously confounds Adler's attempt to translate the centrality of community feeling in the therapy of problem children into a universal pedagogical precept. Piaget demonstrated that the psychological requirements of childhood cooperation and mutuality had little to do with the precepts of sociability that the adult world instilled in the child, but rather hinged on the experiential relations between children. He found that the authority which generated adult constraint produced the child's conception of expiatory punishment, but not a true sense of equalitarian justice, insofar as the latter presupposed that high level of autonomy which only followed the child's own progress in cooperation and mutual respect (pp. 319–322). The ethics of authority were thus not the ethics of community feeling, inasmuch as community feeling necessarily implied mutual respect and cooperation within a community of equals. "Solidarity between equals," for Piaget, is "the source of a whole set of complementary and coherent moral ideas which characterize the rational mentality" (p. 324).

Having said this much, we must pause to consider why exactly we opt for Piaget over Adler. We may note, at the outset, that certain key assumptions of Piaget's theory of moral development—the existence of a universal stage sequence typifying moral development and the dependency of moral development on cognitive development—have been validated by numerous empirical studies (see Hoffman, 1970, pp. 269–273). Above and beyond this relevant fact, however, we must opt for Piaget because he at least approaches the whole question of educability from the standpoint of a bona fide child psychology, i.e., from an epistemological standpoint that dispenses with adultomorphic judgments about inferiority and superiority on behalf of a genetic reconstruction of the child's own cognitive universe. As a commentator on the moral education of the child, in other words, Piaget must at least be taken seriously, whereas Adler cannot be taken seriously insofar as he fails to address the very questions of cognitive development that inform Piaget's observational and experimental work and issue in his psychology of education. Thus, when Piaget invokes the child's "spontaneous egocentrism" to qualify the meaning of the "social bond" between adult and child, he does so from a vastly stronger vantage point than Adler can invoke in pointing to the young child's readiness for community feeling. For Piaget, that is, the imputation of childish egocentrism is a finding with observational referents in the nature of the child's language and thought; it is not simply a therapeutic value judgment foisted on the child by adult sensibilities.

The Moral Judgment of the Child (1932), in this respect, builds on the experimental foundation provided by Piaget's first two books, *The Language and Thought of the Child* (1932) and *Judgment and Reasoning in the Child* (1924). In the first of these two works, in particular, Piaget provided an empirical framework for the verdict reached in the investigation of the child's moral life. How do we arrive at our estimation of the egocentric nature of the child's thought? We do so by apprehending, empirically, that sociality is not an inborn "adult" value but rather a cognitive potential with its own genetic history. By charting the evolution of this potential as it manifests itself in both the use of language and the nature of verbal understanding in early life, Piaget supplied an observational referent for the conclusion that there is "no real social life among children of less than seven or eight years" (1923, p. 61). The "society" of young children, subject to the dictates of an egocentric logic that is essentially subject-centered, intuitive, and syncretistic, "is a society in which, strictly speaking, individual and social life are not differentiated" (p. 61). The educational meaningfulness of "community feeling," for Piaget, necessarily dissolves into a critique of the cognitive constraints that typify the child's early ability to communicate and thereby experience sociality; it is a critique which issues in the finding that "the fact of being or of not being communicable is not an attribute which can be added to thought from the outside, but is a constitutive feature of profound significance for the shape and structure which reasoning may assume (1923, p. 67). Thus, in analyzing the nature of conversations between children, we see empirically that meaningful socialization of thought occurs only at a discrete point in development (around the age of seven or eight) when children are cognitively able to undertake conversations that entail what Piaget terms a "collaboration in abstract thought" (pp. 81ff.). Prior to this time, conversation itself, whether between children or between child and adult, is effectively asocial—i.e., it transpires within the egocentric coordinates that frame the child's ability to think and use language.

The outcome of Piaget's inquiry into the moral judgment of the child is an educational perspective that is anti-Adlerian in its categorical rejection of the traditional assumption that the child can be treated "as a small adult, as a being who reasons and feels just as we do while merely lacking our knowledge and experience" (1970, p. 159). By embracing an epistemology that construes knowledge as a series of operational processes linked to the child's own actions, Piaget arrives at a position that erodes the very premise of Adler's commonsensical approach:

> Whenever it is a question of speech or verbal instruction, we tend to start off from the implicit postulate that this educational transmission supplies the child with the instruments of assimilation as such simultaneously with the knowledge to be assimilated, forgetting that such instruments cannot be acquired except by means of internal activity, and that all assimilation is a restructuration or a reinvention [1970, pp. 39–40].

Adler uncritically adopted this "implicit postulate" with respect to the child's presumed ability to assimilate the verbal call to community feeling. By linking the child's moral education to the continual restraining influence of parent, teacher, and Adlerian therapist alike, he ignored the fact that unilateral respect for the adult and the adult's values frequently consolidates an egocentrism which is both prior and antithetical to the meaningful acceptance of community norms. Unilateral respect issues in this paradoxical effect

> by simply replacing a belief in self with a belief based on authority instead of leading the way toward the reflection and the critical discussion that help to constitute reason and that can only be developed by cooperation and genuine intellectual exchange [Piaget, 1970, p. 179].

But it is not even necessary to follow Piaget this far to explode the fallacious premise of Adler's educational work. The anti-Adlerian verdict follows not only from Piaget's specific conclusions about the sensorimotor origins of intelligence and the egocentric nature of the child's language and thought. It is implicit in the very assumption that the child's power to reason cannot be formed outside the child's cognitive universe. Once we accept the core Piagetian premise, it follows that pedagogy must perforce concern itself with finding "the most suitable methods and environment to help the child constitute [intellectual and moral reasoning power] itself, in other words, to achieve coherence and objectivity on the intellectual plane and reciprocity on the moral plane" (1970, p. 160). But how exactly do we cultivate community feeling from within the child's cognitive and experiential world? Here again, we confront a major question for progressive educators like Dewey, but a question that Adler consistently ignored even though it was centrally implicated in his pedagogical strictures and counseling strategies.

VI.

Despite the social value of Adler's child guidance clinics in Vienna in the period following World War I, the work of Durkheim, Dewey, and Piaget helps clarify the important sense in which his therapeutic precepts failed to provide the basis for a viable philosophy of education. As an elaboration of conventional "supportive" psychotherapy relying on the power of therapeutic suggestion, Adler's counseling technique strove to reeducate the school age delinquent by transplanting his deviant behavior into a preexisting inferiority-superiority paradigm and using the full weight of pedagogic authority to induce the delinquent to rethink the suitability of his behavior within the framework of his preconceptions about the quality of "superior" behavior. To the extent that the delinquent received enough therapeutic support to canalize superiority strivings in socially useful directions, Adler claimed that the delinquent had responded to the demands of community feeling both as social obligation and therapeutic directive. In his writings on the education of children, Adler sought to generalize from his counseling work and make the notion of community feeling an educative precept that would inform the orientation of teachers to pupils. This, however, was as far as he would go. Beyond the hortatory insistence that the child could always be persuaded to conform by the sympathetic, insightful teacher, he completely skirted a central concern of the progressive educators: the problem of transforming the classroom into a viable community in which such pedagogic persuasion would be meaningful to the child himself.

Adler's utter failure to address this problem belies the efforts of sympathetic explicators who have appraised his educational theory only in terms of his own therapeutic effectiveness, and consequently claimed to find in Adler's curative pedagogy "the practical proof of the value of his science" (Bottome, 1939, p. 113).[20] Adler, in the final analysis, had no psychology of the child, and the

---

[20]Traditional adulatory recitals of Adler's counseling activities in Vienna are in Bottome (1939, pp. 112–118, 132–138) and Orgler (1939, pp. 165–192). Ellenberger (1970, pp. 621–623), who also describes Adler's counseling work from inside the internal preconceptions of Individual Psychology, adds nothing to these accounts, and contemporary presentations of Individual Psychology pedagogy (e.g., Mueller, 1973, pp. 114ff.) impart no new critical substance to Adler's explanatory categories.

obvious problem is that for all his therapeutic effectiveness with children, he was continually content to view the child only as a miniaturized carrier of reified adult abstractions about inferiority and superiority. This ingrained tendency was a direct consequence of Adler's therapeutic reliance on community feeling as an uncritical cultural abstraction. Just as he omitted any critical sociohistorical theory to explain what community feeling ought to mean to the adult as adult, so he failed to provide any cognitive psychology to address what community feeling could optimally mean to the child *as child*. For Adler, the child who possessed adequate community feeling was psychologically adult in his knowing acceptance of the principal positive value of adult culture. Conversely, the child who lacked community feeling was also adult, but in a distinctly negative sense: his egoistic tendencies promoted a calculating recourse to interpersonal strategies that were manipulative and exploitative in the fully "adult" sense of these terms.[21]

In his clinical reliance on the inferiority-superiority paradigm, and in his sensitivity to the maladaptive "overcompensatory" ways that inferiorities routinely expressed themselves, Adler wielded a therapeutic tool that may well have enabled him to manipulate the behavior of antisocial children and adolescents in the direction of social conformity. But this calculating use of therapeutic suggestion hardly provides the basis for an educational psychology. By failing to acknowledge (1) that children are not adults and (2) that the classroom must be transformed in its nature if teachers are to inculcate the virtues of community to children *as children*, Adler's educational viewpoint culminates in the commonsensical strictures of the average parent: educate the child by cajoling him, threatening him, preaching to him, and, ultimately, by calling him names. As such, it subserves common mythologies that the best insights of child psychology have long dispelled.

----

[21]For a representative example of Adler's proclivity to reduce the child to a miniature adult, see *Der Sinn des Lebens* (1933a, p. 36; 1933b, p. 56), where he betrays a striking indifference to the psychological frame of reference from which the child makes value judgments: "Talk among children at school about sexual questions can scarcely be avoided. The independent child who looks to the future will reject smut and will not believe foolish statements." See also 1930b (p. 81) and 1930c (pp. 125, 132–133).

9 The Psychologist as Prophet: Adler and *Gemeinschaftsgefuehl*

We have seen how Adler's status as pedagogue hinged entirely on the assumption that the therapeutic goal of *Gemeinschaftsgefuehl*—community feeling— was at the same time a substantive educational precept. It is now time to consider the status of *Gemeinschaftsgefuehl* expressly, with special reference to the evolutionary and political assumptions that both underlay and transcended Adler's pedagogic reliance on this conception. This order of presentation is reasonable because it parallels Adler's own relation to the idea of community feeling. Although he implicitly relied on an assumption about community feeling in explaining the grounds of his break with Freud, and although he explicitly incorporated this assumption into his idea of therapy and pedagogy by World War I, Adler only attributed systemic importance to the idea of community feeling in later lectures following his public educational activities. Initially promulgated in conjunction with practical counseling activities, that is, the norm of community feeling received a formal justification from the standpoint of evolutionary philosophy and social theory only as a sequel to these activities. As such, it is not Adler's ongoing therapeutic *reliance* on the idea of community feeling, but his later *justification* of this reliance that charts the major transition of his later career: that taking him from an established identity as psychologist and educator to the new role of social prophet.

Why exactly do we burden Adler with the "prophetic" ascription? From a pedagogical stress on community as a normative therapeutic ideal, Adler leaped in the 1930s to an estimation of community feeling that transcended his pragmatic therapeutics in its anchorage in a scheme of cosmic evolutionism. Out of this shift, Adler emerged a prophet in the belief that his subjective vision of *Gemeinschaft* foretold a moral destiny to which mankind had to be awakened. Out of his commitment to such spirtual awakening, however, Individual Psychology would be the principal casualty. I will argue that Adler's recourse to vitalistic biology not only undermines the relevance of community feeling to psychological explanation in general; it further vitiates the clinical meaningfulness of the theory of therapy Adler proceeded to erect on such questionable vitalistic premises. That Adler could insistently preach the coming of an age of *Gemeinschaftsgefuehl* without articulating a critical definition of *Gemeinschaft* testifies to the essentially prophetic import of his later work. Frank Manuel, who has written of a coterie of nineteenth-century Parisian prophets whose perspective on community, we shall have occasion to note, bears an uncanny resemblance to Adler's, likens his subjects to "the sorely tried Judeans who were the great moral teachers of their city, sparing neither kings nor commoners, as well as revealers of a divine historical design" (1962, p. 1). In his transcendent estimation of *Gemeinschaftsgefuehl,* Adler too strove to become a moral teacher, the revealer of a moral destiny which, in accord with his vitalistic preconceptions, was at one and the same time man's biological destiny. That Adler's moralizing use of vitalistic biology was subversive to his ability to observe and explain psychologically does not detract from the admirableness of his guiding ideal. But a system of psychotherapy cannot be erected on a moral foundation that is so uncritically intrasubjective. Ultimately, we shall see, the recourse to prophecy leaves Adler's later psychology therapeutically empty, a medley of hortatory admonitions without an epistemological leg to stand on.

I.

Adler's preoccupation with the clinical status of community feeling was not coterminous with his crusading popularization of the idea in his lectures of the 1920s and 30s. Although he ended his career as a social reformer preaching the pervasive human need for community feeling in strident missionary terms, his basic theoretical insight was fully embodied in the clinical writings that followed his split from Freud in 1911. Rather than providing a philosophical supplement to a theory of psychopathology that Adler adumbrated when he took Individual Psychology to the masses, the idea of community feeling was worked out as a direct clinical elaboration of the social theory of neurosis presented in *The Nervous Character* (1912). Indeed, Adler's theory of neurosis, in its dependence on pragmatic social judgments about the admissibility of different kinds of superiority strivings, presupposed from the very outset some implicit criterion that would make these judgments unified and cohesive.

We have already seen how an implicit concept of community feeling informed Adler's presentation in *The Nervous Character*. It is now necessary to document Adler's own explicit acceptance of the normative assumptions of his psychology in the immediate aftermath of the break with Freud. In the two years following the break, Adler quickly recognized the explicit dependence of his theories on community values, and he lost no time in restating his principal conclusions from the vantage point of the community's regulative requirements. Adler did not at this time incorporate into his work any critical elaboration of the specific community values he had in mind. Instead, he implicitly equated positive community values with a voluntary sociability that was conservative and conformist in its acceptance of the irrefragable "logic" of existing social institutions. In addition, Adler's early sense of community values always entailed the implicit identification of the interpersonal obligations that occurred within the family with a transcendent obligation to the community at large.

These assumptions were spelled out in the clinical papers of 1913 and 1914. In "Individual Psychological Treatment of Neuroses" (1913b), Adler characterized neurotic goal-striving as the "distortion and poisoning of all human relationships," adding that the treatment of neurosis meant disclosing to the patient the way his neurotic goal opposed reality as it was embodied in the "logical demands of the community" (*logischen Forderungen der Gemeinschaft*) (pp. 24, 29; Radin, pp. 35, 42). In "Further Main Principles for the Practice of Individual Psychology" (1913d), he added that neurosis led the individual away from social functioning, permitting a "withdrawal from the demands of the community and the decisions of life" (p. 16; Radin, p. 23). In an important summary paper entitled "Individual Psychology, Its Assumptions and Its Results" (1914c), Adler reiterated that the goal of the Individual Psychological viewpoint was the acquisition of a strengthened sense of reality (*Wirklichkeitssinn*), the development of a sense of responsibility, and the substitution of a sense of "mutual goodwill" for "latent hatred." All these goals, he pointed out, "can be gained only by the conscious evolution of community feeling and the conscious destruction of power strivings" (p. 10; Radin, p. 15).

Such was the role Adler assigned to community feeling in articulating the programmatic goals of Individual Psychology. At a more delimited explanatory level, the clinical concepts he employed to illuminate the neurotic life style also presupposed a normative community feeling. The neurotic life plan was judged neurotic, for example, precisely because it opposed the demands of reality (and

Adler claimed reality [*Wirklichkeit*] was the same as community [*Gemeinschaft*])
and eventually compelled the patient to oppose the "normal decisions inherent in
community life" (*den gesellschaftlich durchschnittlichen Entscheidungen*) with
a revolt in the form of an illness. When this kind of life plan remained unnoticed
by the patient and effectively "unconscious," this was because "the neurotic
goal might nullify itself by coming into direct opposition with community feeling." Adler frequently defined the neurotic symptom as a "counter-compul-
sion" (*Gegenzwang*) that was adopted to permit the patient to ignore the "external" compulsions of the community (1913a, p. 164; Radin, pp. 229–230;
1913d, pp. 16–18; Radin, pp. 23–24; 1913e, pp. 148–150; Radin, pp. 208–211;
1914d, p. 73; Radin, p. 102). The "hesitating attitude" (*zoegernde Attituede*),
by which Adler characterized the neurotic's unwillingness to place himself in
situations where his inferiority might be exposed, was invoked to secure the
negative triumph over "normal community demands" (1914d, p. 74; Radin, p.
104). Comparably, the neurotic's "life-lie" (*Lebenluege*), the "arranged" rationalization that freed him from personal responsibility for his failures, was
invoked whenever "socially necessary decisions" arose, and consequently
pointed to the neurotic's diminished community feeling (1914e, pp. 178, 183;
Radin, pp. 236, 244). Lastly, the idea of psychosis, which Adler considered
theoretically continuous with neurosis, was tantamount to the "intellectual suicide of an individual who feels himself unequal to the demands of society or to
the attainment of his own goal" (1914f, p. 192; Radin, p. 257).

II.

In his later writings, and particularly in the lecture series that followed World
War I, Adler no longer referred to community feeling as a negative characterization of what the neurotic lacked; it became instead the positive designation of
what the mentally healthy possessed. This basic shift in emphasis was a necessary part of his transition from psychologist to social prophet. When Adler
decided to make community feeling the vitalistic core of his philosophy of life,
he had to, perforce, recast the import of Individual Psychology beyond the
parameters of inferiority feelings and superiority strivings. In truth, Adler did
even more than this. As a social prophet, his message could not even be contained within the parameters of psychology itself. Instead, new recourse was
made to "evolution" in the largest and most teleological sense.

Adler was not the only renegade psychoanalyst whose differences with Freud
ultimately focused on the question of teleology. Before the outbreak of World

War I, Jung had been more explicit in disowning the limitations of Freudian causal explanation on behalf of the "teleological" meaning of psychological phenomena. Indeed, in 1912, the very year Adler published *The Nervous Character,* Jung published *Transformations and Symbols of Libido* as an index of what he later termed an "internal explosion" against the "reductive causalism" of Freud's whole outlook "and the almost complete disregard of the teleological directedness which is so characteristic of everything psychic" (1952, p. xxiii). Still, there remain fundamental differences between the respective "teleologies" of Adler and Jung. Jung's recourse to a "psychic teleology" met the requirements of a truly "individual psychology" much more adequately than Adler's invocation of a ranging evolutionary teleology. Jung's point, in this respect, was simply that sexual fantasies could be interpreted not only "reductively," but from the standpoint of prospective "metaphysical" needs as well. Indeed, for Jung, all unconscious fantasies acquired teleological meaning in the sense that they were all forerunners of religious and mythological ideas (1912, p. 86; 1913, p. 241; 1917, pp. 294–296). His teleological assumption thereby applied primarily to the projective content of the symbolism that was programmed into individual psychology.

In all his lectures following the split from Freud, Adler, like Jung, increasingly dwelled on the extent to which his Individual Psychology presupposed the "purposiveness" (teleology) of psychic life. Adler's sense of teleology, however, had nothing to do with the content of symbolism called forth by a timeless collective unconscious. Instead, he characterized as teleological a built-in propensity for psychological adaptiveness that corresponded to the predisposition for physical adaptiveness built into biological evolution. Adler's basic assumption was that goal-oriented movement was intrinsic to the very concept of adaptation, and that from the very outset of life, "the first thing we can discover in the psychic trends is that the movements are directed toward a goal" (1927a, p. 13; 1927b, p. 19; cf. 1929c, pp. 1–4). Psychic evolution, in Adler's sense, could only be conceived "within the pattern of an ever-present objective," but the particular objective that oriented behavior was the product of the individual's free choice and not of an impersonal "psychic law." Thus psychic life was lawful in the sense that it always comprised movement towards a goal, but movement in psychic life arose of necessity "only when an appropriate goal has been posited" (1927a, p. 14; 1927b, p. 21).

For Adler, the freely chosen adaptive goals that characterized psychic life transcended mere security from objective danger. They aimed, instead, at a further "coefficient of safety" that "guarantees the continued existence of the human organism under optimum circumstances . . . ." It was this supplementary "coefficient of safety" that superimposed on psychic strivings a new kind of movement: one toward domination and superiority. It was this same postulation of a "coefficient of safety" that made Individual Psychology, from its inception, a social psychology. Because the goals that the psyche set for itself were social goals seeking to overcome the boundaries prescribed by culture, Adler's psychological perspective meant, from the outset, that psychic life was deeply embedded in its "social relationships" (1927a, pp. 17, 18; 1927b, pp. 24, 26).

But Adler did not stop with this assertion. He claimed that despite his ostensibly free will, man could not formulate his goals as a "free agent" because the necessity for solving communal problems constantly intruded upon him, problems that were "indivisibly bound up with the logic of man's communal life." Because the existing conditions of communal life were not final, and because "the meshes of our own relationships" prevented us from illuminating "the dark recesses of the problem of the psychic life," Adler further indicated that we have no psychological base from which to evaluate the epistemological status of the problems of communal life:

> Our sole recourse in this quandary is to assume the logic of our group life as it exists on this planet as though it were an ultimate absolute truth which we could approach step by step after the conquest of mistakes and errors arising from our incomplete organization and our limited capabilities as human beings [1927a, p. 19; 1927b, pp. 26–27].

If Adler's analysis ended at this point, his derivation of the idea of community feeling would be more indicative of philosophical pessimism than of therapeutic optimism. By placing the "purposiveness of psychic life" in a framework of creative evolution, however, Adler made *Gemeinschaftsgefuehl* the crux of an entirely beneficent entelechy. He did so in his most important later work, *The Meaning of Life* (1933). "Individual Psychology stands firmly on the ground of evolution," he wrote, "and in the light of evolution regards all human striving as a struggle towards perfection (*Vollkommenheit*)." Adler's basic conception in this book, which he believed to be a combination of the "fundamental views of Darwin and Lamarck," was that "the 'life-process' must be regarded as a struggle that maintains its direction in the stream of evolution through an external goal of adaptation to the demands of the external world" (1933a, pp. 23, 46; 1933b, pp. 36–37; 69).

To effect the broadening of Individual Psychology into an evolutionary doctrine, Adler read Darwin's *Origin of the Species* (1859) as teleological doctrine, and he appropriated his own idea of community (*Gemeinschaft*) as the "final cause" that would rectify the seeming indifference of natural evolutionary processes.[1] Adler further appropriated for his own purposes the ambitious extension of evolutionary theory that Darwin first charted in *The Descent of Man* (1871), the attempt to understand man's moral and mental qualities as continuous with the evolutionary development of lower animals.

Adler made this late Darwinian view the basis of his optimistic teleology. He claimed that everything grouped under the rubric of "psychical process"—soul, spirit, psyche, reason—was part of the evolutionary "life-process." In its adaptive design, mind, like body, served the principal evolutionary goal, "the ceaseless effort to come to terms victoriously with the demands of the external world. . . . to strive towards the attainment of an ideal and fully adapted final form . . ." Moreover, Adler believed that the impact of evolutionary teleology was to reduce the entire mind-body problem to one fundamental law: the law of "overcoming" (*Ueberwindung*). This law, he said, was variously supported "by the struggle for self-preservation and for bodily and mental equilibrium, by bodily and mental growth, and by the striving for completion (*Vollendung*)" (1933a, pp. 46, 47; 1933b, pp. 70–71). From this point of view, both mind and body became "expressions of life" that were interactive in their adaptive potentialities. On the one hand, mind acted like a motor, "dragging with it all the potentialities which it can discover in the body, helping it bring the body into a position of safety and superiority to all difficulties." On the other, the whole development of the body reflected the errors or deficiencies of the mind (1931a, pp. 27, 40). For Adler, every emotion found some bodily expression, and every bodily expression was "expressive" of some mental attitude.

The offshoot of this interactive reciprocality was Adler's certainty that the evolutionary goal of psychic processes, like the goal of bodily development, was man's progressive mastery of his external environment. It was consequently self-evident for Adler that the "psychic organ" that promoted this mastery was one directed to the development of forms of collective cooperation that compensated for the individual's organic and psychological deficiencies. Only the power of the community, that is, could make good man's status as an individually "inferior" organism and ensure the ongoing achievement of adaptation and security. It thus stood to reason that, for Adler, "the psychic organ must reckon from the very beginning with the conditions of communal life. All its faculties are developed upon an identical basis: the logic of communal life" (1927a, p. 22; 1927b, p. 30). In view of this logic, it stood to reason that the "community feeling" which mobilized the power of the community was to be understood as a "gift of evolution" (1935, p. 4).

---

[1] For a summary of the way *The Origin of the Species* (1859) was read as teleological doctrine, see Himmelfarb (1962, pp. 343–349).

This, then, was the "evolutionary" premise for both the therapeutic and humanistic desirability of *Gemeinschaftsgefuehl*. At the same time, Adler's invocation of community feeling was part of a general trend of the 1920s to explain the purposive aspects of life outside the legitimate field of science. During this decade biologists, influenced by early discoveries in the field of genetics, decided to throw out teleology as a legitimate evolutionary problem. They made this decision on the basis of the current mutationist belief that organisms did not become adapted to a way of life, but simply adopted the way of life that their randomly originating characteristics made possible (Simpson, 1947, pp. 103–104). Biologists who were unsatisfied with this impasse curiously anticipated Adler in attempting to inject into Darwin's account of natural selection a vitalistic ingredient that would account for evolution as purposeful and goal-directed.

In fact, the doctrine of evolutionary vitalism made a serious claim for scientific respectability in the last decade of the nineteenth century under the leadership of Hans Driesch and J. B. S. Haldane. Driesch, a German biologist, and Haldane, a British physiologist, both adduced impressive experimental results that pointed to a teleological reinterpretation of Darwinian selection. Driesch, while pursuing research in experimental embryology, discovered the regenerative capacity of a developing embryo. When a sea urchin embryo that had developed as far as the blastula stage was cut into two (or more) parts, each half developed into an entire embryo, and this happened regardless of the plane along which the original embryo had been sectioned. This experimental finding indicated that, until a very late stage of development, any single part of the embryo somehow "knew" how the other parts of the embryo were going to develop, and could potentially perform any function to complete the predestined development of the organism. Driesch was thereupon led to the conclusion, in 1893, that "teleology is an irreducible peculiarity of the phenomena of life" (1914, p. 176). A decade earlier, Haldane investigated under laboratory conditions the delicate physiological response of the human organism to oxygen deprivation. He found (by direct measurement) that the lung epithelium actively secreted oxygen into the blood in an attempt to rectify the state of oxygen deficiency. On the basis of these experimental findings and analogous demonstrations of "purposive behavior" at the cellular level (e.g., in the reproduction of a newt's limb), Haldane arrived at the conclusion that what appears to belong to the "parts" of an organism independent of their relationship to the whole is really a manifestation in the parts of the influence of the whole. The individual cell, for Haldane (1884), constituted itself not in a blind mechanical fashion but according to its particular function within the whole. Driesch and Haldane were driven to the common verdict that their experimental results could never be described in terms of physics and chemistry. Both had recourse to the "whole" organism as the only possible explanatory unit, and both invoked a vital force to explain the inexplicable tendency of the organismic whole to preserve its form and structure (Driesch) and to maintain optimally favorable conditions for its development (Haldane).

Driesch proceeded to borrow the Aristotelian term "entelechy" to characterize the organism's "intensive manifoldness" to preserve its wholeness.[2] Haldane rejected any formal association with Driesch's vitalism, but his physiological researches pointed to the avowedly vitalist conclusion that the living organism expressed a unified "organic determination" that could never be subject to mechanistic reduction. He criticized nineteenth-century physiology for ignoring the fact that "the body lives as a whole," and he urged future investigations to begin and end with the presupposition that the body was "a living organism, which must be seen as a whole if it is to be seen at all" (1913, pp. 91, 92, 95).

The experimental work of Driesch and Haldane remained influential in the decade following World War I,[3] and it provides the relevant context for understanding the further development of evolutionary vitalism that occurred during this time. Beginning in the 1920s, "mystical" biologists like Pierre Lecomte du Nouey, Edmund Sinnott, and Pierre Teilhard de Chardin countered the reductionist tendency in contemporary evolutionary doctrine by invoking a vitalistic evolutionary theology. These men did not stop with the experimental imputation of a vital force guiding the development of the organic "whole." They supplemented this insight by arguing, from religious premises, that the direction of evolution was toward an irreversible perfection planned by God and, particularly in the case of Teilhard, that the teleological end of evolution was the mystical concentration of consciousness into God (Simpson, 1947, pp. 213–233).

Adler effectively accomplished the sociological secularization of the new religious teleology of these biologists. Although Adler probably never read Driesch and Haldane, much less the later work of Teilhard and Sinnott, he too maintained the religious injunction underlying evolutionary teleology. Adler, however, supplanted the deity with the perfected human community as the pur-

---

[2]My summary of Driesch's research generally follows the account in Needham (1925). For more critical appraisals, see Nordenskioeld (1928, pp. 579–581, 608–610) and von Bertalanffy (1933, pp. 44–45 and 1952, p. 197). For a detailed review of Driesch's experiments, see Hein (1968).

[3]The theories of Driesch and Haldane were popularized and disseminated by C. E. M. Joad, for example, in his *Guide to Modern Thought* (1933, chapter 5). See also the thoughtful defense of Haldane in Woodger's *Biological Principles: A Critical Study* (1929, pp. 242–248, 271).

posive agent of evolution, and he viewed the expanding scope of social cooperation in society as the primary barometer of evolutionary progress. As holistic
doctrine, evolution meant that mental growth buttressed social adaptation. As
teleology, evolution meant that the social product of biological adaptation, the
progressive perfection of the community, was the fulfillment of man's moral
destiny. In his judgment that human evolution posited the final ''good'' from the
standpoint of progressive forms of social organization cemented together by
increasingly perfected forms of community feeling, Adler significantly enlarged
his understanding of the term evolution. Convinced that evolutionary development was tantamount to increasingly perfect forms of social adaptation, he
proceeded to make social adaptation to the existing social order the moral imperative behind biological adaptation. He argued, therefore, that ''the conditions of
our earthly existence actively oppose the person whose contact with them is
insufficient, or who is not in harmony with them'' (1933a, p. 32; 1933b, p. 49).

In this way, Adler meant community feeling to be not only a biopsychological
commentary on the effects and the adaptive aims of evolution, but also a designation for the vitalistic ingredient that fueled evolutionary progress. Henceforth,
the active existence of this vitalistic life force in the individual was to be the sole
measure of mental health, and the potentiation of this force in the neurotic patient
was to be the principal task of the therapist. In turn, this therapeutic transmutation of the collective conditions of evolution into a moral imperative paved the
way for one of the significant incongruities of Adler's later thought. In the years
following World War I, Adler's own devotion to evolutionary development
became the scientific rationale for an inflexible commitment to the existing social
order. He was content to prophesy the timeless preeminence of the form of
community at which humankind had arrived in his time. To this extent, Adler
became the prophet of *Gemeinschaftsgefuehl* only by subverting the evolutionary
rationale that underlay the teleological notion of *Gemeinschaft*. Ultimately, we
shall see, his own reliance on a ''law of movement'' was incapable of taking the
individual beyond the most abject type of social conformism.

III.

Adler viewed community feeling as the original impetus of life passing from one
generation to the next. As such, his term functions as a sociological analogue to
Bergson's *élan vital*, and Adler's entire perspective on evolution is strikingly
reminiscent of Bergson's own vitalistic rendition of evolutionary theory in *Creative Evolution* (1907). The superficial agreement between Bergson and Adler on

the need for a vitalistically "creative" kind of evolution masks important dis-similarities, however, and these dissimilarities in turn point to the conformist sensibilities that dominated Adler's later thought.

Bergson viewed the vital impulsion as dissociating into different elements of vegetative torpor, instinct, and intelligence, and he bemoaned the fact that only man's intellect had been enriched by the *élan vital*. Through the exaggerated development of an intellect directed to the manufacture of artificial tools and the transformation of inert matter into instruments of action, man, for Bergson, could only represent "becoming" as a series of homogeneous fixed states; he could not comprehend the "creative evolution" that was life (1907, pp. 178–179). The intent of evolution could only be realized when the intellect, liberated from its manipulative orientation, could turn inwards on itself and awaken the latent potential for intuition and instinctuality that led to the "inwardness of life" (pp. 194–200).

As evolutionary principle, Adler's community feeling shared a pervasive energic momentum with the *élan vital,* but in all other respects Adler simply turned Bergson on his head. Adler's sense of creative evolution was not transfor-mational, and his therapeutic use of the concept was entirely antithetical to Bergson's conclusion that man represented the "end" of evolution only in the sense that he was the sole medium through which consciousness could break the chain of its mechanistic world view (pp. 287–289). Adler did not view the vitalist force as any kind of basis for transcending contemporary social institu-tions; indeed, it provided a transcendent justification for them. In turn, Adler never viewed the contemporary forms of social organization as "mechanical" representations that restricted the progress of community feeling; instead, they confirmed it in the fullest sense. This was because, for Adler, the vitalist stuff of community feeling was a timeless guarantor of the intrinsic evolutionary moral-ity of all human cooperative strategies. He consequently felt that community feeling both animated and justified every form of social organization on its own sociohistorical terms.

Beyond Bergson, are there any concrete historical referents that illuminate Adler's conservative vitalism? There is only one referent that Adler himself acknowledged, but it is an important one. In later works like *The Meaning of Life,* Adler prefaced the explication of his teleological version of evolution by iterating time and again that everyone "shows a struggle for complete whole-ness" (1933a, p. 45; 1933b, p. 68).[4] To document the universal quality of this tendency and to acknowledge its presumed sponsorship by "the cosmic influ-

---

[4]Literally, Adler says everyone struggles to "become a whole" (*ein Ganzes zu werden*).

ence,'' he repeatedly cited (1933a, pp. 45, 178; 1933b, pp. 68, 270) J. C. Smuts's *Holism and Evolution* (1926). Adler probably read this book in the year of its publication and was sufficiently impressed by it to write Smuts in 1931 and recommend the desirability of a German translation of the work.[5]

Smuts is one of the enigmatic figures in modern British political history. A leading statesman and military leader who made his reputation in British South Africa, he simultaneously pursued serious studies in natural science and philosophy. In *Holism and Evolution,* Smuts's ambitious program was to reconstruct the idea of ''creative evolution'' around the idea of the ''whole'' as the heuristic ''guiding idea'' of all matter. Taking his cue from recent developments in physical theory (especially relativity), Smuts took the Einsteinian space-time continuum as the new relativistic ''field'' of the material world. For Smuts, these recent developments obliterated the pre-Einsteinian concept of matter as inert and simultaneously pointed to a new creative conception of matter that was continuous with organic life. In this essential respect, Smuts's viewpoint coincided with the vitalistic theories of abiogenesis that had been propounded earlier in the decade by S. Alexander (*Space, Time and Deity* [1920]) and C. Lloyd Morgan (*Emergent Evolution* [1923]); with Alexander and Morgan, Smuts embraced the abiogenetic claim that the chain of organisms was continuous with inorganic matter (Wheeler, 1939, pp. 94–95). Convinced that modern physical theory had made the ''fixity'' of types of matter obsolete just as Darwin's theory of descent had destroyed the fixity of life, Smuts's position was that both matter and life consisted of unit structures (i.e., the atom and cell) whose ordered grouping generated natural ''wholes'' (i.e., bodies or organisms). He invoked the term Holism to designate ''this fundamental factor operative towards the creation of wholes in the universe'' (1926, pp. 98, 108, 116–117, 143, 232).

In this recourse to the explanatory power of the ''whole,'' Smuts's scheme presented a distinctive amalgamation of the rival mechanist and vitalist explanations of life that characterize twentieth-century theoretical biology. In his recognition of a transcendent organizational principle that differentiated a sheer aggregation of parts from an organized whole, Smuts argued as a vitalist. Moreover, the thrust of his vitalism was in full accord with the philosophical idealism of contemporary biological organicists, according to whom all individual wholes are ''merely transient moments within the self-realization of an

---

[5]Smuts agreed to have the work translated and even used one of Adler's recommended translators for the job (Erwin O. Krausz). Publication of the German translation could not be financed until 1938, however. Although there is no record of Adler's initial letter to Smuts, Smuts's reply to Adler of 5 March 1931 can be found in *Selections from the Smuts Papers* (Van Der Poel, 1973, p. 472).

all-encompassing whole which is the ground of their being and their scientific rationalization" (Hein, 1969, pp. 238–253).[6]

Smuts's recourse to the "whole" is not singular in the history of biology. He in fact broadened the experimental conclusions that Driesch and Haldane had reached at the turn of the century and anticipated the later work of Edmund Sinnott. Yet, Smuts's invocation of Holism as the regulative evolutionary concept did deviate from the standpoint of biological organicism in one fundamental respect. In *Mechanism, Life and Personality* (1913), Haldane argued that the conception of organism was a higher and more concrete conception than that of matter and energy. For that reason, he submitted, "science must ultimately aim at gradually interpreting the physical world of matter and energy in terms of the biological conception of organism" (pp. 98–99). It fell to Smuts to attempt to implement this imperative. Unlike traditional organicists, however, he did not confine Holism to the realm of organic phenomena; as a vitalistic life force, he saw its rudimentary operation in the entire realm of inorganic phenomena as well. In adopting this abiogenetic assumption, his work parted from the traditional assumptions of vitalism and shared the premise of "mechanistic" molecular biology that the principles which explain inorganic matter are both sufficient and necessary to account for all the characteristics of organic form (see Hein, 1968, 1969). In reality, however, Smuts's integration of organicism and molecular reductionism did not mitigate his vitalistic position, but rather strengthened it by broadening the range of phenomena through which the vitalistic principle itself operated. The principle of the whole not only operated through life; it injected into inanimate matter a developmental impetus that propelled it in the direction of life. It was only because Holism was, for Smuts, the ultimate principle of the universe that it could be construed as the teleological motive force behind evolution, propelling the progressive development of organic wholes out of imperfect inorganic wholes (1926, pp. 99–100).

Clearly it was the vitalistic presupposition of Smuts's schema that exerted a powerful influence on Adler. It was probably on the basis of Smuts's general characterization of biological wholes as self-acting, self-moving organisms with an internal principle of action that Adler invoked his own "law of movement" as the biological basis of human goal striving. Just as Smuts argued that the creative evolution of the "whole" to new levels of "wholeness" effectively eliminated the traditional idea of causality in relation to the activity of an organism, so Adler

---

[6]For critical discussions of this core organicist assumption and of the vitalist-mechanist dispute in general, see two accounts contemporary to Smuts, Woodger (1929, pp. 230–271) and von Bertalanffy (1933, pp. 43–62), along with the more recent assessments of Hein (1969), Phillips (1970), and Hull (1974, chapter 5).

held in his later lectures that psychological impediments to the individual's "law of movement" were not objective "causes" but subjective "meanings." Just as Smuts's progressive realization of the "whole" was viewed as an unending evolutionary advance that increasingly manifested the sociopolitical characteristics of wider human wholes—freedom, individuality, purposiveness (1926, pp. 101, 138–140)—so Adler's inference of a progressively apparent community feeling in human society betokened increased harmony and cooperation between men.

For both Smuts and Adler, evolution was equated with a vitalist agent that determined the direction and the content of evolutionary movement. Adler saw in community feeling not only the effect, but the vitalistic ingredient directing evolution. Correspondingly, Smuts found in his principle of Holism the inner creative factor of Darwinian "variation." It was Holism that "explained" how natural selection was set in motion and how the desired assemblage of small variations that were to be "selected" became correlated and coordinated. For Adler, the social dimension of evolution ensured that society could only evolve in a way that progressively realized the cooperative basis of community feeling. Likewise, Smuts's analogous version of "Holistic selection" meant that minute hereditary variations could be maintained by the individual only if they contributed to the holistic road on which the organism was traveling. Even more remarkably, Smuts's vision of Holistic evolution corresponded to Adler's evolution toward *Gemeinschaftsgefuehl* in its optimistic forecast of the scientific inevitability of social harmony. In opting for Holism, Smuts said he was opting for "the great Darwinian vision of organic evolution" over against the presumed mechanism of Darwinian evolution, the struggle for existence. Smuts termed this Darwinian mechanism "an exceptional procedure of organic Nature" which could have no place in a universe of benignly integrative and interactive wholes:

> This world is at bottom a friendly universe, in which organized tolerant co-existence is the rule and destructive warfare the exception, resorted to only when the balance of Nature is seriously disturbed. Normally Natural Selection takes the form of comradeship, of social cooperation and mutual help [1926, p. 218; cf. pp. 220–221].

For both Adler and Smuts, then, the decoding of the evolutionary imperative ultimately spoke to the benign nature of group psychology, and the vitalistic force directing evolution determined in advance the quality of life within the group that would ensue as evolution reached its happy goal. Smuts did not explicitly refer to "community feeling," but the latter part of *Holism and Evolution* made abundantly clear that the "whole" only realized itself in the broadened organic whole of cooperative human society. Thus, Smuts located in the presence of ''Mind'' an advanced human ''Organ of Wholes'' that entailed the growth of individuality, but he categorically denied that the ''individualistic aspect of Holism'' departed from the general holistic plan of ''extensive coordination and harmonisation.'' The contradiction was only apparent, Smuts claimed, because intensified self-interest inevitably developed into an impersonal endeavor toward the Good, i.e., the broader ''whole'' in which the individual self was symbiotically situated. Paralleling the epistemological presuppositions of Adler's system of therapy, Smuts said that the deepened self ''becomes the center for a fresh ordering and harmony of the universal.'' This happened because Mind was rational and reason was the organ of universality of the spirit (1926, pp. 240–243). Because reason was the direct descendant of organic regulation, the logical direction of reason was inevitably ''holistic,'' and Smuts argued that Mind ''transforms, reorganises, and reconstitutes'' even the purely individualist self, rendering it a ''figment of abstraction.'' Heightened individualism was tantamount to heightened social adaptiveness because self only came to consciousness of itself in society. For Smuts, as for Adler, ''self'' was largely a social construction, and the power and mastery provided by ''Mind'' signified the creation of the social environment appropriate to the development of Mind (pp. 244–251).

The evolutionary goal, in both cases, pointed to the organic *Gemeinschaft*. Personality, the highest phase of Holism, was for Smuts, as for Adler, a discrete approximation of the cooperative principles of *Gemeinschaft* at the level of the individual's internal functioning. As such, personality referred to the unified ''whole'' of body and mind into which Holism shaped the individual on behalf of higher forms of holistic synthesis. Behind Smuts's enveloping ''wholes,'' we easily glimpse the central assumption that informs Adler's conception of personality development as a unity. Psychic activity is not to be unraveled as the outcome of a clash between isolated levels of psychic functioning; it is rather the striving of a unified psychophysiological organism that operates in accord with a unitary ''law of movement.'' The epistemological verdict of vitalistic Holism thus paralleled in essential respects the psychological preconceptions of Adlerian therapy. Smuts's perspective on the mind-body problem clearly paralleled the position Adler consistently took in the lectures following World War I. For Smuts,

> Mind and body as elements in the human personality influence each other because of their copresence in this creative whole of personality. . . . all action of whatever kind, which happens between mind and body in human Personality, is to be traced

to and ultimately accounted for by the holistic Personality itself, and its creative shaping of all that happens to or in it [1926, pp. 271–272].

Comparably, Smuts adduced from Holism the same verdict about mental activity that Adler reached through Individual Psychology:

> All experience, all intuitions, judgments, actions, beliefs and other mental acts are holistic products of Personality. . . . In Personality, even more than in the earlier structures of Evolution, the whole is in charge, and all development and activity can be properly understood only when viewed as being of a holistic character, instead of being the separate activities of special organs, or the separate products of special mental functions [p. 384].

To provide insight into the methodology of a Science of Personality grounded in the principles of Holism, Smuts recommended a method that paralleled in essential respects Adler's method of clinical exegesis. Complementing Adler's clinical preoccupation with the notion of a unified life style, he urged the study of biographies of noted individuals with "real inner histories" because through such study it became clear

> that Personalities follow their own laws of inner growth and development, which will, while conforming to a general plan, show very considerable diversity in detail [p. 289].

Ultimately, this final convergence between Smuts's holistic "Science of Personality" and Adler's therapy of community feeling goes back to the comparably vitalistic premises from which both men began. In the aftermath of World War I, and in an era when biologists themselves generally divorced evolutionary theory from teleological considerations, Adler and Smuts sought to secularize evolutionary vitalism in the direction of renewed social harmony. Both, that is, sought to find in a purposive agent underlying evolution a scientific basis for their personal faith in the inevitability of the cooperative community—in the primacy of the organic, cohesive *Gemeinschaft*. Smuts, for his part, saw Personality, the highest of all wholes, as the embodiment of creativeness, freedom, purity, and wholeness (pp. 304ff). From the vantage point of "scientific" psychology, Adler likewise saw in his norm of community feeling the basis for an "ideal perfection" that represented the ultimate fulfillment of evolution (1933a, p. 182; 1933b, p. 275).

In their respective attempts to justify the coming *Gemeinschaft* in scientific terms, both Adler and Smuts were in touch with a central motif of European thought in the years following World War I. There was widespread longing for *Gemeinschaft* during this period, whether in the guise of the romantically tinged aspirations of the middle-class youth movements or in the political aspirations of young socialists. In Germany, an important manifestation of this preoccupation was the delayed popularity of Ferdinand Toennies' *Gemeinschaft und Gesellschaft* (Community and Society), a major typological exposition of community that was published in 1887 but captured the imagination of a generation of German students only after the experience of the war (see Heberle, 1973, pp. 67–68). In setting forth a typology of community that contrasted *Gemeinschaft* (communal, corporate) with *Gesellschaft* (individualistic, impersonal, contractual) types of human relatedness, Toennies undertook no less than a sociological explanation of the development of the modern state as the political, social, and economic passage of the former into the latter.[7]

Despite his belief that the historical advance of *Gesellschaft* entailed the inevitable disintegration of *Gemeinschaft* forms of relatedness, and despite a discernible nostalgia for the communal forms of society that typified his own upbringing in Schleswig, Toennies did not intend his work as the simple celebration of the premodern community it was taken to be (see Nisbet, 1966 p. 74). Indeed, in the years preceding World War I, Toennies himself came to view the development of *Gesellschaft* positively in accord with his own growing attachment to the German fatherland (Mitzman, 1971). Thus, European students who appealed to *Gemeinschaft und Gesellschaft* to elaborate a refurbished vision of an organic premodern community after World War I generally misunderstood the status of Toennies' ideas as normal concepts (*Normal-Begriffe*) within the framework of what he designated "pure sociology." Toennies opposed *Gemeinschaft* and *Gesellschaft* only as symbols for notional types of relationships analogous to Weber's ideal types; he did not believe that any phase in the evolution of a society corresponded to a pure *Gesellschaft* or a pure *Gemeinschaft*. For Toennies, there are *Gesellschaft* elements in the traditional family and there are *Gemeinschaft* elements in the modern corporation (Nisbet, 1966, p. 76; Herberle, 1973; E. Jacoby, 1973).

Just as Toennies' conceptual distinction between *Gemeinschaft* and *Gesellschaft* cannot be borne out by the empirical human relationships observed by sociologists, so Smuts's and Adler's reliance on a vitalistic agent propelling evolution toward a benign *Gemeinschaft* outcome presupposes a metaphysical conception of progress that has no formal meaning to biologists. Recent discus-

---

[7]Nisbet (1966, pp. 71–73) sees Toennies' typological exposition of community as a fusion of the ideas found in three pioneering works of the 1860s that also made typological use of the notion of "community," Henry Maine's *Ancient Law* (1861), Fustel de Coulanges' *The Ancient City* (1864), and Otto von Gierke's *Das Deutsche Genossenschaftsrecht* (1868).

sions have clarified the important sense in which any ascription of progress implies an act of evaluation, i.e., an axiological standard allowing the terms "better" and "worse" to be applied to events. Given the requisite philosophical judgments that must be made in order to establish such standards, it is generally argued that progress cannot be given a purely biological meaning within the framework of evolutionary theory (see Goudge, 1961, pp. 181–190; Simon, 1971, p. 200). G. G. Simpson has submitted that the only "progressive" change pertaining to life as a whole is the tendency for life to expand, to fill in all available spaces in the livable environments. Apart from this broad tendency

> There is no sense in which it can be said that evolution *is* progress. Within the framework of the evolutionary history of life there have been not one but many different sorts of progress. Each sort appears not with one single line or even with one central but branching line throughout the course of evolution, but separately in many different lines [1967, p. 260].

Inasmuch as any criterion of progress occurs in what Simpson has designated "multiple progressive sequences," the vitalistic self-perfecting progress of Smuts and Adler is undercut at its base, for these variable sequences "are certainly inconsistent with the existence of a supernal perfecting principle, with the concept of a goal in evolution, or with control of evolution by autonomous factors, a vital principle common to all forms of life" (Simpson, 1967, p. 260). If the philosophical implications of evolutionary theory are not conducive to the assumption of one vital principle directing all forms of life, they are equally inhospitable to the assumption of Smuts and Adler that evolutionary progress necessarily culminates in a purified human *Gemeinschaft*. Evolution is necessarily progressive, Michael Simon (1971) has noted, only "in the sense that any inheritable change that gives its bearer a selective advantage is progressive." This fact, however, does not prove man to be the most progressive or highly evolved species, and it hardly requires that cooperative social organization be the most "progressive" dimension of man's evolutionary status. The progressive character of evolution, Simon continues,

> excludes nothing with respect to the nature of the process itself. It is fully compatible, for example, with the possibility that evolutionary change could be regressive in the sense that subsequent generations of organisms might turn out to be inferior in all respects other than the capacity to escape a certain type of environmental danger [pp. 197–198).

The self-perfecting cosmologies of Smuts and Adler never allow for the fact that the adaptive requirements of future environmental conditions might require the decomposition of the attained level of the "whole" or the regressive reactivation of primitive forms of social organization. Yet, this possibility is fully consistent with the evolutionary requirements of survival and propagation. Indeed, its eventuality would be, biologically, just as progressive and just as desirable as the self-perfecting "wholes" of Smuts and the increasingly purified *Gemeinschaft* of Adler.

Such considerations, culled from the philosophy of biology, do not render the schemes of Smuts and Adler worthless. They do, however, clarify anew the principal message of this section: these are vitalistic schemes that metaphysically supplement, but are not derivative from, a strictly biological account of evolution. Adler's own naturalistic protestations notwithstanding, there seems to be no compelling biological reason to consider community feeling the evolutionary outcome of a "law of movement" programmed into the requirements of biological existence.

Adler's recourse to evolutionism supplies the theoretical undergirding of his later career as prophet; it is the naturalistic rationale imputed to *Gemeinschaft* by evolutionary vitalism, that is, which enables *Gemeinschaftsgefuehl* to become both the watchword of Adler's therapeutic faith and the object of his prophetic mission. Having said this much, we must note that the vitalistic underpinnings of the *Gemeinschaft* are largely incidental to Adler's system of psychotherapy. Despite his later contention that the struggle toward a goal of perfection is "fixed by evolution," Adler's therapeutic strategies rely not on "community" as a teleological goal, but on the relative degree of "community feeling"—*Gemeinschaftsgefuehl*—that can be imputed to individual activity (1933a, pp. 155, 164; 1933b, pp. 237, 249). Adler was content to admit that the community which was the "ultimate fulfillment of evolution" was not tantamount to any present-day community, but to an "ideal community" that could only be imagined (1933a, p. 182; 1933b, p. 275; cf. 1933a, pp. 185–186; 1933b, pp. 279–280). This metaphysical inference, however, was irrelevant to the scientific status of his Individual Psychology. Adler wished to make his stand not on the heuristic content of community, but on the clinical significance of community feeling as an objective regulative standard that pertained to the diagnosis and treatment of the emotionally ill. The point was that, in the clinical situation, it was not the *content* of community that was at stake, but the patient's subjective *orientation* toward the goal of community. It was only this subjective orientation that acquired therapeutic meaning in the context of the "life style" which the Adlerian therapist set out to decipher.

This, then, became the crux of Adler's later position. The recourse was once more to that species of neo-Kantian fictionalism he had admired in Vaihinger at the time of his split from Freud. The rationale of his therapy was indeed formulated in terms of dubious vitalistic assumptions; the clinical burden of his therapy, however, rested only on the pragmatic insight that it was clinically efficacious to proceed "as if" the vitalistic assumptions were correct. It is ultimately on the clinical level, in other words, that Adler wanted his invocation of *Gemeinschaft* to be justified, for his philosophy of evolution ultimately served the pragmatic goal of rationalizing and buttressing the clinical categories he had used all his life as physician and psychiatrist. In this section, we have undertaken a substantive critique of Adler's evolutionary vitalism to demonstrate the biological inadequacy of his position. These epistemological considerations are relevant to an evaluation of Adler because they point to Adler's own inability to conceptualize *how* one might accord a superordinate conceptual status to the notion of community feeling, and *why* it might be imperative to do so; these considerations point, in other words, to the impoverished reasoning that underlies Adler's later career as the prophet of *Gemeinschaftsgefuehl*. But it remains to evaluate the strictly pragmatic import of community feeling as a therapeutic tool. We proceed, then, to a question which is not epistemological but frankly therapeutic: is it indeed efficacious to assume, with Adler, that "there is no other standard by which to estimate a person's errors, his symptoms, and his mistaken mode of living (*irrtuemlichen Lebensgang*) than a sufficient measure of right community feeling"? (1933a, p. 138; 1933b, p. 210).

IV.

In all of Adler's later lectures, and especially in *The Meaning of Life*, psychotherapy is made to accommodate the social definition of neurosis at the most pedestrian conceptual level. *Gemeinschaftsgefuehl*, in its varying degrees of absence and presence, becomes the only meaningful therapeutic variable which the psychiatrist can manipulate, and the conformist outcome of *Gemeinschaftsgefuehl*—"social adjustment"—becomes the only normative preconception he may bring to the therapeutic encounter. This clinical implementation of the vitalistic evolutionary imperative rebounded decisively on Adler's answers to the fundamental questions of pedagogy and psychology. The degree of community feeling in the individual was pronounced the "firm standpoint" for the judgment of right and wrong (1933a, p. 68; 1933b, p. 104). "We cannot judge a human being," he wrote in *Understanding Human Nature* (1927), "except by using the concept of community feeling as a standard, and measuring his thought and action according to it'' (1927a, p. 133; 1927b, p. 167). The job of the teacher, correspondingly, was to convince students that the

> great mistakes in life—war, capital punishment, race hatred, hatred of foreign peoples, not to speak of neurosis, suicide, crime, drunkenness, etc.—spring from a lack of community feeling. These mistakes are to be understood in terms of inferiority complexes and destructive attempts to cope with situations in inadmissible and unsuitable ways [1933a, p. 36; 1933b, p. 55].

From the standpoint of personality development, Individual Psychology extolled community feeling as ''the integrating factor in the style of life.'' As its essential ''truth,'' moreover, it posited the ''inexorable demands of an ideal community.'' For the Individual Psychologist, a thought, feeling, or act was characterized as right ''only when it is right *sub specie aeternitatis*'' and only when the welfare of the community is ''incontestably included within it'' (1933a, pp. 111–112, 97; 1933b, pp. 169–170, 146).

Adler arrived at this clinical position by restating the verdict of his evolutionary vitalism in a sociological context. His biological contention was that the ''logic of communal life,'' as the culminating evolutionary advance, had to be assessed as if it were an absolute truth. Correspondingly, ''adaptation to the community'' became ''the most important function of the psychic organ'' (1927a, pp. 19, 23; 1927b, pp. 26–27, 32). From this ''evolutionary'' premise, however, Adler abruptly jumped to the normative characterization of the individual's relation *to* the community. He stated that community feeling had to be the sole evaluative standard of human thought and action,

> because every individual within the body of human society must affirm a deep feeling of the connectedness of life (*ein tiefes Gefuehl fuer die Zusammenhaenge des Lebens*). This necessity causes us to recognize more or less clearly what we owe to others. We exist in the very midst of the agitation of life and are dominated by the logic of human communal life (*der Logik des menschlichen Zusammenlebens*). This determines the fact that we need certain known criteria for the evaluation of other people. As these criteria, we can recognize nothing else but the extent of community feeling. It is impossible for us to deny our mental dependency (*geistige Abhaengigkeit*) on community feeling [1927a, p. 133; 1927b, p. 167].

This translation of evolutionary vitalism into normative sociology ties Adler's system of therapy, once again, to a Durkheimian presupposition. With Durkheim, Adler claimed that ''the individual becomes an individual only in a social context,'' and from here he claimed that the very goal of Individual Psychology was, in fact, social adjustment (1927c, p. 95).

In the course of his later writings, Adler made several passing attempts to mitigate the conformist implications of his conception of social adjustment as the goal of therapy. These attempts proved ill-fated, however, because Adler invoked no critical referent against which to gauge the extent to which present social institutions approximated the guiding *Gemeinschaft* ideal. In *The Meaning of Life*, for example, Adler reiterated that the "right community life" was not the equivalent of present-day communities, but of the community *sub specie aeternitatis*. He admitted, moreover, that "common sense" might justifiably reject present communal achievements "until a higher level of insight into what constitutes the universal welfare has been reached" (1933a, pp. 18n, 179, 160; 1933b, pp. 29n, 271, 243). Beyond this vague concession, however, Adler would not go. He never intimated what a "higher level" in our knowledge would entail, and he never delineated programmatically in what sense a community *sub specie aeternitatis* would differ from present-day communities. In fact, his notion of *Gemeinschaft* is ontologically empty, just as his derivative inference of a *Gemeinschaftsgefuehl,* invoked as a therapeutic covering law, lacks the explicit historical or sociological referents that could convert it into a concept with any critical meaning outside of the Adlerian therapist's subjective intuitions. We see, then, that the emptiness of later Adlerian theory, in its vitalistic evolutionary moorings, necessarily implicates the later Adlerian theory of therapy. Just as Adler's pedagogical perspective includes no theory of cognitive development to explain what "community" can mean to the child as child, so his cosmic vitalism provides no critical referent to determine what "community feeling" *ought* to mean to the therapist as therapist. In the absence of a coherent theory of therapy that ranged beyond the mere supposition of community feeling, the conformist sensibilities of the individual therapist supplied the only superordinate framework within which therapy could be conducted. Ultimately, then, Adler's therapeutic perspective translates into a radical subjectivism reined in only by the overarching injunction that the patient abide by community standards, whatever they may be.

At this point, it is useful to digress briefly in order to justify this sweeping criticism of Adler's basic working concept. The relative emptiness of Adler's formulation is evident in most of his later writings, but it is most apparent when Adler is compared with social theorists who tie man's capacity for "community feeling" to the kind of objective critical referents that Adler ignored. Within the framework of nineteenth-century social theory, Marx and Durkheim are prominent in this respect. Although neither Marx nor Durkheim actually used the concept of "community feeling" as a substantive in the manner of Adler, both theorists relied on key suppositions about man's capacity to experience community feeling that demonstrate Adler's theoretical emptiness in one central respect: Marx and Durkheim both viewed the capacity for community feeling as an emergent property tied to objective historical conditions. For Marx, it was the communist revolution that would transform man into a social being capable of community feeling; for Durkheim it was the consequences of the social division of labor.

In the economic and philosophic manuscripts written early in his career in Paris, Marx transformed the rhetorical invocation of "community feeling" into a critical revolutionary tool by differentiating between man's status as a "social being" before and after the advent of communism. For Marx, man was always a generic social being in the sense that his innate powers and needs could only be realized through productive activity that was collective. In all areas of life, but particularly in production, man was in a close relationship with his fellows because his "needs" (e.g., in sexual relations, in the division of labor) created reciprocal links (see Ollman, 1971, pp. 106–110). Indeed, in *The German Ideology* (1846–47), Marx affirmed that consciousness itself was, from the beginning, "a social product" arising from the necessity of intercourse with other men (p. 51).

Yet, what were the implications of man's generic social condition for the quality of his "feelings" toward the human community? Marx, unlike Adler, hardly equated man's status as a "social being" with any psychological predisposition to act on the basis of beneficent community feelings. He argued instead that man could only actualize his "social" nature when communism abolished the alienated social relations that typified pre-communist society and presented man with sociohistorical conditions that would give free scope to his potential sociability. Under the conditions of capitalism, man could not realize his potential as a free, universal species-being (*Gattungswesen*) because alienated labor reduced his species-life to a mere means of physical existence, thereby preventing the object of man's labor from being an objectification of species-life. To the extent that man was alienated from his own life activity, Marx claimed he was alienated from himself. To the extent that he was in a state of self-alienation, he was, perforce, alienated from his fellow men (1844, pp. 112–115).

With the advent of communism, Marx argued, man would understand that his "social" nature was his "human" nature, because communist society would establish productive relations that enabled the individual to conceptualize others and the necessary objects of others as extensions of himself (1884, p. 136). Indeed, through the conceptual revolution that communism entailed, the "community" would become the new subject with which the individual supplied himself for all but the most personal activities (Ollman, 1971, pp. 109–110; cf.

Tucker, 1961, pp. 150–161). When this happened, man would regain his communal instincts by "return[ing] to himself out of what has historically been known as society, all of whose major institutions have been modes of alienated productive living" (Tucker, 1961, p. 157).

Like Marx, Durkheim posited a critical referent for determining the point in history at which man's social nature would become the basis for genuine community feelings. Durkheim, however, did not tie man's realization of his social potential to a revolutionary upheaval inaugurating new productive relations in society. Instead, he tied the progressive realization of sociability to "organic solidarity," the kind of social connectedness that was related to the evolution of the social division of labor. In distinguishing "organic" solidarity from the "mechanical" solidarity of preindustrial societies, Durkheim made a critical distinction that had no place in Adler's thought. Adler, that is, had nothing to say about the relative quality of different forms of social life. He viewed the division of labor as necessitating social life, but not as a critical referent imparting anything new to the quality of social life. For Adler, the division of labor merely facilitated the linear growth of communality intrinsic to his evolutionary teleology; it enabled the species to continue its existence by "making available to mankind those instruments of offense and defense which are responsible for all its possessions" (1927a, p. 21; 1927b, p. 29; 1933a, p. 38; 1933b, p. 58). Correspondingly, it ensued only after the conditions of evolutionary survival caused men to learn to cooperate (1931a, p. 240).

In *The Division of Labor in Society* (1893), Durkheim's distinction between organic and mechanical forms of social solidarity countered the ahistorical linearity Adler later imputed to social life. Man's communal existence, Durkheim argued, began with a mechanical solidarity that linked the members of primitive societies on the basis of likeness. It was this type of association that fully embodied the integrative requirements of society (i.e., of the *conscience collective*). Durkheim went on to demonstrate, however, that the kind of solidarity that mechanical repressive law expressed was antithetical to the voluntary cooperation and mutuality that followed the division of labor.

Durkheim's verdict about the historical basis of organic solidarity in the division of labor presented the basis, as we have seen, for his prescriptive philosophy of education in *The Moral Education* (1925). The offshoot of his argument was that the cooperative law and restitutive sanctions associated with organic solidarity could not be equated with social life per se. Correspondingly, the kind of community feelings tied to organic solidarity could not be inculcated in the individual as a universal moral requirement of social life. The only requirement of social life was that form of "mechanical" solidarity which reduced men to mechanical compliance to the repressive dictates of the collective conscience. For Durkheim, community feeling (in Adler's sense) was not tantamount to an intensified awareness of community obligations; it presupposed instead concrete historical developments that induced individuals to interact voluntarily in a cooperative division of labor (1893, pp. 266–270).

In this manner, Durkheim, like Marx, elaborated a critical corrective to Adler's blanket equation of social organization with community feeling. He provided, in effect, an *historical* basis for discriminating community feeling from simple communal connectedness. In this respect, the basic anti-Adlerian assumption which Durkheim articulated in opposition to the sociological thought of Herbert Spencer but in agreement with the positivist Auguste Comte, was that cooperation did not produce society, but necessarily presupposed the spontaneous existence of society as a precondition:

> What bring men together are mechanical causes and impulsive forces, such as affinity of blood, attachment to the same soil, ancestral worship, community of habits, etc. It is only when the group has been formed on these bases that cooperation is organized there [1893, p. 278].

Unlike Marx and Durkheim, Adler had no historical referent for determining at what point the mere fact of human communality provided a substantive basis for the human ideal of *Gemeinschaft*. And yet it was precisely to history that Adler was constrained to turn, given his insistence that the status of community as a therapeutic ideal followed from its progressive realization in human history. By failing to consider community feeling as an historically emergent human potential that was discontinuous with the fact of human communality per se, Adler was led to a theory of therapy that is utterly banal in its inability to provide any critical basis for gauging the relative adequacy of different forms of cooperation (cf. R. Jacoby, 1975, pp. 20ff.). In a revealing article written after the outbreak of World War I, he readily conceded the impossibility of educating children to a *Gemeinschaft* modeled on a present-day society torn up into antagonistic fragments (*von Gegensaetzen zerrissene Gesellschaft*). He never elaborated this basic insight, however, and his advice based on the present social reality was tautological rather than critical: "From this consideration we arrive at the self-evident requirement that we should only value as teachers those whose social guiding line at least suffices for the assertion of communal sense (*wenigstens bis zur Behauptung des Gemeinsinnes reicht*)" (1914b, p. 42; cf. 1914a, p. 475). But how do we know when a teacher adequately embodies the sense of the community? Of this, Adler had nothing programmatic to say, beyond his oft repeated insistence that such a teacher would not approve the present cultural depreciation of the female role that complicated the healthy development of girls (1914b, p. 42).

V.

When Adler's heuristic *Gemeinschaftsgefuehl* criterion was extended to the realm of psychopathology, the outcome was predictably subjectivistic. Lacking any critical referent for distinguishing adaptive from maladaptive cooperation, he similarly provided no basis for distinguishing between social adjustment as a therapeutic goal and simple social conformism. From the standpoint of the Adlerian theory of therapy, the two proved functionally identical. In the period following World War I, Adler's basic clinical categories remained identical to those formulated in *The Nervous Character*, but the conformist dimension of "normal" superiority strivings became explicit and central.

Adler argued during this period that neurosis *was* a lack of community feeling, and he characterized neurotic symptoms as "safeguards of persons who do not feel adequately equipped or prepared for the problems of life, who carry within themselves only a passive appreciation of community feeling and interest" (1932, pp. 90, 95). As in his early work, he located the predisposition to neurosis in an exaggerated perception of inferiority, but he now accounted for this inferiority less in terms of organic predisposition than lack of "social preparation" for specific social "tasks" (e.g., coping with the birth of a sibling or entering school). Neurosis, by this analysis, was nothing but a chronic "avoidance" condition precipitated by the "shock" (*Erschuetterung*) that followed the initial inability to meet the social task (1933a, pp. 107–108; 1933b, pp. 162–163). Because his social training had been deficient, the neurotic's latent potential for community feeling had never been activated and had never been able to mitigate the core sense of inadequacy that followed the initial social failures. Sensitized by these early failures to the degrading possibility of being proven worthless, the neurotic was subsequently "trained in his law of movement to retreat from tasks that might, as he feared, through his failing in them injure his self-esteem and interfere with his struggle for personal superiority." Adler said that the neurotic "secured" himself by his retreat, and he additionally characterized neurosis as "the exploiting of the shock experiences for the protection of the threatened nimbus" (1933a, pp. 113–114; 1933b, pp. 171–174). In every case, the proper "solutions" to the "tasks" of life were never at issue. The Adlerian therapist implicitly assumed that the healthy individual accepted community standards of right and wrong and worked toward a sense of self-esteem within the prescribed institutional arrangements.

The conformist mandate implicit in these therapeutic assumptions rever-
berated in two directions. In the explicit contention that neurotics, psychotics,
and delinquents lacked "a correct goal of perfection" (1933c, pp. 33–34), Adler
emphasized the centrality of socioethical values in any psychiatric theory. When
he contended that the cure of neurosis involved the destruction of a "faulty
picture of the world" and the "unequivocal acceptance of a mature picture of the
world" (1936, p. 97), Adler embraced the status of the therapist as a moral and
political agent who had to pass judgment on deviant behavior from certain
normative social premises. Adler's very conceptualization of psychotherapy accepted the political consequences of psychiatric intervention as an integral part of
all therapeutic change, and in this sense he is an important precursor of contemporary critics of a "value-free" psychotherapy like Thomas Szasz (1961), Perry
London (1964), and Seymour Halleck (1971).

There is a sinister implication, however, in Adler's recognition of the therapist as a moral agent reeducating the patient to assume his conformist responsibilities. Since the therapeutic meaning of "social adaptation" resided only in
the therapist's own subjective estimation of the *Gemeinschaft,* the preconceptions guiding therapeutic change were necessarily restricted to the therapist's
own conformist sensibilities. Yet, the Adlerian system presented no formal criteria for gauging the therapeutic adequacy of the mental preconceptions and subjective priorities embodied in a particular vision of the *Gemeinschaft.* In fact, the
thrust of Adler's vitalistic rationale for the desirability of *Gemeinschaft* worked
against any such critical estimation. By making the growing apprehension of
Gemeinschaft—the *Gemeinschaftsgefuehl*—the "scientific" endpoint of evolutionary teleology, Adler effectively imparted a naturalistic sanction to the psychiatrist's therapeutic reliance on his own conformist values. This sanction resulted
from a subtle two-pronged process of reification of an affective substantive
(community feeling) into the "objective" embodiment of evolutionary progress
and sole criterion for gauging mental health. Because the reification of community feeling was made without any critical referent outside the initial vitalistic
inference, however, it inevitably facilitated a second level of reification by which
the therapist's own subjective sense of community feeling became the objective
equivalent of the goal of evolution. To the degree that the very basis for invoking
community feeling as a therapeutic goal was vitalistic, there was never any
theoretical or clinical basis for evaluating the *therapist's* subjective understanding of the concept outside of his formal acceptance of Adler's teleological evolutionary doctrine. In pragmatic terms, this all translated into the compatibility of
the therapist's own intuitive vision of the "ideal society" with that of Adler.

At this point, it is easy to see how the latent authoritarian overtones that were always present in Adler's reeducative therapy became more explicit in the later writings. Believing that his own conformist sensibilities were tantamount to a scientific mandate, he ultimately preached the coming of an era of *Gemeinschaftsgefuehl* as a chiliastic visionary convinced that the day of psychological judgment was at hand. "Whatever changes the future may bring in the methods of the production and distribution of wealth," he enjoined in *The Meaning of Life*, "the changes will necessarily be in better accord with the power of community feeling than there exists today, whether the changes are brought about by force or by mutual consent." He indicated in this work the authoritarian imperative bound up in this crucial evolutionary development: "Every one submits more or less willingly to the iron law of the ideal community" (1933a, pp. 38, 112; 1933b, pp. 59, 171). He ended the book on a prophetic note, claiming that community feeling would become the watchword not only of evolutionary teleology, but of a new ideology as well:

> This community feeling exists within us and endeavors to carry out its purpose; it does not seem strong enough to hold its own against all opposing forces. The justified expectation persists that in the distant future, if mankind is given enough time, the power of community feeling will triumph over everything that opposes it. Then it will be as natural to man as the act of breathing. For the present the only alternative is to understand and to teach that this development is in the necessary course of things [1933a, pp. 189–190; 1933b, p. 285].

In these later writings, the conviction that the coming of community feeling provided the basis for a new ideology rebounded decisively on Adler's diagnostic ascriptions, converting clinical categories into judgmental moral categories. As the prophet of *Gemeinschaftsgefuehl,* Adler was no longer content with the relatively neutral connotations of the term inferiority (*Minderwertigkeit*); he opted instead for the term cowardice (*Feigheit*) to encompass more suggestively the ideological impact of neurosis and delinquency on the evolutionary movement toward *Gemeinschaft*. Neurotics, delinquents, and criminals were all "cowards" in the sense that they denied the naturalistic necessity of community feeling and were unwilling to exercise the restraint and self-control involved in pursuing self-esteem within the prescribed social boundaries. Instead, they chose to pursue "superiority" in antisocial ways that minimized their neurotic vulnerabilities. Therapy for these deviants was tantamount to moral reawakening; it undertook to sensitize them to the fact that the deviant framework in which they pursued superiority really rendered their behavior cowardly and despicable while providing a self-esteem that was sham and transparent. Therapeutic change ensued once the patient accepted the *prerogative* of the Adlerian therapist to pass moral judgment on deviant behavior in a way that was directly relevant to the patient's own inferiority-superiority preconceptions.

This strategy, and the use of the moral categories it entailed, illuminate one of the significant paradoxes of late Adlerian theory. At the same time Adler endorsed a gentle supportive therapy that acknowledged and even dignified the patient's ego needs from within the patient's own subjective preconceptions, his professional diagnostic assessment of these patients became little more than moral condemnation. In this respect, his commitment to community feeling as ideology took him far beyond the more neutral verdict of *The Nervous Character*. In *Understanding Human Nature,* it was no longer a question of merely calling attention to the fact that neurotic superiority strivings were erected on the foundations of neurotic inferiority feelings. Instead, Adler wrote, "we must designate all angry men (*zornige Menschen*) [in whom community feeling has been annulled] as enemies of life" (1927a, p. 217; 1927b, p. 269). The disparity between a man's personal affairs and the welfare of society was no longer a mere clinical denotation of neurotic suffering, but "the measure of hostility (*Feindseligkeit*)" to the community (1927a, p. 186; 1927b, p. 232). From the ideological standpoint of community feeling, the neurotic sufferer who chose maladaptive "psychic detours" to safeguard his precarious ego strength was a deserter (*Ausreisser*), and "society has no place for deserters" (1927a, p. 198; 1927b, p. 246; cf. 1914a, p. 486). As humanity moved toward the realization of the predestined *Gemeinschaft,* it was the psychotherapist trained in Individual Psychological methods who became, for Adler, the legislator and judge of the *Gemeinschaftsgefuehl* content of human behavior. "The problem that the psychiatrist and the psychologist have to face," he wrote, "is the discovery of the norms within us by which we pass judgment on the human form" (1933a, p. 59; 1933b, p. 91). From a clinical standpoint, however, the mission remained an empty one. From the outset, the social content of community feeling was securely tied up with Adler's own conformist sensibilities, and his later writings are virtually authoritarian in their blanket equation of traditional social institutions with the requirements of optimal social adaptation. In these writings, Adler could hardly be further from the socialist politics of his youth. He became a conservative with a vengeance, intent on lodging the values of positive mental health within the bosom of the nuclear family and its sacrosanct institutions. From his evolutionary supposition that love and marriage were "social tasks" that were ultimately "for the sake of the race," he concluded that monogamy was "the highest form of marriage" and the "best active adaptation to evolution" (1929, p. 122;

1931a, pp. 280–281; 1933a, p. 40; 1933b, p. 61). Any deviation from this conventional norm departed from the requirement of "community feeling in love" and could "lead to our exculsion from everlasting existence on this earth in our children and in our cultural achievements." He continued:

> Such trifling with love as is seen in promiscuity, in prostitution, in perversions, or in the hidden retreat of the nudist cults, would deprive love of all its grandeur, of all splendour, and of all aesthetic fascination. The refusal to enter into a lasting union sows doubt and mistrust between the two partners in a common task and makes them incapable of devoting themselves entirely to one another. Similar difficulties, though varying for each individual, can be shown to be signs of diminished community feeling in all cases of unhappy love and marriage, and in all cases characterized by a refusal to perform functions that are justifiably expected [1933a, p. 40; 1933b, p. 61].

Adler's prescriptive guidelines for marital union did not end with this admonishment. Since procreation guaranteed the welfare and the continuity of the race, he further argued that the decision to have children was necessary "for a full solution of the problem of love and marriage." Only couples unwilling to assume their social obligations to the *Gemeinschaft* could "refuse the burden of procreation." Because the institution of marriage could only thrive when there was sufficient community feeling between partners, Adler added that the institution would be best secured "if there have not been sexual relations before the marriage." Moreover, he only endorsed marriages between those of equivalent social status and education, claiming that those who chose partners below them in these respects betrayed an inability to cooperate: "They are afraid of love and marriage and wish to establish a situation in which their partner will look up to them" (1931a, pp. 280, 276–277).

These conformist standards were to be implemented by a select vanguard initiated into the evolutionary requirements of *Gemeinschaft*—the psychologists and psychiatrists trained in the methods of Individual Psychology. Here Adler's faith in liberal democratic values simply ran out. He sought the traditional liberal values, but he questioned the ability of the untutored to perceive the preeminence of these values in psychological terms. When precipitous marriages ended in unhappiness and the "dissolution of the tie of love and marriage" had to be broached, Adler said the decision should not be left to the same people "who themselves are not rightly taught, who themselves do not understand that marriage is a task." Instead, the disinterested perspective of the Adlerian therapist who could judge the marriage from the standpoint of the social welfare had to be invoked. The question, in short, "should be placed in the hands of experienced psychologists who can be relied upon to render judgment in accordance with the requirements of community feeling'' (1933a, p. 40; 1933b, p. 62). Adler presented this claim in *The Meaning of Life,* and he reiterated it elsewhere (e.g., 1931a, p. 283). In *The Science of Living* he wondered, moreover,

> whether it would not be possible to establish advisory councils which could untangle the mistakes of matrimony by the methods of Individual Psychology. Such councils would be composed of trained persons who would understand how all the events in individuals' lives cohere and hang together, and who would have the power of sympathetic identification with the persons seeking advice [1929c, pp. 118–119].

Such councils would not only sanction divorces but would advise divorced persons whether a new love relation or marriage ''had in it any possibility of success'' (p. 119). Beyond the issues of marriage and divorce, whenever an abortion was desired, a ''qualified psychological advisor'' should be called in to ''dismiss any unwarranted reasons adduced for abortion, and if the reasons were sound to give permission for the abortion'' (1933a, p. 41; 1933b, p. 63).

These regulative strictures proceeded from benign therapeutic intent, but they were clearly authoritarian in their implementation and reactionary in their social impact. This is the sinister implication of Adler's teleological belief in ''social adaptation'' as the propelling force behind evolution. To translate this evolutionary supposition into a viable lever for directing psychotherapeutic change, Adler had to make the psychotherapist the sole judge of how socially adapted people would act in the cooperative *Gemeinschaft* of the future. By accepting the therapeutic recommendations of the Adlerian therapist, the Adlerian patient implicitly acknowledged the therapist's status as a member of a natural elite able to equate community norms with the requirements of mental health and able to advise the patient what he must do to behave ''as if'' he were a healthy member of the community.

To the extent that these requirements of mental health dovetail with the specific kinds of social organization that typify present society, Adler's latter-day philosophy of *Gemeinschaftsgefuehl* is strangely reminiscent of the conformist restorationist sociologies that arose in the wake of the French Revolution. Convinced that the Revolution and its ensuing Terror were the necessary culmination of mistaken Enlightenment theories of equality, post-Revolution theocrats like de Bonald and de Maistre retreated to ''organismic'' theories of society that viewed inequalities between men as natural and the institutions that ordered these inequalities as sacrosanct. Like Adler, these men articulated a radically anti-individualist ethic based on the belief that man did not perfect society but society, as God's instrument of salvation, that perfected men. It fell to Saint-Simon, however, to reconcile the organicism of de Bonald and de Maistre with the scientism of the Enlightenment in a way that curiously pre-figured Adler's own amalgamation of social organicism with an evolutionary teleology extracted from nineteenth-century biology. Just as Adler's later preoc-cupation with social adaptation originated in a medical study that defined ''in-ferior'' organs in terms of relative social deficiencies, so Saint-Simon's vision of an organic society reconstructed under the beneficent direction of nineteenth-century industrialism was anchored in his own reading of the eighteenth-century physiologists. From the naturalistic physiological typologies constructed by Cabanis and Bichat, Saint-Simon concluded that inequality was natural, and he elaborated a vision of the future in which a natural elite directed society in accord with objective scientific criteria.

Saint-Simon's scientific model for the perfecting of society was not Darwin and evolution but Newton and physiology. He construed the ordering of society as a project in ''social physiology,'' and he initially turned to a priesthood of scientists who would arrive at the final social physiology able to perfect the human community. Later, in the post-Napoleonic Restoration, he turned to a broad industrial class as the natural elite that could best oversee the triumph of industry and science while bypassing the deceptive overtures of contemporary liberalism. The leadership of the industrial elite was to be accepted gratefully by the different classes composing society because, for Saint-Simon, as for the theocrats, men desired not equality but retention of their traditional social roles. Saint-Simon went beyond the theocrats, however, in contending that this desire was anchored in the ''scientific'' fact that various social roles corresponded to immutable physiological aptitudes.[8] From Saint-Simon's ''social physiology'' it was a short step indeed to the ''social physics'' of Comte and the subsequent transmutation of positivism in the nineteenth century into a doctrine of social ethics and political reconstruction (see Charlton, 1959).

This development was not restricted to the full-blown development of a secu-larized Religion of Humanity in Comte's later writings. It appeared in the origi-nal presentations of positivism and was fully embodied in the early essays Comte wrote for the Saint-Simonian journal *Producteur* in 1825–1826. Already, in these early positivist essays, there is a remarkable anticipation of the late Adlerian program, with the regulative dimension of positivist sociology sup-

---

[8]My discussion of Saint-Simon generally follows Manuel (1956, Part IV and 1962, pp. 103–142). The authoritarian dimension of Saint-Simon's socialism has been especially stressed by Hayek (1955, pp. 123ff.) and G. Iggers (1958).

planting the regulative strictures of Individual Psychology. In both cases the authoritarian organization of social life completed a naturalistic program on behalf of the social "whole." Just as Adler's vision of *Gemeinschaft* satisfied the requirements of biological evolution, so Comte's Social Physics completed the positivistic transformation of the hierarchy of the natural sciences (Comte, 1825, p. 599). Indeed, the sequential rationalization of the hierarchy of sciences imparted a social evolutionary dimension to Comte's scheme. He was led to view the essence of Social Physics as the outcome of "regarding the thorough study of the past as furnishing the true explanation of the present and a general indication of the future" (p. 599).

The political program of positivism comparably mimicked the therapeutic program of Adlerian psychology by sanctifying social conformism with a "positivist" mandate. Just as Individual Psychology therapy sought to educate the patient to accept social adaptation as the distinguishing criterion of mental health, so Comte saw Social Physics as politically necessary "as the condition of a homogenous social education" (1825, p. 606). Moreover, as Adler hoped to place the regulation of social education in the hands of advisory councils of Adlerian therapists, so Comte pointed to a new class of positivist *savants* who would "incorporate themselves anew with society in order to assume, once more, its spiritual guidance" (p. 614). In an essay entitled "Considerations on the Spiritual Power" (1826), Comte plainly delineated the kind of "spiritual guidance" he had in mind. The new *savants* would constitute a veritable "Moral Government" capable of eliminating the reigning intellectual anarchy, social materialism, and corruption of his day, and formulating a unified public morality in its wake. In social structural terms, the spiritual power would strive to mitigate the chief negative effect of the division of labor—the progressive specialization that increasingly rendered the individual unfit to grasp "the relation between his special activity and the entirety of social activity." The new elite would strive "to bring back to the general point of view minds predisposed to diverge, and to impose the common interest upon individualities which constantly tend to deviate from it." To this end it would put forth and enforce positive principles for the regulation of active life "so far as moral means are efficacious for that purpose" (1826, pp. 633–634).

In both directive and repressive ways, Comte consequently viewed spiritual guidance much as Adler would come to view therapeutic guidance—as helping the individual integrate his behavior with the harmonious *ensemble*. His Political Art completed the restorationist program of the Second Empire in terms that accurately prefigured the requirements for a society based on *Gemeinschaftsgefuehl* as Adler would formulate them a century later. To facilitate social harmony, Comte wrote, the individual adaptive tendency needs to be, so to speak, vivified by a moral force, regularly organized, which, continually recalling it to the remembrance of each in the interest of all, can impart the energy that results from such universal adhesion, and is alone capable of overcoming, or even adequately counterbalancing, the force of the antisocial dispositions naturally preponderant in human nature [1826, p. 637].

Adler's appeal to a body of trained psychotherapists to regulate social relations fully approximated the positivist "moral force" that Comte invoked. Although Adler did not anchor his scheme of social regulation in a supposition of social inequality, he invoked a supposition of psychological inequality that had comparable practical consequences. Men, for Adler, through the vicissitudes of organ endowment, social training, sibling placement, and educational opportunities, were unequal as psychological agents. Through different kinds of deficiencies, certain individuals were unable to evaluate their behavior according to the psychological criteria that were compatible with the evolutionary perfection of society. To remedy this inequality, Adler supplanted Comte's authoritarian socialism with a potentially authoritarian psychologism. When Comte, in his later career, elaborated the positivistic mandate for a program of social reconstruction that would place society at the disposal of his spiritual elite, he outlined a scheme that was neither more scientific in its justification, nor more authoritarian in its implications, than Adler's vision of the future *Gemeinschaft*. For the priesthood of scientists, Adler substituted a priesthood of psychologists; for the Religion of Humanity he substituted, in accord with his own evolutionary preconceptions, the Religion of *Gemeinschaftsgefuehl*.

VI.

To compare Adler's conformist therapy of community feeling to European restorationist sociologies that followed the French Revolution is to pose an obvious question: given the obvious parallels that exist, in what sense can Adler be construed as a restorationist? The material that broadly answers this question has figured in much of this study, but it is important at this point to summarize it in terms of the particular issue at hand.

Adler's view of the cooperative *Gemeinschaft* benignly administered by trained Individual Psychologists was first of all a restorationist reaction to World War I. Adler, like the many Germans who were attracted to Toennies during this time, saw *Gemeinschaft* as a vitalistic principle that reduced the aggression of the Great War to an aberrational departure from the main direction of social evolution. To ensure steady movement toward this evolutionary mandate in the future, the precepts of Individual Psychology were to be invoked as beneficent guiding stars. Inherent in this vision was Adler's desire to reduce the problem of social planning to the manageable dimensions of educating children. His collaboration with the Vienna School Board in the immediate aftermath of the war had been his principal public success, and his ultimate view of the good society sought to interpret the kind of educational counseling that occurred in his Vienna child guidance clinics as a fully adequate model for social adaptation.

Beyond this general factor, Adler figures as a restorationist in the more specific context provided by the history of the psychoanalytic movement. There is an important sense, as Karl Mannheim (1936, pp. 229–230) has reminded us, in which conservative utopian thought is actually counterutopian, i.e., it serves as a means of self-orientation and defense against counterideologies that have already been formulated by ascendent classes in society. Adler's vision of a conformist *Gemeinschaft* seems to fit Mannheim's conception of the conservative utopian mentality, and the ascendent class of psychological theorists against which Adler articulated his utopian message was, of course, that of the psychoanalysts.

There seems little doubt that Adler's restorationist sentiments were long fueled by his ongoing antipathy to Freud. Moreover, his later lectures indicate that in the years following the war, he was newly sensitized to the damaging implications of Freud's final instinct theory for his optimistic social forecast. To the end, he claimed insistently that all Freud's metapsychological concepts merely restated the "striving from below to above" in arcane phraseology, reifying in the process different deviant dimensions of the ego's "striving" into anthropomorphic "drives" that were artificial and demonic (1931b). Adler's vision of the regulated *Gemeinschaft* of the future was a concerted attempt to restore a pre-Freudian optimism to depth psychology. He reacted, in this respect, against the pessimistic social philosophy and fatalistic therapeutic strictures contained in Freud's post-World War I formulations. This pessimism did not attach primarily to Freud's derivation of a biological "death instinct" in *Beyond the Pleasure Principle* (1920). It resided, instead, in the clinical and cultural implications of the death instinct that Freud elaborated in monographs like *The Ego and the Id* (1923), *Civilization and its Discontents* (1930), and in his late clinical essay "Analysis Terminable and Interminable" (1937).

The first significant expression of this pessimism is found in *The Ego and the Id*, where Freud integrated his dual instinct theory with the theory of the three psychic agencies—id, ego, superego. By conceptualizing the superego as the psychic reservoir of a death instinct that had been simultaneously internalized and "defused," Freud provided a theoretical explanation for the "negative therapeutic reaction'' that frequently undercut the therapeutic progress of psychoanalytic patients. This negative reaction was, in reality, an ''unconscious sense of guilt,'' and this sense of guilt represented the ''extraordinary harshness and severity'' of the superego toward the ego (Freud, 1923, p. 53; 1937, p. 243; see also Ricoeur, 1970, pp. 296–300 and Stepansky, 1977, pp. 177ff.). If the internalized representative of the death instinct made for clinical fatalism, the externalized enactment of it made for still deeper cultural pessimism. *In Civilization and its Discontents,* Freud formally equated his biological death instinct with an externalized instinct of aggression and destruction that undermined cultural relations and required society to rise as ''the implacable dispenser of justice.'' The rebound of this cultural interpretation on the biological status of the death instinct was dire in its social implications: the ''sense of guilt'' previously viewed as the unwarranted severity of the superego was now designated the necessary instrument used by culture against man's aggressiveness (see Stepansky, 1977, p. 182).

Given these implications of instinct theory, Freud could never share Adler's optimism about the educational status of psychotherapy. Though he readily granted that psychoanalysis had an important role to play in the education of children, it was always a limited prophylactic role that had to accept at face value the bleak verdict of instinct theory. Instead of forecasting the happy *Gemeinschaft* that would ensue when therapy had done its educational work, Freud (1927, pp. 8–9) more characteristically protested that man's modest capacity for education necessarily limited the effectiveness of any cultural transformation that attempted to mitigate the degree of coercion needed in civilization. Moreover, even as educational intervention might help prevent neuroses, Freud saw neurosis itself as ''a risk with all education'' (1916–1917, p. 355). This risk stemmed from the infantile sexual experiences on which early psychoanalytic education would invariably concentrate. Such education might forestall developmental difficulties, but it also ran the risk of accomplishing either too much or too little sexual suppression. The gains of an education enriched by psychoanalysis were thereby rendered tentative and problematic. Such education, for Freud, had no choice but to ''find its way between the Scylla of noninterference and the Charybdis of frustration'' (1933, p. 149).

Freud's eventual acceptance of the description of psychoanalysis as a kind of aftereducation (*Nacherziehung*) merely underscored the confessed inability of analysis to generate an educational theory that could succeed in its prophylactic work. In his Preface to Aichhorn's *Wayward Youth* (1925b), he characterized the work of education as *sui generis* and accordingly rejected the idea that it could be replaced by psychoanalytic influence. Psychoanalysis, wrote Freud, was an auxiliary means of dealing with a child, "but it is not a suitable substitute for education" (1925b, p. 274).

Teamed with this skeptical estimation of "psychoanalytic" education was Freud's own summary dismissal of "social feelings" as secondary phenomena reducible to the primary instincts. The group spirit (*Gemeingeist*), he admonished in *Group Psychology and the Analysis of the Ego* (1921), was in reality a reaction formation deriving from original feelings of envy and hostility. Such communality only arose when original rivals "succeeded in identifying themselves with one another by means of a similar love for the same object." Thus, "social feeling is based upon the reversal of what was first a hostile feeling into a positively toned tie in the nature of an identification" (pp. 119–121). According to psychoanalysis, in other words, social feeling could only emerge when "aggressive inclinations" toward a "formerly hated object" had been surmounted (Freud, 1922, pp. 231–232; 1923, pp. 37, 43; on the origins of Freud's group psychology, see Rieff, 1956).

Adler's regulated *Gemeinschaft* was articulated as a pointed rejoinder to these pessimistic psychoanalytic deductions. In a letter to the Hebrew novelist Yohanan Twersky of 1 April 1929, Adler protested that the "fundamental difference" between psychoanalysis and Individual Psychology lay in their respective points of departure. "While Freud's 'Unconscious' is full of egoism, cruelty (*Grausamkeit*), and the yearning for sexual gratification" as innate remnants of development, Individual Psychology upheld "the better supported conception . . . that the human being always had a friendly, good essence (*Wesen*), full of communal interest. This latter quality is destroyed and turned to evil only through bad incidents and severely malignant relationships (*schlimme Zwischenfaelle und starke Ungunst der Verhaeltnisse*)." "It seems," he continued, "that the scholarly and general perception is turning more and more to Individual Psychology's perception, which sees as its goal an optimistic world view, the strengthening of individual responsibility, and a harmonic formation of our individual and universal life" (Adler to Twersky, 1 April 1929, Jewish National and University Library [Jerusalem], Schwadron autograph collection).

In his final published comparison of psychoanalysis and Individual Psychology in 1931, Adler reaffirmed these optimistic sentiments by disavowing Freud's assumption that man only sought satisfaction of instinctual drives and was therefore "completely bad" from the viewpoint of culture. "Individual Psychology," he countered,

> states that the development of man, by virtue of his inadequate physique, is subject to the redeeming influence of community feeling, so that all his drives can be

guided in the direction of the generally useful. The indestructible destiny of the human species is community feeling. In Individual Psychology this is the truth; in psychoanalysis it is a trick [1931b, pp. 210–211].

Freud's "death wish," in this connection, was no more than "an unrecognized confession of weakness in the face of reality." It betokened a lack of community feeling characteristic of "the weak in heart" (pp. 208–209).[9] In *The Meaning of Life,* Adler betrayed his ongoing preoccupation with Freud's pessimism in comparable terms. Freud's "distorted nomenclature" invariably described the failings of "pampered children"; his "evil instincts" (*boesen Triebe*) were the consequence of pampering and embodied wishes and fantasies that had been artificially nurtured in the child. Impulses of hate (*Hassregungen*) and death wishes "are the familiar artificial products of an incorrect training in community feeling." They arose from "the inferiority complex of pampered children" (1933a, pp. 140, 152, 166; 1933b, pp. 213–214, 232, 253).

In these polemical protestations, Adler's restorationist ethic was always transparent. He sought to restore faith in the positive function of psychotherapy as social education, and he strove to convince others that this kind of therapy would be instrumental in ensuring the evolutionary march of social progress. The priesthood of the psychologist was a small price to pay to inculcate the moral ideals that would disprove Freud's dire prognosis and inaugurate a new *Gemeinschaft* at peace with itself.

---

[9]Adler made the common error of equating Freud's "death instinct" with a veritable "death wish." There is no basis for this identification in Freud's writings. See Stepansky (1977, pp. 17–18).

Appendix
The Hidden Adler in Freud

There is one final paradox built into Freud's perspective on Adler and the "aggressive instinct" during the period following the split. This concerns the degree to which Freud continued to incorporate implicit Adlerian premises into his clinical writings of the time despite the fact that these papers tried to subsume Adler's "masculine protest" under psychoanalytic formulations of castration anxiety and penis envy.[1]

This is one of the ironic offshoots of Freud's heightened sensitivity to the drive status of Adler's "aggressive instinct": it blinded him to the full interpretive range of the masculine protest as Adler himself understood it. Consequently, when Freud encountered what appeared to be a "masculine protest" in his clinical material, he was generally content to offer a summary judgment that sidestepped without successfully resolving the interpretive issue at stake. To a large extent, the very criticism that Freud made of Adler—that he innovated terminologically without going beyond the explanatory range of psycho-analysis—came full circle in these clinical discussions. When Freud was content

---

[1]This statement pertains only to Freud's construal of the masculine protest in his published clinical writings. Kardiner (1977, pp. 70–71) suggests that, as a therapist, Freud could be quite unequivocal in his reliance on the masculine protest qua masculine protest. In this connection, Kardiner recounts Freud's interpretation of a dream that occurred during his personal analysis with Freud of 1921–1922: " 'But I see from your second dream that you are not necessarily willing to surrender. You do have intercourse with your stepmother. That's the assertive part of your character and part of your masculine protest. There's a lot of fight in you. It was a life-or-death struggle for your survival. You undoubtedly felt very insignificant in your childhood' " (pp. 55–56).

to translate the apparent fact of a masculine protest into the language of castration anxiety and penis envy, that is, he transformed without effectively undercutting the possibility of the Adlerian interpretation of the same clinical facts. Freud's psychoanalytic rendering of the masculine protest in his clinical presentations was never more than partially successful, then, because his contentment with summary terminological refutation always permitted an Adlerian rejoinder by which castration anxiety itself could be attributed to a preexisting (i.e., a pre-oedipal) masculine protest. Thus, Freud's repudiation of Adler's masculine protest, in its summary imputation of a "masculine" libidinal or narcissistic component, often involved the very type of terminological sleight of hand of which Adler, for Freud, stood accused. Furthermore, even as Freud construed the masculine protest as one evaluative component of libidinal development, he unwittingly demonstrated how Adlerian assumptions could be tacitly incorporated into clinical discourse without formal recourse to Adlerian terminology. In the following analysis, I wish to take the position of an Adlerian advocate in order to demonstrate the equivocal and ultimately unsatisfactory nature of Freud's published disavowal of the masculine protest. My intention is neither to defend Adler nor to sustain the viability of an Adlerian critique of libido theory. Rather, I am only interested in presenting further evidence for my historical claim that Freud's objections to Adler in the period surrounding the split are essentially "symptomatic" in nature (see chapter 5, section IV).

I should reiterate my belief that Freud's critique of Adler could have been conducted along radically different and more substantial lines (cf. the critique of Lou Andreas-Salomé reviewed in chapter 6). Moreover, we shall see that Freud was in fact able to challenge Adler's sexualized theory of repression in a more meaningful theoretical way in the essay " 'A Child is Being Beaten' " of 1919. In the years surrounding the split, however, the unsatisfying polemical quality of Freud's critique refers back to the host of personal, professional, and political factors that induced him to be selectively inattentive to the grounds of Adler's ego psychology. I shall not discuss these factors further here, but I would certainly invoke them in offering the following analysis as a continuation of my critique of Freud's published evaluation of Adler (see chapter 7, section II).

A key example of Freud's convoluted maneuverings toward Adler's theory is his *Psycho-Analytic Notes upon an Autobiographical Account of a Case of Paranoia (Dementia Paranoides)* published in 1911, the famous "Schreber" case history. It is clear that Freud was preoccupied with Adler while he prepared this study; he had confided to Jung that it was only the Adler affair that disturbed his "peace" during the work on paranoia (letter of 22 December 1910, *Freud/Jung Letters*, p. 382). Freud's awareness of the deteriorating situation with Adler was undoubtedly at the heart of his clinical interpretations in the Schreber case; he clearly construed the piece as a successful defense against Adler's theoretical incursions. When, in March, 1911, he called its forthcoming appearance in the *Jahrbuch* to the attention of his friend Ludwig Binswanger, he characterized it as "a bold stroke at the heart of the enemy position and at the problem of Paranoia" (quoted in Binswanger, 1957, p. 31). Freud sought to execute his "bold stroke" by demonstrating how the particular delusional formations that accompanied a paranoid psychosis had to undergo a secondary revision that reconciled them with masculine ego needs. In the case in question, Schreber's homosexual attachment to his physician Flechsig and homosexual fantasies of being transformed into a woman could only achieve delusional representation when Schreber's "masculine indignation" toward these fantasied productions was neutralized (1911, p. 33). For Freud, this intact dimension of Schreber's "masculine protest" accounted for the transformation of his interpersonal delusions into the Redeemer fantasy that was at the heart of his religious delusions. Schreber's sensual, feminine attitude toward God represented an ego-syntonic embodiment of passive homosexual fantasies toward his physician, in other words, because his masculine protest could only tolerate this overt acceptance of the female role if "it was God Himself who, for His own satisfaction, was demanding femaleness from him" (p. 33).

Given the "libidinal" nature of the feminine fantasies, Freud was content to construe the resulting "delusion of persecution" in true Adlerian fashion: as the end product of the "ensuing defensive struggle" prompted by the "intense resistance" of Schreber's personality to his feminine fantasy. When Freud referred to the ego needs served by the symptomatic transformation, he was presupposing a decidedly "masculine" ego feeling in the Adlerian sense. He formally viewed these masculine ego needs as secondary phenomena that worked over without etiologically "arranging" the homosexual libido. Yet, it is curious that, even in the case of this delusional psychotic, Freud emphasized that the emergent symptomatology was fully dependent on masculine valuational criteria existing outside the libidinal psychopathology. Psychosis, from this perspective, presupposed a veritable compromise analogous to the compromise typifying neurosis. With psychosis, however, this compromise did not involve reality aspects of the ego instincts, but the internalized masculine sense of adequacy adhering to the ego apart from its ties to the real world. Thus, Freud observed that

> It was impossible for Schreber to become reconciled to playing the part of a female wanton towards his doctor; but the task of providing God Himself with the volup-

tuous sensations that He required called up no such resistance on the part of his ego [p. 48].

Again, commenting on Schreber's vision of the universal redemption that would proceed from his sexual submission, Freud made the same point and invoked, uncharacteristically, Adler's idea of compensation:

> By this means an outlet was provided which would satisfy both of the contending forces. His ego found compensation in his megalomania, while his feminine wishful phantasy made its way through and became acceptable [p. 48].

Clearly, Freud's formulation invoked Adlerian considerations in accounting for the "choice of delusion" in psychotic symptomatology, and it is in this respect that his clinical discussion betrays implicit Adlerian assumptions that range beyond the formal "mechanism of paranoia" he elucidated in the case study. In the third part of the case, Freud characterized paranoia as a clinical disorder typified by a withdrawal of libido from objects back to the ego. This withdrawal signaled a regression back to the stage of narcissism that resulted in the "aggrandizement of the ego." Paranoid delusion formation, according to this formulation, was not a pathological product of the regression, but a restitutional attempt to reestablish object relationships in the real world (1911, pp. 70–72). Freud's perception of the Schreber fantasies, however, supplied an additional evaluative component for appreciating the distinguishing content of the delusions that served restitutional ends: they satisfied the ego's need for a sense of masculine adequacy. This was the way the paranoid psychotic renewed his libidinal investment in the outer world—by fantasizing precisely those "arranged" situations in which the libidinal investment subserved the quest for interpersonal leverage and the desired masculine ego feeling.

Freud actually made the presumed Adlerian connection explicit. In the incubation period between the first and second outbreaks of illness, he observed, Schreber's apparent "affectionate dependence upon his physician" blossomed into a full feminine fantasy. This fantasy, "which was still kept impersonal, was met at once by an indignant repudiation—a true 'masculine protest' to use Adler's expression, but in a sense different from his" (p. 42). In the appended footnote, Freud spelled out the intended distinction in this way:

> According to Adler the masculine protest has a share in the production of the symptom, whereas in the present instance the patient is protesting against a symptom that is already fully fledged [p. 42n].

This distinction is noteworthy because it highlights both the qualified sense in which Freud attempted to subsume Adler's theoretical constructs within psycho-analysis, and the degree to which this subsumption essentially begs the funda-mental area of disagreement. Freud redefined the scope of the masculine protest by reserving the right to invoke it at that point in his clinical explanation at which it was theoretically convenient: as a secondary, ego-directed attempt to manage what he construed as the exciting cause of illness—"an outburst of homosexual libido" (p. 43). Adler, however, could have retained his own theoretical pre-rogative to reduce the libidinal outburst itself to an "arranged" expedient of masculine goals, and Freud's explanatory reference to Schreber's "fully fledged" symptoms merely reiterated his belief in the "authenticity" of libido without undercutting the possibility of such an Adlerian rejoinder. Furthermore, Adler could have argued just as easily that Schreber's concretized libidinal "symptoms" toward his exphysician were the masculine protest's "feminine" means of insuring manipulative control over the physician. In this way, Adler could argue that the return of Schreber's nervous disorder (as heralded by the repeated premonitory dreams to this effect during the incubation period [pp. 13, 42]) embodied "safeguarding tendencies" (*Sicherungstendenzen*) designed to escape the heightened responsibilities of his new appointment as a regional *Senatspraesident* and the failure of his marriage to produce children—to escape, in other words, the heightened potentiality for experiencing "feminine" catas-trophe.[2] It would have been Schreber's psychotically exaggerated idealization of masculinity and heightened anxiety that he would continue to fall short of his masculine goals which fueled his recourse to escapist homosexual fantasies. In this manner, Adler might well have attributed to the masculine protest "a share in the production of the symptom."

Elsewhere in his writings, Freud managed to incorporate clearly Adlerian assumptions into his clinical arguments while taking scrupulous care to avoid drawing outright "Adlerian" conclusions. The first of his "Contributions to the Psychology of Love," written in 1910, illustrates important aspects of this strategy. In "A Special Type of Choice of Object Made by Men," Freud out-lined the characteristics of male object choice in adults that betrayed an infantile oedipal fixation on the mother. He included in this typology the frequent "rescue fantasies" that men directed toward their love objects. Such fantasies stemmed from the male conviction that the object of affection was disreputable and had to be "rescued" from the dire fate that awaited her. Freud traced these adult rescue fantasies back to the early rescue ideas that the young child formed when he

---

[2]See, in this connection, Schreber's own explanation of the second outbreak of his illness (p. 12).

understood his infantile dependence on his parents and sought vindication from a relationship perceived as compromising:

> When a child hears that he *owes his life* to his parents, or that his mother *gave him life*, the feelings of tenderness unite with impulses which strive at power and independence, and they generate the wish to return this gift to the parents and to repay them with one of equal value. It is as though the boy's defiance were to make him say: "I want nothing from my father; I will give him back all I have cost him." He then forms the phantasy of *rescuing his father from danger and saving his life;* in this way he puts his account square with him [1910b, p. 172; emphasis in the original].

Freud thereby assumed that when rescue fantasies were directed to the father they proceeded from a "defiant meaning." As applied to the mother, on the other hand, the rescue fantasies allegedly proceeded more from a "tender meaning" deriving from the child's grateful recognition of the fact that the mother gave him life. The idea of rescuing the mother thereby subserved the Oedipus complex: in "rescuing" the mother, the child repaid her for the gift of life by giving her a child or making one for her. In this fashion, Freud contended, the child identified himself with his father: "All the instincts, those of tenderness, gratitude, lustfulness, defiance and independence, find satisfaction in the single wish *to be his own father*" (p. 173; emphasis in the original).

Now Freud's consideration of infantile dependence certainly antedated his dialogue with Adler. As far back as 1905, in the *Three Essays on the Theory of Sexuality*, he had recognized the important contribution of an "instinct for mastery" to "masculine sexual activity."[3] The essay on male object choice is noteworthy, however, because Freud here took an essential plank of Adler's theory of development—the male child's early realization of his inferiority and compensatory longing for "power and independence"—and turned it into a motivational component of oedipal attachment to the mother. The maternal rescue fantasy proceeded from an Adlerian supposition, that is, but only acquired "significance" when the content of the rescue coincided with the aim of oedipal attachment: to possess the mother and have a child by her. Since Freud was discussing subsequent rescue fantasies as residual traces of infantile fixation on the mother, it is hardly surprising that he should construe the child's fantasied possession of the mother as a manifestation of "tender" oedipal feelings toward her. Yet, as in the Schreber case, Freud seemed to recast Adlerian observations

---

[3]See Freud (1905, p. 188), but note that Freud only elaborated the "instinct for mastery" in the additions he prepared for the third edition of the work in 1915 (see pp. 193, 194, 198).

without really undercutting the possibility of an Adlerian reading of the same material. Here, for example, Adler could certainly have argued that the sexual form of the child's "rescue fantasy" did not subserve genuine libidinal attachment to the mother. Insofar as the child's longing to requite himself to *both* parents proceeded from the wish to gain "power and independence," Adler could surely have claimed that the sexual formulation of the rescue fantasy was merely the "arranged" expedient for attaining this masculine goal. The wish to be the father would thereby proceed less from the oedipal wish to supplant him sexually than from an identification with him as the embodiment of the masculine strength and power that subdued the mother and permitted the tactical possibility of "rescuing" her for the child as well.

The theoretical culmination of Freud's attempt to subsume the phenomena of the masculine protest within psychoanalytic categories occurred three years after Adler had actually left him. In "On Narcissism: An Introduction" (1914b), he contended that Adler's masculine protest originated from the early mental epoch in which the sexual and ego instincts operated in union and made their joint appearance as "narcissistic interests." The "protest" was directed against the fear of castration (or in little girls, against the loss of the penis) that impinged on the child's original sense of narcissistic well-being. Thus Freud argued that

> Psycho-analytic research has from the very beginning recognized the existence and importance of the "masculine protest," but it has regarded it, in opposition to Adler, as narcissistic in nature and derived from the castration complex. The "masculine protest" is concerned in the formation of character, into the genesis of which it enters along with many other factors, but it is completely unsuited for explaining the problems of the neuroses, with regard to which Adler takes account of nothing but the manner in which they serve the ego-instincts. I find it quite impossible to place the genesis of neurosis upon the narrow basis of the castration complex, however powerfully it may come to the fore in men among their resistances to the cure of a neurosis. Incidentally, I know of cases of neurosis in which the "masculine protest," or as we regard it, the castration complex, plays no pathogenic part and even fails to appear at all [1914b, pp. 92–93].[4]

---

[4]See p. 93n where Freud later retracted the last sentence of this passage in a subsequent letter to Dr. Edoardo Weiss. Freud further undercut his own refutation of Adler in his late clinical essay "Analysis Terminable and Interminable" (1937). He did so by broadening his conception of the castration complex to include not only penis envy and castration anxiety proper, but the male's "struggle against his passive or feminine attitude to another male." Freud admitted, in this connection, that Adler's term masculine protest "fits the case of males perfectly," though he would have preferred "repudiation of femininity" as a more accurate description of "this remarkable feature in the psychical life of human beings" (1937, pp. 250–251, but see also the qualifying footnote on pp. 252–253).

Freud's theoretical explanation of the masculine protest mimics the evasive strategy which typifies the clinical writings that preceded it; it sets back the necessity for invoking a masculine protest one step without providing a detailed argument that would preclude the possibility (or desirability) of invoking it at all. Freud did not present a non-Adlerian justification for the significance of the castration complex from the standpoint of preoedipal development. His explanation consequently did not preclude the reasonableness of invoking a preexisting masculine protest to provide an evaluative component for appreciating the momentousness of the discovery of the anatomical distinction between the sexes when it in fact occurred.

In this respect, Schafer's (1974) review of Freud's psychology of women has perceptively illuminated the incompleteness of Freud's concept of ''penis envy'' in young girls in a way that dramatically highlights the possibility (though Schafer does not say so) of injecting an Adlerian rationale beneath the ''libidinal'' explanatory base. He notes that Freud's inability to anchor his understanding of the castration complex in the prephallic phase of development effectually undermines the adequacy of his psychology of childhood (pp. 468–477). With reference to his psychology of women, for example, Freud simply took for granted the little girl's catastrophic response to the discovery of the anatomical difference between the sexes without explaining *why* she was so mortified and envious after discovering that she lacked a penis. This was the very question that Karen Horney forcefully raised in the early 1920s. She traced the origins of primary penis envy to the demonstrable inferiority of the little girl's genital apparatus in providing sexual component gratifications linked to urethral erotism, scoptophilia, and masturbation. In this way, she was able to tie the typicality of penis envy to experiential referents showing that ''little girls *are* at a disadvantage compared with boys in respect of certain possibilities of gratification'' (Horney, 1923, p. 42; cf. 1926, p. 63). Freud rejected Horney's theories for various reasons (see Fliegel, 1973), but he provided no satisfactory explanation for the girl's precariousness of self-esteem in the face of genital discovery, however and whenever it occurred. Schafer (1974), arguing here in the spirit of Horney, reiterates the important assumption that must necessarily supplement Freud's conception of castration anxiety in the girl: one must assume that before the time of mortification and envy, it was already terribly important to the little girl that there be no differences between herself and boys.

Self-evidently, the supplemental corrective *can* be of an Adlerian nature. It is conceivable that a ''masculine protest'' extending back to the pregenital stages of life potentiates the cognitive impact of the first perceptions of the genital distinction between the sexes. The desirability of functioning at a level of optimum "masculine" adequacy may not only be socially imprinted at the preoedipal stage of development, that is, but may actually constitute the valuational criterion for understanding why castration anxiety occurs in the first place. The little girl may be envious of the penis and the little boy fearful for the penis because both of them bring their sense of childish inferiority and desire for masculine superiority into the arena of genital confrontation.

This Adlerian construction is further compatible with Horney's argument that the female "masculinity complex" only arises after the little girl has renounced her oedipal attachment to the father. Her claim was that the little girl first sought "a strong and wholly womanly love relation to the father," but following her invariable disappointment and frustration, relinquished her "womanly" orientation and replaced it with an active identification with the father (1923, pp. 48–50; 1926, p. 64). Adler could easily have agreed that the little girl fled to a "fictitious male role" after failing to win her father through a "womanly love relation." He would have disagreed, however, with Horney's subsequent claim (1926, pp. 66–67) that this desire to be a man subserved the girl's repression of her libidinal fantasies toward the father. The Adlerian counterclaim would be that the little girl's recognition of "masculine" superiority preceded and guided her libidinal aspirations from the outset, that her initial "womanly" orientation was nothing but a feminine "tactic" utilized by the masculine protest.

This kind of Adlerian rejoinder not only explains castration anxiety as an instance of the masculine protest, but, in so doing, undercuts Freud's subsequent methodological objection, for Adler would have been the first to agree that the castration complex constituted much too "narrow" a basis for explaining the genesis of neurosis. Unlike Freud, however, Adler did not view the castration complex as tantamount to the masculine protest; rather, it was but one kind of mask the masculine protest could assume at certain stages of development.

In fact, Freud himself implicitly conceded the "masculine" predisposition actuating castration anxiety in the greatest of his case histories, *From the History of an Infantile Neurosis* (1918), the case history of the "Wolf Man." Freud's clinical exegesis here embodied fairly explicit Adlerian assumptions, a fact all the more remarkable because the case history was written in 1914, the same year that saw the disavowal of Adler's theories in *On the History of the Psycho-Analytic Movement* (1914) and "On Narcissism: An Introduction" (1914b). In this work, Freud analyzed in elaborate detail a dream of his patient that harkened back to a "primal scene" in which the Wolfman witnessed sexual intercourse *a tergo* between his parents and reached the infantile conviction of the reality of castration based on his observation of his mother's genitals (1918, p. 45). Freud observed that the wishful motive behind the dream was his patient's inverted oedipal attachment to his father. The dream followed the emergence of the Wolfman's passive homosexual attachment to his father and the recollection embedded in the dream thoughts represented his wishful attempt to reconstruct the conditions for obtaining sexual satisfaction by the father. Freud thus remarked that the dream should have presented to the child "this picture of sexual satisfaction afforded through his father's agency, just as he had seen it in the primal scene, as a model of the satisfaction that he himself was longing to obtain from his father" (p. 41). Instead of issuing in a wish fulfillment, however, these dream thoughts resulted in an anxiety dream that issued in a subsequent phobia of "wolves" and other father substitutes. The reason for this was that the "picture of sexual satisfaction" was accompanied by the concomitant realization that castration was a necessary condition of sexual satisfaction from the father (pp. 42ff.). Through the mediating impact of the castration anxiety, the Wolfman's passive sexual attitude toward his father succumbed to repression and his fear of his father appeared in the guise of the wolf phobia. In conceptualizing the "driving force" of this repression, Freud had recourse to plainly Adlerian considerations about masculinity as the guiding value that accounted for the momentous impact of his patient's emergent castration anxiety:

> And the driving force of this repression? The circumstances of the case show that it can only have been his narcissistic genital libido, which, in the form of concern for his male organ, was fighting against a satisfaction whose attainment seemed to involve the renunciation of that organ. And it was from his threatened narcissism that he derived the masculinity with which he defended himself against his passive attitude towards his father [p. 46].

Freud partially disguised the seeming recourse to Adler by lodging the operation of the masculine protest within the "narcissistic genital libido" of his patient, but he was characterizing the genital libido of a four-year-old child whose "narcissistic" concern for his male organ obviously transcended the limited perception of the organ as an instrument of sexual intercourse. As Freud related here and elsewhere (1908), the child understands intercourse itself as an act of violence. There is consequently nothing in his argument that precludes the rendering of the child's "concern" for his sexual organ from the standpoint of masculine superiority per se. To contend, as Freud did, that the Wolfman "derived" his masculinity from his "threatened narcissism" is to reverse the *explanans* and *explanandum* in a way that obscures the implicit Adlerian premise. Castration anxiety can only represent a "threat" to narcissism if narcissistic well-being is tied up with preexisting beliefs about "masculine" adequacy and, more particularly, the kind of masculine domination that can be achieved with the male genitals. The masculinity does not derive from the "threatened narcissism"; rather, the "threat" to narcissism derives from the fact that the Wolfman had certain masculine goals that preceded his castration anxiety and conditioned the repressive significance of his castration anxiety in terms of his "passive" attachment to his father. To the extent that sexual satisfaction by the father required castration, the Wolfman actively opposed the former goal and his pleasure was transformed into anxiety. This was tantamount, in Freud's words, to "a clear protest on the part of his masculinity" (1918, p. 47). The very content of the Wolfman's phobia, moreover, the fear of being eaten by a wolf, corresponded to a further regressive move from the sexual aim of being copulated like a woman to the aim of oral incorporation "owing to the opposition of his narcissistic masculinity."

In the subsequent development of the Wolfman's obsessional neurosis, Freud had further recourse to the masculine evaluative component in explaining his patient's identification with Christ as a vehicle for expressing a homosexual attitude toward his father. Just as Schreber's masculine ego feeling could only be reconciled with his passive homosexuality when he viewed his libidinal task as providing God Himself with "voluptuous sensations," so the Wolfman's homosexual attachment to his father could only be symptomatically enacted in the fantasied service of Christ to the Divine Father. Only through identification with Christ, that is, did the Wolfman become "something great and also . . . a man" (p. 64), someone for whom feminine service to the father was no longer threatening. Through his religious sublimations, the Wolfman protected himself against "a direct outbreak of dread of the feminine attitude towards men" (p. 70; cf. pp. 78, 83–84).

Freud was a more effective critic of Adler when he abandoned the attempt to translate the masculine protest into an analogous castration complex and simply took issue with the underlying claim that the motive forces of repression could be "sexualized" at all. To Adler's claim that the "repressing" agency was always a "masculine" instinctual impulse and the "repressed" a feminine one, Freud juxtaposed the case of masochistic men who voluntarily transferred themselves into the role of women. In " 'A Child is Being Beaten' " (1919), Freud traced the masochistic attitude of such patients to early incestuous attachments to the father and analyzed their childhood beating fantasies as regressive substitutes for the forbidden genital relation with the father. This incestuous attachment was used to account for beating fantasies in which the male did not give up the "feminine line" and for subsequent masochistic fantasies in which he chose not to be "on top" (pp. 197ff.).

Freud conceded the possibility that such fantasies could be symptoms of the "failure" of the masculine protest. In this eventuality, however, he was at a loss to explain why female patients developed analogous beating fantasies. These female patients, as young girls, also fantasized being beaten by their fathers, but, like their male counterparts, they saw themselves being beaten as boys in accord with their budding "masculinity complex" (p. 191). If, in these oedipal fantasies, the masculine protest had "completely achieved its object," Freud queried, why would the beating fantasy appear as a "symptom" in the first place? His verdict was that the masculine protest could not satisfactorily explain this development, just as it could not explain, in general, why the content of repression was not only passive "feminine" tendencies but active "masculine instinctual impulses" as well. If the "feminine" posited the only criterion for repression, that is, why did the masochistic male repress sadistic oedipal fantasies that were fully compatible with his masculine self-esteem? Freud concluded that "the doctrine of the masculine protest is altogether incompatible with the fact of repression" and that "the motive forces of repression must not be sexualized" (p. 203; cf. 1918, pp. 110–111).

Adler, of course, could have replied to these arguments by simply retranslating Freud's clinical observations into his own terminology. He might have questioned the "symptomatic" status of the young girl's "masculine" beating fantasies, claiming that the fantasy was actually a "guiding fiction" embodying one "passive" strategy for retaining control over the father—offering herself as a masochistic sexual object. Correspondingly, he could have argued that the boy's repression of his "active" oedipal fantasies was a mere expedient, a "safeguard" designed to avoid a direct encounter with the father that would necessarily highlight the "inferiority" of the child. Indeed, Adler could have appealed to Freud's insistence on the centrality of the Oedipus complex in establishing future object relations to bolster the claim that the "masculine" dimension of oedipal striving was only temporarily "safeguarded" and retained as a permanent model for future "masculine" conquests.[5]

So where does my hypothetical dialogue between Adler and Freud leave us? With a renewed appreciation, I believe, of the pseudoscientific quality of the *actual* dialogue surrounding Adler's "dissent" from psychoanalysis. For Freud, the masculine protest was merely an instance of castration anxiety. For Adler, castration anxiety was merely an instance of the masculine protest. The easy

---

[5]It is interesting that Jean Lampl de Groot, who accepted Freud's conception of female sexuality, offered this very interpretation as far back as 1928: "If however, forced by the superior power of that far stronger rival, his father, he renounces the fulfillment of his desire, the way remains open to him at some later period to fight his father with greater success and to return to his first love-object, or, more correctly, to her substitute. It seems not impossible that this knowledge of a future chance of fulfilling his wish . . . may be a contributing motive in the boy's temporary renunciation of the prohibited love-craving" (pp. 333–334).

translatability of clinical observations from the language of libido theory to the language of the masculine protest (with its provision for libidinal "arrangements" safeguarding the feeling of masculine adequacy) highlights the very methodological shortcomings that would eventuate in Popper's (1934) falsifiability criterion of demarcation. In the period surrounding the split, in any event, "crucial tests" were not available to arbitrate between the explanatory strength of statements framed in terms of libido theory and statements framed in terms of the masculine protest. In the absence of such tests, Freud and Adler both had ongoing recourse to polemical stratagems that generated unfalsifiable claims in the original Popperian sense. The counterproductive nature of the dialogue is highlighted by Freud's largely unsuccessful attempt to incorporate Adlerian observations into his clinical discourse at the same time as he sought to dissociate himself from the masculine protest which was the embodiment of these observations at the level of clinical generalization (cf. Waelder, 1962, pp. 251–252). Freud's attempt to subsume the masculine protest within the fold of libido theory did not constitute a *refutation* of the theory of the masculine protest because it merely begged the underlying issue of the relative explanatory primacy of libido theory *versus* the theory of the masculine protest.

References

Abrahamsen, D. (1946), *The Mind and Death of a Genius*, New York: Columbia University Press.

Adler, A. (1898), *Gesundheitsbuch fuer das Schneidergewerbe.* Berlin: Heymanns.

———— (1902a), Eine Lehrkanzel fuer Soziale Medizin. *Aerztliche Standeszeitung*, I, No. 7 (15 October), pp. 1–2.

———— (1902b), Das Eindringen Sozialer Triebkraefte in die Medizin. *Aerztliche Standeszeitung*, I, No. 1 (15 July), pp. 1–3.

———— (1903a), Stadt und Land. *Aerztliche Standeszeitung*, II, No. 18 (15 September), pp. 1–3; No. 19 (1 October), pp. 1–2; No. 20 (15 October), pp. 1–2.

———— (1903b), Staatshilfe oder Selbsthilfe? *Aerztliche Standeszeitung*, II, No. 21 (1 November), pp. 1–3; (15 November), pp. 1–2.

———— (1904), Der Arzt als Erzieher. In: *Heilen und Bilden: Aerztlich-paedagogische Arbeiten des Vereins fuer Individualpsychologie*, ed. A. Adler & C. Furtmueller. Muenchen: Reinhardt, 1914, pp. 1–10.

———— (1907a), Die Theorie der Organminderwertigkeit und ihre Bedeutung fuer Philosophie und Psychologie. In: *Heilen und Bilden: Aerztlich-paedagogische Arbeiten des Vereins fuer Individualpsychologie*, ed. A. Adler & C. Furtmueller. Muenchen: Reinhardt, 1914, pp. 11–22.

———— (1907b), Entwicklungsfehler des Kindes. In: *Heilen und Bilden: Aerztlich-paedagogische Arbeiten des Vereins fuer Individualpsychologie*, ed. A. Adler & C. Furtmueller. Muenchen: Reinhardt, 1914, pp. 33–40.

———— (1907c), *Studie ueber Minderwertigkeit von Organen.* Berlin und Wien: Urban und Schwarzenberg.

_____ (1907d), *Study of Organ Inferiority and its Psychical Compensation: A Contribution to Clinical Medicine*, trans. S. E. Jelliffe. New York: Nervous and Mental Disease Publishing Company, 1917.

_____ (1907e), Zur Aetiologie, Diagnostik und Therapie der Nephrolithiasis. *Wiener Klinische Wochenschrift*, 20:1534–1539.

_____ (1908a), Ueber Vererbung von Krankheiten. In: *Heilen und Bilden: Aerztlich-paedagogische Arbeiten des Vereins fuer Individualpsychologie*, ed. A. Adler & C. Furtmueller. Muenchen: Reinhardt, 1914, pp. 41–49.

_____ (1908b), Der Aggressionstrieb im Leben und in der Neurose. In: *Heilen und Bilden: Aerztlich-paedagogische Arbeiten des Vereins fuer Individualpsychologie*, ed. A. Adler & C. Furtmueller. Muenchen: Reinhardt, 1914, pp. 23–32.

_____ (1908c), Das Zaertlichkeitsbeduerfnis des Kindes. In: *Heilen und Bilden: Aerztlich-paedagogische Arbeiten des Vereins fuer Individualpsychologie*, ed. A. Adler & C. Furtmueller. Muenchen: Reinhardt, 1914, pp. 50–53.

_____ (1908d), Zwei Traeume einer Prostituierten. *Zeitschrift fuer Sexualwissenschaft*, 1:103–106.

_____ (1909a), On the Psychology of Marxism. In: *Minutes of the Vienna Psycho-Analytic Society, vol. II: 1908–1910*, ed. & trans. H. Nunberg & E. Federn. New York: International Universities Press, 1967, pp. 172–174.

_____ (1909b), Ueber neurotische Disposition. Zugleich ein Beitrag zur Aetiologie und Frage der Neurosenwahl. *Jahrbuch fuer Psychoanalytische Forschungen*, 1:526–545.

_____ (1910a), Trotz und Gehorsam. In: *Heilen und Bilden: Aerztlich-paedagogische Arbeiten des Vereins fuer Individualpsychologie*, ed. A. Adler & C. Furtmueller. Muenchen: Reinhardt, 1914, pp. 84–93.

_____ (1910b), Der psychische Hermaphroditismus im Leben und in der Neurose. In: *Heilen und Bilden: Aerztlich-paedagogische Arbeiten des Vereins fuer Individualpsychologie*, ed. A. Adler & C. Furtmueller. Muenchen: Reinhardt, 1914, pp. 74–83.

_____ (1910c), Ein erlogener Traum: Beitrag zum Mechanismus der Luege in der Neurose. *Zentralblatt fuer Psychoanalyse*, 1:103–108.

_____ (1910d), Ueber maennliche Einstellung bei weiblichen Neurotikern. *Zentralblatt fuer Psychoanalyse*, 1:174–178.

_____ (1910e), Syphilidophobie: Ein Beitrag zur Bedeutung der Phobien und der Hypochondrie in der Dynamik der Neurose. *Zentralblatt fuer Psychoanalyse*, 1:400–406.

_____ (1910f), Beitrag zur Lehre vom Widerstand. *Zentralblatt fuer Psychoanalyse*, 1:214–219.

_____ (1910g), Book Review of *Psychische Grenzzustaende* by Karl Pelman. *Zentralblatt fuer Psychoanalyse*, 1:78–79.

———— (1910h), Book Review of *Der Sexualverbrecher* by E. Wulffen. *Zentralblatt fuer Psychoanalyse,* 1:118–119.

———— (1910i), Book Review of *Drei Vortraege aus dem Gebiete der Unfall-Neurologie* by Paul Schuster. *Zentralblatt fuer Psychoanalyse,* 1:122.

———— (1910j), Book Review of ''Ueber Konflikte der kindlichen Seele'' by C. G. Jung. *Zentralblatt fuer Psychoanalyse,* 1:122–123.

———— (1911a), Zur Kritik der Freudschen Sexualtheorie der Nervositaet: I. Die Rolle der Sexualitaet in der Neurose. In: *Heilen und Bilden: Aerztlich-paedagogische Arbeiten des Vereins fuer Individualpsychologie,* ed. A. Adler & C. Furtmueller. Muenchen: Reinhardt, 1914, pp. 94–103.

———— (1911b), Zur Kritik der Freudschen Sexualtheorie der Nervositaet: II. 'Verdraengung' und 'Maennlicher Protest'; Ihre Rolle und Bedeutung fuer die neurotische Dynamik. In: *Heilen und Bilden: Aerztlich-paedagogische Arbeiten des Vereins fuer Individualpsychologie,* ed. A. Adler & C. Furtmueller. Muenchen: Reinhart, 1914, pp. 103–114.

———— (1912a), *Ueber den Nervoesen Charakter: Grundzuege einer vergleichenden Individual-Psychologie und Psychotherapie.* Wiesbaden: Bergmann.

———— (1912b), *The Neurotic Constitution: Outline of a Comparative Individualistic Psychology and Psychotherapy.* New York: Moffat, Yard, 1916.

———— (1912c), *Ueber den Nervosen Charakter: Grundzuege einer vergleichenden Individual-Psychologie und Psychotherapie,* 4th ed. Munich: Bergmann, 1928.

———— (1912d), An die Leser. In: C. Furtmueller, *Psychoanalyse und Ethik: Eine vorlaeufige Untersuchung.* Muenchen: Reinhardt, p. iii.

———— (1913a), Zur Rolle des Unbewussten in der Neurose. In: *Praxis und Theorie der Individualpsychologie,* 2nd ed. Muenchen: Bergmann, 1924, pp. 22–35.

———— (1913b), Individualpsychologische Behandlung der Neurosen. In: *Praxis und Theorie der Individualpsychologie,* 2nd ed. Muenchen: Bergmann, 1924, pp. 22–35.

———— (1913c), Kinderpsychologie und Neurosenforschung. In: *Praxis und Theorie der Individualpsychologie,* 2nd ed. Muenchen: Bergmann, 1924, pp. 42–54.

———— (1913d), Weitere Leitsaetze zur Praxis der Individualpsychologie. In: *Praxis und Theorie der Individualpsychologie,* 2nd ed. Muenchen: Bergmann, 1924, pp. 16–21.

———— (1913e), Zur Funktion der Zwangsvorstellung als eines Mittels zur Erhoehung des Persoenlichkeitsgefuehles. In: *Praxis und Theorie der Individualpsychologie,* 2nd ed. Muenchen: Bergmann, 1924, pp. 148–150.

———— (1914a), Soziale Einfluesse in der Kinderstube. *Paedagogisches Archiv,* 56:473–487.

——— (1914b), Kindliches Seelenleben und Gemeinsinn. *Annalen der Natur- und Kulturphilosophie,* 13:38–45.

——— (1914c), Die Individualpsychologie, ihre Voraussetzungen und Ergebnisse. In: *Praxis und Theorie der Individualpsychologie,* 2nd ed. Muenchen: Bergmann, 1924, pp. 1–10.

——— (1914d), Das Problem der 'Distanz.' In: *Praxis und Theorie der Individualpsychologie,* 2nd ed. Muenchen: Bergmann, 1924, pp. 71–76.

——— (1914e), Lebensluege und Verantwortlichkeit in der Neurose und Psychose. In: *Praxis und Theorie der Individualpsychologie,* 2nd ed. Muenchen: Bergmann, 1924, pp. 177–184.

——— (1914f), Melancholie und Paranoia. In: *Praxis und Theorie der Individualpsychologie,* 2nd ed. Muenchen: Bergmann, 1924, pp. 185–196.

——— (1918a), Bolschewismus und Seelenkunde. *Internationale Rundschau,* 4:597–600.

——— (1918b), Book Review of Wilhelm Fliess, *Das Jahr im Lebendigen. Vossische Zeitung* (Berlin), 29 December, pp. 2–3.

——— (1919), *Die Andere Seite: Eine Massenpsychologische Studie ueber die Schuld des Volkes.* Wien: Heidrich.

——— (1923), Danton, Marat, Robespierre: Eine Charakterstudie. *Arbeiter-Zeitung* (Vienna), 25 December, pp. 17–18.

——— (1924), Die Strafe in der Erziehung. *Arbeiter-Zeitung* (Vienna), 14 June, p. 12.

——— (1925), Unerziehbarkeit des Kindes oder Unbelehrbarkeit der Theorie? Bemerkungen zum Falle Hug. *Arbeiter-Zeitung* (Vienna), 5 March, p. 6.

——— (1927a), *Menschenkenntnis.* Leipzig: Hirzel.

——— (1927b), *Understanding Human Nature,* trans. W. B. Wolfe. New York: Greenberg, 1946.

——— (1929a), *Problems of Neurosis: A Book of Case Histories,* ed. P. Mairet. New York: Harper & Row, 1964.

——— (1929b), *Guiding the Child on the Principles of Individual Psychology,* trans. B. Ginzburg. London: Allen & Unwin, 1930.

——— (1929c), *The Science of Living.* New York: Greenberg, 1929; Anchor Books, 1969.

——— (1929d), *Individualpsychologie in der Schule: Vorlesungen fuer Lehrer und Erzieher.* Leipzig: Hirzel.

——— (1930a), Something About Myself. *Childhood and Character,* 7:6–8.

——— (1930b), *The Problem Child.* New York: Capricorn, 1963.

——— (1930c), *The Education of Children,* trans. E. & F. Jensen. New York: Greenberg.

——— (1931a), *What Life Should Mean to You,* ed. A. Porter. Boston: Little, Brown.

——— (1931b), The Differences between Individual Psychology and Psychoanalysis. In: *Superiority and Social Interest,* ed. H. & R. Ansbacher. New York: Viking, 1973, pp. 206–218.

———— (1932), The Structure of Neurosis. In: *Superiority and Social Interest,* ed. H. & R. Ansbacher. New York: Viking, 1973, pp. 83–95.

———— (1933a), *Der Sinn des Lebens.* Wien und Leipzig: Passer.

———— (1933b), *Social Interest: A Challenge to Mankind,* trans. J. Linton & R. Vaughan. New York: Putnam, 1939.

———— (1933c), On the Origin of the Striving for Superiority and of Social Interest. In: *Superiority and Social Interest,* ed. H. & R. Ansbacher. New York: Viking, 1973, pp. 29–40.

———— (1935), The Prevention of Delinquency. *International Journal of Individual Psychology,* 1(3):3–13.

———— (1936), The Neurotic's Picture of the World: A Case Study. In: *Superiority and Social Interest,* ed. H. & R. Ansbacher. New York: Viking, 1973, pp. 96–111.

———— (1963), *The Practice and Theory of Individual Psychology,* trans. P. Radin. Paterson, N.J.: Littlefield, Adams.

———— (1973), *Superiority and Social Interest: A Collection of Later Writings,* 3rd rev. ed., ed. H. & R. Ansbacher. New York: Viking.

Aichhorn, A. (1925), *Wayward Youth.* New York: Viking, 1963.

———— (1936), On the Technique of Child Guidance: The Process of Transference. In: *Delinquency and Child Guidance: Selected Papers,* ed. O. Fleischmann, P. Kramer, & H. Ross. New York: International Universities Press, 1964, pp. 101–192.

Alexander, F. (1923), The Castration Complex in the Formation of Character. *International Journal of Psycho-Analysis,* 4:11–42.

———— (1930), The Neurotic Character. *International Journal of Psycho-Analysis,* 11:292–311.

———— (1935), *Psychoanalysis of the Total Personality: The Application of Freud's Theory of the Ego to the Neuroses,* trans. B. Glueck & B. Lewin. New York: Nervous and Mental Disease Publishing Co.

———— (1938), Remarks About the Relation of Inferiority Feelings to Guilt Feelings. *International Journal of Psycho-Analysis,* 19:41–49.

———— (1942), *Our Age of Unreason.* Philadelphia: Lippincott, 1951.

———— (1960), *The Western Mind in Transition.* New York: Random House.

———— & French, T. (1946), *Psychoanalytic Therapy: Principles and Application.* New York: Ronald.

———— & Healy, W. (1935), *Roots of Crime: Psychoanalytic Studies.* New York: Knopf.

———— & Selesnick, S. (1965), Freud-Bleuler Correspondence. *Archives of General Psychiatry,* 12:1–9.

Alexander, S. (1920), *Space, Time & Deity.* London: Macmillan.

Amacher, P. (1965), *Freud's Neurological Education and its Influence on Psychoanalytic Theory. Psychological Issues* [Monograph 16]. New York: International Universities Press.

Andreas-Salomé, L. (1912–1913), *The Freud Journal of Lou Andreas-Salomé,* trans. S. A. Leavy. New York: Basic Books, 1964.

———— (1951), *Lebensrueckblick.* Zurich.

Ansbacher, H. (1959), The Significance of the Socio-Economic Status of the Patients of Freud and Adler. *American Journal of Psychotherapy,* 13:376–382.

———— (1962), Was Adler A Disciple of Freud? *Journal of Individual Psychology,* 18:126–135.

———— & Ansbacher, R. R. (1956), *The Individual Psychology of Alfred Adler: A Systematic Presentation in Selections from his Writings.* New York: Harper & Row, 1967.

Bateson, G., Jackson, D. D., Haley, J., & Weakland, J. H. (1956), Toward a Theory of Schizophrenia. *Behavioral Science,* 1:251–264.

———— ———— ———— ———— (1963), A Note on the Double Bind—1962. *Family Process,* 2:154–161.

Baumer, F. L. (1949), Intellectual History and its Problems. *Journal of Modern History,* 21:191– 203.

Becker, C. L. (1932), *The Heavenly City of the Eighteenth-Century Philosophers.* New Haven: Yale University Press, 1971.

Becker, P. (1966), Edward Hitschmann. In: *Psychoanalytic Pioneers,* ed. F. Alexander, S. Eisenstein, & M. Grotjahn. New York: Basic Books, pp. 160–168.

Beckh-Widmanstetter, H. A. (1965), Zur Geschichte der Individualpsychologie: Julius Wagner-Jauregg ueber Alfred Adler. *Unsere Heimat,* 36:182–188.

———— (1966), Alfred Adler und Waehring. *Unser Waehring,* 1:38–42.

Bergson, H. (1907), *Creative Evolution,* trans. A. Mitchell. New York: Modern Library, 1944.

Bernfeld, S. (1944), Freud's Earliest Theories and the School of Helmholtz. *Psychoanalytic Quarterly,* 13:341–362.

———— (1949), Freud's Scientific Beginnings. *American Imago,* 6:163–196.

———— (1951), Sigmund Freud, M.D., 1882–1885. *International Journal of Psycho-Analysis,* 32:204–217.

Bibring, E. (1934), The Development and Problems of the Theory of the Instincts. *International Journal of Psycho-Analysis,* 22:102–131, 1941.

Binion, R. (1968), *Frau Lou: Nietzsche's Wayward Disciple.* Princeton: Princeton University Press.

Binswanger, L. (1957), *Sigmund Freud: Reminiscences of a Friendship,* trans. N. Guterman. New York: Grune & Stratton.

Birnbaum, F. (1935a), The Individual Psychological Experimental School in Vienna. *International Journal of Individual Psychology*, 2:118–124.

———(1935b), Applying Individual Psychology in School. *International Journal of Individual Psychology*, 1(3):109–119.

Blau, P. (1964), *Exchange and Power in Social Life*. New York: Wiley.

Bottome, P. (1939), *Alfred Adler: Apostle of Freedom*. London: Faber & Faber.

Braunthal, J. (1965), *Victor und Friedrich Adler: Zwei Generationen Arbeiterbewegung*. Wien: Wiener Volksbuchhandlung.

Brome, V. (1967), *Freud and His Early Circle*. London: Heinemann.

Bruegel, L. (1925), *Geschichte der oesterreichischen Sozialdemokratie*, vol. 4. Wien: Wiener Volksbuchhandlung.

Carotenuto, A. (1982), *A Secret Symmetry: Sabina Spielrein Between Jung and Freud*, trans. A. Pomerans, J. Shepley, & K. Winston. New York: Pantheon.

Charlton, D. G. (1959), *Positivist Thought in France during the Second Empire*. Oxford: Clarendon Press.

Clark, R. W. (1980), *Freud: The Man and The Cause*. New York: Random House.

Colby, K. M. (1951), On the Disagreement between Freud and Adler. *American Imago*, 8:229–238.

Comte, A. (1825), Philosophical Considerations on the Sciences and Savants. In: *Early Essays on Social Philosophy*, trans. H. D. Hutton, published as an appendix to *System of Positive Polity*, vol. 4. New York: Franklin, 1877.

——— (1826), Considerations on the Spiritual Power. In: *Early Essays on Social Philosophy*, trans. H. D. Hutton, published as an appendix to *System of Positive Polity*, vol. 4. New York, Franklin, 1877.

Copleston, F. (1963), *A History of Philosophy*, vol. 7. London: Search.

Coser, L. (1956), *The Functions of Social Conflict*. New York: Free Press.

Cranefield, P. F. (1970), Some Problems in Writing the History of Psychoanalysis. In: *Psychiatry and its History: Methodological Problems in Research*, ed. G. Mora & J. L. Brand. Springfield, Ill.: Thomas, pp. 41–55.

Dahrendorf, R. (1958), Toward a Theory of Social Conflict. *Journal of Conflict Resolution*, 2:170–183.

——— (1959), *Class and Class Conflict in Industrial Society*. Stanford: Stanford University Press.

Darwin, C. R. (1859), *On the Origin of Species by Means of Natural Selection, or, The Preservation of Favoured Races in the Struggle for Life*. London: Murray.

——— (1871), *The Descent of Man, and Selection in Relation to Sex*, 2 vols. London: Murray.

Decker, H. (1971), The Medical Reception of Psychoanalysis in Germany, 1894–1902: Three Brief Studies. *Bulletin of the History of Medicine*, 45:461–481.

———— (1977), *Freud in Germany: Revolution and Reaction in Science, 1893–1907. Psychological Issues* [Monograph 41] New York: International Universities Press.

Deutsch, H. (1940), Freud and his Pupils: A Footnote to the History of the Psychoanalytic Movement. *Psychoanalytic Quarterly,* 9:184–194.

Deutsch, J. (1929), *Geschichte der oesterreichischen Gewerkschaftsbewegung, I: Von den Anfaengen bis zur Zeit des Weltkrieges.* Glashuetten im Taunus: Detlev Auvermann KG, 1975.

Dewey, J. (1897), My Pedagogic Creed. In: *The Philosophy of John Dewey: The Lived Experience,* ed. J. J. McDermott. New York: Capricorn, 1973, pp. 442–454.

———— (1899), *The School and Society.* In: *The Child and the Curriculum and The School and Society.* Chicago: University of Chicago Press, 1971.

———— (1902), *The Child and the Curriculum.* In: *The Child and the Curriculum and The School and Society.* Chicago: University of Chicago Press, 1971.

———— (1916), *Democracy and Education: An Introduction to the Philosophy of Education.* New York: Macmillan, 1937.

———— (1938), Experience and Education. In: *The Philosophy of John Dewey: The Lived Experience,* ed. J. J. McDermott. New York: Capricorn, 1973, pp. 506–511.

Dorer, M. (1932), *Historische Grundlagen der Psychoanalyse.* Leipzig: Meiner.

Dottrens, R. (1930), *The New Education in Austria.* New York: Day.

Dreikurs, R. (1933), *Fundamentals of Adlerian Psychology.* New York: Greenberg.

Dunn, J. (1968), The Identity of the History of Ideas. *Philosophy,* 43:85–104.

Durkheim, E. (1893), *The Division of Labor in Society,* trans. G. Simpson. New York: Free Press, 1964.

———— (1897), *Suicide,* trans. J. Spaulding & G. Simpson. New York: Free Press, 1951.

———— (1898), Individual and Collective Representations. In: *Sociology and Philosophy,* trans. D. F. Pocock. New York: Free Press, 1974, pp. 1–34.

———— (1911), Value Judgments and Judgments of Reality. In: *Sociology and Philosophy,* trans. D. F. Pocock. New York: Free Press, 1974, pp. 80–97.

———— (1925), *Moral Education: A Study in the Theory and Application of the Sociology of Education,* trans. E. Wilson & H. Schnurer. New York: Free Press, 1961.

Eissler, K. R. (1948), August Aichhorn: A Biographical Outline. In: *Searchlights on Delinquency: New Psychoanalytic Studies.* New York: International Universities Press, pp. ix–xiii.

———— (1971), *Talent and Genius: The Fictitious Case of Tausk contra Freud.* New York: Quadrangle.

Ellenberger, H. F. (1970), *The Discovery of the Unconscious: The History and Evolution of Dynamic Psychiatry*. New York: Basic Books.

Ermers, M. (1932), *Victor Adler: Aufstief und Groesse einer Sozialistischen Partei*. Wien: Epstein.

Fancher, R. (1971), The Neurological Origin of Freud's Dream Theory. *Journal of the History of the Behavioral Sciences*, 7:59–74.

Federn, E. (1963), Was Adler a Disciple of Freud? A Freudian View. *Journal of Individual Psychology*, 19:80–81.

Federn, P. (1913), Beitraege zur Analyse des Sadismus und Masochismus. *Internationale Zeitschrift fuer Aerztliche Psychoanalyse*, 1:29–49.

Ferenczi, S. (1911), On the Organization of the Psycho-Analytic Movement. In: *Final Contributions to the Problems & Methods of Psycho-Analysis*, ed. M. Balint, trans. E. Mosbacher et al. London: Hogarth Press, 1955, pp. 299–307.

Fermi, L. (1971), *Illustrious Immigrants: The Intellectual Migration from Europe, 1930–1941*. Chicago: University of Chicago Press.

Fischl, H. (1929), *Wesen und Werden der Schulreform in Oesterreich*. Wien: Deutscher Verlag fuer Jugend und Volk.

———— (1950), *Schulreform, Demokratie und Oesterreich, 1918–1950*. Wien: Verlag Jungbrunner.

Flavell, J. (1963), *The Developmental Psychology of Jean Piaget*. Princeton: Van Nostrand.

Fleming, D. & Bailyn, B., ed. (1969), *The Intellectual Migration: Europe and America, 1930– 1960*. Cambridge: Harvard University Press.

Fliegel, Z. O. (1973), Feminine Psychosexual Development in Freudian Theory: A Historical Reconstruction. *Psychoanalytic Quarterly*, 42:385–408.

Flugel, J. C. (1945), *Man, Morals & Society*. New York: International Universities Press.

Frank, O. (1928), *Max von Gruber*. Muenchen: Bayer.

Freud, A. (1951), Obituary, August Aichhorn. *International Journal of Psycho-Analysis*, 32:51–56.

Freud, S. (1895), Project for a Scientific Psychology. In: *The Origins of Psycho-Analysis. Letters to Wilhelm Fliess, Drafts and Notes: 1887–1902*, ed. M. Bonaparte, A. Freud, & E. Kris, trans. E. Mosbacher & J. Strachey. New York: Basic Books, 1954, pp. 347–445.

———— (1900), The Interpretation of Dreams. *Standard Edition*, 4 & 5. London: Hogarth Press, 1953.

———— (1901), The Psychopathology of Everyday Life. *Standard Edition*, 6. London: Hogarth Press, 1960.

———— (1905), Three Essays on the Theory of Sexuality. *Standard Edition*, 7:130–245. London: Hogarth Press, 1953.

———— (1908), On the Sexual Theories of Children. *Standard Edition*, 9:209–226. London: Hogarth Press, 1959.

———— (1909), Analysis of a Phobia in a Five-Year-Old Boy. *Standard Edition,* 10:5–149. London: Hogarth Press, 1955.

———— (1910a), The Psycho-Analytic View of Psychogenic Disturbance of Vision. *Standard Edition,* 11:211–218. London: Hogarth Press, 1957.

———— (1910b), A Special Type of Choice of Object Made by Men (Contributions to the Psychology of Love I). *Standard Edition,* 11:165–175. London: Hogarth Press, 1957.

———— (1911), Psycho-Analytic Notes on an Autobiographical Account of a Case of Paranoia (Dementia Paranoides). *Standard Edition,* 12:9–82. London: Hogarth Press, 1958.

———— (1914a), On the History of the Psycho-Analytic Movement. *Standard Edition,* 14:7–66. London: Hogarth Press, 1957.

———— (1914b), On Narcissism: An Introduction. *Standard Edition,* 14:73–102. London: Hogarth Press, 1957.

———— (1915), Instincts and Their Vicissitudes. *Standard Edition,* 14:117–140. London: Hogarth Press, 1957.

———— (1916–1917), Introductory Lectures on Psycho-Analysis (Part III). *Standard Edition,* 16. London: Hogarth Press, 1963.

———— (1918), From the History of an Infantile Neurosis. *Standard Edition,* 17:7–122. London: Hogarth Press, 1955.

———— (1919), 'A Child is Being Beaten': A Contribution to the Study of the Origin of Sexual Perversions. *Standard Edition,* 17:179–204. London: Hogarth Press, 1955.

———— (1920), Beyond the Pleasure Principle. *Standard Edition,* 18:7–64. London: Hogarth Press, 1955.

———— (1921), Group Psychology and the Analysis of the Ego. *Standard Edition,* 18:69–143. London: Hogarth Press, 1955.

———— (1922), Some Neurotic Mechanisms in Jealousy, Paranoia and Homosexuality. *Standard Edition,* 18:223–232. London: Hogarth Press, 1955.

———— (1923), The Ego and the Id. *Standard Edition,* 19:12–66. London: Hogarth Press, 1961.

———— (1925a), An Autobiographical Study. *Standard Edition,* 20:7–74. London: Hogarth Press, 1959.

———— (1925b), Preface to Aichhorn's *Wayward Youth. Standard Edition,* 19:273–275. London: Hogarth Press, 1961.

———— (1927), The Future of an Illusion. *Standard Edition,* 21:5–56. London: Hogarth Press, 1961.

———— (1930), Civilization and its Discontents. *Standard Edition,* 21:64–145. London: Hogarth Press, 1961.

———— (1933), New Introductory Lectures on Psycho-Analysis. *Standard Edition,* 22:5–182. London: Hogarth Press, 1964.

———— (1937), Analysis Terminable and Interminable. *Standard Edition,* 23:216–253. London: Hogarth Press, 1964.

_____ (1963), *Psychoanalysis and Faith: The Letters of Sigmund Freud and Oskar Pfister*, trans. E. Mosbacher. London: Hogarth Press.

_____ (1965a), *Sigmund Freud-Karl Abraham: Briefe*. Frankfurt: Fischer.

_____ (1965b), *A Psycho-Analytic Dialogue: The Letters of Sigmund Freud and Karl Abraham*, trans. B. Marsh & H. Abraham. New York: Basic Books.

_____ (1972), *Sigmund Freud and Lou Andreas-Salomé: Letters*, ed. E. Pfeiffer, trans. W. & E. Robson-Scott. New York: Harcourt Brace Jovanovich.

_____ (1974), *The Freud/Jung Letters*, ed. W. McGuire, trans. R. Manheim & R. F. C. Hull. Princeton: Princeton University Press.

Friedlander, K. (1947), *The Psycho-Analytical Approach to Juvenile Delinquency*. London: Routledge & Kegan Paul.

Friedman, P. (1967), *On Suicide, with Particular Reference to Suicide Among Young Students*. New York: International Universities Press.

Fromm, E. (1959), *Sigmund Freud's Mission*. New York: Harper.

Fuchs, A. (1949), *Geistige Stroemungen in Oesterreich, 1867–1918*. Wien: Globus.

Furth, H. G. (1969), *Piaget and Knowledge*. Englewood Cliffs, N.J.: Prentice-Hall.

Furtmueller, C. (1912), *Psychoanalyse und Ethik: Eine vorlaeufige Untersuchung*. Muenchen: Reinhardt.

_____ (1946) Alfred Adler: A Biographical Essay. In: Alfred Adler, *Superiority and Social Interest*, ed. H. & R. Ansbacher. New York: Viking, 1973, pp. 330–394.

Ganz, M. (1953), *The Psychology of Alfred Adler and the Development of the Child*, trans. P. Mairet. New York: Humanities Press.

Gedo, J. E. (1979a), Magna Est Vis Veritatis Tuae et Praevalebit. *The Annual of Psychoanalysis*, 7:53–82. New York: International Universities Press.

_____ (1979b), *Beyond Interpretation: Toward a Revised Theory for Psychoanalysis*. New York: International Universities Press.

_____ (1983), *Portraits of the Artist: Creativity and its Vicissitudes*. New York: Guilford Press.

_____ & Goldberg, A. (1973), *Models of the Mind: A Psychoanalytic Theory*. Chicago: University of Chicago Press.

Gloeckel, O. (1939), *Selbstbiographie*. Zurich: Verlag Genossenschaftsdruckerei.

Glover, E. (1960), *The Roots of Crime: Selected Papers on Psychoanalysis*. New York: International Universities Press.

Goudge, T. A. (1961), *The Ascent of Life: A Philosophical Study of the Theory of Evolution*. Toronto: University of Toronto Press.

Graf, M. (1942), Reminiscences of Professor Sigmund Freud. *Psychoanalytic Quarterly*, 11:465–476.

Gruber, M. (1923), Kleine Mitteilungen. *Muenchener Medizinische Wochenschrift* (3 August), 31:1038–1039.

Gruenbaum, A. (1977), How Scientific is Psychoanalysis? In: *Science and Psychotherapy*, ed. R. Stern et al. New York: Haven, pp. 219–254.

———— (1979), Is Freudian Psychoanalytic Theory Pseudo-Scientific by Karl Popper's Criterion of Demarcation? *American Philosophical Quarterly*, 16:131–141.

———— (1980), Epistemological Liabilities of the Clinical Appraisal of Psychoanalytic Theory. *Noûs*, 14:307–385.

Haldane, J. S. (1884), Life and Mechanism. *Mind*, 9:27–47.

———— (1913), *Mechanism, Life and Personality*. London: Murray.

Hale, N., ed. (1971), *James Jackson Putnam and Psychoanalysis: Letters Between Putnam and Sigmund Freud, Ernest Jones, William James, Sandor Ferenczi, and Morton Prince, 1887– 1917*. Cambridge: Harvard University Press.

Halleck, S. (1971), *The Politics of Therapy*. New York: Science House.

Hartmann, H. (1939), *Ego Psychology and the Problem of Adaptation*, trans. D. Rapaport. New York: International Universities Press, 1958.

————Kris, E., & Loewenstein, R. (1949), Notes on the Theory of Aggression. *The Psychoanalytic Study of the Child*, 3/4:9–36. New York: International Universities Press.

Hayek, F. A. (1955), *The Counter-Revolution of Science*. New York: Free Press.

Heberle, R. (1973), The Sociological System of Ferdinand Toennies: An Introduction. In: *Ferdinand Toennies: A New Evaluation*, ed. W. J. Cahnman. Leiden: Brill, pp. 47–69.

Hein, H. (1968), Mechanism and Vitalism as Meta-Theoretical Commitments. *Philosophical Forum* (New Series), 1:185–205.

———— (1969), Molecular Biology vs. Organicism: The Enduring Dispute Between Mechanism and Vitalism. *Synthese*, 20:238–253.

Hendrick, I. (1942), Instinct and Ego during Infancy. *Psychoanalytic Quarterly*, 11:33–58.

———— (1943a), Work and the Pleasure Principle. *Psychoanalytic Quarterly*, 12:311–329.

———— (1943b), Discussion of the "Instinct to Master." *Psychoanalytic Quarterly*, 12:563.

Himmelfarb, G. (1962), *Darwin and the Darwinian Revolution*. New York: Norton.

Hodges, H. (1944), *Wilhelm Dilthey: An Introduction*. London: Routledge & Kegan Paul, 1969.

———— (1952), *The Philosophy of Wilhelm Dilthey*. London: Routledge & Kegan Paul.

Hoffer, W. (1949), Mouth, Hand, and Ego-Integration. *The Psychoanalytic Study of the Child*, 3/4:49–56. New York: International Universities Press.

_____ (1950a), Development of the Body Ego. *The Psychoanalytic Study of the Child*, 5:18–23. New York: International Universities Press.

_____ (1950b), Oral Aggressiveness and Ego Development. *International Journal of Psycho-Analysis*, 31:156–160.

Hoffman, M. L. (1970), Moral Development. In: *Carmichael's Manual of Child Psychology*, vol. 2, ed. P. H. Mussen. New York: Wiley, pp. 261–350.

Homans, G. (1974), *Social Behavior: Its Elementary Forms*, rev. ed. New York: Harcourt Brace Jovanovich.

Horney, K. (1923), On the Genesis of the Castration Complex in Women. In: *Feminine Psychology*, ed. H. Kelman. New York: Norton, 1967, pp. 38–53.

_____ (1926), The Flight from Womanhood. In: *Feminine Psychology*, ed. H. Kelman. New York: Norton, 1967, pp. 54–70.

_____ (1950), *Neurosis and Human Growth*. New York: Norton.

Hughes, H. S. (1961), *Consciousness and Society: The Reconstruction of European Social Thought, 1890–1930*. New York: Vintage.

_____ (1975), *The Sea Change: The Migration of Social Thought, 1930–1965*. New York: Harper & Row.

Hull, D. (1974), *Philosophy of Biological Science*. Englewood, N.J.: Prentice-Hall.

Iggers, G. (1958), *The Cult of Authority*. The Hague: Nijhoff.

_____ (1968), *The German Conception of History*. Middletown, Conn.: Wesleyan University Press.

Iggers, W. (1967), *Karl Kraus: A Viennese Critic of the Twentieth Century*. The Hague: Martinus Nijhoff.

Jacoby, E. G. (1973), Three Aspects of the Sociology of Toennies. In: *Ferdinand Toennies: A New Evaluation*, ed. W. J. Cahnman. Leiden: Brill, pp. 70–102.

Jacoby, R. (1975), *Social Amnesia: A Critique of Contemporary Psychology from Adler to Laing*. Boston: Beacon.

Janik, A. & Toulmin, S. (1973), *Wittgenstein's Vienna*. New York: Simon & Schuster.

Jenks, W. (1960), *Vienna and the Young Hitler*. New York: Columbia University Press.

Joad, C. E. M. (1933), *Guide to Modern Thought*. London: Faber & Faber.

Johnston, W. (1972), *The Austrian Mind: An Intellectual and Social History, 1848–1938*. Berkeley: University of California Press.

Jones, E. (1955), *The Life and Work of Sigmund Freud*, vol. 2. New York: Basic Books.

_____ (1957), *The Life and Work of Sigmund Freud*, vol. 3. New York: Basic Books.

_____ (1959), *Free Associations: Memories of a Psycho-Analyst.* London: Hogarth.

Jung, C. G. (1907), The Freudian Theory of Hysteria. *Collected Works,* 4:10–24. New York: Pantheon Books, 1961.

_____ (1912), The Theory of Psychoanalysis. *Collected Works,* 4:83–226. New York: Pantheon Books, 1961.

_____ (1913), General Aspects of Psychoanalysis. *Collected Works,* 4:229–242. New York: Pantheon Books, 1961.

_____ (1917), Prefaces to "Collected Papers on Analytical Psychology." *Collected Works,* 4:290–297. New York: Pantheon Books, 1961.

_____ (1952), Symbols of Transformation. *Collected Works,* 5. Princeton: Princeton University Press, 1967.

Kahane, M. (1908), *Medizinisches Handlexikon fuer Praktische Aerzte.* Berlin und Wien: Urban und Schwarzenberg.

Kant, I. (1787), *Critique of Practical Reason,* ed. L. W. Beck. Indianapolis: Bobbs-Merrill, 1956.

Kanzer, M. (1971), Freud: The First Psychoanalytic Group Leader. In: *Comprehensive Group Psychotherapy,* ed. H. I. Kaplan & B. J. Sadock. Baltimore: Williams & Wilkins.

Kardiner, A. (1977), *My Analysis with Freud: Reminiscences.* New York: Norton.

Kaufmann, W. (1968), *Nietzsche: Philosopher, Psychologist, Antichrist,* 3rd ed. New York: Vintage.

_____ (1980), *Discovering the Mind, III: Freud versus Adler and Jung.* New York: McGraw Hill.

Kluback, W. (1956), *Wilhelm Dilthey's Philosophy of History.* New York: Columbia University Press.

Kohn, C. (1963), *Karl Kraus.* Paris: Didier.

Kohn, H. (1962), *Karl Kraus, Arthur Schnitzler, Otto Weininger: Aus dem judischen Wien der Jahrhundert.* Tuebingen: Nohr.

Kohut, H. (1977), *The Restoration of the Self.* New York: International Universities Press.

Kris, E. (1938), Review of *The Ego and the Mechanisms of Defense* by Anna Freud. In: *The Selected Papers of Ernst Kris.* New Haven: Yale University Press, 1975, pp. 343–356.

Kuppe, R. (1947), *Dr. Karl Lueger: Persoenlichkeit und Wirken.* Wien: Hollinek.

Lampl de Groot, J. (1928), The Evolution of the Oedipus Complex in Women. *International Journal of Psycho-Analysis,* 9:332–345.

Lesky, E. (1965), *Die Wiener Medizinische Schule im 19. Jahrhundert.* Graz-Koeln: Boehlaus.

Levin, K. (1978), *Freud's Early Psychology of the Neuroses.* Pittsburgh: University of Pittsburgh Press.

Lewin, K. (1935), *A Dynamic Theory of Personality*. New York: McGraw-Hill.

Loewald, H. (1960), On the Therapeutic Action of Psychoanalysis. In: *Papers on Psychoanalysis*. New Haven: Yale University Press, 1980, pp. 221–256.

———— (1971), On Motivation and Instinct Theory. In: *Papers on Psychoanalysis*. New Haven: Yale University Press, 1980, pp. 102–137.

———— (1977), Book Review Essay on *The Freud/Jung Letters*. In: *Papers on Psychoanalysis*. New Haven: Yale University Press, 1980, pp. 405–418.

———— (1978), Instinct Theory, Object Relations, and Psychic Structure Formation. In: *Papers on Psychoanalysis*. New Haven: Yale University Press, 1980, pp. 207–218.

London, P. (1964), *The Modes and Morals of Psychotherapy*. New York: Holt, Rinehart & Winston.

Mach, E. (1897), *Contributions to the Analysis of Sensations*. London: Open Court.

Mahony, P. (1979), Friendship and Its Discontents. *Contemporary Psychoanalysis*, 15:55–109.

Malinowski, B. (1944), *A Scientific Theory of Culture and Other Essays*. Chapel Hill: University of North Carolina Press.

Mannheim, K. (1936), *Ideology and Utopia*, trans. L. Wirth & E. Shils. New York: Harvest.

Manuel, F. (1956), *The New World of Henri Saint-Simon*. Cambridge: Harvard University Press.

———— (1962), *The Prophets of Paris*. New York: Harper & Row.

Marmor, J. (1962), Psychoanalytic Therapy as an Educational Process: Common Denominators in the Therapeutic Approaches of Different Psychoanalytic "Schools." In: *Psychoanalytic Education*, ed. J. Masserman. New York: Grune & Stratton, pp. 286–299.

Marx, K. (1844), *Economic and Philosophic Manuscripts of 1844*, trans. M. Milligan. New York: International Publishers, 1964.

———— & Engels, F. (1846–1847), *The German Ideology*, ed. C. Arthur. New York: International Publishers, 1970.

Maslow, A. H. (1962), Was Adler a Disciple of Freud? A Note. *Journal of Individual Psychology*, 18:125.

Maus, H. (1962), *A Short History of Sociology*. New York: Philosophical Library.

McGrath, W. (1974), *Dionysian Art and Populist Politics in Austria*. New Haven: Yale University Press.

Mitchell, G. D. (1968), *A Hundred Years of Sociology*. Chicago: Aldine.

Mitzman, A. (1971), Toennies and German Society, 1887–1914: From Cultural Pessimism to Celebration of the *Volksgemeinschaft*. *Journal of the History of Ideas*, 32:507–524.

Montessori, M. (1912), *The Montessori Method*, trans. A. E. George. New York: Stokes.

Morgan, C. L. (1923), *Emergent Evolution*. London: Williams & Norgate.

Mueller, A. (1973), *Grundlagen der Individualpsychologie: Beitraege zur Verhaltensweise des Menschen und zur individualpsychologischen Paedagogik*. Zurich: Classen.

Needham, J. (1925), Mechanistic Biology and the Religious Consciousness. In: *Science, Religion and Reality*, ed. J. Needham. New York: Braziller, 1955, pp. 223–261.

Nietzsche, F. (1887), On the Genealogy of Morals. In: *Basic Writings of Nietzsche*, ed. & trans. W. Kaufmann. New York: Modern Library, 1968, pp. 449–599.

Nisbet, R. A. (1966), *The Sociological Tradition*. New York: Basic Books.

Nordenskioeld, E. (1928), *The History of Biology*, trans. L. B. Eyre. New York: Tudor.

Nunberg, H. (1959), "Introduction." In: *Minutes of the Vienna Psychoanalytic Society, vol. I: 1906–1908*, ed. & trans. H. Nunberg & E. Federn. New York: International Universities Press, 1962, pp. xvii–xxxii.

———— (1969), *Memoirs: Recollections, Ideas, Reflections*. New York: Psychoanalytic Research and Development Fund.

———— & Federn, E., ed. & trans. (1962), *Minutes of the Vienna Psychoanalytic Society, vol. I: 1906–1908*. New York: International Universities Press.

———— ———— ed. & trans. (1967), *Minutes of the Vienna Psychoanalytic Society, vol. II: 1908–1910*. New York: International Universities Press.

———— ———— ed. (1974), *Minutes of the Vienna Psychoanalytic Society, vol. III: 1910–1911*, trans. M. Nunberg. New York: International Universities Press.

Ollman, B. (1971), *Alienation: Marx's Conception of Man in Capitalist Society*. Cambridge: Cambridge University Press.

Orgler, H. (1939), *Alfred Adler: The Man and His Work*. Ashington, England: Daniel.

Papanek, E. (1962), *The Austrian School Reform: Its Bases, Principles and Development—The Twenty Years Between the Two World Wars*. New York: Fell.

Peters, H. F. (1962), *My Sister, My Spouse*. New York: Norton.

Phillips, D. C. (1970), Organicism in the Late Nineteenth and Early Twentieth Centuries. *Journal of the History of Ideas*, 31:413–429.

Piaget, J. (1923), *The Language and Thought of the Child*, trans. M. Gabain. New York: Meridian, 1974.

———— (1924), *Judgment and Reasoning in the Child*, trans. M. Warden. New York: Harcourt, Brace & World, 1926.

———— (1932), *The Moral Judgment of the Child*, trans. M. Gabain. New York: Free Press, 1965.

———— (1937), *The Construction of Reality in the Child*. New York: Basic Books.

———— (1970), *The Science of Education and the Psychology of the Child,* trans. D. Coltman. New York: Orion.

Popper, K. (1934), *The Logic of Scientific Discovery.* London: Hutchinson, 1959.

———— (1963), *Conjectures and Refutations: The Growth of Scientific Knowledge.* New York: Harper & Row.

———— (1974), Autobiography. In: *The Philosophy of Karl Popper,* ed. P. A. Schilpp. La Salle, Ill.: Open Court.

Puner, H. (1947), *Freud: His Life and His Mind.* n.p.: Howell, Soskin.

Rank, B. (1949), Aggression. *The Psychoanalytic Study of the Child,* 3/4:43–48. New York: International Universities Press.

Rapaport, D. (1951), The Autonomy of the Ego. In: *The Collected Papers of David Rapaport,* ed. M. Gill. New York: Basic Books, 1967, pp. 357–367.

———— (1954), Clinical Implications of Ego Psychology. In: *The Collected Papers of David Rapaport,* ed. M. Gill. New York: Basic Books, 1967, pp. 586–593.

———— (1957), Letter [Response to Robert W. White's Review of Heinz L. and Rowena R. Ansbacher's *The Individual Psychology of Alfred Adler*]. In: *The Collected Papers of David Rapaport,* ed. M. Gill. New York: Basic Books, 1967, pp. 682–684.

Reitler, R. (1911), Kritische Bermerkungen zu Dr. Adler's Lehre vom 'maennlichen Protest.' *Zentralblatt fuer Psychoanalyse,* 1:580–596.

Ricoeur, P. (1970), *Freud and Philosophy: An Essay on Interpretation,* trans. D. Savage. New Haven: Yale University Press.

Rieff, P. (1956), The Origins of Freud's Political Psychology. *Journal of the History of Ideas,* 17:235–249.

Roazen, P. (1969), *Brother Animal: The Story of Freud and Tausk.* New York: Vintage.

———— (1975), *Freud and His Followers.* New York: Knopf.

Rom, P. (1966), *Alfred Adler und die wissenschaftliche Menschenkenntnis.* Frankfurt am Main: Kramer.

Rosenstein, G. (1910), Die Theorien der Organminderwertigkeit und der Bisexualitaet in ihren Beziehungen zur Neurosenlehre. *Jahrbuch fuer Psychoanalytische Forschungen,* 2:398–408.

Rubinstein, B. B. (1975), On the Clinical Psychoanalytic Theory and its Role in the Inference and Confirmation of Particular Clinical Hypotheses. *Psychoanalysis and Contemporary Science,* 4:3–58. New York: International Universities Press.

———— (1978), Psychoanalytic Hypotheses and the Problem of their Confirmation. In: *Theory, Language, and Consciousness,* ed. K. D. Irani & G. Myers. New York: Haven.

Sachs, H. (1944), *Freud: Master and Friend.* Cambridge: Harvard University Press.

Sandler, J. (1960), On the Concept of the Superego. *The Psychoanalytic Study of the Child,* 15:128–162. New York: International Universities Press.

Schafer, R. (1974), Problems in Freud's Psychology of Women. *Journal of the American Psychoanalytic Association,* 22:459–485.

Schilder, P. (1938), The Social Neurosis. In: *On Neuroses,* ed. L. Bender. New York: International Universities Press, 1979, pp. 161–178.

———— (1950), *The Image and Appearance of the Human Body.* New York: International Universities Press.

Schopenhauer, A. (1819), *The World as Will and Representation,* trans. E. F. J. Payne. New York: Dover, 1969.

Schur, M. (1972), *Freud: Living and Dying.* New York: International Universities Press.

Seidler, R. (1936), School Guidance Clinics in Vienna. *International Journal of Individual Psychology,* 2(4):75–78.

———— & Zilah, L. (1929), The Vienna Child Guidance Clinics. In: *Guiding the Child on the Principles of Individual Psychology,* ed. A. Adler et al., trans. B. Ginzburg. London: Allen & Unwin, 1930, pp. 9–27.

Shengold, L. (1976), The Freud/Jung Letters. In: *Freud and His Self-Analysis,* ed. M. Kanzer & J. Glenn. New York: Aronson, pp. 187–201.

Siegl, M. H. (1933), *Reform of Elementary Education in Austria.* New York.

Simmel, G. (1923), *Conflict.* In: *Conflict & The Web of Group-Affiliations,* trans. K. H. Wolff & R. Bendix. New York: Free Press, pp. 11–123.

Simon, M. (1971), *The Matter of Life: Philosophical Problems of Biology.* New Haven: Yale University Press.

Simpson, G. G. (1947), *This View of Life: The World of an Evolutionist.* New York: Harcourt, Brace & World, 1964.

———— (1967), *The Meaning of Evolution.* New Haven: Yale University Press.

Skinner, Q. (1969), Meaning and Understanding in the History of Ideas. *History and Theory,* 8:3–53.

Smuts, J. C. (1926), *Holism and Evolution.* New York: Macmillan.

Soper, P. H. & L'Abate, L. (1980), Paradox as a Therapeutic Technique: A Review. In: *Advances in Family Psychiatry,* vol. 2, ed. J. G. Howells. New York: International Universities Press, pp. 369–384.

Sorokin, P. A. (1928), *Contemporary Sociological Theories.* New York: Harper & Row.

Spehlmann, R. (1953), *Sigmund Freuds Neurologische Schriften: Eine Untersuchung zur Vorgeschichte der Psychoanalyse.* Berlin: Springer.

Sperber, M. (1926), *Alfred Adler: Der Mensch und seine Lehre.* Muenchen: Bergmann.

———— (1970), *Masks of Loneliness: Alfred Adler in Perspective,* trans. K. Winston. New York: Macmillan, 1974.

Spiel, O. (1956), The Individual Psychological Experimental School in Vienna. *American Journal of Individual Psychology,* 12:1–11.

Spitz, R. A. (1953), Aggression: Its Role in the Establishment of Object Relations. In: *Drives, Affects, Behavior,* ed. R. Loewenstein. New York: International Universities Press, pp. 126–138.

Stekel, W. (1950), *Autobiography: The Life Story of a Pioneer Psychoanalyst.*
New York: Liveright.

Stepansky, P. (1976), The Empiricist as Rebel: Jung, Freud, and the Burdens of
Discipleship. *Journal of the History of the Behavioral Sciences,* 12:216–239.

_____ (1977), *A History of Aggression in Freud. Psychological Issues*
[Monograph 39]. New York: International Universities Press.

_____ (1983), Perspectives on Dissent: Adler, Kohut, and the Idea of a Psychoanalytic Research Tradition. *The Annual of Psychoanalysis,* 11 (in press).
New York: International Universities Press.

Stockert-Meynert, D. (1930), *Theodor Meynert und seine Zeit.* Wien: Oester-
reichischer Bundesverlag.

Sullivan, H. S. (1953), *The Interpersonal Theory of Psychiatry.* New York.
Norton.

Sulloway, F. (1979), *Freud, Biologist of the Mind: Beyond the Psychoanalytic
Legend.* New York: Basic Books.

Swales, P. J. (1982), Freud, Fliess, and Fratricide: The Role of Fliess in Freud's
Conception of Paranoia. Privately printed.

Szasz, T. (1961), *The Myth of Mental Illness.* New York: Harper & Row.

_____ (1976), *Karl Kraus and the Soul-Doctors: A Pioneer Critic and His
Criticism of Psychiatry and Psychoanalysis.* Baton Rouge: Louisiana State
University Press.

Toennies, F. (1887), *Community and Society,* trans. C. P. Loomis. New York:
Harper & Row, 1957.

Trotsky, L. (1970), *My Life.* New York: Pathfinder.

Tucker, R. (1961), *Philosophy and Myth in Karl Marx.* Cambridge: Cambridge
University Press.

Vaihinger, H. (1911), *The Philosophy of 'As If',* trans. C. Ogden. New York:
Harcourt, Brace, 1935.

_____ (1923), Wie die Philosophie des Als Ob entstand. In: *Philosophie der
Gegenwart in Selbstdarstellungen,* ed. R. Schmidt. Leipzig: Meiner, pp.
183–212.

Van Den Berghe, L. (1963), Dialectic and Functionalism: Toward a Theoretical
Synthesis. *American Sociological Review,* 28:695–705.

Van Der Poel, J. (1974), *Selections from the Smuts Papers,* vol. 5. Cambridge:
Cambridge University Press.

Von Bertalanffy, L. (1933), *Modern Theories of Development: An Introduction
to Theoretical Biology,* trans. J. H. Woodger. London: Oxford University
Press.

_____ (1952), *Problems of Life: An Evaluation of Modern Biological
Thought.* New York: Wiley.

Waelder, R. (1956), Sigmund Freud Centennial Lecture. In: *Psychoanalysis: Observation, Theory, Application,* ed. S. A. Guttman. New York: International Universities Press, 1976, pp. 1–13.

———— (1962), Psychoanalysis, Scientific Method, and Philosophy. In: *Psychoanalysis: Observation, Theory, Application,* ed. S. A. Guttman. New York: International Universities Press, 1976, pp. 248–274.

———— (1963), Historical Fiction. *Journal of the American Psychoanalytic Association,* 11:628–651.

Wasserman, I. (1958), Letter to the Editor. *American Journal of Psychotherapy,* 12:623–627.

Watzlawick, P., Weakland, J., & Fisch, R. (1974), *Change: Principles of Problem Formation and Problem Resolution.* New York: Norton.

Way, L. (1950), *Adler's Place in Psychology.* New York: Macmillan.

Weininger, O. (1903), *Sex and Character,* trans. from the 6th German edition. London: Heinemann, n.d.

Weiss, E. (1966), Paul Federn. In: *Psychoanalytic Pioneers,* ed. F. Alexander, S. Eisenstein, & M. Grotjahn. New York: Basic Books, pp. 142–159.

Weisz, G. (1975), Scientists and Sectarians: The Case of Psychoanalysis. *Journal of the History of the Behavioral Sciences,* 11:350–364.

Wexberg, E. (1929), *Individual Psychology,* trans. W. B. Wolfe. New York: Cosmopolitan.

Wheeler, L. R. (1939), *Vitalism: Its History and Validity.* London: Witherby.

White, R. (1957), Adler and the Future of Ego Psychology. In: *Essays in Individual Psychology,* ed. K. Adler & D. Deutsch. New York: Grove, 1959, pp. 437–454.

———— (1960), Competence and the Psychosexual Stages of Development. In: *Nebraska Symposium on Motivation,* ed. M. R. Jones. Lincoln: University of Nebraska Press, pp. 97–141.

———— (1963), *Ego and Reality in Psychoanalytic Theory: A Proposal Regarding Independent Ego Energies. Psychological Issues* [Monograph 11]. New York: International Universities Press.

Winnicott, D. W. (1956), Primary Maternal Preoccupation. In: *Through Paediatrics to Psycho-Analysis.* New York: Basic Books, 1975, pp. 300–305.

———— (1960), The Theory of the Parent-Infant Relationship. In: *The Maturational Processes and the Facilitating Environment.* New York: International Universities Press, 1965, pp. 37–55.

Wittels, F. (1924), *Sigmund Freud: His Personality, His Teaching, and His School,* trans. E. & C. Paul. New York: Dodd, Mead.

———— (1933), Revision of a Biography. *Psychoanalytic Review,* 20:361–374.

Woodger, J. H. (1929), *Biological Principles: A Critical Study.* New York: Harcourt, Brace & Co.

Index

A

Abiogenesis, 253, 254
Abortion, 272
Abraham, K., 125, 138, 140, 141, 142, 190
Abrahamsen, D., 69n
Adaptation, social, 251
see also conformism
Adler, A.
and Austrian educational reforms, 214–217
on Bolshevism, 29–30
childhood illnesses of, 8–9
concept of neurotic conflict, 51, 62
conservatism of, 270–272, 275
critique of repression, 118–119
critique of sexuality in neurosis, 113–117
education of, 10–11
as educational counselor, 217–222
as emigré, 6
evolutionary theory of, 245–248, 250–251, 255–257, 260–261

expressions of indebtedness to work of, 2
formative years, 8–10
on Freud and psychoanalysis, 276, 278–279
Freud's critique of, 175–205
and Judaism, 9–10
influence of, 7
influence of others on, 5
and Marx, 12, 17, 19, 22, 31, 93, 120–121, 168, 184
medical training, 10–11
military service, 11, 27
on Oedipus complex, 75–76
as president of Vienna Psychoanalytic Society, 101, 112
and preventive medicine, 18
as prophet, 242–243, 251, 261, 269
as psychoanalyst, 77–78
on punishment, 231
relationship with Freud, 4, 77, 79–80, 81–111; issue of "discipleship," 81–84, 181–182, 202–205

Adler, A. (*cont.*)
  reminiscences of, by colleagues
      and protégés, 1–2
  as restorationist, 275–276, 279
  social medicine and, 13–14, 19,
      20
  as social reformer, 208
  social theory of neurosis, 160–166
  socialism and, 11–14, 20, 30, 270
  split with Freud, 2, 4, 32–33, 81,
      83–87, 104, 112, 130, 150,
      182, 206
  status as a Freudian, 4
  subjectivism of, 221
  theory of organ inferiority, 33–48
  theory of sexual types, 68–73
  theory of therapy, 267–272
  in the United States, 6, 7
  World War I, reaction to, 27–29
Adler, Leopold (father), 9
Adler, Victor, 12–14, 15
  as *Armenarzt*, 13
Adlerian educational guidance
    clinics, 216–222, 240
Adlerian experimental school,
    215–216
Adlerian psychology, accounts of, 1
Adlerians, Adler as seen by, 2, 4
Affection, child's need for, 64–65
Aggression, 90–91, 184–189,
    194–197
  Adler on, 59–62
  as issue in Freud's critique of
      Adler, 182–191, 194–197,
      202
  and organ compensations, 59
Aggressive drive, 45, 59–60, 75,
    90–91, 94, 98, 105, 183, 280
  and death instinct, 277
  and ego psychology, 60
  Freud's resistance to, 197
"Aggressive Drive in Life and in
    Neurosis, The" (Adler), 42–46,
    59–60, 66, 90–91

Aichhorn, A., 222–225, 232, 277
Alexander, F., 222–223, 225–230,
    232
  Adlerian presuppositions of,
      225–228
  on psychoanalytic therapy, 227
Alexander, S., 253
Alienation, Marx on, 264
Altruism, 231
America, Adler and, 6, 7
Andreas-Salomé, L., 150–151,
    166–174, 175, 182, 193–194,
    196, 205, 281
  critique of Adler's ego psychol-
      ogy, 168–173
  critique of "guiding fiction,"
      170–171
  on narcissism, 172
Antisocial behavior, therapy and,
    218–220, 223, 241
"As if," philosophy of; *see*
    Vaihinger
Asthma, 99
Austrian school reforms, 211–214
  Adler and, 214–217
  Einheitsschule as governing idea
      of, 212–213
  see also Gloeckel
Austrian trade unionism, growth of,
    15
Authoritarianism, in Adler, 269–272,
    275

B

Bach, D., 149n
Baden school, neo-Kantian, 158
Baldwin, G. M., 232
Bateson, G., 219n
Beckh-Widmanstetter, H., 9, 10n,
    11n
Behavior modification, 218
Bergson, H., 251–252
Bernfeld, S., 50n

Bertalanffy, L. von, 250n, 254n
Bichat, X., 273
Binion, R., 166n, 172n
Binswanger, L., 282
Biologist, Freud's critique of Adler
    as, 95, 98, 99, 105–106,
    126–127, 131, 136, 181
Biology
    and *Gemeinschaft*, 259–260
    and psychoanalytic dissidents,
        126n
    and psychoanalytic instinct theory,
        134–135
    and vitalism, 249–250, 254
    see also evolution
Birnbaum, F., 215, 216n
Bisexuality, 197–201
    in Adler and Fliess, 197–198
    influence of concept on Freud, 199
    see also psychic hermaphroditism
Bjerre, P., 166
Blau, P., 107
Bleuler, E., 109n, 139, 140, 142
"Bolshevism and Psychology"
    (Adler), 29–30
Bonald, L. de, 272, 273
Bottome, P., 81, 104n, 215n, 240n
Brill, A. A., 139, 140
Brome, V., 83n
Buehler, C., 215
Buehler, K., 215

C

Cabanis, G., 273
Capitalism, 29, 30, 264
Castration anxiety, 191, 280, 281,
    286, 287, 288–290, 291
    and Freud's critique of masculine
        protest, 191, 286–287
Causality, Adler on, 209
Child guidance clinics; *see* Adlerian
    educational guidance clinics

Childhood defects (*Kinderfehler*), 46,
    52, 53, 54, 55, 59
    and awkwardness, 62
    and oversensitivity, 59
    and sexuality, 53
    see also organ inferiority
Children
    Adler on education of, 206–241
    Adler on welfare of, 21–26
Clark, R., 70n, 84n, 88
"Coefficient of safety" (Adler),
    246–247
Colby, K., 86
Collective conscience (Durkheim),
    162, 230
Communism, 264
Community; *see Gemeinschaft*
Community feeling; *see*
    Gemeinschaftsgefuehl
Community hygiene, 18–25, 31
    and Adler's notion of prophylaxis,
        18
    role of government in promoting, 19
    and working-class reform, 18, 20
    see also prophylaxis
Compensation, 41, 46–47, 59
    and "brain activity," 46
Compulsion, 48
Comte, A., 266, 273–275
Conflict, 51–52
Conflict groups, 144, 146
Conformism, as psychopedagogical
    goal, 218, 221, 241, 251, 263,
    267–272, 275
Consciousness, Marx on, 264
Conversion neurosis, 174
Copleston, F., 158n
Coulanges, F. de, 258n
Counter-fiction, Adler's notion of,
    164–165
Courage, as pedagogical goal, 208,
    217–218, 221
Cowardice, 218, 269
Criminality, 227, 269

Cruelty impulse, 185, 197
  see also aggression, aggressive
    drive
Culture
  and aggression, 277
  and drive satisfaction, 119
  and neurosis, 153
  and theory of organ inferiority, 23,
    36, 39–40, 66

D

Dahrendorf, R., 144
Darwin, C., 247–248, 249, 253,
  273
  Adler on, 247–248
Death instinct, 276–277, 279n
Death wish, 279
Decker, H., 108n, 109n
Defiance, 66–70, 75, 114, 121–122,
  185
  and aggression, 185
  and feeling of inferiority, 67
"Defiance and Obedience" (Adler),
  65–69, 73–74
Delinquent behavior, therapy and,
  222–225, 227–229, 240, 269
  Aichhorn on, 223–225
  Alexander on, 227–230
Deutsch, H., 193n
Deviant behavior, therapy and,
  218–220, 240, 269–270
Dewey, J., 232–235, 236, 240
  on community feeling, 233, 234
  on manual training, 233, 234
  philosophy of experience, 234–235
  on school curriculum, 234
Dilthey, W., 5, 6
Discipline, 230
Division of labor, 265–266
Divorce, 272
"Don Juan" characteristic, 124
Dorer, M., 50n

Dottrens, R., 213n
Driesch, H., 249–250, 254
Drives, 60, 113, 120, 184–185
  see also instinct theory
Dunn, J., 7n
Durkheim, E., 161, 162, 163, 184,
  230–232, 240, 262, 263–266
  on community feeling, 265–266
  pedagogy of, 230–232

E

Education of children, Adler on; see
  pedagogy
Educators, as Adlerian psychologists,
  208–211
Ego, 44, 119, 225–226
Ego instincts, 118–119
Ego psychology, 3, 6–7, 96, 113,
  121, 125, 127, 131, 132, 168,
  193
  and aggression, 184–185
Egocentrism, in intellectual develop-
  ment, 238
Eissler, K., 86–87, 192n
Élan vital (Bergson), 251–252
Ellenberger, H., 1, 6–7, 9n, 10n,
  11n, 30, 240n
Ellis, H., 114
Epilepsy, 35
Ermers, M., 13
Erythrophobia, 92
Evolution, 245–260, 268, 272
  Bergson on, 251–252
  and communal life, 248
  community as goal of, 256–257,
    259–260
  Driesch on, 249–250
  Haldane on, 249–250
  Smuts on, 253–257
  and teleology, 246–247, 268
  and vitalism, 249–250, 268
Exchange structuralism, 107–108

F

Falsifiability (Popper), 37n–38n, 292
Fancher, R., 49n
Federn, E., 85, 88–92, 100, 102,
     103, 104, 109, 111, 117, 130
Federn, P., 111, 147–148, 149n,
     167
Female sexuality, 75–76, 287–288
Femininity, 69–70
Ferenczi, S., 140–141, 199n
Fischl, H., 212, 213n, 215n
Fliess, W., 183, 197–202, 205
     Adler on, 198, 198n
Flugel, J. C., 3
Frank, O., 13n
French, T., 226
Freud, A., 96n
Freud, S.
     Adler's relationship with, 4, 77,
          79–80, 81–206
     Adler's split with, 2, 4, 32–33,
          81, 83–87, 104, 112, 130,
          150, 182, 206
     chronology of changing estimation
          of Adler, 178–182
     critique of Adler's "aggressive
          drive," 186–191
     and Fliess, 197–199; Adler as a
          "little Fliess," 197, 200–201
     hidden Adler in, 280–292
     influence on Adler, 5
     on psychoanalysis and education,
          277–278
     strategy of "systematic toler-
          ance," 146–147, 205
     structural theory, 44, 276–277
     theory of primary and secondary
          psychic processes, 49–51
     view of Adler as "paranoid,"
          181, 190
Freudians, Adler as seen by, 2, 4
Friedlander, K., 223n

Friedman, P., 161n
Fromm, E., 7, 192
Furtmueller, C., 10n, 11, 12, 82, 96,
     102, 128, 154, 202, 215

G

Ganz, M., 216n
Gedo, J. E., 176n
Gemeinschaft (community)
     and conservative utopian men-
          tality, 276
     and Gesellschaft (society), 258
     as goal of evolution, 247,
          250–251, 257, 268; biological
          critique of, 259–260
     and holism, 255–256
     Toennies and, 258
Gemeinschaftsgefuehl (community
     feeling)
     in Adler's theory of neurosis,
          243–245, 267
     and Adler's theory of therapy,
          261–263, 266; conformist im-
          plications of, 267–272
     and Bolshevism, 30
     and child's need for affection, 65
     and counter-fiction, 164–165
     Dewey on, 233–235
     and evolutionary theory, 246–248,
          251, 268
     and holism, 255–257
     as pedagogical goal, 207, 211,
          214, 217; critique of,
          240–241
     Piaget on, 235–237, 238
     and restorationist sociologies,
          272–275
     and superiority strivings, 207, 217
     and World War I, 28–29, 30
Gesellschaft (society), Toennies on,
     258
Gierke, O. von, 258n

Gloeckel, O., 212–215
Glover, E., 223n, 224n
Graf, M., 92, 149n, 193n
Griesinger, W., 35
Gruber, M., 12–13
Gruen, H., 18
Gruenbaum, A., 37n–38n, 137n
Guidance clinics; see Adlerian educational guidance clinics
Guiding fiction, Adler's notion of, 3, 153, 155–157, 160, 170–171
  "healthy" versus "neurotic," 156–157, 160

H

Haldane, J. B. S., 249–250, 254
Halleck, S., 268
Hartmann, H., 3, 60, 96n
Hate, 185
Hayek, F. A., 273n
Health Book for the Tailoring Trade (Adler), 11, 15–18
Healy, W., 222
"Heightened brain performance" (Adler), 46
Hein, H., 250n, 254n
Heller, H., 149n
Hendrick, I., 2
Hermaphroditism; see psychic hermaphroditism
Himmelfarb, G., 248n
Hitschmann, E., 88–92, 102, 103, 104, 109, 111, 127, 128, 147, 148, 149n
Hoffer, W., 60
Holism, 253–257
  see also Smuts, vitalism
Holism and Evolution (Smuts), 253–257
Homans, G., 107, 110n
Homosexuality, 96

Horney, K., 7, 122, 184, 287, 288
Hull, D., 254n
Hygiene; see community hygiene
Hysteria, 176, 177

I

Id, 44, 276
Iggers, G., 158n, 273n
Iggers, W., 70n
Impotence, 90, 116
"Independent ego energies" (White), 3
Individual Psychology
  Adler as founder of, 1, 8
  Adler's comparison of psychoanalysis and, 278
  analysts' opinion of, 3
  development of, 4, 24
  as evolutionary doctrine, 245–257
  and goal of social adjustment, 262
  origins of, 8
  theory of therapy of, 267–272
Infantile Sexuality
  Adler's critique of, 115–116
  and education, 277
  and organ pleasure, 135
  and theory of organ inferiority, 53–54
Inferiority feelings, 56, 67–71, 131, 151–152, 185, 209, 211, 226, 229
  and education, 2–6, 211
  and theory of organ inferiority, 56
  and theory of sexual types, 70–71
Influence, in history of ideas, 6–7
Insight, 139n, 218
Instinct theory
  Adler's critique of, 119–121, 184–185
  and biology, 135
  psychoanalytic, 276–277

"Instinct to master" (Hendrick), 2
Instincts; *see* instinct theory
International Psychoanalytic Association, 140–149, 203
    founding of, 140–142

J

Jacoby, R., 3n
James, W., 232
Janik, A., 70n
Joad, C. E. M., 250n
Joffe, A. A., 12
Jones, E., 32, 33, 85–86, 104n,
    110n, 139, 140, 182–183, 188,
    192, 194, 196
Jung, C. G., 78–79, 89, 95, 96,
    101, 106, 109n, 110, 138–143,
    175–182, 188, 246
    Adler's critique of, 78–79
    Freud's relationship with, 176–178
    and Nuremberg Congress, 141
    and politicization of psycho-
        analysis, 143
    and teleology, 246
Justice, acquisition of sense of,
    236–237

K

Kahane, M., 147, 148
Kalmar, A., 70n
Kant, I., 158, 159
Kanzer, M., 87–88
Kardiner, A., 111, 180n
Kaufmann, W., 85n, 88
Kidney stones, 34n
Klemperer, P., 134
Knowledge, thirst for, 115
Koch, R., 13
Kohn, C., 70n
Kohn, H., 69n

Kohut, H., 119n, 204n
Kraus, K., 69–70
Krausz, E. O., 253n
Kris, E., 3, 96n

L

L'Abate, L., 219n
Lamarck, J. -B., 247
Lamarckism, 23
Lampl de Groot, J., 291n
Lange, F. A., 158
"Law of movement" (Adler),
    254–255, 256, 260, 267
Lecomte du Nouey, P., 250
Leseverein der deutschen Studenten
    (Reading Society of Viennese
    and German Students), 12–13
Lesky, E., 9n, 10n
Levin, K., 35n, 49n
Levy-Bruhl, L., 162
Libido, 91, 97–100, 105, 116, 124,
    132–134, 136–138, 177, 178,
    195, 224
    and Adler's "aggressive drive,"
        188–189, 195
    as "arranged," 116, 133, 134
    Freud as champion of, 97
    Freud's response to Adler's re-
        evaluation of, 136–138
    masculine character of, 98, 107
    see also infantile sexuality,
        sexuality
Life-process, 247–248
"Little Hans," case of, 186–188
Loewald, H., 120n, 176n
Loewenstein, R., 96n
London, P., 268
Love
    and Adler's "world system," 189,
        197
    as social task, 270–271

"Lowered self-esteem," Adler's work on, 3
Lueger, K., 15

M

Mach, E., 158, 196
Mahony, P., 199n
Maine, H., 258n
Maistre, J. de, 272, 273
Male object-choice, 93–94, 284–285
Malinowski, B., 144n
Mannheim, K., 276
Manuel, F., 243, 273n
Marmor, J., 137n–138n
Marriage, 270–272
Marx, K., 31, 120, 168, 184, 263–266
  on community feeling, 263–265
Marxism, 38n, 93, 120
  Adler and, 12, 29, 31
Masculine protest, 54, 56, 57, 62, 68, 72–78, 97, 100, 102–104, 105, 113, 114–115, 117–118, 119, 123, 151, 182–186, 188, 191, 228, 280–292
  and Adler's theory of neurosis, 72–73, 114–117
  and aggressive instinct, 183–185
  Andreas-Salomé on, 172–173
  and castration anxiety, 191, 286, 287, 288, 289, 290
  and the feminine role, 185
  Freud's critique of, 97–99, 191
  and narcissism, 286, 289–290
  in the transference, 74–75
Masculinity, 69–70
  preeminence as "arch evil" of culture, 26, 68
  see also masculine protest
Maslow, A., 82
Masturbation, 53, 64, 100, 115–116

and masculine protest, 100, 115–116
  premature, 63, 122
Maus, H., 163n
Mauss, M., 162
McGrath, W., 13n
Mead, G. H., 236
The Meaning of Life (Adler), 247, 252–253, 261, 269
Medicine; *see* community hygiene, organ inferiority, preventive medicine, prophylaxis, social medicine
Merrick, J., 25n
Meynert, T., 13, 35, 43
Migraine, 161
Mind, Smuts on, 256
Mitchell, G. D., 163n
Moebius, P., 198
Monogamy, 270
Montessori, M., 232, 236
Morality
  Durkheim on, 230
  Piaget on development of, 235–237
Morgan, C. L., 253
Mueller, A., 240n

N

Narcissism, 135, 172, 173, 191, 286, 289–290
  and masculine protest, 191, 286, 289–290
Natural selection, 255
Needham, J., 250n
Neo-Adlerians, 7
Nervous Character, The (Adler), 62, 64, 67, 150–174, 186, 206, 210, 243, 244, 267
Neurosis, 32, 47–48, 57–73, 89–100, 103, 105, 113–124,

127–128, 132, 150–174, 186,
    244, 267, 277
Adler's social theory of, 160–166;
    as Durkheimian, 162–164,
    230
Alexander's theory of, 225–226
and community feeling, 243–245,
    267
Neurotic character, Adler on, 62–64,
    122–124, 151–153
Neurotic conflict, 51, 62–63, 79, 98,
    161–162
Adler versus Freud on, 161–162
and libido, 98
"Neurotic Disposition, On The"
    (Adler), 57–59, 61–64
Neurotic predisposition, 32, 34, 61
Neurotic symptoms, Adler on,
    52–53, 55
Nietzsche, F., 166, 210, 220
Nisbet, R., 258n
Nordenskioeld, E., 250n
Nothnagel, H., 148
Nunberg, H., 85, 149n
Nuremberg Congress, 101, 136,
    140–149, 179, 205
    and institutionalization of psycho-
        analysis, 140–142, 146, 149

O

Obedience, 66–69, 121
    and feeling of inferiority, 67
Oedipus complex, 57, 75–77, 99,
    124, 138, 161, 204, 285
    and the masculine protest, 75–76,
        124, 133
Organ drives, Adler on, 43–45
    as socially regulated, 119
Organ inferiority, theory of
    Andreas-Salomé on, 173
    and awkwardness, 62–63

and conflict theory, 45, 51
and cultural requirements, 36,
    40–41, 66, 68, 73
and embryological damage, 39
and functional inferiorities, 34, 35
as incompatible with psychoana-
    lytic theory, 52–54
as mediator between organ drives
    and cultural demands, 44–45
and morphologic inferiorities, 34,
    35
and neurophysiological change,
    45–47
as nonfalsifiable, 37, 40
and oversensitivity, 59
and pathoanatomical psychiatry, 35
and psychogenesis, 47–48, 50–51
Schilder on, 174
and sexuality, 53–54, 114,
    133–134
Wagner-Jauregg on, 33–34
Organicism, 254
    and theories of society, 272–273
Orgler, H., 240n
Other Side, The (Adler), 27
Overcompensation, 41, 89, 114
Oversensitivity, Adler's notion of,
    57–63, 67, 79, 136
    and aggression, 60–61
    and awkwardness, 62–63, 65
    and cultural attitudes, 68
    as hereditary expression of organ
        inferiority, 59
    and masculine protest, 62
    and sexuality, 63

P

Pacher, R., 212
Papanek, E., 213n
Pedagogical Institute (Vienna), 215
Pedagogical psychology, 21–25

Pedagogy
    Adler's optimism regarding,
        208–210, 277
    and Adler's therapeutic assump-
        tions, 206–207
    and child development, 207
    Dewey's, 232–235
    and *Gemeinschaftsgefuehl,* 207,
        231, 239, 240–241
    heredity and, 209
    and parents, 208
    Piaget's, 239
    as prophylaxis, 208
Penis envy, 280, 281, 286n,
    287–288
Periodicity (Fliess), 198n
Pernerstorfer, E., 13
Personality, Science of (Smuts), 257
Pfister, O., 189
Phillips, D. C., 254n
Philosophy of education, Adler's,
    240–241
    see also pedagogy
"Physician as Educator, The"
    (Adler), 21–22, 24, 31
Piaget, J., 152, 232, 235–239, 240
    and development of morality,
        235–237
    versus Adler on education,
        237–239
Pleasure principle, 48
Poincaré, H., 158
Popper, K., 37n–38n, 170, 292
Positivism, 273–274
Prelinger, E., 57n, 109n
Premature ejaculation, 116
Preventive medicine, 18, 20–22, 23
Procreation, 271
Progress, 259
Progressive educators, 232, 240
Prophylaxis, 18, 20–26, 208
    depoliticization of, 24
    and education, 208

Psychic hermaphroditism, 70–73, 79,
    97
    Freud's critique of, 98
    in the transference, 74–75
    see also bisexuality
Psychic life, purposiveness of, 246,
    247
"Psychic organ" (Adler), 248
Psychic processes, 49–51
"Psychical Hermaphroditism in Life
    and in Neurosis" (Adler),
    70–74, 97, 198
Psychoanalysis, Freud's concept of,
    277–278
Psychoanalytic movement
    institutional consolidation of,
        140–149, 204
    sectarian character of, 192,
        192n–193n, 195
    and "Society for Free Psycho-
        analytic Research," 202–203
Psychogenesis, Adler on, 47
"Psychological superstructure"
    (Adler), 36, 42, 44, 51, 222
    and aggressive drive, 42
    and localization theory, 43
Psychoneurosis, 226
    see also neurosis, neurotic charac-
        ter, neurotic conflict
Psychosis, 245, 282
Psychotherapy, 206–207, 261, 268
    "value-free," 268
Punishment, 230–232, 237
Putnam, J. J., 139, 140, 182

R

Rank, B., 60
Rank, O., 79n, 85, 88–92, 99, 102,
    120, 129, 130, 149n
Rapaport, D., 3
Raschke, H., 213
Reason, 256

Reframing, 219n
Reich, W., 22
Reitler, R., 88, 89, 104, 118, 147, 148
Relgis, E., 27n–28n
Religion of Humanity (Comte), 275
Resistance, Adler on, 76
Repression, 48, 93, 98, 103, 118–119, 153, 191, 197–198, 281, 289–291
  Adler's critique of, 118–119
  Freud on sexualized theories of, 290–291
Rescue fantasies, 284–286
Rickert, H., 158
Rilke, R., 166
Roazen, P., 83n, 192n
Rom, P., 8n
Rosenstein, G., 32n, 127–128
Rubinstein, B. B., 38n
Ruehle, A., 12, 210
Ruehle, O., 12, 210

S

Sadger, I., 100, 107, 149n
Sadism, 185
  see also aggression, aggressive drive, cruelty impulse
Safeguarding tendencies (Adler), 76, 115, 117, 119, 121
  defiance and obedience as, 121–122
Saint-Simon, H., 273
Salzburg Congress, 141
Schafer, R., 287
Schilder, P., 162n, 174
Schiller, F. von, 91–92
Schopenhauer, A., 158, 159, 160
Schreber, case history of, 178, 281–284, 285, 290
  Adlerian rendering of, 284
Schur, M., 200–201

Seidler, R., 216–217
Self-alienation, Marx on, 264
Self-esteem, 267, 269–270
  lowered, 3, 57
Sexual types, theories of
  Adler's, 68–73, 97
  Kraus's, 69–70
  Weininger's, 69
  see also masculine protest, psychic hermaphroditism
Sexuality
  Adler on, 93–94, 134
  and education, 277
  Freud on Adler's devaluation of, 125, 127, 132–133, 194
  and "instinct for mastery," 285–286
  and masculine protest, 75–76, 115–117
  in neurosis (Adler), 113–117
  and role confusion in childhood, 68, 76
  as "safeguard," 115
  and theory of organ inferiority, 53–54, 115–116
  in the transference, 75
  traumatic impact of early awareness of, 63
Shengold, L., 176n
Siegl, M., 213n
Simmel, G., 147
Simon, M., 259
Simpson, G. G., 259
Sinnott, E., 250, 254
Skinner, Q., 7n
Skopec, M., 9n
Smuts, J. C., 5, 253, 260
Social adjustment, 262–263, 267, 268, 272
  see also conformism
Social conscience, 226
Social Democrats, Austrian, 15, 212, 214

Social feeling, 64, 278
  see also *Gemeinschaftsgefuehl*
Social medicine, Adler and, 11,
    13–14, 19, 20, 24
  see also community hygiene,
    prophylaxis
Social physics (Comte), 274
Social power
  Adler's within Vienna Psycho-
    analytic Society, 110–111
  concept of, 107–108
Socialism, 15, 214
  Adler and, 11–14, 20, 30
Society for Free Psychoanalytic Re-
    search, 131, 202, 203
Soper, P., 219n
Sorokin, P. A., 162, 163n
Spencer, H., 266
Sperber, M., 8n, 10n, 12, 210
Spiel, O., 216n
Spielrein, S., 190n
Spiritual guidance (Comte), 274
Spitz, R., 60
Staub, H., 222
Stekel, W., 74, 78, 81n, 83n, 88,
    89, 90, 91, 100, 102, 103, 107,
    110, 111, 124–125, 127, 129,
    130, 147, 148
Stepansky, P., 60n, 110n, 119n,
    177n, 204n, 279n
Stuttering, 99
Suicide, 160–161, 184
Sullivan, H. S., 7, 175n, 184
Sulloway, F., 23n, 49n, 84n–85n,
    108n, 126n, 199
Superego, 44, 225, 226, 276–277
Superiority strivings, 220–221, 229,
    240, 267, 270
  and community feeling, 207, 217
  and educational counseling,
    220–221, 240
Swales, P., 154n, 199n, 201n
Swoboda, H., 198n, 201
Szasz, T., 70n, 268

T

Tausk, V., 100, 118, 192n
Teachers and teaching; *see* educators,
    pedagogy
Teilhard de Chardin, P., 250
Teleology, 245–254, 265, 268, 269
  see also evolution, vitalism
Toennies, F., 258, 275
Toulmin, S., 70n
Transference, 57, 74–75, 224
Trotsky, L., 12

U

Unconscious
  absence in Adler's system, 194
  Adler on, 132, 278
  and Freud's primary process, 51
Understanding Human Nature
    (Adler), 208, 261, 270
United States, Adler in, 6, 7

V

Vaihinger, H., 153–160, 171, 260
  Adler's indebtedness to, 154
  as neo-Kantian, 157
  notion of "fiction," 157–159
Van Den Berghe, L., 144n
Vienna Psychoanalytic Society
  Adler as president of, 101, 112
  founding of, 79n, 81
  medical character of, 147–148
  rival interpretations of Adler's sta-
    tus in, 81–84
Vitalism
  Adler's theory as, 246–249
  Bergson and, 251–252
  Driesch and, 249–250
  Haldane and, 249–250
  Smuts and, 253–260
Vitalist-mechanist dispute,
    253–254

W

Waelder, R., 4, 193n, 292
Wagner-Jauregg, J., 33, 34, 54
War, Adler on, 27–29
Watzlawick, P., 219n
Wedekind, F., 89
Weininger, O., 69, 70, 198, 201
Weiss, E., 148, 286n
White, R., 3
"Will to power," 2, 30, 42, 210, 220
Windelband, W., 158
Winnicott, D. W., 120n

Wittels, F., 70n, 110n, 124–125, 149n, 192, 192n–193n
"Wolf Man," case history of the, 288–290
Woodger, J. H., 250n, 254n
Wulffen, E., 78

Z

*Zentralblatt fuer Psychoanalyse: Med-
izinische Monatsschrift fuer
Seelenkunde,* 56, 74–79, 101, 149
Zweig, A., 202